QUEER LIVES ACROSS THE WALL

GERMAN AND EUROPEAN STUDIES SERIES

General Editor: Jennifer L. Jenkins

Queer Lives across the Wall

Desire and Danger in Divided Berlin, 1945–1970

ANDREA ROTTMANN

UNIVERSITY OF TORONTO PRESS
Toronto Buffalo London

© University of Toronto Press 2023
Toronto Buffalo London
utorontopress.com

ISBN 978-1-4875-4780-6 (paper)

ISBN 978-1-4875-4781-3 (EPUB)
German and European Studies   ISBN 978-1-4875-4783-7 (PDF)

Printed and bound by CPI Group (UK) Ltd, Croydon, CR0 4YY

Library and Archives Canada Cataloguing in Publication

Title: Queer lives across the wall : desire and danger in divided Berlin, 1945–1970 / Andrea Rottmann.
Names: Rottmann, Andrea, author.
Series: German and European studies ; 50.
Description: Series statement: German and European studies ; 50 | Includes bibliographical
    references and index.
Identifiers: Canadiana (print) 20230136044 | Canadiana (ebook) 20230136079 |
    ISBN 9781487547806 (paper) | ISBN 9781487547837 (PDF) | ISBN 9781487547813 (EPUB)
Subjects: LCSH: Gays – Germany – Berlin – History – 20th century. | LCSH: Transgender people –
    Germany – Berlin – History – 20th century. | LCSH: Gay culture – Germany – Berlin – History –
    20th century. | LCSH: Homosexuality – Germany – Berlin – History – 20th century. |
    LCSH: Gender identity – Germany – Berlin – History – 20th century.
Classification: LCC HQ76.3.G42 B4785 2023 | DDC 306.76/6094315509045 – dc23

Cover design: Alexa Love
Cover image: Passionate kisses under the roses. Feminist FFBIZ Archives, Berlin.

A version of chapter 2 was first published in German as "Gefährdete Geselligkeit: Queeres Nachtleben
in West Berlin zwischen Überschwang, Überwachung und Überfall, 1945–1970," in *Räume der deutschen
Geschichte*, ed. Teresa Walch, Sagi Schaefer, and Galili Shahar (Göttingen: Wallstein, 2022), 217–65.

A version of chapter 4 was originally published as "Bubis behind Bars: Seeing Queer Histories in
Postwar Germany through the Prison," *Journal of the History of Sexuality* 30, no. 2 (May 2021): 225–52.
Copyright © 2021 by the University of Texas Press. All rights reserved. Used by permission.

This publication was financed in part by the open access fund for monographs
and edited volumes of the Freie Universität Berlin and a contribution of the
Arbeitskreis Historische Frauen- und Geschlechterforschung (AKHFG).

The German and European Studies series is funded by the DAAD with funds from the German
Federal Foreign Office.

DAAD   Deutscher Akademischer Austauschdienst
        German Academic Exchange Service

We wish to acknowledge the land on which the University of Toronto Press operates. This land is
the traditional territory of the Wendat, the Anishnaabeg, the Haudenosaunee, the Métis, and the
Mississaugas of the Credit First Nation.

University of Toronto Press acknowledges the financial support of the Government of Canada, the
Canada Council for the Arts, and the Ontario Arts Council, an agency of the Government of Ontario, for
its publishing activities.

Canada Council   Conseil des Arts
for the Arts   du Canada

ONTARIO ARTS COUNCIL
CONSEIL DES ARTS DE L'ONTARIO
an Ontario government agency
un organisme du gouvernement de l'Ontario

Funded by the   Financé par le
Government   gouvernement
of Canada   du Canada

Contents

Illustrations

Acknowledgments

This book is the result of years of work in different scholarly contexts in the United States and in Germany. In many ways, it is a collaborative achievement, and I would like to express my gratitude to the many people who contributed to it. Since they were so many, it is likely that I am not naming everyone here – my sincere apologies if your name is missing.

First off, thanks to all those who helped me find or get access to sources: Roman Klarfeld and Dagmar Noeldge of the Feminist FFBIZ Archives; Jens Dobler, Kristine Schmidt, and Karl-Heinz Steinle at the Schwules Museum, as well as the volunteers who staff the library-archives there; at the Magnus-Hirschfeld-Gesellschaft, Raimund Wolfert and Ralf Dose; at the Police Historical Collection Berlin, again Jens Dobler; at the Landesarchiv, Bianca Welzing-Bräutigam; and at the Archive of Other Memories, Daniel Baranowski and Andreas Pretzel. Thanks also to Birgit Bosold for the opportunities she gave me during an internship at the Schwules Museum.

This book draws heavily on the memories of queer Berliners who have trusted me or other researchers to preserve, publish, and interpret their life narratives. My gratitude goes to Hans-Joachim Engel, who shared his memories with me directly, and to Klaus Born, Orest Kapp, Christine Loewenstein, Fritz Schmehling, and Rita "Tommy" Thomas, as well as to their careful interviewers at the Archive of Other Memories. I was also so lucky to meet Tommy and her partner Helli, who generously shared memories of their life together. Christiane von Lengerke kindly invited me to her home to survey the papers of Kitty Kuse. I would also like to thank Carsten Repke at the Stasi Archives, Jörg-Uwe Fischer at the German Radio Archives, Niki Trauthwein of the Lili Elbe Archives, and the archivists of the Bundesarchiv. I conducted further research at Spinnboden Lesbenarchiv as well as at the Stiftung Berliner Stadtmuseum. Even if these materials did not end up in the book, archivists at both institutions were welcoming and helpful. Much of this book was written in libraries – many thanks to the staff at Hatcher Library in Ann Arbor, the Staatsbibliothek Berlin at Potsdamer Straße, the Berliner Stadtbibliothek, and the library of the Friedrich-Meinecke-Institut at Freie Universität Berlin.

This project took shape amid the intellectual community and generous collegiality at the University of Michigan. I am indebted to my teachers and mentors there, in particular Kerstin Barndt, Scott Spector, Helmut Puff, Clare Croft, Victor Mendoza, Julia Hell, Kathleen Canning, Johannes von Moltke, Gayle Rubin, and Esther Newton, as well as to the community of grad students that accompanied this project's development over years. Thank you, Naomi Vaughan, Katy Holihan, Calder Fong, Domenic DeSocio, Emma Thomas, Hannah Pröbsting, Mary Hennessy, Onyx Henry, Duygu Ula, Bri Gauger, Joey Gamble, and everyone in the Institute for Research on Women and Gender's 2018 Community of Scholars summer workshop. Teaching at Michigan was fun and a great balance to research, and I am so glad that I got to work with my many fabulous students and my wonderful colleagues, especially Hartmut Rastalsky, Andrew Mills, and Mary Gell. Jennifer Lucas was an invaluable part of my Michigan experience.

In Germany, Martin Lücke has shown support and enthusiasm for my work for many years now and has eased the transition from the United States back to Germany. Danke Dir, Martin. I am grateful also for the exchange and encouragement given by my colleagues: Maria Bühner, Mirjam Höfner, Elisa Heinrich, Teresa Tammer, Adrian Lehne, Veronika Springmann, Lotte Thaa, Nina Reusch, Jan-Henrik Friedrichs, Sonja Dolinsek, Sébastien Tremblay, Josh Armstrong, Lorenz Weinberg, Merlin Bootsmann, and Greta Hülsmann.

During my research, I had the fortune of meeting many of the most eminent historians of German queer history. Jens Dobler, Ralf Dose, Ilse Kokula, Kirsten Plötz, Claudia Schoppmann, Karl-Heinz Steinle, and Raimund Wolfert each very generously offered their expertise and memories. Maria Borowski shared transcripts and contacts of her oral history partners, and Barbara Wallbraun shared her research on Stasi surveillance of lesbians. Thank you all.

Since this book is the culmination of a learning process that began long before graduate school, I would like to acknowledge some teachers who early on spurred my interests in writing and thinking about stories and histories. In high school, Hildegard Vierhuff trusted my storytelling, Jörg Bernauer taught me how to engage with historical complexity, and Friedemann Ries introduced me to historical hermeneutics. At the Freie Universität Berlin, Luita D. Spangler taught me how to write compellingly in English. Andreas Etges, also at Freie Universität, and

Michael Edmonds of the Wisconsin Historical Society introduced me to the Progressive Midwest, where I don't think I would have ended up otherwise. Two beautiful summers in Madison, Wisconsin, are the real reason this book exists, even if it was written in Michigan and Berlin. Thinking of you, Michael, Jane, Jesse, Bret, Kristina, Anna, Elise, Abby, Sandra, Seth, Taylor, Mike, and everyone at Friends Coop.

This project would not have been possible without the generous funding provided by the University of Michigan's Department of Germanic Languages and Literatures, the Rackham Graduate School, the Institute for Research on Women and Gender, and the Freie Universität Berlin. The dissertation prizes that the Coalition of Women in German and the Arbeitskreis Historische Frauen- und Geschlechterforschung awarded me provided much-needed support while I revised the manuscript, and I thank my colleagues for their support and encouragement. This book is available open access thanks to the Freie Universität Berlin's open access funding and to my father Dieter Rottmann's *Spendierhosen*. Papa, ich wünschte, du hättest es auch noch in den Händen halten können.

I revised this book's manuscript during the Covid pandemic. Working with my spot-on, steady, and friendly editor Stephen Shapiro gave me much-needed structure and motivation. I am very grateful for my three anonymous readers, especially reader A-1. There is little that has been comparably uplifting and motivating in my career as your in-depth reading and suggestions for improving the book. A version of the chapter on bars was previously published in German in the collected volume *Räume der deutschen Geschichte*, and editor Teresa Walch's comments significantly improved the text. The same is true of the chapter on prisons, a first version of which appeared in the *Journal of the History of Sexuality*, and which benefited from editor Annette Timm's comments as well as those of the anonymous readers. As I finished this manuscript during a difficult time, Lauren Beck's help made things much easier. Many thanks to the Press's cover designer Alexa Love for the beautiful design. Managing editor Mary Lui and copy editor Carolyn Zapf smoothly directed the final steps of the revision process. In Berlin, special thanks to Andrea Ladányi, who made sure all bills were paid on time.

Finally, of course, this book wouldn't exist without my friends and family, who have tolerated me over years of doubt and stress, and have reminded me that there are other things in life. Thank you, Johannes, Uli, and Sophie, Ali, Ali and Claudia, Andrew, April, Ariana, Bettina and Henning, Bri and Brett, Calder and Michelle, Charlotte, Conni, Doro, and Mia, Dete, Domenic, Duygu and Begüm, Emily, Emma, Eylem, Guy, Hanna, Hannah, and Hannah, Herbie, Jan, Janni, Joris, Lauren, Lotte, Luise and Hans with Juri, Lia, and Mara, Katy, Maria and

Melina, André, Mary, Naomi, Onyx, Prestyn, Sarah, Sigrid, Siiri, Stella and Josephine with Karlotta and Jolanda, Veronica, and Zazie. The stories, curiosity, and encouragement of my grandmothers Anneliese Kohleiss, Tante Lise, and Charlotte, all great lovers of learning, accompanied me on this long journey. My sisters Doro and Netti are my great luck in life. Jakob, thanks for karaoke! Mama und Papa, danke für eure Liebe und euer Vertrauen, euer Interesse und eure Unterstützung. Tilly and Joku: I'm so glad you're here, and I am curious to see what stories and histories will be meaningful to you.

Abbreviations

BArch	Bundesarchiv Berlin (Federal Archives Berlin)
BMH	Bundesstiftung Magnus Hirschfeld (Federal Magnus Hirschfeld Foundation)
BStU	Der Bundesbeauftragte für die Unterlagen des Staatssicherheitsdienstes der ehemaligen Deutschen Demokratischen Republik (Federal Commissioner for the Records of the State Security Service of the Former German Democratic Republic)
CDU	Christlich Demokratische Union Deutschlands (Christian Democratic Union)
FDP	Freie Demokratische Partei (Free Democratic Party)
FDGB	Freier Deutscher Gewerkschaftsbund (Free German Union Corporation)
FFBIZ	Feministisches Archiv FFBIZ (Feminist FFBIZ Archives)
FRG	Federal Republic of Germany (West Germany)
GDR	German Democratic Republic (East Germany)
HAW	Homosexuelle Aktion Westberlin (Homosexual Action West Berlin)
HIB	Homosexuelle Interessengemeinschaft Berlin (Homosexual Interest Community Berlin)
KPD	Kommunistische Partei Deutschlands (Communist Party of Germany)
LAB	Landesarchiv Berlin (Berlin State Archives)
LAZ	Lesbisches Aktionszentrum Westberlin (Lesbian Action Centre)
LGBTTIQ	lesbian, gay, bisexual, transsexual, transgender, intersexual, and queer people
MHG	Magnus-Hirschfeld-Gesellschaft
OdF	Opfer des Faschismus (Victims of Fascism)

PHS	Polizeihistorische Sammlung Berlin (Police Historical Collection Berlin)
PrV	Politisch, rassisch oder religiös Verfolgte (Persecuted for Political, Racist, or Religious Reasons)
PRV-Amt	Amt für politisch, rassisch oder religiös Verfolgte (Office for the Politically, Racially, or Religiously Persecuted)
SED	Sozialistische Einheitspartei Deutschlands (Socialist Unity Party of Germany)
SMB	Schwules Museum Berlin (Gay Museum Berlin)
SPD	Sozialdemokratische Partei Deutschlands (Social Democratic Party of Germany)
TKK	Teilnachlass Kitty Kuse (Kitty Kuse Personal Papers)
VVN	Vereinigung der Verfolgten des Naziregimes (Association of Those Persecuted by the Nazis)

QUEER LIVES ACROSS THE WALL

Introduction: "Mamita Invites You In"

Let us remember those glittering ball nights we celebrated after the collapse of the disastrous Third Reich, in a way as continuation of the year 1933. Hundreds of our friends rushed towards the Tefi ballroom when Mamita called them.

> – O.Z., "Mamita läßt bitten!"[1]

A call to remember glittering ball nights seems like a fitting way to begin a book on the history of queer Berlin. It was uttered in 1962 by an anonymous writer in the West German homophile magazine *Der Weg* in the piece "Mamita Invites You In," a text that was both an obituary for the entertainer and community organizer Mamita and an elegy for a carefree time that had since passed. It conjures the moment of liberation from the Nazis, when "hundreds of our friends" – the word "friend" was long used as a self-designation among queer men and women – danced in celebration in the city's resurrected queer ballrooms.[2] With its reference to the time before the Nazi ascent to power in 1933 and its lamenting the loss of tolerance that Berlin had witnessed recently, the article sketches the temporal coordinates that also frame this book: the queer publics of the Weimar Republic, their destruction by the Nazis, the moment of freedom between the end of the war and the founding of the new German states in 1949, and the growing social conservatism that characterized the 1950s and early 1960s.

Mamita invites you into this book because her non-normative embodiment of gender illustrates one of this book's key claims: that gender was a crucial aspect of queer lives in Germany in the mid-century. In the article, the writer describes Mamita, a "keen waiter by trade," as a cross-dressing "homophile" man whose "unusual" cross-dressing challenged many within the queer community and who was subject to "much animosity."[3] In the end, this "friend's" charm won over everyone, however.

Even the custodians of the law put up with Mamita the way she was, and even the cynical critics would at the end laugh along with her. Because Mamita had humour and did not just make fun of others, but also of herself. At her balls, she would stand on the flight of stairs as Grand-Dame and personally welcome all her dears; and then she would present the best show too. The vaudeville program was quite something, and she herself was definitely the top act. She recited as Countess Strachwitz, she sang the Zarah Leander, and she danced the dying swan, and everyone convulsed with laughter.[4]

The writer, shifting between feminine and masculine pronouns, not only admires Mamita's skills as a community organizer and her stamina in the face of hostilities, but also fondly remembers her talent for entertainment: she performed classics like "The Dying Swan" from Tchaikovsky's ballet and German wartime favourites like the songs of Zarah Leander to great acclaim. The wistful memory of Mamita stands out sharply against the changed situation at the time of publication. The piece ends on the sad note that, a decade after Mamita's famous balls, the "newly won freedom and tolerance" had given way again to "prohibition" and a "skewed morality."[5] Nevertheless, the writer insists that "Berlin is still worth a trip, even if a stupid political conception has badly mutilated the city."[6] This "stupid political conception" is the Cold War, of course, and the mutilation it has wrought on the city is the Berlin Wall, constructed one year before the article's publication.

With Mamita, the non-binary star of postwar Berlin's "resurrected social life" who has since been forgotten, I invite you in to explore the subjectivities and spaces of queer Berlin from the end of Nazism to the beginnings of the gay and lesbian liberation movements of the early 1970s. Subjectivity refers to the processes of making the self: how queer Berliners understood themselves, their gender, sexuality, and relationships with others, and how they expressed themselves through styling their bodies, through gestures and movements, through having their photograph taken, or through writing. Space refers to the material and immaterial sites whose meaning for queer Berliners was made through their own practices and the practices of those trying to control and suppress them, be they representatives of the state or fellow Berliners. Ballrooms and the Berlin Wall are two locations in this queer world. Other locations include bars but also more mundane spaces such as private homes and streets and parks. A final chapter is devoted to prisons, which, as we will see, were significant spaces for queer Berliners of different genders. While "glittering ball nights" were and continue to be important aspects of Berlin's queer culture, this book argues that it is worth our while to ask about the daylight and everyday spaces too.

Broadening the scholarly gaze from its current focus on nightlife and politics brings into focus queer lives that historians of queer Berlin have had little to say about in the past, particularly those of lesbian women and trans people. But only by examining lesbian, gay, and trans[7] lives together, and by paying close attention to how gender, sexuality, and class were intertwined, can we understand how the two German postwar states and societies dealt with non-normative genders and sexualities, and what exclusionary processes were at work in constructing East and West German norms of gender and sexuality. Other identity markers such as race, ethnicity, and migration are largely absent from this book, even if Mamita's Spanish name alone hints at the multiple and complicated ways in which the queer Berlin of the postwar decades was entangled with the world. Their intersection with the city's queer history deserves its own study. This absence, and others that I will discuss later, demonstrates that archival absences and imbalances continue to shape queer urban and German histories in different ways. Rather than just replicating these absences, historians interested in intersectional analyses can discuss them and thus make visible historical inequities that often extend into the present.[8]

This book also addresses historiographical imbalances. Most research in queer history focuses on male homosexuality, and this focus is particularly striking in urban queer history and German queer history. Classic histories of queerness and the city, such as George Chauncey's *Gay New York* and Matt Houlbrook's *Queer London*, offered a nuanced analysis of the multiple and shifting gendered subjectivities of queer men, but neither of them analysed lesbian women in the city.[9] The same is true of recent studies of queerness and sexuality in Berlin, for instance Jennifer Evans's *Life among the Ruins* or Robert Beachy's *Gay Berlin*: they ignore lesbian and trans subjectivities and relationships.[10] In German queer history, the scarcity of research on lesbians remains dramatic, and the situation in trans history is even worse.[11] Given that through much of the twentieth century, liberal as well as conservative commentators grouped different forms of non-normative gender and sexuality together as various aspects of "immorality," this research imbalance has severely skewed our understanding of the historical meanings of queerness.[12] When around the turn of the last century, sexual science, sexual subcultures, and activism in Berlin and elsewhere shaped the sexual identities that we continue to use today, it was not just a modern gay male identity but also lesbian and trans identities that came into the world.[13] It thus appears consequential to jointly examine these different queer subjectivities.

A study thus conceptualized must go beyond a history of §175, the German law prohibiting sex between men, and beyond a merely legal history, though of course laws played a significant role in framing the lives not just of cis gay men but also of trans people and lesbian women. As the reader will see, going beyond criminalization results in an account of queer everyday lives that encompasses aspects of the pleasures of living queerly as much as its dangers. Gay male history will also profit from moving away from a history focused overwhelmingly on persecution. At the same time, this book shows how the construction of heterosexuality and the gender binary in postwar Germany was built on more than the criminalization of male homosexuality. State practices, such as the inclusion of gendered markers in identification documents, and the policing of feminine masculinities through police officers but also through neighbours and youth gangs all contributed to the stabilization of normative sexuality and gender. For this reason, rather than offering an account of political activism for legal change, this book tells a more broadly political history of belonging and exclusion.

By exploring some of Berlin's queer spaces from the beginnings of the Cold War through the construction of the Berlin Wall in 1961 and the first decade of the city's complete division, this study also contributes to the historiography of Berlin as a divided and entangled city. Its close examination of the meanings of the Wall for queer East and West Berliners suggests that the East German government harnessed homophobic discourses to distract its own citizens and the world public from its murderous border regime, highlighting a neglected dimension of the Berlin Wall and the political uses of homophobia in German history.[14]

In this book, I use "queer" to describe people who found themselves outside the sexual or gender norms of their time because of their same-sex desires or practices, or because they "perceived themselves and were perceived by their societies as gender nonconforming."[15] I hence use it as an umbrella term that can describe subjectivities whose same-sex desires or non-normative gender positioned them against, outside, or deviating from the norm. While it is true that lesbian women, trans people, and gay men have at times faced vastly different legal and social situations, they were put together in the same space of criminalization, medicalization, or stigma because of their same-sex desires and/or gender identities at other times. My choice to use "queer" as an integrative term may come across as outdated in light of trans scholars' long-standing critiques of "queer theory's erasure of transgender subjectivity" and recent theorizations of trans studies that have argued for "breaks from the established epistemological frameworks of women's studies and queer studies."[16] However, as this book shows, it is impossible to always draw clean analytical borders between non-normative genders and sexualities in recent German history. Rather, this study follows Kadji Amin's suggestion that "critical transgender studies" might include

> foregrounding modes of gender variance inseparable from homosexuality; returning to a feminist understanding of gender not simply as a neutral category of social difference but as a site invested with relations of power; and capitalizing on transgender's associations with public sex, economic marginality, racialized inequality, and policing to promote a politics of structural transformation rather than identity.[17]

While I thus posit that "queer" remains an adequate and helpful umbrella term for this study, a varied terminology will describe the actors in the chapters that follow. I use "gay" as an analytic term for men who sought love and sex with men and "lesbian" for women who sought love and sex with women. I use "trans" for individuals of non-conforming gender who did not identify as gay or lesbian and who may or may not have identified as transgender, or rather as "transvestite" in the terminology of the day. The latter term was coined in 1910 by sexual scientist Magnus Hirschfeld to describe "a range of cross-gendered characteristics and desires."[18] From the 1920s on, it was also used as self-identification by some cross-gendered individuals. Whenever possible, I use specific terms from my historical sources, including *Bubi* (butch woman), *Freundin* and *Freund* (female and male friend), *Homophiler* (male homophile), *Homosexueller* (male homosexual), *Lesbierin* (lesbian), *Mäuschen* (femme), *Schwuler* (gay man), *Strichjunge* (streetwalking boy, that is, male selling sexual services), *Transvestit* (trans person), and *Tunte* (feminine gay man or queen).[19] Part of the work of this book is to disentangle the meaning that these terms held for their speakers. The multitude of terms has to do with the history to which this book seeks to add: that of sexuality and gender, in particular non-normative sexualities and genders, acting as central sites of societies' negotiations of power, or, in Michel Foucault's terms, "as an especially dense transfer point for relations of power."[20] There are so many words because there was so much talk: between bar acquaintances, friends, and lovers; in homophile magazines and in the mainstream press; between sexologists, doctors, psychologists, and patients; among legislators, politicians, administrators, and police; between historians and their subjects.

The different terms speak of those who participated in the negotiations about non-normative genders and sexualities; the multiplicity of terms hence reflects the many voices that held a stake in these debates. Scholars have long argued that Berlin was a central arena of these negotiations.

Berlin, Queer Eldorado? Myths and Histories

Berlin holds a mythical space in queer imaginations as a utopia where queer subcultures were allowed to flourish decades before anywhere else. Christopher Isherwood's memoir *Goodbye to Berlin*, as well as *Cabaret*, the musical and films based on the memoir, have been central to this myth. More recently, television shows such as *Transparent* and *Babylon Berlin* have continued it. Since the 1970s, this popular image has been both undergirded and complicated by historical research. Early studies of queer Berlin came from scholars rooted in the gay and lesbian movements.[21] The 1984 student-initiated exhibition *Eldorado: Homosexuelle Frauen und Männer in Berlin 1850–1950* made a powerful case for Berlin's special role as a catalyst of a modern homosexual identity: that in the rapidly growing industrial metropolis and capitol of the German empire, a large queer subculture, the new discipline of sexual science, and a political movement for ending the criminalization of sex between men developed in close connection from the end of the nineteenth century until the Nazi takeover in 1933.[22] Since *Eldorado*, many Berlin-specific studies have explored the Kaiserreich and Weimar periods, focusing on the policing of queer spaces and subjects; the flourishing nightlife; the close collaboration between sexual scientists and activists for decriminalization and emancipation; the emergence of gay, lesbian, and trans identities; the role of scandal in disseminating sexual knowledge; the world's first Institute for Sexual Science, founded in Berlin in 1919; and the diverse queer publics of the Weimar Republic. They have uncovered a city that was no Eldorado but that had indeed produced a diverse, if not uncensored, queer public. Recent scholarship has stressed the limits of this queer public, however, arguing that the "Weimar settlement on sexual politics" entailed keeping "immoral" sexualities out of the public sphere.[23] When the Nazis came to power in early 1933, they very quickly targeted the Institute for Sexual Science and shut down the queer bars and ballrooms, as well as the queer press.[24] In 1935, the Nazis tightened §175, the section prohibiting sex between men, potentially making even short touches criminal. The Nazis also introduced a new §175a, making a man's sex with a male dependent or a male minor, as well as homosexual prostitution, punishable with up to ten years in prison.[25] §175 did not extend to lesbian women, and the Nazis did not directly target them because they believed that, unlike gay men, whose virility was lost to the state, lesbian women's fertility would still be available to the *Volksgemeinschaft*.[26] Despite persecution and risks, queer Berliners continued socializing. Bars catering to gay men did so more covertly throughout the Nazi period in some parts of the city. Private circles of friends continued meeting throughout the Nazi era too.[27] The lesbian club "Jolly Nine," masked as a bowling club, organized queer balls where predominantly lesbian women, but also gay men and "transvestites," gathered until at least 1940.[28] Research on the queer Berlin of the early postwar decades, up to 1970, has focused on the re-emergence of queer nightlife and its policing, on the ambivalent figure of the "streetwalking boy," on political organizing, and on the denial of justice or rehabilitation of gay victims of the Nazis, who instead faced continued criminalization and persecution.[29] Research on lesbian and trans subjectivities in Berlin during this time remains exceedingly scarce.[30]

Sexuality and Gender in the Postwar Germanies

Sexuality, gender, and the family were central concerns in both German postwar states, the Federal Republic of Germany (FRG, West Germany) and the German Democratic Republic (GDR, East Germany), and despite the major political, legal, economic, and cultural differences, the two countries saw remarkably similar developments in this area in the 1950s and 1960s. In both East and West Germany, a sexual conservatism took hold in the 1950s, leading to at times intense persecution of those who deviated from the path of normalcy, whether same-sex desiring men, women seeking sex outside marriage, or rebellious youth, called "Halbstarke" or "Rowdies."[31] Both countries shared the "homophobic consensus" coined by historian Susanne zur Nieden for the pre-1945 German states, even if this homophobia manifested quite differently in the two societies.[32]

The immediate postwar period has been described as one of violence, chaos, and crisis: the mass rapes of women at the hands of occupying soldiers, Soviet soldiers in particular; families broken up by death, flight, and imprisonment; and a crisis of masculinity as men returned home from the war with physical and psychological injuries.[33] At the same time, the years following German defeat are also remembered as a period of openness and possibility, when the end of the old and the promise of a new order made for realities beyond any traditional family models and allowed for hopes of a less restrictive future.[34] The absence of fathers and of the heterosexual couple changed everyday understandings of the family.[35] As historian Elizabeth Heineman has shown, in the "crisis years" between the defeat of the German army at Stalingrad in 1942 and the foundation of the two German states in 1949, the "woman standing alone" whose husband was at war, dead, or in captivity was the norm rather than the exception.[36] In the case of the "women families," families headed by two "women standing alone," this postwar queer reality even became the subject of political debate in West Germany. During the deliberations for the West German rump constitution, the *Grundgesetz* or Basic Law, conveners considered expanding the definition of the family to include such "women families."[37]

Similarities and Differences in the Legal Frameworks in East and West

Hopes for a new beginning quickly faltered after the 1949 foundation of the two German states. Instead of protecting different existing families, the West German Basic Law favoured a traditional family model and guaranteed the state's "special protection" of "marriage and the family." Over the course of the 1950s, gender roles and ideas of the family became increasingly rigid. With a shortage of men, unmarried women were viewed with suspicion, and female couples, who had formerly been seen as inconspicuous as long as they did not display public affection, were increasingly understood as non-normative.[38] Married women were treated as second-class citizens and were dependent on their husbands for permission to work and to open a bank account.

Both East and West Germany reintroduced the German criminal code established during the late nineteenth century. Both countries also adopted some Nazi changes to the criminal law, though with important differences regarding sex between men. Allied efforts to denazify German criminal law and reintroduce the pre-1935 version of §175 quickly fell victim to Germany's Cold War division.[39] In 1951, the GDR reintroduced §175 in its old, less encompassing version.[40] The new socialist criminal code, passed in 1968, abolished §175, though the new §151 introduced a different age of consent for sex between men or between women, thus continuing to criminalize certain same-sex relationships.[41] The numbers of men persecuted under §175 in East Germany had already dwindled since the late 1950s. The FRG, by contrast, kept the Nazi version of §175, prompting a contemporary to observe that, for gay men in West Germany, "the Third Reich only ended in 1969."[42] West German judges, many of them former Nazis, repeatedly denied that the law presented a Nazi injustice, and until the Great Criminal Law

Reform of 1969, they sentenced 50,000 men under §175.[43] Both East and West Germany held on to the Nazis' addition of §175a, which criminalized male prostitution as well as male sex with a male dependent or underage partner, and prosecutions under this section were comparably high in the GDR and the FRG.[44] Apart from §175 and §175a, the laws against public nuisance, which remained largely unchanged since the nineteenth century, also affected non-normative genders and sexualities. §183, "Public Causation of a Sexual Nuisance," punished those "who give a public nuisance by acting indecently" in both states with up to two years in prison or a fine, and additionally allowed for the withdrawal of civil rights.[45] §360 made "engaging in disorderly conduct" punishable by a fine of 150 Marks or imprisonment.[46] These laws remained in place in both German postwar states until the law reforms of the late 1960s: the new socialist criminal law codified in the GDR in 1968 and the West German Great Criminal Law Reform of 1969. The GDR also created new laws that served to penalize deviance and to police public space. The 1961 "Ordinance about the Limitation of Stay" and §249 of the new criminal code, "Endangering Public Order through Asocial Behaviour," passed in 1968, allowed the state to prohibit citizens from entering certain areas as well as force them to work if they were found to be "work-shy" (*arbeitsscheu*). These laws were used against different groups who deviated from the socialist norm, in particular people who did not hold a steady job, rebellious youth, and women who sold sexual services. Legal scholar Sven Korzilius has shown that the law targeted deviant sexualities more broadly: "From the perspective of the state authorities and the jurists, homosexuals and people suffering from sexually transmitted diseases bordered on 'asocials.'"[47] Being convicted under the 1961 ordinance or the 1968 law could mean being sent to "labour education commandos," as well as prohibited from visiting certain areas – usually cities frequented by Western tourists. §249 allowed for prison sentences too, and courts made frequent use of it throughout the existence of the GDR.[48]

Discourses about Sexuality

Despite the continued legal repression of non-marital sexuality, both East and West Germany also experienced "sexual revolutions," which involved massive changes in their citizens' sexual mores.[49] Historian Dagmar Herzog has famously interpreted West Germans' desire for moral cleanliness as a way to distance themselves from sexual permissiveness in Nazi Germany and thus as a response to avoid dealing with German crimes.[50] Historian Sybille Steinbacher has further argued that the 1950s debates over sexuality represented the resurfacing of discourses of sexual morality, or *Sittlichkeit*, that emerged at the turn of the century.[51] She has accordingly interpreted the postwar debates as a continuation of the struggle over the meaning and shape of modernity. West Germany's economic boom, the *Wirtschaftswunder*, allowed its citizens to participate in these debates as consumers too: purchasing erotica from Beate Uhse's mail-order catalogues and, later, sex shops, they became educated about different varieties of sex by the marketplace and "learn[ed] liberalism through sexuality."[52] On the one hand, aspects of sexual repression remained in place in West Germany during and beyond the 1950s, well into the 1960s, in fact: convictions of men for transgression of §175 continued to be high, and marriage rates soared to previously unknown levels, making other forms of cohabitation less acceptable and entrenching the "normal family" – the married couple with children – as the dominant social model.[53] On the other hand, ideas and attitudes about sex were changing rapidly, with 50 per cent of West German households ordering erotica, whether self-help literature, contraceptives, toys, or sexual imagery, from mail-order catalogues by the early 1960s.[54] Accordingly, what is often referred to as the "sexual revolution" of the late 1960s and early 1970s began much earlier in postwar West Germany and was, rather than "a sudden, fundamental overthrow of … sexual interests and behaviours … a long-term, complicated process."[55] In East Germany, changes in ideas about and practices of sexuality were comparably vast and followed a similar trajectory despite immense differences between the two political systems, prompting historian Josie McLellan to speak of an "East German sexual revolution."[56] In the socialist state too, the 1950s and the first half of the 1960s were marked by sexual conservatism and a concern with deviant behaviour, and the mid-to-late 1960s and 1970s characterized by a trend towards liberalization.[57] The place for sex in the GDR was within loving, long-term heterosexual relationships. Practices other than reproductive, monogamous sexuality were discouraged, with sexological handbooks condemning masturbation, anal sex, and sadomasochistic practices.[58]

Same-sex desiring East Germans faced a contradictory situation that scholars have recently described as "persistent ambivalence" or "schizophrenic."[59] While the GDR never persecuted sex between men with a zealousness comparable to West Germany, and the government abolished §175 in its 1968 criminal code, it continued to criminalize queer lives through the new §151 and §249. Additionally, the lack of a free public sphere meant that queer publications and organizations could not exist, severely hampering East Germans' possibility to organize queer communities and live queer lives. "Persistent homophobia" thus appears as a more apt description of the East German state and society's dealings with queer citizens.

Theories and Methods

This book contributes both to a re(dis)covery of queer lives *and* an analysis of how sexual "normality" and "difference" were produced. It thus sits squarely in the middle of the decades-long argument among queer historians on whether their work is about searching for lesbian, gay, bisexual, or trans (LGBT) ancestors who have been "hidden from history" and must be rediscovered, or if it is rather the study of how sexual and gender norms were produced through the making of sexual and gendered difference.[60] Historian Laura Doan has described the two strands as "the history of us," an ancestral history or genealogy, on the one hand, and a "critical queer history," on the other, with the first looking for "queerness-as-being" and the latter interested in "queerness-as-method."[61] While this division is, to some extent, a false dichotomy – most recent work partakes in both approaches – many authors of recent studies in the histories of urbanity and sexuality appear compelled to situate their work in this way.[62] Following David Halperin, I pursue a genealogical approach that takes the modern concepts of homosexuality, lesbianism, and being trans as vantage point and traces back their developments.[63] As I will show, this approach is possible without ahistorically mapping contemporary identities onto subjects in the past who were both similar and different from us.

Though their work is not framed as a contribution to the "queerness-as-being"/"queerness-as-method" debate, Laurie Marhoefer has argued in a similar vein for a "queer methodological approach, generating a history of 'immorality' rather than a history of just one faction of 'immorality.'"[64] They note that Weimar Republic contemporaries understood sexual phenomena that we would differentiate today, for instance homosexuality, prostitution, or birth control, as really just "a single, capacious phenomenon." Their descriptions of "immorality" or "moral degeneration," Marhoefer argues, reflected the interconnectedness of these different issues.[65] While I agree with them on this point, this book demonstrates that asking about queer subjectivities continues to be a productive route for historians of gender and sexuality. We simply do not know enough about queer lives between 1945 and the 1970s to *not* ask how lesbian women, gay men, and trans people lived during that time.

Like Marhoefer's book, *Queer Lives across the Wall* considers women and men, as well as people embodying shifting genders.[66] This approach sets it apart from the overwhelming majority of queer histories, particularly queer urban histories. In *Queer London*, Matt Houlbrook offered a rationale for excluding lesbian subjectivities from his analysis, arguing that "women's access to public space was more problematic" and that "lesbianism remained invisible in the law."[67] Despite women's more limited access to funds and public spaces, however, lesbian publics existed in cities like London, New York, and Paris. For Berlin, we can even speak of a trans public during the Weimar Republic, however small it was. Furthermore, private urban spaces warrant scholarly analysis too, though researching them requires different methods and archives than examining public spaces. By disregarding the lives of urban women, these studies reproduce the state's (apparent) ignorance and are complicit in upholding an image of the city as a male-only space. As a result, their analysis of the gendered experience of city life will remain insufficient. In this book, I have attempted to privilege female and trans voices, and to be particularly attentive to lesbian and trans subjectivities and their space-making practices, even when their traces, particularly in public spaces, were fleeting.

Indeed, the transient nature of lesbian and trans spaces in particular challenges scholars to come up with alternative ways to theorize the production of space.[68] Feminist theorist Sara Ahmed has noted that lesbian spaces often "come and go with the coming and going of the bodies that inhabit them."[69] She points out the spatial origin of the term "queer":

We can turn to the etymology of the word "queer," which comes from the Indo-European word "twist." Queer is, after all, a spatial term, which then gets translated into a sexual term, a term for a twisted sexuality that does not follow a "straight line," a sexuality that is bent and crooked. The spatiality of this term is not incidental. Sexuality itself can be considered a spatial formation not only in the sense that bodies inhabit sexual spaces, but also in the sense that bodies are sexualized through how they inhabit space.[70]

Ahmed's return to queer's semantic origin directs readers to think about the metaphorical meanings of the terms used to describe spaces and the movement of bodies in them. It is a richly productive direction of thought for a queer urban history. Consider, for example, how she describes queer sexuality as "not follow[ing] a 'straight line.'" All kinds of lines come to mind: lines drawn on city maps to represent streets, buildings, rail tracks; subway lines; the itineraries of city dwellers from sleep to school, work, leisure, and back. In German, one translation of the word for line, "*Strich*," denotes the location of public commercial sex. "*Auf den Strich gehen*," walking on the line, hence means selling sexual services in public space, and the "*Strichjunge*," a figure that will be present in multiple chapters and that I have translated as "street-walking boy," is the name of a youth or young man offering them.

Lines also play a role in geographer Jen Jack Gieseking's theorization of lesbian and queer space-making practices. They compare the sporadic and unfixed quality of lesbian and queer places to "stars and other celestial objects" that are "scattered and visible only when you know where and when to look."[71] The networks and lines drawn by lesbian and queer city dwellers in their everyday movements, for instance from a bar to the LGBT centre to their home, make up constellations: "By tracing the contingent production of virtual, physical, and imagined places and the lines and networks between them, I show the formation of constellations as an alternative, queer feminist practice … of the production of urban space."[72] Gieseking introduces constellations as an alternative to more fixed queer space-making practices associated with cis gay men, namely the "gayborhood," a neighbourhood characterized by the long-term concentration of cis gay men's commercial venues, community spaces, and residences.[73] The spaces around which this book is organized belong to both categories: the bar chapter highlights neighbourhoods in which queer nightlife concentrated, often over a period spanning multiple decades, whereas the chapters on homes and prisons analyse spaces whose queerness remained potential until it became realized through the presence of queer bodies doing queer things.

I assembled the archive for this book from materials that I found at the archives of the feminist and LGBTIQ* movements as well as from sources collected at state institutions, where they are often not catalogued as such. Here, queer historians, like other scholars of marginalized communities, have found success by reading against the grain, or "reading queerly": reading against the intent of those who authored and collected the documents. In the case of Berlin, the city's Cold War division has created further challenges for the researcher. Two administrations produced two archives, and even though the city has now been reunited for over thirty years, some records from East Berlin remain less accessible than those from West Berlin. The resulting archival imbalances structure this book; I have attempted to make them visible throughout the chapters.

This book is committed to privileging queer voices over those of the state. Hence, I started building my archive at the feminist and LGBTIQ* movement archives, where I found oral history interviews, movement publications, and personal papers that included correspondence, calendars, diaries, memoirs, fiction, and personal photographs. My account also draws heavily on sources produced by the state, however, such as West Berlin police records, court documents, and files of the East Berlin Stasi. Whereas the first group of sources was produced from the perspectives of people who made queer social spaces, the second was produced by the state actors who surveilled them, attempted to delimit them, and criminalized them. Because both German postwar states were concerned about the dangers that queer desires and subjectivities presented to "the fragility of heterosexuality," they surveilled queer public spaces intensely and produced ample documentation of the process.[74] In using these sources, I focus on the self- and space-making practices of queer Berliners, even if they are often rendered through homophobic language and perspectives.

By contrast, queer voices from the postwar decades are relatively scarce, for many reasons. The study of gay and lesbian history did not begin until the 1970s and 1980s in West Germany, and the 1980s in East Germany, with trans history only emerging in the 2000s. Intergenerational tensions between postwar queer Berliners and those socialized during the gay and lesbian liberation and rights movements did not always foster an atmosphere of trust necessary to sharing personal stories and documents. Often, survivors of postwar criminalization, stigmatization, and homophobia destroyed "evidence" of their queer lives during this period so that it could not be used against them. Finally, many aspects of everyday life, of producing queer spaces, making the self, and emotional and sexual practices may have been perceived as trivial or unworthy of recording.

Additional imbalances in my archive stem from the fact that sources on West Berlin outnumber sources on East Berlin, and materials about sex between men, non-normative masculinities, and male-to-female trans people outnumber materials about sex between women, non-normative femininities, and female-to-male trans subjects. Concerning queer-produced sources, the East-West imbalance has to do with the differences in gay and lesbian activism and scholarship in West and East. Whereas activists in West Berlin started researching "their" history in the 1970s, and through the 1980s institutionalized it by founding archives, a museum, and workshops, East Berlin activists did not have access to publishing and other resources, though they began much of the same work in the 1980s. Of the movement archives that I visited – the Feminist FFBIZ Archives (Frauenforschungs-, Bildungs- und Informationszentrum), the Gay Museum, the Magnus Hirschfeld Society, the

Spinnboden Lesbian Archives, the Kitty Kuse papers at Christiane von Lengerke's home, the Lili Elbe Archive for Inter Trans Queer History, and the Archive of Other Memories of the Federal Magnus Hirschfeld Foundation – only the last two were *not* founded in pre-1989 West Berlin.[75] The West Berlin archives also collected materials from East Berlin, and some, like the Gay Museum, have significantly enlarged their GDR-related collections since German reunification. Nevertheless, they remain predominantly West German archives. As for East Berlin movement archives, the Robert Havemann Society, dedicated to the history of the opposition in the GDR, has records related to queer lives from the 1980s, but not before.[76] The Lila Archive in Meiningen, founded by East Berlin lesbian activist Ursula Sillge and dedicated to "preserving cultural artefacts relevant to women," does not have personal papers of lesbian women.[77]

State-produced sources for East Germany remain difficult to access, even thirty years after German reunification. For instance, at the Police Historical Collection Berlin (Polizeihistorische Sammlung Berlin), where archivist Jens Dobler pointed me to some crucial sources for West Berlin, the files from the East Berlin People's Police are not indexed at all. Since this archive relies on private funding, it has neither the staff nor the resources to make indexing happen in the near future. At the Stasi Archives, researchers cannot search the catalogue and must instead rely on the archive's staff and trust that they know how to search for the issue at hand. In my case, the staff member assigned to me provided me with materials about gay men but claimed there were no files about lesbian women for my period of interest, a result of the lack of the criminalization of sex between women, he explained. Late in my research, I met a documentary filmmaker from Leipzig, Barbara Wallbraun, who had come across Stasi files about lesbian women in Berlin in the 1960s.[78] She was so generous as to share the relevant call numbers, which the archivist then pulled for me. This episode demonstrates just how damaging a criminalization-focused approach to queer history can be.

As for same-sex relationships between women, scarcity of sources is a problem that generations of lesbian historians have grappled with and productively engaged. Already in 1987, Hanna Hacker noted that "the wish to represent their 'reality' [that of women-loving women] requires a different method and a different language than the analysis of male-male dialogues."[79] More recently, Martha Vicinus, summarizing different paradigms in lesbian history, has suggested "the usefulness of examining the 'not said' and the 'not seen' in order to discover women's sexual lives in the past," or, "in other words, silence is not empty, nor is absence invisible."[80] In my analysis, I have marked silences and described invisibilities; however, for postwar Berlin, lesbian lives did leave traces in both movement and state archives. In movement sources from the period, such as homophile magazines, there is a small yet significant lesbian presence. West Berlin lesbian activists of the 1970s and 1980s bridged generational differences, forming organizations that focused on older women, interviewing them for books and documentary films, and founding archives that collected their personal papers, thus creating a rich archive for the historian. But even in state archives, lesbian lives are present, despite the lack of an explicit criminalization of sex between women.[81]

To overcome the sole focus on cis gay men, I conducted a broad archival search, often following the suggestions of archivists and lesbian historians.[82] At the movement archives, I looked at all available personal papers and oral histories from people who had lived in Berlin during my period of interest, in addition to homophile publications. At the Landesarchiv, the archivist helped me create a list of terms that described deviant sexual behaviour and subjectivities, which might have been used to police queer subjectivities, as well as a list of the sections of the German criminal code relevant to policing gender and sexuality. The list of terms that she helped me come up with included the terms "lesb," for variations of lesbian; "homo," for homosexual; "aso," for asocial; "kuppelei," the German legal term for procuration; "GeKra," for sexually transmitted disease; "lid," "erregung," and "grober unfug," for causing a public nuisance; "unzucht," the German term for fornication; "sittl," for morality; "betrug," for fraud; and the sections of the German criminal code relevant to policing gender and sexuality, §175, §180, §181, §181a, §183, §360, §327, and §361; as well as "trans" and "strich" for streetwalking boys. I then searched the police, prison, and court files for these terms, looked through samples, and probed deeper if I found material relevant to queer subjectivities.

Oral histories present an important body of sources for this book, and they have been an indispensable source for queer histories of the recent past from the beginning of the discipline.[83] In light of the challenges of the queer archive spelled out earlier, oral histories have the potential to mitigate some of the imbalances of traditional archives and to go beyond what is traditionally deemed worthy of archiving. However, oral histories also come with significant challenges for queer history. Nan Alamilla Boyd has described how "it is nearly impossible for oral history or ethnographic narrators to use language outside the parameters of modern sexual identities."[84] Narrators' knowledge of the purpose of their interviews for preservation in a gay and lesbian history archive not only prompted them to identify in the categories of that archive but also made them self-censor parts of their life stories that they felt would run counter to the community's respectability, specifically sexual practices.[85] This bias is a problem for a queer history whose inquiry is directed not towards finding stable gay and lesbian identities in the past but towards analysing how the construction of normative and non-normative sexual subjectivities has changed over time. The oral history archive that I have primarily worked with, the Archive of Other Memories in Berlin, was founded as part of the German federal government's efforts to rehabilitate men persecuted under §175.[86] Its nature as a recuperative, government-sponsored project also creates imbalances; specifically, the narratives told for it may tend to emphasize stories of victimhood over stories of success.[87] Keeping these methodological challenges in mind, oral histories are crucial to this study. I quote extensively from five interviews from the Archive of Other Memories, as well as one interview that I conducted myself, and from oral history passages reprinted in published histories. In approaching these sources, I was most interested in how narrators talked about spaces in Berlin, what the spaces meant to them and how they used them, and how narrators described their sexual and gendered subjectivities. Thus, while I listened to the complete interviews, I did not analyse the whole narrative, only the episodes that addressed Berlin specifically.

Chapter Overview

The book begins in the moment of Berlin's liberation from Nazism in early May 1945, as we follow lesbian communist Hilde Radusch and her girlfriend Eddy Klopsch marching back from their rural hideout into the city centre. The first chapter, "Homes," examines both how the realities of postwar housing played out for queer Berliners and the domestic, political, social, and sexual practices they engaged in to make queer homes. Bringing together oral history narratives, photographs, fiction, and personal papers, I explore what challenges and opportunities the material realities of the postwar moment, particularly the lack of housing and the absence of men, held for queer Berliners. My analysis follows feminist theorizations of home as a space of resistance and of homemaking as fundamental to the making of the self. In my discussion of queer practices of homemaking, I consider queer Berliners' living quarters but also their bodies as important sites of creating a sense of self and belonging.

From the precarious privacy of the home, the second chapter, "Surveilled Sociability: Queer Bars," moves into a semi-public space often called a "second home": the bar. Opening with party photos that were collected and captioned by the West Berlin police, this chapter examines bars as spaces of surveilled sociability. It discusses personal narratives of going out in (West) Berlin against the backdrop of police records that document constant surveillance, frequent raids, and the targeted persecution of those categorized by the police as "transvestites" or "streetwalking boys." The chapter tracks changing reactions against this harassment, showing how bar-goers and owners both creatively subverted surveillance and fought it head-on during the 1960s. It also demonstrates the competing agendas of different authorities in regulating West Berlin's nightlife, as morality began losing out to the mandate of marketing the isolated city to tourists. Finally, it discusses the impact that the division of the city's public by the Wall had for queer East Berliners, who were mostly cut off from these spaces of sociability after August 1961.

Chapter 3, "Passing Through, Trespassing, Passing in Public Spaces," ventures out into the streets and parks of the city to examine what public spaces meant to queer Berliners and how their presence in public was perceived and policed. In personal narratives and police records, streets and parks appear as spaces of seeing and being seen, of flirting, cruising, and sex, but also of slurs, name-calling, and assault, of surveillance and arrest. One major focus of the chapter is the policing of non-normative gender by authorities and bystanders. I examine an oral history account of a feminine man who describes the difficult process of learning normative masculinity, as well as a police file that documents a changing policy of regulating "transvestites" in West Berlin. Another focus of this chapter is "streetwalking boys," who again emerge as central figures who attracted the police's attention, both for their public offers of sexual services and for crimes against their clients. In the chapter's third part, I analyse how the East German regime used the stigmatized figure of the streetwalking boy to detract attention from the violent death of Günter Litfin, the first person to be shot at the Berlin Wall. I argue that, through Litfin's death and the ensuing obliteration of his reputation, the Wall came to signify queer death for the city's queer community. From a distance, however, the Wall could also serve as a template for erotic fantasies, as a short story from Swiss homophile magazine *Der Kreis* demonstrates.

The final chapter, "Bubis behind Bars: Prisons as Queer Spaces," examines queer inmates' experiences of incarceration in both East and West Berlin, with a focus on women's prisons. In oral history accounts and prisoner files, penal institutions emerge as sites that simultaneously regulated and accommodated queer subjectivities. Lesbian relationships and non-normatively gendered subjectivities have left traces in records from both the East and West Berlin's women's prisons. In the late 1960s, prison officials in East Berlin repeatedly linked newly criminalized "asocial" women with "lesbian love" and female masculinity.[88] In West Berlin, the file of prisoner Bettina Grundmann offers an opportunity to assess the possibilities and limits of prisoner agency. It also testifies to queer working-class subjectivities that are rarely found in movement archives. In these sources, prisons appear as spaces whose relatively isolated same-sex environment facilitated erotic relationships between women, turning a site designed to instill social norms into delinquents into a space of queer possibility.

1 Homes

"Schöneberg – old home!" Hilde Radusch began her diary entry for 8 May 1945.[1] Her exclamation expressed her exhilaration at coming home and no longer having to hide after years of a precarious existence as a communist. Born in 1903, Radusch joined the Communist Party as a young adult and was active in party and union politics in Berlin throughout the Weimar Republic. The Nazis arrested and imprisoned her for just under six months in 1933. After she was released from prison, Radusch briefly continued her undercover political work and then led a quiet life. When an acquaintance tipped her off that she was about to be arrested again in 1944, she and her girlfriend Eddy Klopsch fled and lived undercover in a garden shed in Prieros, southeast of Berlin. Now, they returned to the city on the very day that the German army capitulated. Berlin had been under Soviet control for days – the Soviets had raised the red flag on the Reichstag on 30 April, and the German military had capitulated in Berlin on 2 May. Already on 28 April, the Soviet military administration had issued its first order and begun to reorganize public life in the city. German communists returning from their Soviet exile, and from the liberated concentration camps, quickly took charge of the urgent tasks of providing food and shelter and rebuilding infrastructure in the vastly destroyed city.[2] Though Klopsch and Radusch were both weak from hunger and sickness, they had walked almost fifty kilometres from Prieros to Schöneberg, found temporary shelter at a friend's apartment, registered with the district office, run into communist comrades there, and even acquired their ration cards, all within two days. With these necessities taken care of, Radusch's next errand took her to the police station close to Alexanderplatz. Here, she sought the files that the authorities kept on her but realized that they had been burned.[3] Her search unsuccessful, she continued walking north to Pankow, where she had been told that the Soviet commander-in-chief resided. This information turned out to be false, and she turned around, walking south to her former apartment in the Mitte district. She found it partially destroyed by bombs but packed a steamer trunk on a handcart with her belongings and began her walk back to Schöneberg through the "completely wiped out city centre – still burning. Dust; people are stealing whatever they can."[4] When she arrived at her temporary home, she was feverish. Despite feeling "3/4 dead," she left the apartment again the next morning, first to take her girlfriend's place in line for bread, then to the Soviet commandant's office to give her report on the war's end as she had experienced it in Prieros.[5] Between describing her errands, Radusch made notes on the ruined cityscape she traversed, on the mood among the population, and on conversations about the political future that she had with other communists. On 10 May, her wartime diary ends with two questions: "Where should I report for work? What about an apartment of our own?"[6]

Physical survival and the making of a new political future are the main themes in Hilde Radusch's immediate postwar diary. In her account, bread, work, an apartment, police files, and politics appear as equally urgent necessities in the immediate aftermath of the Nazi war. Hence, both literal and figurative notions of home are at the centre of this chapter. Investigating the realities of postwar housing as well as domestic practices, I trace what challenges queer Berliners faced in making actual homes – in living by themselves, with a partner, or in other constellations. What did the affective work of making a *Zuhause*, or, in a more old-fashioned term, a *Heim*, look like?[7] What homes were queer Berliners envisioning and building? For many Berliners who had opposed the Nazis, these were also questions of political belonging, often envisioned as a continuation of the progressive politics of the Weimar Republic. Communists like Hilde Radusch hoped, now that fascism had been defeated and Berlin was under the control of the Soviet army, that the city would be governed by socialists, herself among them. Others, such as trans man and activist Gerd Katter, sought to salvage the legacy of sexologist Magnus Hirschfeld and recreate the Institute for Sexual Science. This chapter documents their efforts, as well as those of dog groomer Rita "Tommy" Thomas and others, to make political and personal homes. Radusch's and Katter's aspirations for a new political beginning were soon disappointed in both East and West Berlin, and close analysis of archival documents will show some of the different forces at work to quell their political endeavours. "The private sphere was less a zone of immunity than a social assertion and even political claim," as historian Paul Betts has argued for the GDR, and it was a space of queer articulation and embodiment in both West and East.[8]

Not everyone persecuted by the Nazis returned home like Hilde Radusch. Some of the between 5,000 and 6,000 men whom the Berlin Landgericht Court convicted of crimes related to homosexuality between 1933 and 1945 did not survive.[9] Three-quarters of them received a prison sentence, and at least 138 men died in incarceration and never came home again.[10] Other queer Berliners were racialized as Jews and murdered in the Holocaust, such as young Gad Beck's boyfriend Manfred Lewin or Felice Schragenheim, known from the 1999 feature film *Aimée und Jaguar*.[11] Journalist and writer Eva Siewert's short story "The Oracle," published in 1946, mourns and memorializes her lover Alice Carlé, who was Jewish and was deported to Auschwitz in 1943 and murdered there. The story and their relationship stand at the beginning of the chapter's first part, which explores home as belonging.

Theorizing Queer Homes

"Home" is a productive concept to study queer lives in postwar Berlin, not just because the close etymological relationship of *Heim* (home) and *heimelig* (cozy, homely) to *heimlich* (secret, clandestine) appears promising in this period in which queer lives were often lived *heimlich*, meaning both in the privacy of people's homes *and* hidden. Sigmund Freud has famously tracked the etymology of the word "*unheimlich*" in his essay "Das Unheimliche" (The Uncanny). Setting out from the assumption that *unheimlich* (uncanny) is the opposite of *heimlich, heimisch, vertraut* (homely, familiar), he found that the ambivalence of *heimlich* as the "*Vertrauten, Behaglichen*" *and* the "*Versteckten, Verborgengehaltenen*" leads to the incorporation of *unheimlich* in *heimlich*.[12] Home's ideological inscriptions as the site of familial reproduction, as a peaceful haven from a menacing world, and as a female space opposed to a male public space all make it a pre-eminent site for any study of gender and sexuality. Feminist thinkers have long critiqued the notions of home as a safe space of belonging and of rigid boundaries between private and public. Rejecting the conceptualization of homes as spaces outside politics, they have instead pointed to the inherent instability of the boundaries between private and public,[13] stressed the home's significance as a space of resistance,[14] and made the case for homemaking to be considered as fundamental to the making of the self.[15] Recent publications in gender and sexuality studies have continued feminist inquiries as well as pushing beyond them, investigating the home as a key site of constructing and maintaining heteronormativity and attending to processes of queering the home.[16] Here, scholars have questioned the field's focus on "exceptional sites" such as bars and clubs, cruising spots, marches, or festivals at the expense of quotidian spaces. Instead, they have highlighted "the role of the politics of domesticity in social change, the subversive possibilities of the home and the continued significance of a home-space for self-worth and well-being."[17]

This chapter's inquiry of queer domesticity in postwar Berlin is guided by this theoretical framework. My discussion of sources will explore homes' significance as spaces of rest and recovery, and as sites of self-constitution through sexual and gendered practices. The sources also exemplify the inherent instability of the boundaries between inside and outside, private and public. While the second half of this chapter is dedicated to case studies of queer domesticity, its first half discusses queer Berliners' efforts to create a home in the sense of a place of belonging. For Hilde Radusch, it meant contributing to the political reconstruction of Berlin as a long-time communist. For Gerd Katter, it meant commemorating Magnus Hirschfeld and his Institute for Sexual Science, where he had found refuge as a trans teenager. Memory was also a driving force for Eva Siewert, who had lost her lover Alice Carlé in the Holocaust and mourned and memorialized her in her short story "The Oracle" (Das Orakel).

I. Home as Belonging

No Homecoming: Eva Siewert and Alice Carlé

Eva Siewert (1907–94) was a well-known radio journalist and speaker during the 1930s. The Nazis destroyed her career and severely damaged her health, and after the war, she was unable to achieve comparable success. Her life and works have recently enjoyed renewed interest thanks to historian Raimund Wolfert, who came across her during research on writer and activist Kurt Hiller and has since published on her biography and works.[18] My discussion of Siewert's life and writing is indebted to Wolfert's work, particularly as access to the files of Siewert's estate proceedings is limited to the "circle of involved parties (potential heirs, creditors, etc.)," but not researchers.[19] Recently, new information about Siewert has surfaced, and a monograph about her and Alice Carlé is in the works.[20]

Born in Breslau (today, Wrocław, Poland) in 1907 to concert singers Hans and Frieda Siewert, Eva Siewert grew up in Berlin. From July 1932 until March 1938, she was chief editor and speaker at Radio Luxemburg, a private radio station, and became a popular radio personality. She was featured in newspaper and magazine articles across German-speaking Europe and sent autographed postcards to her fans (figure 1.1).

Eva Siewert
Radioansagerin und Redakteurin
Phot. Ed. Kutler

Figure 1.1. Star postcard of Eva Siewert, 1930s. Collection of Raimund Wolfert, Berlin.

Her elegant masculinity attracted attention. For instance, a newspaper portrait by the Czernowitz (today, Chernivtsi, Ukraine) writer Franz Porubsky noted with "utmost surprise" that she wore "gentlemen's garb" in two star postcards. Siewert, who was also quoted as "hoping to stay unmarried for a long time still," explained that "she prefers gentlemen's garb because it suits her best, is practical and comparatively cheaper, but still elegant."[21]

Fearing the outbreak of war, Siewert attempted to leave Europe in 1938 for Teheran, Iran, where she had worked for a German company in 1930–31. She travelled to Berlin to apply for a visa at the Iranian embassy, but her application was denied and her passport was seized, making it impossible for her to leave. With a "fully Jewish" mother according to the Nuremberg Laws, Siewert was categorized as a "half Jew" by the Nazis and prohibited from working for the radio or the press.[22] She got by as a translator and typist but was repeatedly arrested and incarcerated for sharing anti-Nazi jokes. Soon after her arrival in Berlin, she met the clerk Alice Carlé (1902–43), and the two became close, likely lovers. How they met remains unknown. In her autobiographical short story "The Oracle," published in 1946, Siewert worked through the loss of Alice, who was murdered in Auschwitz.[23] The story, a moving account of a queer relationship between two women persecuted by the Nazis, is both a starting point and an end point: a starting point for grappling with the years of persecution, separation, uncertainty, and death; and an end point to that uncertainty, the coming to terms with Alice's death through the process of writing. By fictionalizing her own story and by leaving uncertain the nature of the relationship between the narrator and Alice, Siewert mourned and memorialized a relationship between two women considered illegitimate by most of her contemporaries.

"The Oracle" appeared in the 8 November 1946 issue of *Der Weg: Zeitschrift für Fragen des Judentums* (The Path: Journal for Questions of Judaism). *Der Weg* came out weekly beginning in March 1946. Its publishers envisioned it as both a medium to educate non-Jews and a forum for discussion in the Jewish community. Among the weekly's features were not only news of Jewish congregational life, advice for those who wanted to emigrate, and personal ads of Jewish Berliners mourning their dead, asking for information about missing relatives and friends, or seeking marriage partners. *Der Weg* also offered space for personal reflections on the years of persecution, testimonials, and literary explorations of Nazism and the Holocaust, most often in the form of poetry.

Set between reprints of original documents about the "Kristallnacht" (November Pogrom, or Night of Broken Glass) of November 1938, short news dispatches, a longer piece detailing the question of postwar housing, and the personal ads section, the story's title "The Oracle" evokes ancient myth, the transcendental, and the sense of an unknown future – the latter a central theme of the story. The narrative begins with the November Pogrom:

> At that point it became clear to us that staying meant risking our lives. Until 9 November 1938, the desire to emigrate had been a desire for freedom. Now it became a necessity. We had to save ourselves.[24]

Waiting anxiously for a possibility to emigrate together, the narrator and Alice seek out a fortune-teller in the hope of gaining certainty. Her oracle tells them that the narrator will get away first, then Alice, "very far away," giving them cause for relief. The oracle continues, however: they will then never see each other again. This oracle appears to have been mistaken when the pair find a sponsor in London who agrees to host them. But his letter comes late, in August 1939, and they do not manage to leave before the war begins. Leaving is not as urgent for the narrator, who describes herself as "only 'half.'" Alice and her sister, however, are racialized as fully Jewish according to the Nuremberg Laws of 1935. When the narrator is imprisoned for anti-Nazi jokes and comments, a sympathetic guard lets Alice know that her friend leaves the prison in the mornings and returns at night from an outside work camp. Twice a week, Alice comes to the prison, standing on the other side of the street, which is busy with shoppers.

> Twice a week we greeted each other with our eyes. More could not happen. Even a smile or a nod meant the greatest danger for her and *Kellerstrafe* for me. During this time of special punishment, we could not have seen each other ... In this way, we always saw each other for six minutes. Precious minutes. We both knew of the other that we were alive.[25]

This precious contact is interrupted when the narrator's work gets moved to a site within the prison, but Alice now sends weekly letters to keep in touch. She has gone underground and lives in a garden shed outside Berlin, and mutual friends serve as intermediaries for their mail exchange. Once Alice's letters stop coming, the narrator is left with an agonizing ignorance about Alice's whereabouts. When the narrator is released from prison, she runs to Alice's house, hoping that the sympathetic concierge ("She was considered a secret ally") might know something. But the whole block is in ruins. Her friends have found out that Alice and her sister were discovered and deported, probably to Auschwitz. This name has no meaning for the narrator, who consults an atlas to make sense of it. "I picked up the big atlas and looked for Auschwitz. So it was down there." Then, she asks around, getting dramatically different answers: one person tells her that those in Auschwitz don't have it so bad, being only required to work on farms; another one says: "They are long dead." She refuses to believe it. In recurring dreams, Alice knocks on her door, asking her to hide her. When the war ends, the narrator inquires about Alice wherever she can, writing to search committees, going through lists, and contacting Alice's brother in Tel Aviv. All her inquiries remain unanswered, however: "The oracle had fulfilled itself."

At the beginning, Siewert's narrator is "wir," the first-person plural. Yet, as soon as her characters are torn apart, the story is told from the perspective of an unnamed, single, first-person narrator. While their relationship is not described in any detail, and the narrator never refers to Alice by any other referent than her name, it is evident that the narrative "wir" denotes the two of them. Their plan to emigrate together, the fact that they have their fortune told together, and their desperate hope that "we would find each other again somehow. Some ship would depart one day that would carry one to the other" leaves little doubt as to their coupledom.

While Siewert fictionalized the story, it still bears many autobiographical traces. She was "half" Jewish in Nazi race categorization. Like the narrator in "The Oracle," she tried to leave Germany before the war. Like her narrator, she was imprisoned twice for jokes and critical comments about the Nazis. While little is known about Alice Carlé, Siewert's statement that Carlé sometimes stayed overnight at her apartment was confirmed by multiple witnesses after the war when Siewert applied for recognition as a Victim of Fascism. After Siewert's arrest, her apartment was no longer accessible as a hideout for Alice. Alice and her sister Charlotte were arrested in August 1943, deported to Auschwitz, and murdered in the same year.[26]

"The Oracle" thus allowed Siewert to begin working through some of the traumatic events that she had experienced. Her use of the past tense and of temporal markers such as "back then" and "one day," as well as phrasings such as "Berlin lay in ruins back then" and "the war ended," create a temporal distance at odds with the date of the story's publication, just one and a half years after the end of the war, when Berlin was still very much in ruins. By shifting the events back in time, Siewert distanced herself from the continuing pain of losing Alice. By conceding that the oracle had been fulfilled, she put an end point to the nagging uncertainty about her fate, creating a closure that reality had not yet provided. Writing the story may thus have helped Siewert to orient herself in the present and to turn from the future she had imagined with Alice to a future without her. At the same time, "The Oracle" is, of course, a memorial to Alice and to their relationship. Fictionalizing their story and leaving readers in the dark about the exact nature of their friendship allowed her to mourn her queer love.

For years after the end of the war, Eva Siewert attempted to find out about Alice Carlé's fate, unsuccessfully (figure 1.2).[27] She also sought to continue her career in journalism. Until 1947, she worked as a translator

Figure 1.2. Eva Siewert in the immediate postwar years. Collection of Raimund Wolfert, Berlin.

and interpreter for the Soviet-controlled Berliner Rundfunk radio station.[28] She wrote for magazines and newspapers, among them the West Berlin *Telegraf* and, briefly, for the East Berlin *Weltbühne*. It was an article Siewert penned for the latter in 1947 that attracted the attention of the author Kurt Hiller, a major protagonist of the homosexual emancipation movement during the Weimar Republic who at the time was still living in his London exile. In the correspondence that ensued, Siewert reported on mounting political tensions in the Berlin media, but also shared glimpses of her personal life. She was pessimistic about the impact of her work and the prospects for a democratic Germany. "I write for many newspapers, but it serves little purpose," she wrote in her response to Hiller's initial letter.

> Already, incorrigible compatriots have left notes at my door again: "Germany shall live!" ... The majority of Germans sympathize with our informers, who once turned us in and are now running free. There is no point anymore in steering this mad ship with a hostile crew as a reasonable person or, in trying to do that, with the shadows of the dear dead floating around us.[29]

Despite her well-founded pessimism and the threat that the note on her apartment door may have meant, Eva Siewert was a highly productive writer in the immediate postwar years. By 1950, she had published over 130 short stories, reviews, opinion pieces, and translations, all this oeuvre despite significant health problems that resulted from her incarceration.[30] With Hiller, she also exchanged notes about continuing the pre-Nazi homosexual activism, and for a short while in 1949–50, she served as a member of the Berlin chapter of the refounded Scientific-Humanitarian Committee. Two book manuscripts that Siewert wrote in the postwar years are lost: A memoir about her time in the women's prison did not appear after the publisher Volk und Zeit went bankrupt in 1949.[31] A manuscript on the topic of female homosexuality likewise was not published, despite her high hopes for public interest in light of the "major spread of this phenomenon, due to the mere lack of men."[32] Two years after her initial response to Hiller, Siewert remained depressed about the political situation. "We have not progressed in the past years, quite in contrast!" she wrote to him in April 1949. "We were further in 1945 than we are now. At times I give up all hope; at other times I get so angry that I want to fight more than ever."[33] In her despair about Germany, Siewert also considered emigration, but in the end she stayed in Berlin until her death in 1994. Her grief for Alice Carlé did not stop her from falling in love again – in her letters to Hiller, she mentions crushes and relationships with other women. Little is known about the second half of her life, whether West Germany's liberalization in the 1960s made her feel less at odds with the Germans, or what she thought about the politics of the gay and lesbian movements of the 1970s.

More than twenty years after Eva Siewert's death, and more than seventy years after Alice Carlé's murder, public memorials made their love and their lives visible in Berlin and on the internet. In February 2017, three of Berlin's queer archives, the Magnus-Hirschfeld-Gesellschaft, Spinnboden Lesbenarchiv, and the Schwules Museum laid out *Stolpersteine* (memorial stepping stones) for Carlé, her siblings, and parents.[34] In 2018, the Magnus-Hirschfeld-Gesellschaft launched an online memorial space, "In Memoriam Eva Siewert," commemorating the two women and making some of Eva Siewert's oeuvre available.[35]

Siewert's struggle for survival in the postwar years is paralleled in some ways by the attempts of communist Hilde Radusch to gain political footing, contribute to Germany's political renewal, and pursue a career amid personal threats from hostile men and escalating Cold War tensions.

Hilde Radusch: Purged from Her Political Home

The beginning of this chapter saw Hilde Radusch and Eddy Klopsch making their way from the countryside through the outskirts into the city centre, seeking to be part of the rebuilding of German politics after fascism. The following section examines how their queerness affected Radusch's ability to do so. To reconstruct the couple's lives in the postwar years, I draw primarily on Hilde Radusch's extensive papers at the Feminist FFBIZ Archives, which include calendars, housekeeping books, correspondence, unpublished manuscripts, and photo albums.[36] I triangulate her personal papers with the couple's Victim of Fascism (*Opfer des Faschismus*) files at the Landesarchiv, as well as the historiography on communist power consolidation in postwar Berlin. What emerges in my reading of these sources is a deeply precarious life endangered by economic hardship, hostility, and threats of violence. Radusch's papers also demonstrate, though, how these two middle-aged women stubbornly pursued a dignified livelihood, withstanding continued hostility and not shying away from long exchanges with the authorities.

Else "Eddy" Klopsch and Hilde Radusch experienced the end of the war in their garden plot in the village of Prieros, southeast of Berlin. After returning to the city, they first found temporary refuge in a sublet, but they could soon move into their own apartment in Schöneberg – a privilege they likely enjoyed because of Radusch's communist merits.[37] Born in 1903 into a family devoted to the German emperor, Hilde Radusch became a leftist as a young adult. At age eighteen, she entered the Communist Youth. After training as an after-school children's caretaker, she joined the ranks of Weimar Germany's new female white-collar workers as the prototypical *Fräulein vom Amt* in 1925, operating switchboards. She was active in the communist Roter Frauen- und Mädchenbund (Red Women's and Girls' Association), gave lectures, and wrote for different communist publications. She served in the union of the postal service and as a representative for the Communist Party on the Berlin Mitte District Council from 1929 to 1932. Because of the latter function, the Nazis arrested her in April 1933 and sent her to jail for just short of six months. After her release, she continued performing some underground party work, but stopped because she was, according to her own estimation, "conspicuous and unfit for clandestine work."[38] She survived the rest of the Nazi reign doing various clerical jobs.

Hilde Radusch and Eddy Klopsch's relationship began in 1939, when Radusch moved from her former home district Schöneberg to a new apartment in Mitte (figure 1.3). Klopsch lived in the same building.[39]

Figure 1.3. Hilde Radusch and Eddy Klopsch at Tiergarten, 1939. Hilde Radusch Papers, Feminist FFBIZ Archives, Berlin.

The two became friends and then quickly girlfriends. Looking back, Radusch recalled Klopsch's mention of Damenklub Violetta, a lesbian social group active until 1933, as the shibboleth that allowed them to know each other's queerness and thus made their relationship possible. Much less is known about Klopsch than about Radusch, and most of what little can be reconstructed is based on Radusch's papers. Klopsch was born in Berlin on 12 May 1906, likely with a heart deficiency.[40] As a young woman, she worked in a tobacco factory, but at age twenty-two she had to stop because of her disability.[41] In the early 1940s, the two women ran a cheap lunch restaurant in Mitte. In 1944, a friend of

Figure 1.4. Passport photo of Hilde Radusch, 1946. Feminist FFBIZ Archives, Berlin.

Klopsch's informed her of Radusch's imminent arrest during the *Aktion Gitter*, the concerted arrest of former representatives from non-nationalist parties in the national, state, and city parliaments on 22 August. From then on, Radusch, soon joined by Klopsch, hid on their garden plot southeast of Berlin, where they witnessed the arrival of the Red Army.

Back in the city in May 1945, Radusch quickly found work in her old neighbourhood of Schöneberg, heading the Opfer des Faschismus (OdF, Victims of Fascism) Department in the district office (figure 1.4). Initiated by a communist survivor of the Nazi camps, the OdF had a dual role: as a political body making decisions about who to acknowledge as a victim of fascism and as a welfare department in charge of supplying survivors with food, clothes, housing, jobs, and compensation.[42] Radusch's lifelong political work for the Communist Party served as her entrance ticket to the job. Her task was to help those who had survived the Nazi prisons and concentration camps, or an underground existence like herself, to survive and get compensation for what they had suffered. Within months, however, Radusch's work for the OdF led to conflicts with the party. In late November, its Berlin leadership summoned her to appear in front of a "control commission."[43] On 1 January 1946, she was asked to appear before another investigation committee "to resolve a number of questions."[44] The day of the meeting, 7 January 1946, marks the end of her membership in the Communist Party, after almost twenty-five years. Just five days later, she quit her position with the Schöneberg OdF Department.[45] But Radusch left neither her party nor her job voluntarily. A series of letters, pencil-written in clumsy handwriting, detail the reasons for her termination, painting a messy picture of postwar greed, political intrigue, and vicious misogyny. In an undated letter that is part of Radusch's OdF file, a Heinz S. writes to his unnamed comrade:

> Ms. Radusch had to leave too, after all, because she treated all four parties in the same way and rejected Jure's order to give everything to those with a KPD [Communist Party of Germany] membership.[46]

In a second letter to his comrade M., Heinz S. further reveals:

> Comrade. I can no longer stand being seen as a rascal in your eyes therefore I make a confession to you … Before Christmas Jure, Binz, Krüger, Steinfort said How do we get rid of Radusch she is too smart and dangerous as a broad [*Weib*] I give 100 cigars and 5 jackets if somebody helps us. I was there and asked what one would have to do. I was then told take out a few bills and a package from the desk directly in front of the door to the right in Room I. They said after Christmas all will be put back inside. However in the meantime I found that that was not done but you and Ms. Radosch were kicked out of the office.[47]

Heinz S. wrote a similar letter to Hilde Radusch herself, kept in her personal papers, in which he identified himself as a Social Democrat.[48] Though none of the letters are dated, he likely wrote them in late February or early March 1946, when the US military administration filed a lawsuit against Schöneberg mayor Gerhard Jurr (misspelled Jure in the letters) and other communists.[49] In this third letter, afraid to be implicated in the lawsuit, Heinz S. pleads with Radusch to save his skin by not testifying in the trial. His letters offer two explanations for her termination: when distributing goods in her OdF job, she refused to favour her comrades. She was thus an obstacle to enrichment. To get rid of her, the local clique of Communist and Social Democrat men arranged for the theft of valuables and documents from her office.[50] The theft, and the likely indictment for embezzlement, rapidly ended what had appeared as a promising postwar career in city administration.[51] At the same time, S. also writes that Radusch "as a broad" (*als Weib*) had become "too smart and dangerous." The phrasing does not leave much room for doubt: Radusch's gender was perceived as a menace; she directly threatened male power.

In an oral history interview she gave in 1979–80, Radusch, who became an activist in the lesbian movement of the 1970s as well as a much-sought-after speaker on Weimar Berlin, the Nazi period, and the postwar years, herself gave an additional reason for her resignation from the Communist Party.

> Yeah, as long as you collaborate with the Communists, helping them with their work, etc., everything is splendid. But back then, when I quit, I was told, well, yeah, we would let you join again if you promise to let your girlfriend go. [I] thumped the table with my fist, said: "My girlfriend is none of your business," and handed in my membership book myself.[52]

In Radusch's memory, it was her relationship with Eddy Klopsch, then, that made her unbearable for the party. She does not say here what her comrades had against her girlfriend specifically – if it was something she did or was, or rather their relationship that they objected to.[53] It seems entirely plausible that it was homophobia that motivated them. As historian Susanne zur Nieden has shown, the anti-fascists who worked for the OdF shared the German "homophobic consensus" and deprived both gay men and lesbian women whom the Nazis had persecuted of recognition and material help.[54] Heinz S.'s plea letter to Radusch helps untangle the men's motivation. He writes:

> You've been wanted dead for a long time but your girlfriend did not leave your side and once when she threw somebody out they noticed unforeseen forces in her that woman must have some kind of training because otherwise she could not throw a strong man into the air like paper after that one was afraid when she was present.[55]

According to Heinz S., Radusch might long be dead had it not been for her girlfriend, whose constant presence and physical strength protected her. This assertion comes as a surprise, given Klopsch's fragile health – the heart defect that she was born with, her later disability. What is more, she was about a head shorter than Radusch, who herself was only 5 feet 4 inches (1.62 metres) tall, as figure 1.3 shows.[56] It appears, then, that in their case, being visible as a queer couple created a presence that made it harder to attack them. For them, their openly lived relationship was a safeguard, not a hazard. Even if their relationship saved Radusch from a physical assault, however, it could not protect her from intrigue, from the heartbreak of losing her political home, and from the poverty that resulted from her comrades' bullying. In the second part of the chapter, I will discuss how the couple dealt with these emotional and financial challenges, and how their home, while providing space for self-care and the constitution of sexual selves, could not keep misogyny and homophobia completely outside.

Gerd Katter: Memorializing Magnus Hirschfeld as Homemaking

Like Hilde Radusch and Eddy Klopsch who had socialized at Damenclub Violetta in the 1920s, Gerd E. Katter had also discovered his queerness during the Weimar Republic. For his coming out as trans, it was not Berlin's subculture that had played the key role, but the homosexual and transvestite magazines of the era, his subsequent visits to the Institute for Sexual Science, and his acquaintance with Magnus Hirschfeld, who he came to regard as a father figure. After the defeat of the Nazis, Katter started his personal campaign to commemorate the former mentor. In June 1947, his impassioned letter reached the desk of Anton Ackermann, head of the cultural department of the Sozialistische Einheitspartei Deutschlands (SED, Socialist Unity Party of Germany) and functionary of the Kulturbund, a forum for intellectuals and cultural workers.[57] Katter introduced himself as a "cultural creator, member of the Kulturbund, and especially comrade and SED functionary."[58] He was deeply upset that the new Germany had so far neglected to commemorate "an eminent man of German science," a man who was also a "victim of fascism" and deserved recognition as a "fighter for social reform and human rights, as a friend of the Soviet Union … [a] staunch pacifist." The man that the writer wanted to see memorialized and commemorated was Magnus Hirschfeld. Gerd E. Katter, a resident of Birkenwerder, a village just outside the northern Berlin city limits, was inspired to start a campaign to honour Hirschfeld and to rebuild his Institute for Sexual Science from his experience of the institute in the Weimar Republic, a place that he remembered as a place of belonging. Katter was not the only one fighting to procure Hirschfeld his rightful place in German collective memory in postwar Berlin.[59] What makes Katter's case particularly interesting are his motivation and his social standing. In contrast to other postwar activists for Hirschfeld's cause, Katter was neither a scientist nor an intellectual or politician, but rather a working-class person driven by his warm personal memory of Hirschfeld. The difficulties that he ran into shed light on the politics of memory in East Germany in the immediate postwar years. Before discussing his postwar activism, however, it is important to understand his prewar biography, especially his encounter with sexual science, Magnus Hirschfeld, and the institute.

Katter was born in Berlin-Britz in 1910 and registered and raised as female, but never felt at home in that gender.[60] As a teenager, he came across an article by Max Hodann, sexual scientist and colleague of Magnus Hirschfeld, and subsequently discovered the homosexual and transvestite magazines published by Radszuweit Verlag, which he bought at kiosks and hid at home. Katter's parents, first unhappy about their child's gender nonconformity, soon became supportive.[61] His father helped him find an apprenticeship as a carpenter, a male profession. In the carpenter union's library, Katter found Hirschfeld's *Geschlechtskunde*, which contained sections on homosexuality and transvestism. A communist acquaintance told his parents about the Institute for Sexual Science, and an uncle who was a direct neighbour of sexual scientist Max Hodann put them in touch. In 1927, Katter visited the institute for the first time, accompanied by his mother. Remembering the friendly welcome, he described the experience as life-altering: "This meant the end of doubts and fears; I had nothing to fear from such friendly people."[62] For the following two years at least, Katter became a regular at the institute. Hirschfeld helped him procure a *Transvestitenschein* (transvestite pass), a document identifying its bearer as known to the police to wear the clothing of the opposite sex (figure 1.5). Holders could show the pass to the police to avoid being arrested for causing a public nuisance. In 1929, Katter applied to have his first name changed officially to Gerd, and he also underwent surgery, likely a mastectomy.[63] At the institute, Katter met other teenage patients. He hung out with archivist Karl Giese, and even imagined a professional future for himself as Giese's successor or assistant. "After all, my trade, though I practised it with joy, was not something that could satisfy my mind!"[64] Looking back on his years in the institute sixty years later, Katter called them "the most interesting of my life."[65] He met international visitors, "many Americans, English, and Japanese."[66] Even more meaningful to him were meetings with members of the German parliament, who came to the institute to learn about homosexuals first-hand as they discussed a reform of §175. Perhaps most importantly, he developed a close relationship with Magnus Hirschfeld, who, according to Katter, endearingly called him "*Katterchen*" and on one occasion even "my dear son."[67] Hirschfeld's role as paternal figure, and the institute's significance as a place of safety, comfort, community and kinship, learning, and political engagement would motivate Katter's postwar activism, and he cherished the memory of his time spent there into old age. In a way, he continued inhabiting the institute long after it was gone.

Figure 1.5. Katter's transvestite pass, 1928. Courtesy of Magnus-Hirschfeld-Gesellschaft Berlin.

Little is known about Katter's life during National Socialism.[68] He worked for an insurance company during the war years and, following his passion for the stage, took private acting lessons.[69] After the war, he settled in Birkenwerder with his mother. It was from there, from the outskirts of Berlin, that he campaigned for a refounding of the Institute for Sexual Science and for the recognition and memorialization of Hirschfeld. Katter claimed that he had begun these efforts in 1945, but the earliest documentation is his letter to the Kulturbund dated 24 June 1947.[70] In his appeal, Katter constructed both himself and Hirschfeld as good socialists and anti-fascists. He stressed that he had actively fought for Hirschfeld's honour already during National Socialism.[71] By describing Hirschfeld as a "victim of fascism" and a "fighter," Katter used the terms of the emerging socialist recognition categories for survivors of the Nazis. *Opfer des Faschismus* (OdF, Victim of Fascism) was the official term for those survivors who were recognized as such by the state.

Katter put particular emphasis on Hirschfeld's quality of being a "fighter": he was a "fighter for social reform and human rights," led the "fight against ignorance and mindlessness," saved hundreds from suicide by giving them purpose as "fellow fighters," was a "fighter for the truth," in short, a "gigantic fighter."[72] Constructing Hirschfeld as a fighter appeared as an especially promising rhetorical strategy because it echoed the OdF distinction of "active fighters" and "passive victims," with the latter less deserving of recognition and tangible help. But Katter also appealed to his readers' national pride. He called Hirschfeld a "German hero," famous around the world, where he stood "in the bright lights ... of the world's public."[73] He asked: "What will the world think of us" with no attention given to Hirschfeld's memory three years after the end of Nazism? And he ended his letter with a warning penned by none other than the quintessential German poet, Johann Wolfgang von Goethe: "Noble man! Woe the century that pushed you away! Woe the progeny that misjudges you!"[74] It is noteworthy that Katter stressed Hirschfeld's Germanness but remained silent on his Jewishness. Apparently, he – correctly – did not believe that mentioning it would help his cause. Rather, it would have undermined his construction of Hirschfeld as a "fighter," since the OdF hierarchy denigrated the Jewish victims of the Nazis as "passive victims."

Katter bolstered his appeal for Hirschfeld's recognition, and the continuation of his work, by finding prominent supporters for his endeavour. He contacted writers Friedrich Wolf and Arnold Zweig; Paul Krische, scientist and sexual reformer; Felix Bönheim, director of Leipzig's university hospital; Harry Damrow, chief press officer of Berliner Rundfunk, the East Berlin radio station, and member of the Kulturbund's Berlin leadership; among others.[75] They were all sympathetic to his concern, but at the same time, as merited anti-fascists, they now held important functions in the cultural and medical sectors and were all extremely busy. Krische reported that he had contacted newspapers to feature memorials to Hirschfeld in celebration of his birthday. Wolf promised that he would try to write a memorial for him in the magazine of the Vereinigung der Verfolgten des Naziregimes (VVN, Association of Those Persecuted by the Nazis).[76] Damrow answered that he had contacted the federal leadership of the Kulturbund and would steer the attention of his station's cultural editors to Hirschfeld. Zweig, who had returned to Berlin from Palestine in October 1948, called Katter's letter one of the "most thanks-deserving events since my return to Germany."[77] He cautioned him that Hirschfeld's rehabilitation would take some time, and he offered an explanation why nobody seemed interested in him.

> You must realize that the public's attitude towards the memory and life's work of Magnus Hirschfeld is not only an act of sexual displacement ... but in addition, it also represents a pause in dealing with the psychological side of social processes.[78]

Zweig thus read the German public's disinterest in Hirschfeld as an expression of German guilt for the Holocaust. Indeed, the resistance that Katter encountered can be explained as the result of an overlay of different discourses. By portraying Hirschfeld as a pacifist and an early friend of the Soviet Union, Katter had given good arguments to celebrate Hirschfeld as a hero for the new socialist Germany. But the Nazis' defamation of Hirschfeld as a Jewish pervert, built on an earlier identification of Jews and sexual liberalism, and sexual science as a Jewish science, continued to reverberate in the postwar era.[79] Hirschfeld's membership in the Social Democratic Party (SPD, Sozialdemokratische Partei Deutschlands) would likely not have counted in his favour after the unification of the SPD and the Communist Party of Germany (KPD, Kommunistische Partei Deutschlands), resulting in the creation of the Socialist Unity Party (SED) in the East, was rejected in the sectors controlled by the Western Allies. Additionally, many of the leading figures of the East German SED had adopted the reactionary sexual politics that they witnessed in exile in Stalin's Russia, despite the sexual progressivism of the KPD during the Weimar Republic.[80] When a 1947 Kulturbund article called for the creation of "a new, clean, and decent life," "in the area of mind and culture too," the terms anticipated the East German state's emphasis on moral cleanliness and decency that became party policy in the 1950s.[81] Thus, it is not surprising that the prominent support for Katter's project failed to lead to a recognition of Hirschfeld through the Kulturbund. If Zweig, Damrow, or Wolf did lobby for his memory, their efforts have left no traces in the archives.[82] If one of the Kulturbund's Berlin district chapters organized a talk about Hirschfeld and the Institute for Sexual Science in 1948, as Harry Damrow vaguely remembered, it was not recorded.[83]

Framing Hirschfeld, and himself, as socialists and the appreciation of Hirschfeld's legacy as a task of the new, anti-fascist Germany did not keep Katter from appealing to possible partners in West Germany. In February 1951, he wrote to the West German periodical *Liebe und Ehe*.[84] This short-lived advice journal served as a forum for discussions of sex in and outside marriage, oscillating, as Dagmar Herzog has shown, between distancing itself from and reaffirming Nazi attitudes towards sex.[85] Here, Katter's request fell on deaf ears, however. The editor, Dr. Kaltofen, informed him that the new Institute for Sexual Science, which had been founded in Frankfurt am Main, sought to distance itself from Hirschfeld. Kaltofen associated Hirschfeld with "extreme" positions in the debates about §175 and claimed that his ideas had been "misunderstood" and used as "licence or justification," resulting in Hirschfeld becoming "a victim of his own, by all means sincere, efforts." Kaltofen also voiced hesitations about the continuing validity of Hirschfeld's research, mirroring the distancing moves of leading West German sexologists.[86] Kaltofen's criticism of Hirschfeld remained imprecise. Since Alfred Kinsey's research was not published in German until a few years later, the scientific doubts that he referred to were likely those of Nazi sexology. Kinsey's volume on women's sexual behaviour was translated into German in 1954; his report on men became available in German in 1955. However, Germans had known about Kinsey's studies for years, as magazines had reported his spectacular findings, and an array of summaries written in understandable, non-jargon language were available at low cost in the early 1950s.[87] In light of the violent destruction of Hirschfeld's institute, and the Nazis' repeated defamation of him, the editor's suggestion that Hirschfeld himself was to blame for his demise was nothing but pure hostility. Kaltofen's response is an example of the continuity of Nazi attitudes in *Liebe und Ehe*. As Dagmar Herzog has shown, the magazine gave voice to anti-semitic sentiment both implicitly, through the denigration of Freud and psychoanalysis, and through an explicit linking of Jewishness and sexual depravity.[88]

Gerd Katter was not alone in his efforts to memorialize Hirschfeld, of course. In Saxony, psychiatrist Rudolf Klimmer appealed to authorities and the Kulturbund to resume Hirschfeld's work and establish a sexological institute.[89] Homophile publications such as Switzerland-based *Der Kreis* periodically published commemorative pieces, often penned by Hirschfeld's friend and comrade-in-arms Kurt Hiller.[90] Hiller was himself active in West German efforts to continue Hirschfeld's work, though quickly became disenchanted by the cautious politics of postwar sexologists.[91] In 1952, *Die Freunde*, another homophile magazine, reprinted a short note from the West Berlin night paper *nacht-depesche* on a commemoration held for Hirschfeld at Kreuzberg's chamber music hall in Hallesche Straße in November 1951.[92] The event was organized by the Adolf-Koch-Institut and the Bund für Körperkultur und Erziehung, two Weimar-era organizations dedicated to working-class nudist culture and refounded after the war with the support of the Kreuzberg district office. Speakers were Kreuzberg mayor Willy Kressmann as well as former colleagues of Hirschfeld's from medical and activist circles.[93] The brief note gives no further information about the memorial, such as how large the attendance was or what the speakers said. Still, the fact that it was sponsored by the district administration and held in a festive hall show that Hirschfeld was not universally forgotten or rejected. In Kreuzberg, a working-class district that had been home to a queer subculture since the late nineteenth century, Hirschfeld was celebrated even in the early 1950s. Hallesche Straße, where the memorial took place, was in walking distance of the bars and ballrooms that Hirschfeld had often visited and described in his works. The name change of the Bund für Menschenrecht, a prewar homosexual rights organization reregistered after multiple attempts at the Charlottenburg district office in 1951, to Magnus-Hirschfeld-Gesellschaft may have been inspired by heightened attention to Hirschfeld's name after the Kreuzberg memorial. That first postwar group bearing Hirschfeld's name had its office, as well as an Archiv für Sexualwissenschaft, on Skalitzer Straße, also in Kreuzberg.[94] As with all other organizations dedicated to fighting the criminalization and stigmatization of homosexuality, its traces disappear by the end of the 1950s, however.

Despite the efforts by Katter, Klimmer, Hiller, and others, Hirschfeld and the Institute for Sexual Science remained lost to German memory, both East and West, until the 1980s, a long-term result of the Nazis' destruction of the institute and the discipline of sexual science, more generally, and the active suppression of memory after the war.[95] In 1970, the West Berlin postal office denied a request to memorialize Hirschfeld through a stamp. The office claimed – falsely – that the sexual scientist had not been known to the general public.[96] Research and commemoration of Hirschfeld and the institute only took off in the 1980s. In 1982, a group of young West Berliners active in the gay and lesbian movements founded a new Magnus-Hirschfeld-Gesellschaft (MHG), dedicated to researching Hirschfeld, the institute, and German sexual science; and in 1986, Charlotte Wolff, who had studied medicine and enjoyed the queer nightlife in Weimar Berlin, published her Hirschfeld biography.[97] Katter, who was still living just outside East Berlin, heard about the MHG on a West Berlin radio station in 1985. He immediately wrote to them, evading possible censorship by giving his letter to a friend who took it to West Berlin. Katter understood the MHG's efforts as a continuation of his own attempts

to bring into being, or rather resurrect in honour of the humanist Magnus Hirschfeld and to the benefit of those people whom he cared for, an institution that will finally close the gap that had emerged since his expulsion from Hitler's Germany and the shattering of the institute, which he had generously given to the German state.[98]

His own efforts had failed, Katter thought, "through the lack of a respective mandate from a non-existing responsible authority" – an adequate analysis given the lack of a free public sphere in the GDR and the difficulties that the nascent gay and lesbian organizations faced in the 1970s and 1980s.[99] Katter's lifelong quest to memorialize Hirschfeld was finally successful when he recorded his memories and donated his papers to the archives of the MHG.[100] Sharing the shelves with the books and magazines that were so important to his self-making as a young person, and with the personal papers of others who inhabited the space of the institute, they have, in a way, returned home.

The first part of this chapter has traced queer Berliners' efforts at finding belonging in postwar Berlin. The sources analysed here produce an ambivalent image. Eva Siewert memorialized her lover Alice Carlé through fiction. By not spelling out the romantic or sexual terms of their relationship, she created a space to mourn her queer love. Gerd Katter passed; he did not discuss his being trans publicly. His queerness remained invisible and did not affect his work negatively. Hilde Radusch's homosexuality was well known among her socialist comrades, who pressured her to break up with her girlfriend. Whether their motive was homophobic or sexist, or both, they knew that the relationship with Eddy Klopsch protected Radusch. While they did not succeed in destroying the couple's bond, their intrigue ended Radusch's promising career in city administration and resulted in decades of precarity and poverty. How their home and practices of homemaking helped them cope with this difficult situation, and how domesticity looked for other queer Berliners in the postwar years, is the subject of the second part of this chapter.

II. Queer Domesticity

In May 1945, one-third of Berlin's prewar apartments were uninhabitable, destroyed by the Nazis' plans for turning the city into their imperial capital Germania, allied bombs, and the battle of Berlin in spring 1945. Only a quarter of the apartments that existed in 1939 were left undamaged; all others were in need of repair.[101] The population had also shrunk: through the Nazis' exiling, deportation, and murder of the city's Jewish population; civilians killed by bombs or leaving town to escape the bombings; and the death or war imprisonment of German soldiers. After 1945, refugees from formerly German or German-occupied regions in Russia, Poland, and Czechoslovakia flocked into the city in great numbers.[102] While the Soviet city commander issued a prohibition to move to Berlin and attempted to steer refugees to other parts of Germany, they continued to arrive in Berlin and stayed, often in camps that had previously housed forced labourers or in makeshift accommodation such as the British Nissenhütten.[103] These huts had a floor area of forty square metres and were often shared with a second party, the occupants separated only by a thin wall.[104]

The housing problem was urgent, but building materials were hard to come by. Additionally, the city administration did not have the necessary funds for large-scale reconstruction in the first years after the war, and state-administered programs for urban planning and public housing did not begin until after the foundation of the two German states in 1949.[105] As a consequence, most households were home not to a nuclear family but to women and children, more distant relatives, or people not related at all. As Kirsten Plötz has shown, this reality found its way into the debates over the *Grundgesetz* (Basic Law, rump constitution) for West Germany. Female-female couples raising children together were so prevalent that there was discussion of including these families, *Frauenfamilien* (women families), in the *Grundgesetz*'s protection of families – a radical, if ultimately unsuccessful challenge to prevailing ideas of family and the ideology of the nuclear family that would become dominant in the 1950s.[106] In East Berlin, large households accommodating various parties – close as well as distant family members and non-related occupants – remained the predominant reality for residents into the late 1960s.[107] In West Berlin, funds became available for public housing from the federal government and the United States in the mid-1950s, and construction of apartment buildings moved ahead faster than in East Berlin, where the development of heavy industry and representative architecture took precedence over housing.[108] At the same time, in West Berlin too, "few Berliners lived in nuclear-family households before the mid-fifties, and thereafter the numbers increased but incrementally over time."[109] In sum, Berlin's housing situation remained extremely tense well beyond the founding of the two German states. Privacy was a luxury, not the norm for most of the city's inhabitants. And most Berliners, whether they resided in East or West Berlin, did not live the nuclear-family model throughout the 1950s and 1960s.

What did the shortage of housing mean for queer Berliners? While a lack of privacy affected most middle- and working-class Berliners, its repercussions varied immensely. Working-class men living in hotels, sublets, or communal accommodation could not bring other men to their home. This restriction was the case for Fritz Schmeh-ling, who had moved to West Berlin from West Germany in the early 1960s because of its reputation as a gay haven.[110] As a skilled labourer, he was able to escape military conscription in exchange for commit-ting to two years of work in West Berlin, an opportunity that he took gladly as soon as he was twenty-one. The job that the West German employment office found for him came with accommodation in a Nissenhütte in the West Berlin district of Spandau. Because of its lack of privacy, Schmehling had little choice but to pursue sex outside the home. I will pick up his narrative in my discussion of public spaces in chapter 3.

In personal ads in pen-pal services such as Berlin's *Amicus-Briefbund*, same-sex love and friendship were sometimes sought in combination with accommodation. *Amicus-Briefbund* was a monthly list of pen-pal ads, published since 1948 with the permission of the American mili-tary command.[111] Its name, *Amicus*, was Latin for "friend," a term long understood to signify a same-sex partner and used concurrently in Weimar-era queer publications such as *Freundschaft* or *Die Freundin*. The publisher described its purpose in words that sounded neutral to the ignorant but were well understood by the list's intended subscribers: the *Briefbund* was for those seeking "honest cameraderie" and "like-minded people," "also across zonal and country borders." He promised an end of loneliness to those in want of "pure friendship, valuable life cameraderie" and appealed to those who wanted to be particularly cau-tious and did not want to be recognized right away. Subscribers looking for others who shared their hobbies or for business partners were also welcome to post an ad, though.[112] While ads came from across postwar Germany, Berliners placed the majority, and most of them resided in the western sector.

In *Briefbund*'s February 1950 issue, one man from Berlin's east sector placed an ad in search of a "long-term friendship," adding: "I would be thankful for a job and accommodation."[113] In the same issue, three men and one woman from the city's west mention in their ads that they own a home, signalling a higher sense of privacy for the same-sex encounters they sought as well as possible accommodation for a new "friend." In June 1951, Hamburg homophile magazine *Die Freunde* called on its readers to give the editors notice of available rooms to help those "friends" who had to start from scratch after being sub-jected to a lawsuit or even prison time for a violation of §175.[114] The same magazine collected addresses for temporary stays around Ger-many and Europe, including not just the big cities but also mid- and small-sized towns.[115]

Frauenfamilien

By contrast, female couples living together were generally less con-spicuous, even a "respectable part of society," which tolerated possible intimacies between women – as long as they did not publicly show or speak about them.[116] As seen earlier, many households consisted of two women raising their children together in their husbands' absence. The perception of female couples began to change in West Germany, however, as conservatives established marriage as the only legitimate model of cohabitation over the course of the 1950s and into the late 1960s.[117] In the following, I discuss two examples of lesbian love rela-tionships in a *Frauenfamilie*. The first is the relationship of Käthe "Kitty" Kuse and Ruth Zimmel. Käthe "Kitty" Kuse is a well-known figure of Berlin lesbian history. Of the same generation as Hilde Radusch, she too participated in the activism of elderly women in West Berlin's lesbian movement in the 1970s, befriended a group of young lesbian activists, and was the subject of oral history interviews, publications, and docu-mentaries in the 1980s.[118]

Born in Schöneberg in 1904, Kuse had lived in lesbian relationships since the 1920s.[119] Through the Weimar and Nazi years, she worked as a typist and accountant. After the war, she continued her education, got her *Abitur* (high school diploma), and enrolled at Humboldt University for a degree in economics.[120] Her education and her membership in SED and Freier Deutscher Gewerkschaftsbund (FDGB, the state-sponsored union in the GDR), which she joined in July 1946, became the basis for a stellar career in East Berlin, and Kuse earned extremely well by the early 1950s, making more than four times the median income. She worked in different agencies in East Berlin: the Zentralverband der Deutschen Industrie, later Deutsche Wirtschaftskommission, from 1946 until 1950; then in the Regierungskanzlei of the GDR; then the Patentamt from 1951 until 1954, where she held leadership positions; and finally the VEB Forschungs- und Entwicklungsbetrieb für Turbinen und Transfor-matoren from January until September 1955.[121] In 1952, while recover-ing from a breakdown at Weissensee hospital, she met Ruth Zimmel, another patient and a refugee from East Prussia. Born in 1911, Zimmel had worked in retail and later in her husband's grocery store, whose direction she took over when he was drafted into the army. When Zim-mel met Kuse, she was married, but she divorced her husband in the same year, and she and her two daughters moved in with Kuse, whose income supported the whole family.[122] While Kuse lost her well-paying job when the family moved to West Berlin in 1955, she and Zimmel remained a couple until 1970.

In Kuse's large collection of photos, there is a black-and-white one that shows Ruth Zimmel and her daughters in what appears to be a joyous, carefree moment.[123] It is dated for 1952, the year that Kuse and Zimmel met. Just off the centre of the image is Zimmel, smiling broadly, if somewhat awkwardly, her eyes looking directly at the photographer. In front of her, to her left and her right, are her daughters, beaming at each other and their mother. The image is taken on a sunny day outside, and a tall object made of wicker, reminiscent of a beach chair, is in the background. In the gazes and smiles that the photographed direct towards each other and the camera, and in their body postures, turned towards one another, the children's arms touching their mother's upper body, the photo exudes lightheartedness, intimacy, and trust. The combination of sunlight and wicker evokes an association of the beach, and their casual but trim dresses suggest Sunday outfits. In these qualities, the photo appears as an exemplary family snapshot. The lack of a second parent does not hamper the impression of familial bliss; rather, it is a common feature of such images, since one of the parents is often behind the camera. Whether that was Kitty Kuse in this instance or not, her inclusion of the photo in her personal papers suggests that the scene represented something important to her: that her role as parent and, at least for a while, family provider was a significant part of the life story that she decided to leave to posterity.

A second example of a lesbian relationship in a *Frauenfamilie* comes from an anecdote that Christine Loewenstein shared in a 2018 oral history interview for the Archive of Other Memories. Her narrative demonstrates how the inconspicuousness of *Frauenfamilien* depended on keeping signs of a lesbian relationship within the home.[124] Loewenstein was born in 1946 or 1947 and grew up in the Johannisthal district in Berlin's southeast. In the interview, when discussing how she realized that she herself was attracted to women, Loewenstein begins to explain that she did not know any lesbian women in her childhood, but quickly corrects herself:

I did not know any lesbian, I mean, that's not entirely true, but in my childhood, in my youth, that term did not really exist. The word did not exist either. I heard it from my husband, well, my boyfriend at the time … It was funny, we were visiting my friend … we are going out, and then he says: "Well, since when, since when has your mother been lesbian?" And we [gesticulates] did not know at all, how, what. And then it turned out that the mother of my friend was living together with her girlfriend. And it was quite obvious, but I did not see, we both did not see it. She herself [Loewenstein's friend] did not see it. They had a real, a, a, a marital bed

[*Ehebett*], with nightstands left and right, and were both sleeping there and were clearly one of those traditional lesbian couples. The wife [*Frau*] always a bit with suits, her with the skirt. And we did not ... We did not know that. We did not have a word for that. And that's why, if you don't have a word, you can't bring things into your consciousness, either, right? And therefore, that was not a way for me either.[125]

Loewenstein explains her and her friend's inability to see the nature of the women's relationship with a lack of words. They did not know the word "lesbian," and this ignorance meant they did not see that the two women embodied lesbian subjectivities and (ostensibly) had a sexual relationship, or at least furnished their home like a married couple. Once Loewenstein's boyfriend introduces the term, the pieces fall into place: the women's embodiment of a masculine-feminine, or butch-fem[126] couple (suits and skirts), their sharing a bed. It seems to me, though, that the key moment in the teenagers' understanding of the women's relationship is their entering the family's home: it is right after their visit, after they leave the house, that the boyfriend blurts out his question. It is seeing their shared household, in particular the "marital bed with nightstands left and right," that lets him know that the two women are "lesbian." In other words, seeing the inside of their *Heim* brought their *Geheimnis* into the open. Loewenstein's anecdote is hence an apt example of Sara Ahmed's notion that bodies "are sexualized through how they inhabit space."[127] It shows, too, that the home, even its most intimate parts, often is not completely sealed off or private, but rather porous. The theme of the porosity and precarity of home continues in my discussion of Eddy Klopsch and Hilde Radusch's homemaking work in the following section.

West Berlin Domesticities: Hilde Radusch and Eddy Klopsch

After Hilde Radusch had been ousted from her job in the Schöneberg district office and shut out from the nascent socialist postwar order, she and Eddy Klopsch struggled to make ends meet. They lived on the verge of poverty well into the late 1950s, getting by just barely through a mix of temporary city jobs, small business ventures, writing gigs, and compensation and pension benefits. Eddy Klopsch died sick and poor in 1960, just fifty-three years old. The materials that Hilde Radusch left behind in her personal papers allow for a reconstruction of their day-to-day efforts to get through an economically, physically, politically, and spiritually difficult time. They also document the couple's relationship practices and speak of lesbian subjectivities in mid-century Berlin.

Finally, they show the instability of a notion of home as private, secure, and separate from the public sphere and its power struggles.

As soon as Hilde Radusch was out of her OdF job, in February 1946, the couple applied to open a restaurant, then began peddling with waste glass and scrap metal.[128] Beginning in May 1946, they ran a second-hand store in Mitte. For two and a half years, business was good – they even hired an employee – and the store provided their income despite what appears to have been continuous harassment by Radusch's former comrades. Indeed, two anonymous letters in Radusch's papers show that the threats against the couple did not cease after she left the party and her job at the OdF district office in Schöneberg. Presumably written in 1947–48, these letters threaten the couple's lives openly. Like the letters discussed earlier, they are written in pencil, in clumsy handwriting and in colloquial language, disregarding spelling or punctuation rules. They were delivered to their home address by hand.[129] One letter writer makes a brutal, sexualized threat, its graphically violent language recalling the mass rape of Berlin women at the end of the war. The letter writer postulates: "We are still in charge and Nobody will change that here."[130] Who is meant by "we" is clarified in the second letter. "Those who become an inconvenience will be finished no matter how we are still in charge and not broads [*Weiber*]."[131] The two women are threatened precisely because they endanger male power. Moreover, abuse calling Radusch a "cranky old woman, hysterical and moody" is a stereotypically gendered insult: a colloquial reference to the medicalization of outspoken or otherwise conspicuous women as "hysterical" and, more generally, to women's alleged inability to control their emotions, in contrast to men's sober, level-headed demeanour.[132] The fact that the letters were delivered by hand, as evidenced by the lack of a stamp on the envelopes and the delivery instructions, "Drop off before seven only otherwise after dusk," suggests that the writer had observed Radusch and Klopsch and knew their everyday rhythm.[133] Their home was clearly not safely remote from outside intrusion.

Radusch and Klopsch thus continued to fear the Schöneberg Communist Party clique, but also more generally the SED. Radusch made notes in her 1947 daily calendar about a man who ostensibly shadowed them.[134] In 1948, their store was broken into six times in a period of six months, and they noticed intensified surveillance. Their complaints to the police did not lead to arrests.[135] In November of that year, Klopsch wrote down a conversation that she overheard in the hallway in front of their store between two men who were apparently assigned to harm them.[136] The following two weeks, they were constantly observed, and they took the summons for "personal consultation" sent to them by the Mitte Housing Office as a signal to leave the Eastern sector head over heels.[137] They deregistered their store and returned to Schöneberg in the American sector in November 1948, where they went back to peddling for a few months.[138] In 1951, Radusch found employment for six months in the West Berlin Senate's emergency program for municipal workers.[139] Four years later, the same program took her on again for six months.

Another source of income was financial compensation for health damage and career obstacles resulting from Radusch's activism against the Nazis, but these payments were always precarious too. Already in March 1948, during a revision of all OdF benefit recipients, Radusch's status as OdF had been revoked, though she was allowed to keep an enhanced ration card.[140] Her incarceration had been too short, and she could not prove that her relocation to Prieros had been motivated by imminent arrest rather than fear of allied bombings, the committee argued. In 1948, as a consequence of the escalating Cold War and the growing separation between East and West Berlin during the Berlin Blockade of 1948, the OdF committee ceased to be responsible for West Berlin, with an Amt für politisch-religiös Verfolgte (PRV-Amt, Office for the Politically, Racially, or Religiously Persecuted) instead taking care of victims of Nazi persecution there.[141] Here again, Radusch was denied recognition for many of the same reasons as in East Berlin. She appealed the decision successfully and was granted a one-time compensatory sum of 870 DM, appealed again and received another 500 DM, still less than she believed to be adequate.[142] From January 1953, she was granted a monthly disability pension in the amount of 165 DM for the rheumatism she suffered as a result of Nazi persecution, allowing the couple a somewhat stable existence, albeit in poverty.[143] This pension was cancelled in February 1954, however, because the Senator for Work and Welfare found "the occupational disability no longer extant," according to her latest medical exam.[144] Radusch appealed, and nine months later, the PRV-Amt again confirmed her rheumatism, though to a lesser degree, reducing her disability pension to 60 DM. Radusch's struggle for compensation dragged on until 1963, when the PRV-Amt Berlin granted her a final redress of 24,570 DM for "career damage" suffered as a result of Nazi persecution.[145]

How did Eddy Klopsch and Hilde Radusch cope with these challenging years of financial insecurity, political disillusion, and constant threats? Radusch's calendars and some love letters written by Klopsch document how they experienced this difficult time and how the couple structured their everyday lives. Brief jottings in Radusch's calendars concern her mood, her and Klopsch's health, their economic situation, work, political and personal events, and the weather.

The drama of her resignation from the Communist Party and her OdF job at Bezirksamt Schöneberg in early 1946 becomes palpable despite the brevity and soberness of many of the notes: 7.1. "quit KPD"; 12.1. "quit OdF wailed to Hagen"; 16.1. "last day Hauptstraße 19 Balke takes over"; 18.1. "bed"; 19.1. "bed"; 20.1. "sorted out all OdF stuff"; 5.2. "drank."[146] Her frequent dentist appointments (20.2. "1 tooth filled"; 11.3. "dental treatment"; 30.4. "11:30 teeth"; 31.5. "first tooth pulled"; 5.6. "3:30 getting tooth pulled"; 6.6. "10:45 dentist"; 21.6. "picked up teeth") indicate the health cost of the physical and psychical strains that Radusch endured at the time.

In 1949, when the couple had relocated to West Berlin, the year began with a joyous event, the celebration of their ten-year anniversary on 7 January. Hard times notwithstanding, the "neat celebration" boasted "coffee, torte, cake, schnapps/cigarettes, head cheese, tomato salad, potato salad, tea."[147] To afford the party, Radusch had sold her mother's necklace and two skirts. At the end of the week, she notes: "did not work at all/just walked around for the celebration on the 7th and spent money." Despite this pessimist bottom line and a toothache, she records "good mood" on most days.[148]

As the year continued, there was little occasion for good moods, however. After hastily giving up their store in Mitte, they needed new jobs in Schöneberg, especially once Radusch lost her status as OdF in May 1949 and was not recognized as a *Politisch-Rassisch Verfolgte* (PrV, Persecuted for Political, Racist, or Religious Reasons) by West Berlin's PRV-Amt.[149] Radusch wrote articles for newspapers and the radio (the British-controlled NWDR, the US-controlled RIAS), but most were not published. They continued to sell valuables to get by, received a small amount of welfare, and sometimes friends helped them out. The two took turns being sick and depressed, as testified by notes such as "E sad" (19–20 January), "Quite desperate" (25 January), "Vati [Daddy] heart" (22 January), "E gall and heart" (28–29 January), "desperate, toothache" (1 February), "E crying" (21–22 March), "E gall" (25–26 March), "Everything too much for E" (15 April), "E rails against everything" (16 April), "E heart attacks/falls asleep during breakfast and cries from pain" (27 June).[150] Accordingly, Radusch's weekly summaries for 1949 remained deeply pessimistic: week four, "no money, no prospects"; week five, "no prospects"; week twelve, "no prospects"; week thirteen, "no money"; week eighteen, "no rent for May"; and week thirty-two, "the year progresses and nothing gets better."[151]

The couple's 1950 housekeeping book sheds light on their economic situation five years after the war had ended. Monthly expenses ranged from about 190 DM (November) to 260 DM (December), with the biggest chunk of their budget going to rent (114 DM) and food (between 55 and 80 DM). Other sizable positions were light (14 DM), the newspaper (7 DM), tobacco (6 DM), and public transport (between 4 and 10 DM). Housekeeping was Eddy Klopsch's responsibility, whereas Radusch checked the book, often adding laudatory comments such as "a commendation for good economizing. Vati" or "Oh how thrifty! One extra kiss! Vati."[152] Cleaning the apartment was a duty shared between "Mutti" and "Vati." Their choice of gendered terms of endearment, *Mutti* (Mommy) and *Vati* (Daddy), suggests that the couple embodied gendered roles, with husbands as breadwinners and wives responsible for keeping the books on domestic expenses. In their relationship, Radusch, the "Vati," appeared in public – getting involved in party politics, writing for magazines, looking for wage jobs. Klopsch's fragile health kept her from work outside the home. At the same time, as seen in the first part of this chapter, when it mattered, her physical strength was superior to Radusch's, and "Mutti," not "Vati," protected their bodily integrity.

Some pieces in Radusch's papers inspire reflections on the couple's love life. In rare letters to Radusch, Klopsch sometimes called her "my sweet chappie."[153] For her birthday one year, she asked "Vati" for "10000000 sweet little kisses everywhere, and where they can't be applied right now, later on" as well as "So much love that Mutti doesn't know where anymore," adding "How? Sweetly, Vati must know how it's best done."[154] In another note, "Mutti" asked the "sweet man of the house" for a follow-up examination, and "the family doctor" reported his diagnosis: "healthy on both cheeks and most of all in the middle."[155] Frequent "x" markings in Radusch's calendars, sometimes preceded by the letter "E" or "H," likely documented their sex, possibly their orgasms.[156] The fact that Radusch made these notes – if indeed they record their sexual encounters – shows that sex was important to her, something she wanted to track and keep in her memory. During these years of physical weakness and pain from hunger and sickness, of emotional turmoil and financial and political instability, sex may have been especially significant for Radusch as an assurance of her body's continued ability to give and receive pleasure. The calendar markings structure a time otherwise characterized by material want as one of simultaneous sexual fulfilment.

Eddy Klopsch died in March 1960 in their home in Staaken. She had designated her girlfriend to take care of her funeral and final affairs.[157]

Radusch sought to bury her in her own mother's grave in Sophien Cemetery in Mitte, the cemetery that was also the final home of many members of the Klopsch family. She organized Klopsch's cremation and a memorial ceremony at Wilmersdorf Krematorium, where she delivered the eulogy. She then had her neighbour, a pastor, inquire with the cemetery about the possibility of rededicating Radusch's mother's grave to accommodate Eddy and, after her own death, herself. The pastor's letter stated that Klopsch had "no relatives apart from her friend, Frau Radusch."[158] This statement was not true – Eddy's sister, Hertha Kaufmann, was alive and living in East Berlin. The two were not on good terms, however. The cemetery's administrator wrote back a week later, informing the pastor that Klopsch's ashes would be buried next to the ashes of her deceased husband, Otto Klopsch, and that all fees had been paid by Klopsch's sister, Hertha Kaufmann. It was the sister who had suggested that Eddy Klopsch had been married. Otto Klopsch, however, was Eddy's father.[159] Dismayed, Radusch tried to mobilize the West Berlin media for her cause. She wrote to the *Tagesspiegel* daily paper: "Out of hate I have been deprived of the ash urn of my deceased (girl)friend."[160] In her letter, she described their life together, as well as their agreement to be buried together and the power of attorney letters they had written for each other. Klopsch's spiteful sister had neither held a memorial service nor installed a gravestone, she continued. The *Tagesspiegel* declined to cover the story and had no advice for Radusch either. She herself came up with a way to fulfil her girlfriend's wish, however. Even if Eddy could not be buried with her, she could be memorialized in the way the two of them had devised. She commissioned a stonemason to add Eddy Klopsch's name and life dates to her mother's tombstone and, because she believed she would not live much longer, to add her name and birth date too.[161]

East Berlin Domesticities

In the Hilde Radusch papers, the domestic has emerged as space that facilitated the formation and performance of sexual subjectivities and intimacy between a long-term lesbian couple. This function of the home was not particular to West Berlin, of course. The photo collection of East Berlin dog groomer Rita "Tommy" Thomas, and the oral history conducted with her for the Archive of Other Memories, allow glimpses into East Berlin domestic spaces as sites of lesbian subjectivity formation and sociability.[162] Consisting mostly of portraits and snapshots of parties, Tommy's photos document lesbian butch-fem subjectivities and queer community in East Berlin from the 1950s into the 1980s. They not only bring into sight previously unseen subjects, however. They also make visible "desire as a fundamental feature of historical self-knowledge," as Jennifer Evans has suggested of West Berlin photographer Herbert Tobias's 1950s erotic photos of streetwalking boys.[163] Rather than focusing solely on the role of images as tools of discipline, for instance, as evidence collected or produced by the police in their persecution of gay men, she points out that "erotic photographs can create a much-needed space for historicizing the productive role and potential of desire, opening up 'new acts of seeing' the past, politically, aesthetically, as well as emotionally."[164] I argue that this point is true not only for explicitly erotic photographs but also for portraits of butches and fems, gendered identities in lesbian subculture that carried political and sexual meanings.

The terms "butch" and "fem" are best known as denoting masculine and feminine gender identities in US lesbian subcultures of the mid-twentieth century. In the German context, gender-differentiated female couples have been known since the turn of the twentieth century, when Magnus Hirschfeld described various names for masculine-presenting lesbian women, among them *Bubi* (lad).[165] During the Weimar Republic, the feminine partner of a *Bubi* was called *Dame* (lady), variously *Mädi* (girl), and Rita "Tommy" Thomas reported being introduced to the terms *Bubi* and *Mäuschen* (little mouse) in the mid-century.[166] For the US context, Madeline Davis and Elizabeth Kennedy have described the sexual and political significance of these gendered identities in their seminal oral history study *Boots of Leather, Slippers of Gold*, an analysis of the lesbian working-class community of Buffalo, New York, at mid-century.[167] They argued that, by appearing publicly in gender-differentiated female couples and thus demonstrating the possibility of living without men, these women paved the way not only for the gay and lesbian liberation movements emerging in the late 1960s but also, more generally, for women's sexual empowerment.[168] Whereas middle-class lesbians had much to lose by becoming public and hence took care not to become conspicuous, working-class lesbians could make their sexual difference visible without having to fear social decline. In their interviews with butches and fems who had participated in 1940s and 1950s bar culture, Davis and Kennedy found that, to their interviewees, "the erotic was as important as the political in the system of meanings created by butch-fem roles."[169] In the erotic butch-fem system, the masculine-presenting butches were usually the active sexual part. Their role was to satisfy their fem partners, from whose satisfaction they then derived pleasure. The role of fem women was that of receiving pleasure.[170] Historical scholarship on German lesbian subcultures has overwhelmingly been limited to the study of published sources, and butch-fem roles have not seen in-depth analysis. While it may no longer be possible to determine whether German gender-differentiated lesbian subcultures adhered to a similar sexual system as those in the United States, butch-fem couples were as visibly different in Berlin as in Buffalo, and their public appearance is proof that alternatives to the postwar heteronormative order, be it capitalist or socialist, existed. The photo collection of Rita "Tommy" Thomas at the Feminist FFBIZ Archives in Berlin opens a window into how butch-fem couples styled and presented themselves in East Berlin in the 1950s and 1960s, and documents the embodiment of lesbian subjectivities as well as the making of lesbian communities in the domestic spaces of garden and apartment.

Rita "Tommy" Thomas was born in Berlin-Weissensee in 1931.[171] She trained as a dog groomer and then worked in the profession all her life. In her early twenties, she met seventeen-year-old Helli on the job. The two fell in love and remained lifelong girlfriends until Tommy passed away in 2018. Tommy was an avid photographer, and she and Helli donated hundreds of their photos to the Feminist FFBIZ Archives. The images range from Tommy's childhood to her old age. Some of them were taken in public spaces, but most of them are party snapshots, captured at private parties since the mid-1960s. The most prominent spaces in the collection are Tommy and Helli's apartments and Tommy's garden.

Like many Berliners, Tommy rented a garden plot in the city. For a period in the 1950s and 1960s, her garden in an allotment just beyond the S-Bahn circle line between Greifswalder and Landsberger Allee stations served as her home where she slept, ate, kept animals, and entertained guests. When she first met Helli, Tommy was living in her garden cottage. "She was with me a lot, and we were mostly living in the garden. That was nice," she remembered of their early time together in an oral history interview in 2016.[172] "[Helli's] mom cooked for us, and we would take the pots of food with us to the garden. I was only ever at the garden."[173] Tommy raised ducks, geese, and chickens, and her dogs had space to play in the garden. She may also have lived there full time because of the continuing housing shortage in the city, though she never brought this problem up herself as a reason. Photos of the inside of the cottage, taken in 1966, show a radio, sofa, and a poodle poster on the wall. It is a site of socializing with friends and family, and of the couple's Christmas celebrations with a Christmas tree (figures 1.6 and 1.7). In the spring and summer, the leaves of the greenery shield the garden from the outside, allowing for erotic play and passionate kisses under the roses (figures 1.8–1.10). As the photos show, Tommy and Helli embodied

Figure 1.6. Tommy and Helli celebrating Christmas in the garden cottage, 1966. Feminist FFBIZ Archives, Berlin.

Figure 1.7. Tommy in the garden cottage with friends, 1966. Feminist FFBIZ Archives, Berlin.

Figure 1.8. Erotic play in the garden. Tommy (on the right) with two friends. Feminist FFBIZ Archives, Berlin.

a butch-fem couple, as did some of their friends. Helli and the other fems had long hair, and they wore pumps and skirts or dresses and figure-hugging tops, or in the summer, bikinis. Tommy and her butch friends expressed their masculinity through hair and clothing: their hair kept short, wearing button-down shirts combined with a leather vest or a cardigan, long or short pants, boots or clunky sandals.

Figure 1.8 suggests that sexual aggression, here performed through the two butches' grabbing of the centre woman's breast and crotch, could also be part of butch subjectivity. The photos also demonstrate, however, that butch and fem subjectivities were far from uniform. Instead, they could encompass a range of femininities and masculinities. The young butch holding and kissing her fem partner embodies

Figure 1.9. A young butch-fem couple in Tommy's garden. Feminist FFBIZ
Archives, Berlin.

what might be called a feminine masculinity, with pants that accentuate
her hips and simple, but elegant slippers (figures 1.9 and 1.10).

   The collection also includes a series of party pictures from the same
year, taken on two different occasions and at two different apartments.
They show party guests conversing, flirting, having a laugh, drinking,
dancing, and making out. The first apartment evokes turn-of-the-century
coziness with a tiled stove, floral wallpaper, an Oriental rug hung on
the wall, a dark wooden credenza, and guests crammed together tightly
on a bench (figure 1.11). They are women of different ages. Other
photos from the same night show a male couple partying along with
the women. The interior of the other apartment is brighter and more

Figure 1.10. Passionate kisses under the roses. Feminist FFBIZ Archives, Berlin.

Figure 1.11. Tommy and friends partying at home, 1966. Feminist FFBIZ Archives, Berlin.

Figure 1.12. Helli and friends dancing at home, 1966. Feminist FFBIZ Archives, Berlin.

modern. Dancers are moving their bodies alongside a mid-century sideboard with a glass front (figure 1.12). Many of the women are wearing white shirts, combined with dark vests, sweaters, or jackets, but most are decidedly feminine in cut. Likewise, the short hair that many of them sport is in tune with 1960s women's hair fashion. The different embodiments of gender that are apparent in the party pictures may mirror broader social developments, as the body ideals of the 1950s with their clear gender demarcations gave way to the more androgynous fashion of the 1960s.

The collection includes more shots from both parties. It is noteworthy that the different images, though taken at one occasion, bear the imprints of different photo studios on their backs. Tommy may have ordered extra prints to give to friends, or some of the pictures may have been taken by other party guests and then given to her. Josie McLellan, in her analysis of Heino Hilger's photos of gay male sociability in 1960s and 1970s East Berlin, has pointed out that the practice of taking and exchanging photos was important in constituting queer community in East Germany: "Taking group photographs and circulating them were part of the building of communities away from the mass organizations and official loyalties of the socialist state."[174] The photos from Tommy's collection demonstrate that lesbian women in the GDR also used photography as a means to constitute queer subjectivity and community.

It is no coincidence that these pictures, taken in 1966, document house parties. Until 1961, Tommy and Helli regularly hit the West Berlin queer bars; in fact, bar-going was an integral part of their weekly routine in their early relationship, when Tommy lived in the garden. Tommy described her life in those years:

> I continued running the dog salon and looking after the animals, all the ducks and chickens, three ducks and three chickens, not so many. And in the evenings we always went out to number 21. Adalbertstraße 21. There was dance in the evening, at eight p.m. there was dance, and some coziness, you could talk to others. Most of the time there were women there only, no men.[175]

Adalbertstraße 21 in Kreuzberg, just across the Spree River from Friedrichshain, where Tommy's garden and dog salon were located, was home to Fürstenau, a club popular with lesbian women. When the East German regime completely sealed off the border in August 1961, those bars, even though just a couple of kilometres away, became utterly out of reach for East Berliners. As we will see in the next chapter, queer bars were few and far between in the socialist capital. With the state controlling the public sphere and shutting down all efforts of queer community organization, the domestic served as the main site for queer sociability in East Germany until the 1980s, when gay men and lesbians began congregating under the roof of the Protestant church.

Conclusion

This chapter has brought together narratives and images of diverse queer subjects to explore how queer Berliners went about making homes in the postwar years, literally and figuratively. The first part of the chapter explored Eva Siewert's, Hilde Radusch's, and Gerd Katter's efforts to find belonging in postwar Berlin. Siewert, a well-known radio personality before the war, had lost her lover Alice Carlé in the Holocaust. After the war, she commemorated her through the autobiographical short story "The Oracle," though she remained vague about their love relationship. Siewert's political and personal hopes for a new beginning were soon crushed, as she found most Germans all too eager to forget Nazi crimes, and her journalistic prospects disappointed.

Radusch, who had been active in Communist Party politics during the Weimar years, hoped to contribute to rebuilding the city in a leadership position in the Victims of Fascism section at the Schöneberg district office, but her male comrades quickly bullied her out of her job as well as out of the party. Faced with her comrades' sexism and homophobia, her relationship with Eddy Klopsch protected her from bodily harm and mentally sustained her. Gerd Katter, a working-class trans man with fond memories of Magnus Hirschfeld and the Institute of Sexual Science, used socialist rhetoric to bring Hirschfeld back into public memory and to continue his emancipatory legacy. His appeals to key cultural and medical figures in Germany's Soviet-controlled zone met with interest but remained ultimately unsuccessful. In their struggles for belonging in socialism, both Katter and Radusch kept their queer genders and sexualities out of public discussion. In Radusch's case, this discretion did not stop the Communist Party from demanding that she end her lesbian relationship.

The case of Hilde Radusch and Eddy Klopsch acted as a link to queer domesticity, the subject of the chapter's second half. Their home, and their practices of homemaking, emerged as crucial sites of constituting lesbian subjectivities. In their terms of endearment for each other, *Mutti* and *Vati*, and their distribution of tasks, such as housekeeping and earning income, they embody a model of a gender-differentiated relationship reminiscent of both German prewar lesbian cultures and contemporaneous butch-fem ones in the United States. Their calendars and letters reveal sex as an important practice of sustaining the self, one for which their home provided a private space. At the same time, the threatening letters that were delivered to their house demonstrate that their home was not a safe haven, that the violence of postwar politics did not stop at their door. Though less dramatic, the years of pleading for recognition and restitution with different bureaucratic authorities equally endangered their home's security.

In the photos from East Berlin dog groomer Rita "Tommy" Thomas's collection, two kinds of domestic spaces appeared as sites of the constitution of lesbian subjectivities and communities: the apartment and the garden. The latter provided sheltered space for the relationship between Tommy and Helli, as well as for socializing with other lesbian couples. Produced at different photo studios, the photo prints point to a practice of sharing party photos among East Berlin queers. Documenting their celebrations, constituting their queer subjectivity by posing for the camera, and sustaining the fleeting community of a party by circulating these photos were crucial strategies for creating and maintaining queer community in the deeply homophobic GDR.

The chapter has also shown that, in postwar Berlin, the conditions for making homes were difficult, with privacy a rare luxury. At the same time, the absence of many male heads of household and the presence of extended family or strangers in the home collapsed the nuclear-family model, creating new realities of kinship. One of these was *Frauenfamilien*, and in my discussion of this widespread family model, I have shown how the postwar moment created queer possibilities: for women previously married to men to enter into long-term relationships with a woman and for women who had been in relationships with other women all their lives to take on parenting responsibilities.

However, well into the 1960s, the accommodations of many queer Berliners were neither private enough for sex nor *heimelig* enough to serve as spaces for socializing among friends. The next chapters will turn to spaces outside the home where queer Berliners sought and found community, sociability, and sex, beginning with one often described as a "second home": the bar.

2 Surveilled Sociability: Queer Bars

The photos in the album have captured moments of what looks like a fabulous party: partygoers around a table raising their champagne glasses in a toast, big smiles directed at each other and the camera (figure 2.1), a pair of dancers embracing each other while holding on to a bottle (figure 2.2), and what might be a flirting scene, crashed by a goofy-looking third person. A handwritten sign on the wall indicates the party's occasion and location. "To celebrate the third anniversary of Boheme, Tuesday, 25 October 1955, we're presenting a fashion show! ... You're warmly invited by Willy Lorenz."[1] The occasion, hence, was the third anniversary of the Boheme bar, situated on Lausitzer Platz in the district of Kreuzberg. The space of the bar looks crowded and cozy. The dark wood panelling and flowered wallpaper, lit by lamps hanging from the ceiling and installed on the walls above the tables, together with the flower-patterned table-cloths on the wooden tables, make for a rustic *Heimeligkeit*, or coziness (figure 2.1).

Taken at various points of the evening, the photos show guests enjoying drinks and conversation, swaying to the music of the jukebox, crowding the dance floor, competing for the prize for the best ballroom dancers, clapping to a dance performance by a couple in drag (figure 2.3), watching a solo dancer in exoticized drag (figure 2.4), and participating in a beauty contest (figure 2.5).

These scenes of buoyant sociality, of a carefree-looking evening spent in a place where everybody felt very much at home, were *not* arranged by bar owner Willy Lorenz as a keepsake to leaf through in later years. They were *not* kept in a cabinet in a private home to reminisce with friends or family. Instead, it was a police officer in West Berlin who carefully glued them into an album, supplied them with captions, and stored the album in the police archives. The album's

Figure 2.1. Boheme bar. Polizeihistorische Sammlung Berlin.

Figure 2.2. Boheme bar. Polizeihistorische Sammlung Berlin.

location stands in tension with the familiarity, even intimacy, between camera and subjects suggested by the images. What does it mean that this testimony to queer exuberance is found in the archives of an institution that played a key part in surveilling, shutting down, and sanctioning the very scenes displayed in its pages? The tension that the

Bild 16: Tanzvorführung Homosexueller.
Beide Tänzer zeigen sich in der Öffentlichkeit
nur in Frauenkleidern

Figure 2.3. Boheme bar. Polizeihistorische Sammlung Berlin. The caption by the police reads: "Dance performance by homosexuals. Both dancers appear in public only in women's clothing."

Figure 2.4. Boheme bar. Polizeihistorische Sammlung Berlin.

Figure 2.5. Boheme bar. Polizeihistorische Sammlung Berlin.

Boheme photo album embodies, I argue in this chapter, is precisely what characterizes the space of the queer bar in postwar Berlin: play *and* persecution, sociability *and* surveillance, dancing *and* detention.[2] In the following pages, I will describe these dynamics as they changed over the period of the two and a half decades after the war. I will do so by highlighting the practices of space-making that different actors who held a stake in queer bars engaged in. As I will show, queer bar-goers and the West Berlin police were only two players in a large cast of characters, which included the West Berlin city government and district offices, newspapers, bar owners, as well as West Berlin's tourism office, which had an acute interest in marketing the city's nightlife as the most thrilling this side of the Iron Curtain. At least until 1961, the Stasi, the East German secret police, also kept an eye on West Berlin's bars, both to control its own queer citizens and to gather information about "the class enemy," whether represented by West Germans or members of the Allied forces.

As spaces long identified as nodes of deviant sexualities and criminality by the police and the state more generally, queer bars are a key site to study the regulation of same-sex sexuality and gender "deviance." State policy is thus a guiding interest in this chapter, and I will attempt to chart the dynamics of bar regulation in West and East Berlin, though the scarcity of sources for the latter will make for an imbalanced account.[3] As in the other chapters, I will also trace queer Berliners' practices of space-making in bars. Simply by patronizing and running queer bars, they ensured their continued existence. By conversing and flirting, drinking and dancing, cross-dressing and performing in drag, they created a different, queer, mode of sociability. They confronted the regulations of police and city administrators by controlling access to queer bars through visual, verbal, and aural codes: drawn curtains, passwords to be whispered, or bells to be rung. The chapter's third conceptual layer are discourses: of homosexualities, deviant genders, prostitution, asociality, juvenile delinquency. The multitude and diversity of discourses woven into the sources on queer bars are testimony to their centrality to the topography of postwar Berlin.

After a review of how bars have figured in the existing scholarship on queer Berlin before 1945, the chapter returns to the first postwar decade. The section following focuses on the second half of the 1950s, when more prohibitive police policies appear to have replaced an earlier laissez-faire approach to queer bars. The construction of the Berlin Wall in 1961 defines the rest of the period of analysis: it meant that East Berliners could no longer go out to West Berlin's bars, but it also meant that West Berlin became further isolated. This isolation changed the significance that nightlife had for the city's economy, and it eventually led to West Berlin's becoming a playground for alternative lifestyles, such as student communes, radical politics, and a growing queer subculture.

Queer Nightlife in Berlin before 1945

In the history of homosexualities, the bar has played a pivotal role as one of the spaces understood to be crucial in the formation of a homosexual identity. Historians Jeffrey Weeks, John D'Emilio, and others have linked the emergence of a homosexual identity to the dramatic socio-economic changes brought about by industrial capitalism, which released individuals from their families as they moved to the cities to work in factories. The rapidly expanding cities provided the conditions for a homosexual subculture to form: large numbers of people with unfulfiled sexual needs and anonymity. Urban taverns, pubs, and bars thus became places of congregation for men looking for sex with men.[4] For Berlin, Magnus Hirschfeld and other contemporary observers have documented that, at least since the second half of the nineteenth century, a large number of restaurants and bars existed where men, and to a lesser extent, women, socialized and found same-sex partners; around the same time, a queer ball culture also emerged.[5] The Berlin police kept a close watch on these queer sites, ensuring that no "overtly sexual behaviour" occurred, but from the mid-1880s on, and through the Weimar Republic, it did not raid them.[6] This policy changed even before the Nazis came to power, however. In 1932, the newly appointed police president declared a campaign against "Berlin's immoral night-life," prohibited queer dances, and soon ordered the shutdown of many of the city's known queer bars.[7] In 1933, the Nazis continued the bar closures, and those that were not shut were in danger of being raided by police.[8] Nevertheless, queer socializing in bars did not disappear completely. Patrons sought out new locales, and some queer bars may have survived through the end of the Nazi reign, as historians have suggested was the case in other German cities, such as Hamburg, Munich, and Frankfurt.[9] After the end of the war and Nazism, queer nightlife quickly re-emerged in Berlin, despite continuities in the police force.[10] Jennifer Evans has described "burgeoning and competing homosexual subcultures that came back into view after the war and despite the police regulation and morality enforcement in the 1950s and 1960s," summarizing detailed studies by historians Jens Dobler, Andreas Pretzel, and Karl-Heinz Steinle.[11] Centres of queer nightlife were located in the West Berlin districts of Schöneberg, Charlottenburg, and Kreuzberg, as well as along East Berlin's Friedrichstraße, though historians agree that East Berlin had much less to offer in terms of queer nightlife (figure 2.6).[12] What is missing in the existing studies are two things: first, an analysis of the development of the bars over time, taking into account the different actors involved in the making and unmaking of these queer spaces; second, while some of the studies mention bar patrons' gender as an important factor in the way that police dealt with them, it is not a central analytic, and the evidence remains anecdotal.[13] By contrast, I argue that gender centrally determined whether queer Berliners could live their lives free from harassment and is thus a crucial component of any analysis of queer bar culture.

The Early Postwar Years: "Resurrected Social Life"

The photos from Boheme bar's three-year anniversary capture a specific moment, place, and mode in postwar queer social life in West Berlin: the end of what was almost a decade of relatively carefree bar-going and, more generally, rebuilding of a queer public in Berlin; a dense network of queer bars in a small pocket of West Berlin's Kreuzberg neighbourhood; and a mode of working-class social life that reached across sexualities. In East Berlin, queer bars re-opened and thrived in the immediate postwar period, but were shut down in the early 1950s,

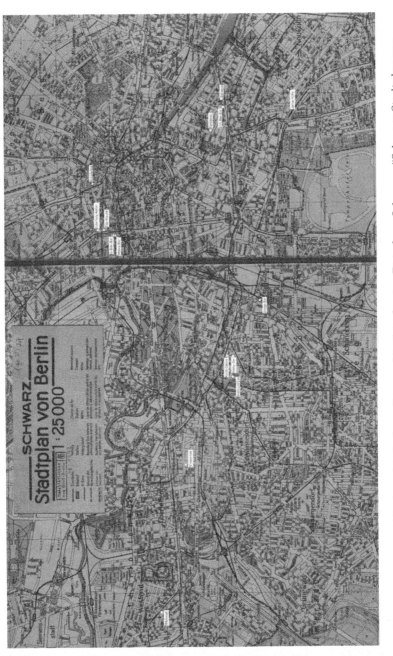

Figure 2.6. 1947 map of Berlin with the bars discussed in this chapter. Data from Schwarz, "Schwarz Stadtplan von Berlin." Digitale Landesbibliothek Berlin/the author.

likely because party leaders regarded queer commercial spaces in the
GDR's capital as incompatible with the project of building a socialist
morality.[14] This book opened with Mamita, the non-binary star of the
rich ball culture that quickly emerged in Berlin after the war had ended,
and with an elegy for the years of "newly won freedom and tolerance."[15]
Doubts are in order to how tolerant those years really were. After all,
Richard Gabler, who had led the detective squad's (Kriminalpolizei, or
Kripo) homosexual section (Homosexuellendezernat) from 1944, served as
head of the vice squad from 1946 until at least 1947.[16] Between 1948 and
1951, under the direction of Gustav Nitsch (1948–50) and Kurt Linke
(1950–52), the West Berlin criminal squad regularly controlled "meeting
places of homosexual persons," particularly public toilets but also, to a
lesser extent, bars.[17] The police reports do not mention raids, however.
Thus, at least into the early 1950s, the city boasted a rich and varied
queer nightlife, as advertisements in Berlin's same-sex pen-pal newsletter Amicus-Briefbund document. In its February 1950 issue, readers were
invited not just to the three weekly ball nights at Mamita's Ballhaus im
Wiener Grinzing, Fasanen-Straße 78, but to an additional nine other
balls at locations in Moabit, Neukölln, Kreuzberg, Schöneberg, and
Steglitz, all Western districts.[18] In March, dancers could choose between
a "Great Spring Festival" at Kreuzberg's Fürstenau and Schöneberg's
Kleines Eldorado bei Gerda Kelch, a "Spring Awakening Under Real
Blossoms" at Schöneberg's Kleist-Casino, a "Bad Boys Ball" at Charlot-
tenburg's Bart, a "Great Mask Ball" at Neukölln's Delmonico, a "Ladies'
Opening Ball" at Kreuzberg's Imperial, or the "House Ball" at Thefi
and Kleines Eldorado. There was just plain dancing at Delmonico and
Bart every night, Sunday afternoon "Tea Dance" at Kleist-Casino, "Vari-
ety Night" Wednesdays and "Glee and Gaiety" Sundays at Fürstenau,
fashion shows at Kleines Eldorado and Imperial, open stage cabaret
Thursdays at Delmonico, and "Elite-Evenings" at Kleist-Casino and
F13.[19] The advertisements show that some bars catered to particular
groups of patrons, such as women or an older crowd. In 1950, "Ladies'
Nights" were offered on all week nights: Mondays and Wednesdays
at Casa Tulenda in Moabit, Thursdays at Fürstenau or at Kathi und
Eva im Grinzing, Fridays at Kreuzberg's Bier-Bar, Saturdays at Imperial
and later also at Fürstenau.[20] Lotti und Bobby in der Wittenbergklause
advertised equally "For the Lady – For the Gentleman," and Mimi
of Die Bohème at nearby Nollendorfplatz welcomed women Tues-
days and Fridays.[21] A bar on Kreuzberg's Friesenstraße, F 13, advertised as "Treffpunkt der alten Freundschaft" (variably "Treffpunkt
der alten Freunde"), indicating both its origin in the earlier, possibly
prewar location Oase on Grünstraße/Jakobstraße and the older age of

its customers.[22] Zum Grünen Anker at Nollendorfplatz billed "Social Nights for Young and Old," signalling that older patrons were welcome too.[23] Two years later, in 1952, some of the same bars still advertised in *Amicus-Briefbund*, and new ones had arrived on the scene too. Live music and dance, long hours, and "solid prices" continued to be among the attractions most frequently praised. Mamita's Ballhaus was still in operation.[24] Around the same time, Mamita took over a corner bar on Kreuzberg's Lausitzer Platz, just across the square from Boheme bar.[25] Indeed, she was among the guests at Boheme's third-anniversary festivities. She is announced on a poster advertising the event in the pub (figure 2.1) and may be among the participants of a fashion show that formed part of the evening's entertainment (figure 2.5).

It is not just the image of Mamita, however, that warrants returning to Boheme bar. The photo album documents a mode of neighbourhood sociality across sexualities, an atmosphere of familiarity and coziness that is also described in another source speaking of the Kreuzberg bar scene of the 1950s, Peter Thilo's unpublished novel *Ein Igel weint Tränen aus Rosenholz oder Die Kulturluftschiffer Berlins aus der Sicht des Bodenpersonals betrachtet* (A Hedgehog Cries Tears of Rosewood or the Cultural Air Skippers of Berlin Seen from the Perspective of the Ground Personnel).[26] The novel narrates the life of Karl Simon, born in 1931 and living in Berlin since 1946, his coming out as a gay man, his education, and his career in West Berlin's cultural administration.[27] After some disappointments with men whom he found through personals in the homophile magazines, twenty-one-year-old Karl decides to look for love in the bars. He makes his first visit to Skalitzer Platz, where "on each of the four corners, there was a pertinent bar."[28] The bar on the southeastern corner, the location of Boheme bar, is his first destination. In the narrator's description of the outside and inside of the bar and the scene he finds inside, further practices of queer space-making become visible.

> Like most bars of this kind, it was only furnished with a neon beer sign on the outside, but those in the know recognized it by the curtains drawn in the windows, which made it impossible to peek inside. Karl felt shy, he did not know what to expect, but since he had made a plan to go for direct contacts now, he entered. It was dim, everything was bathed in reddish light which reflected the thick red curtains and the red wallpaper. The place was half full, men of different ages were sitting at some of the tables, making an impression of being old acquaintances. There were men sitting at the bar, mostly younger ones, who appeared to have come there only to drink beer … They seemed friendly, peaceful, and bored … What Karl did not know was that bars of this kind only get crowded around midnight.

Those who come around this time, shortly past nine, don't come for adventures of any sort. They want to drink beer and talk to acquaintances … Karl felt that he was in the wrong place. It was too cozy here, people didn't stray, they stayed.[29]

Thilo's description of the bar sketches a moment different from the photos, an early weeknight at the bar. Nevertheless, both the photos and the narrative transport a familiar and cozy atmosphere. In Thilo's manuscript, it is the warm red colour of the curtains, wallpaper, and light that contributes to this coziness. Curtains in the windows protect patrons, all men, from outside gazes, thus ensuring the privacy necessary to create a relaxed, familiar mood: the bar's *Heimeligkeit* depends on keeping the identities of its patrons *geheim*, secret. At the same time, the curtains serve as a marker for those "in the know" that the bar caters to queer patrons. They hence have a double function: they both conceal and unveil.

Returning to the photos of the bar in the police album, features of its interior design, such as the floral pattern of wallpaper and tablecloths, the wood panelling, and wooden door-frames, also help create this impression of a rustic, petty bourgeois sociality. In addition, though, it is the relationship between photographer and subjects that suggests familiarity. The big smiles directed at the camera show that the photographer was no stranger to Boheme. An undercover officer may have been among the bar's frequent guests. Alternatively, the pictures may have been sold to the police, or seized during a raid or house search. In a way, in its incorporation of queer space-making practices, the categories of sexual science, and police surveillance, the album stands for a resurfacing of the familiarity between queer Berliners, sexologists, and the police that characterized Berlin at the beginning of the century, almost half a century later. The police classified same-sex sexuality, gender transgression, and commercial sex together, and the list of sexually deviant characters described in the captions of some photos – identifying guests as "homosexuals" (figure 2.3), "homosexual transvestite," "prostitutes," "bar girls," and "pimps" – partly relies on the language invented by sexology in the late nineteenth and early twentieth centuries.[30]

Boheme bar can also serve as an example for a variety of practices of queer space-making. It was run by an allegedly gay man who provided a space of low-key relaxation for an all-male afterwork crowd as well as for a glittering party of patrons of mixed genders and ages.[31] The party's program included two different dance performances. The two dancers captured in figure 2.3, in matching gowns, ribbons on their heads and necks, and high heels, have clearly carried the audience along: the seated guests appear to be clapping in the rhythm of the music, their faces beaming, while the host overlooks the scene, his gaze towards the dancers and photographer showing pride. The night's other drag performance featured a dancer in racialized drag: a headpiece with a feather, heavily made-up eyes and a bindi, creole earrings, a band around the neck, a band of bananas on top of a shiny bra top, and a straw skirt, painted fingernails, and the rest of their body unclothed (figure 2.4). Rather than just the dancer's take on a racialized and sexualized "exotic" femininity, the banana skirt is also a reference to Black performance artist Josephine Baker, who had performed in Berlin during the 1920s. Postwar drag performers hence drew on femininities popular during Nazism, such as actor and singer Zarah Leander, as well as earlier divas who represented the cosmopolitan moment of Weimar Germany, such as Josephine Baker.

On the album's last page is a glued-in envelope full of photographs of a group of gangsters who went by the name Sparverein West.[32] The fact that these two groups of photographs were archived together, those depicting the patrons of Boheme and those showing the members of Sparverein West, suggests that the police were interested in the bar as a hang-out of organized crime as well as illegitimate sexuality. West Berlin's burgeoning queer nightlife as documented in these photos, in advertisements, articles, and Thilo's manuscript was soon disturbed as police began not just surveilling but also raiding bars.

In East Berlin, authorities began shutting down queer nightlife even earlier. Bars in East Berlin did not advertise in *Amicus-Briefbund*, though East Berliners read the paper, as their ads in the personal ad section attest. But according to Charlotte von Mahlsdorf, the trans museum curator, collector, and activist from East Berlin, "transvestite" and "homosexual bars" re-opened in the Soviet-controlled part of the city after the war had ended. "The old audience was back all of a sudden, since many did, after all, manage to survive. And the prostitutes, of course, they were back again too."[33] The East Berlin police kept track of queer bars, listing "pederast and gay broad bars" among other "sketchy bars" in their precinct guidebooks, a tool for police work.[34] The pub Mulackritze in the Scheunenviertel neighbourhood in Mitte had catered to a queer clientele throughout the Nazi period and continued to do so in the postwar period.[35] In her memoir, Charlotte von Mahlsdorf described in great detail how the new owners, Minna Mahlich and her husband, were harassed by the district office within months of taking over the bar.[36] She cited Mahlich's rendition of a district office employee asking her to no longer serve "hookers, lesbians, and gays." When she did not comply,

Mahlich lost her *Opfer des Faschismus* pension and her bar license.[37] Though both were reinstated after Mahlich's brother, the Belgian resistance fighter Max Levinthal, intervened, the bar could only continue until 1951, when the police irrevocably withdrew Mulackritze's license as part of a clean-up of the area. Von Mahlsdorf claimed that another thirty-one bars in the Scheunenviertel were shut down.[38] Cleansing the area of queer bars may have been a result of the SED's turn towards a restrictive sexual morality in the early years of the GDR.[39] In the same year, 1951, the East Berlin radio station Berliner Rundfunk laid off eight men because, as "homosexuals," they were prone to attending queer bars, which, according to the staff report's author, only existed in West Berlin.[40] In this case, SED officials worried primarily that homosexuals, long considered unreliable citizens because of their transnational networks, would connect with "biologically congenial individuals" from the other side of the Iron Curtain.[41] The report author's insistence that no such meeting places existed in East Berlin was wishful thinking rather than fact; certainly, the statement shows that queer bars were not wanted in the socialist capital. The shutting down of queer bars on East Berlin's Friedrichstraße in the 1960s and 1970s may have been caused by a similar concern for presenting a clean socialist city. Both areas, Scheunenviertel and Friedrichstraße, would see massive construction projects after the construction of the Berlin Wall in 1961.[42]

Repression Returns in West Berlin in the 1950s

In West Berlin too, the "newly won freedom and tolerance" reminisced about in the Mamita article in *Der Weg* did not last forever. The first reports of West Berlin police raids on queer bars appear in the homophile magazines in the fall of 1954, and they continue into the late 1960s. On 18 September 1954, the West Berlin police raided three Neukölln bars, checking the IDs of all patrons present and registering everyone on a list. *Der Weg* reported on the incident in its November 1954 issue and reprinted brief articles from the boulevard paper *B.Z.* and the left-leaning daily *Der Telegraf*, which had criticized both the raid and especially the lists, suggesting that the practice was considered unusual.[43] The *Telegraf*'s evening edition, the *nacht-depesche*, voiced what can be read as the strongest critique of the raids.[44] The article's author used the term "persons of same-sex sentiment" to describe the bar guests, indicating sympathy for and, possibly, familiarity with the homophile cause.[45] The author then devoted more than half of the article to a direct quotation of a protest letter written by a "Kreuzberg citizen" who was subjected to the raid. The man, who had – self-confidently, if unsuccessfully – asked the police officer who was registering him to reveal his identification number, argued from a perspective of democratic citizenship. He criticized the raids as an attack on German democracy, comparing them both to Nazi methods and to the practices he imagined to be in place in communist East Berlin.[46] As the journalist did not comment on the letter, the letter writer's opinion came across as the newspaper's to the reader. Such direct critique of police action against queer people on the first page of a widely read newspaper is remarkable. The fact that the raid was so widely reported on, and the critical assessment of the police across different newspapers, speaks for the novelty of the practice: it is likely that the 1954 raid in Neukölln was the first postwar raid on a queer bar. The West Berlin police thus broke with the long-standing policy of surveilled tolerance of queer nightlife that the city's police had followed from the 1880s until the end of the Weimar Republic.[47] Unfortunately, the newspapers remain silent on why the police changed course so drastically. One reason might be changes in the West Berlin police force. Police president Johannes Stumm (1897–1978, in office 1948–62) and Wolfram Sangmeister (1912–78), head of the criminal squad from 1952 to 1969, did not have a Nazi past, at least not one that was publicly known.[48] But Erich Duensing, who in 1951 became director of the regular police (Schutzpolizei, or Schupo), was a former German army colonel who then recruited multiple former army officers for leadership positions in the police force.[49] Also in 1951, article 151 of the Grundgesetz became effective in West Berlin, making former Nazi party members entitled to employment in an office equivalent to their former positions.[50] This policy meant an exchange of personnel in the precincts, as many of the police officers hired after 1945 had to make room for former Nazis. After the Christian Democratic Union (CDU, Christlich Demokratische Union Deutschlands) and the Free Democratic Party (FDP, Freie Demokratische Partei) won the Berlin elections in 1952, the West Berlin police hired hundreds of former SA and SS men.[51] It appears likely that these personnel changes in the force had repercussions in the police's dealings with queer Berliners too. Additionally, the fact that the first raids took place in September 1954, less than three months before the Berlin government elections in early December, suggests that the CDU/FDP government sought to present itself to its voters as the guarantor of law and order. Though they lost the 1954 election, the police's approach to queer bars remained repressive under the following SPD-led governments.

The raids may also have been a reaction to the scandalous disappearance of the president of the West German Federal Office for Protection of the Constitution (Bundesamt für Verfassungsschutz),

Dr. Otto John, on 19 July 1954, and his reappearance in East Berlin a few days later. Both the general and the homophile press commented on his case and discussed John's alleged homosexuality. Even today, scholars debate whether John left West Germany on his own accord, or whether he was kidnapped, as he himself claimed upon his return in 1955.[52] An article in *Der Spiegel* magazine published on 28 July 1954 included multiple allusions to John's "peculiar disposition," which supposedly had led to his arrest in Portugal in 1944, as well as to his visits to "homosexual bars in Berlin" during private stays in the city.[53] "Rolf," editor of the Swiss homophile magazine *Der Kreis*, worried that the scandal would have repercussions for the situation of all homosexuals in Germany. He wrote: "Should it turn out to be true that John is homosexual and has shared classified information about the Western defense with the East, then I am pessimistic for the comrades in Germany."[54] In *Der Weg*, another homophile magazine, Larion Gyburg-Hall expressed his hopes that the "John case" would pave the way to decriminalizing homosexuality in West Germany. Now, the judges at the Federal Constitutional Court would have to accept the "sour consequences" of the prohibition of sex between men: that, evidently, §175 made men who were in charge of state secrets vulnerable to blackmail and thus had to be abolished in the interest of national security.[55] This hope was deceptive, as the Federal Constitutional Court confirmed the constitutionality of §175 in 1957.[56] Even if none of the reports about the fall 1954 raids in the Berlin bars linked them to the John case, a connection appears plausible. Research in the archives of the German and Allied secret services might confirm or falsify this thesis.

The critical press coverage of the raids affected police rhetoric, but not practice. In 1955, criminal squad director Wolfram Sangmeister rejected raids, declaring them an inappropriate measure during a press conference on §175 and crimes committed by "streetwalking boys," teenagers or young men who sold sexual services to men.[57] The press conference was covered in almost all West Berlin newspapers, signalling a strong public interest.[58] The conference's immediate occasion was the successful investigation of the murder of a sixty-five-year-old homosexual man, who had died at the hands of a twenty-six-year-old streetwalking boy. The case was one of eight murders of homosexual men investigated by the police in West Berlin since 1948. Sangmeister presented himself as a proponent of decriminalizing sex between adult men but took a tough stance on streetwalking boys. He pledged to prosecute them and mentioned the possibility of sending "repeat offenders" and "incorrigible cases" to the workhouse.[59]

Despite Sangmeister's claim that these streetwalking boys were "uncharted territory" for the police, the figure of the male prostitute had occupied a central position in discourses around deviant sexuality since the turn of the twentieth century, as Martin Lücke has shown.[60] Sexual scientists, legal professionals working on a reform of German sexual law, homosexual emancipation activists, and social workers were all concerned with streetwalking boys.[61] Often, sexual scientists described them as particularly feminine, distinguishing them from more respectable, conventionally masculine homosexuals.[62] Since 1909, all efforts at reforming Germany's sexual laws singled out men engaging in same-sex sex "for profit": men selling sexual services but also men of legal age who had sex with male minors or who abused "a dependency resulting from a service or work relationship."[63] These cases were described as "complex [*qualifizierte*] homosexuality" and distinguished from "simple homosexuality," or consensual, non-commercial same-sex relationships between men of legal age. The bills for a reformed sex law created a hierarchy between male prostitutes and the men purchasing their services: whereas the latter continued to be understood and punished as "simple homosexuals," "streetwalking boys" were to receive much more severe penalties. These suggestions for legal reform, drawn up by legal professionals in Wilhelmine and Weimar Germany, served as the basis for the Nazis' changes to §175 and introduction of §175a in 1935. As discussed in the introduction, West Germany kept both laws until 1969, whereas East Germany adopted §175a but brought back the Weimar-era version of §175. The "increasing demonization of streetwalking boys" described by Lücke continued in the postwar era, as Jennifer Evans has shown. For the immediate postwar years, she has described a shift in attitudes towards streetwalking boys from "endangered victims" of the wartime and postwar disruptions to family life – hunger, homelessness, becoming orphans, parental neglect – to "capricious villains" who presented a danger to national renewal in both East and West.[64] The two states employed ideologically different understandings of streetwalking boys, but both "inherit[ed] a similar strand of pre-1945 criminology, especially Lombrosian-inspired analysis of prostitution as passive asociality."[65]

But authorities also understood the streetwalking boy phenomenon as rooted in problems particular to the postwar moment and the city's division. In reaction to Sangmeister's press conference on streetwalking boys, an employee of West Berlin's youth services office explained that a quarter of the streetwalking boys who were known at the office lived in East Berlin. For those under age eighteen, the office contacted their parents, sometimes successfully stopping them from returning to West

Berlin. Another 25 per cent of the known streetwalking boys were homeless, however. "We cannot take care of them because they are East-West-migrants and in part unrecognized refugees, or they have not continued their process at the refugee office," the office employee explained.[66] Rather than refugees from formerly German areas in central and eastern Europe as in the immediate postwar years, the refugees described here were East German citizens fleeing the GDR. Their number increased over the 1950s as the East German economy increasingly lagged behind its West German counterpart and as the GDR further curtailed its citizens' political rights and freedom of movement. Consequently, the East-West divide continued to serve as an explanation for "the problem of streetwalking boy activity." A 1960 West Berlin police statement claimed

> the not insignificant rise in the number of streetwalking boys [can] be traced back in large part to the so-called currency differential and the refugee misery. Apart from the streetwalking boys who have their residency in the Soviet-occupied district [of Berlin] or the Soviet-occupied zone [of Germany], among those working as streetwalking boys are also such male persons who have come to Berlin as alleged refugees, but who have been denied admission according to the Federal Law for Provisional Accommodation ... According to police experience, streetwalking boys are almost always work-shy and only interested in an effortless "breadwinning." When it comes to "earning" money without effort, many of them – animated by the milieu they have chosen and freed of the natural inhibitions – do not shrink back from murder or other violent crime. This is proven by the number of such crimes committed by streetwalking boys in Berlin in the past few years.[67]

The "currency differential" mentioned here refers to the unequal value of the West and East Mark, and more generally to the economic disparity between West and East Berlin.[68] In West Berlin, streetwalking boys were hence seen primarily as East Germans who profited from the porousness of the city's division, whether out of need or greed. Both sources stress the refugees' lack of state recognition, and their unclear resident status further made them suspicious. Streetwalking boys' mobility made them suspect in the eyes of East Berlin authorities too, as I will discuss in chapter 3. The construction of the Berlin Wall in 1961 would stop the mobility of people, services, and goods that had characterized the city since 1945, rendering its Cold War division concrete. In neither East nor West Berlin did it end the presence of streetwalking boys, proof that the explanations given had fallen short.

Despite *Kripo* director Sangmeister's acknowledgment of the inefficacy of raids in fighting the "streetwalking boy plight," the West Berlin police continued raiding queer bars into the late 1960s.[69] The meticulous police documentation of the raids on three bars in Schöneberg and Kreuzberg in the fall of 1957 allows reconstruction of how raids were prepared and conducted, and what outcome they had. On the night of Saturday to Sunday, 26–27 October, under the direction of Sangmeister and a *Schupo* officer, over one hundred policemen came down on the popular Amigo-Bar in Schöneberg, where between 180 and 250 patrons were enjoying a night out.[70] Just two weeks later, on the weekend of 9–10 November, the vice department and *Schutzpolizei* raided Kreuzberg's Elli's Bier-Bar on Skalitzer Straße.[71] And another two weeks later, on the night of 21–22 November, the same happened at Robby-Bar in Schöneberg.[72]

The police intensified the fight against the "streetwalking boy plight" in November of that year, with police department E I (S), usually responsible for robberies and break-ins, taking over raids and patrols, whereas the vice squad, M II 2, took care of interrogations.[73] Patrols toured bars that were known as meeting spaces for non-conforming people of different sorts: rebellious youth, women selling sexual services and their clients, gay men, streetwalking boys, lesbian women, and trans people. Sometimes, professionals involved in state efforts to regulate sexuality and control juveniles, such as judges and district attorneys, joined the officers.[74] Journalists were also at times taken for a tour of the city's nightlife. For instance, a French cameraman came along on a 1959 patrol of bars in Charlottenburg, Schöneberg, and Kreuzberg.[75] The patrols thus served multiple functions. They kept law enforcement informed about the clientele and character of bars and ensured that owners and patrons remained aware that they were under observation. As tours of the underworld for select visitors, they also played into the city's reputation as Europe's nightlife capital, simultaneously penalizing, participating in, and thus also generating the spectacle. Finally, in their enumeration of conspicuous individuals, of the "homosexuals," "streetwalking boys," "transvestites," "prostitutes," and "lesbian women," the officers created and reinforced a typology of sexually suspicious personalities.

In preparation for the 1957 raids on queer bars, officers noted the license plates of cars that were parked in front of the establishments, documenting their owners' data in the files. They observed what kind of crowd gathered in the bars, what patrons were doing, and at what time of the night places were busiest.[76] With this information collected, meticulous action plans for the raids were written and sketches of the bars' interiors drawn, complete with exits, windows (barred or not), music box, toilets, and tables and chairs (figure 2.7). The "Xs" in the

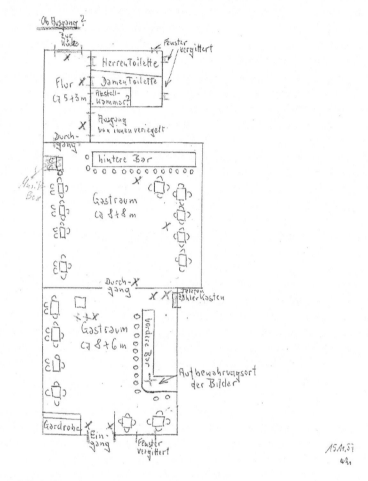

Figure 2.7. Police sketch of Robby-Bar. Polizeihistorische Sammlung Berlin.

sketch show where officers were to be positioned to stop patrons from fleeing.

The raids were conducted by a handful of officers from the detective squad and dozens of regular policemen, as well as a small number of female officers (*Weibliche Kriminalpolizei*, WKP). *Schupos* blocked all exits and moved into the bar, immediately detaining those suspected of being streetwalking boys and, sometimes, transvestites.[77] They were escorted right away to the police vans that were waiting outside and then driven to the State Office of Criminal Investigations (*Landeskriminalamt*, LKA). All other guests were shoved towards the back of the bar. Officers sat down at a table and checked the patrons' IDs. They compared them with their records (*Fahndungsbuch*) and wrote down names, birth dates, addresses, and sometimes occupations.

The lists from the fall 1957 raids at Elli's Bier-Bar in Kreuzberg and Robby-Bar in Schöneberg give insight into who patronized these bars, even if they lack those identified as "streetwalking boys" or "transvestites" by police. Thirty-four individuals were recorded at the raid at Elli's.[78] Most guests were from the immediate neighbourhood (fourteen from SO36) or from areas nearby (six from other parts of Kreuzberg or Neukölln). Patrons also came from other central West Berlin districts (seven from Charlottenburg, Wilmersdorf, and Schöneberg) and from the outskirts (Tegel, Reinickendorf, Lichtenrade, and Britz). An East Berliner and a man from Bonn were also at the bar that night. The thirty-two men and two women ranged in age from twenty-three to sixty-two years, though most were in their thirties. Most of them were craftsmen, blue- and white-collar workers, and businessmen, but among the crowd were also a civil servant and a journalist, as well as three men "without profession." At Robby-Bar, the crowd was more international. The raid yielded information on twenty-two German men between the ages of twenty-five and sixty-four, many of them visiting from West Germany, others from across West Berlin, with one East Berliner in attendance too. The fifteen foreigners at the bar, "Americans, English, Austrians, Brazilians, and Italians," were asked for identification, but then let go without documentation of their names. Whereas Elli's served mostly working-class and petty bourgeois locals, then, Robby-Bar in Schöneberg was popular with tourists from West Germany and abroad. While all the bars raided catered overwhelmingly to cisgender men, women – both cisgender and transgender – were also often among the guests. Female customers were dealt with in contradictory ways. An October 1957 article about the raid on Amigo-Bar in *der neue weg* notes that women were given particular scrutiny.[79] Female officers examined the gender identity of a female patron and the bar owner's wife. The article does not give details on how the examination went about, but its description of the procedure as "tactless" and "embarrassing and bureaucratic" suggests that the women had to undress or were patted down so that police could determine that they were not "transvestites." Officers singled out transvestites and young men suspected of being streetwalking boys directly and put them in police vans that were waiting in front of the bars. By contrast, a police report of a 1958 raid on Kleist-Casino notes that tables occupied by mixed groups were left alone.[80] It appears, then, that it was not a normatively gendered appearance alone, but rather the semblance of heterosexuality that could protect patrons at a queer bar from police attention.

With their massive police presence, these raids did not go unnoticed by the public. Police files and reporting have recorded immediate reactions to the raids, as well as bar owners' efforts to cut their losses from the negative press. At Elli's Bier-Bar, two patrons protested against police taking down their names. According to the police officer in charge, the raid was conducted in a generally calm atmosphere. Outside the bar, however, the atmosphere was far from quiet.

> In front of the bar a large crowd of people, several hundred persons, had congregated, and they openly proclaimed their approval of the police action. Only one male person tried to cause unrest. This person was arrested, however … After the action was finished, a group of officers remained close to the bar for security reasons, as the bar owner had expressed her worries that an "upset crowd might storm and demolish her bar after the police have left!" No incidents occurred, however.[81]

Hundreds of people congregating in front of the bar, voicing their approval for the raid – the bar owner certainly had reason to be worried. It is unclear from the officer's narrative whether the male individual trying to cause unrest echoed the crowd's sentiment or whether he expressed frustration or anger with the police. The report does not explain, either, why the crowd approved of the raid. Were they upset with the bar's clientele for its queerness, or was Elli's simply too noisy? According to the police, complaints "from residents" had led to their previous raid on Amigo-Bar, suggesting that neighbours were another actor in struggles around queer spaces.[82]

Even if the West Berlin press was often critical of the raids, there were also newspapers whose homophobic reporting contributed to hostile attitudes towards queer bars. The 7 Uhr Blatt am Sonntag Abend's coverage of the raid at Elli's was titled "Fight the Vice," and its report mixed images of crime and disease to create an impression of imminent threat at the hands of streetwalking boys.[83]

> The Berlin detective squad has declared a massive fight against the "street-walking boy" vice, which has been spreading in our city like a foul plague and has become a nourishing ground for multiple other crimes. After a notorious meeting place of these elements, who are mostly work-shy and adverse to any orderly life, was raided just two weeks ago in Schöneberg, the police struck last night in Kreuzberg.[84]

The article did not mention the bar's name, but its description as a "bar on Skalitzer Straße that is known as a meeting place of homosexual circles" left little doubt as to which establishment was meant.[85] It is thus not surprising that the owner of Robby-Bar, raided two weeks after Elli's, pleaded with the officer in charge to inform the press only in a factual manner, if at all, and asked for confirmation of his "exemplary and correct" behaviour – his cooperation in a smooth and quiet raid.[86] Indeed, the report notes that, in contrast to the events at Elli's, not a single guest at Robby-Bar protested against having their information recorded.

Despite the enormous effort undertaken by the police, the success of the raids, purportedly conducted to arrest "streetwalking boys," was questionable. The police carted off those patrons who were detained at the beginning of the raids to the State Office of Criminal Investigations, where they interrogated and photographed them and took their fingerprints, even if they could not make any charges against them.[87] Once personal information was on record in the "pink lists," it could be used in any arising court case, and it was accessible to federal and city governments.[88] Of the around one hundred individuals arrested in the three raids, only six seem to have been sentenced.[89] All of them were residents of East Berlin or the GDR, and at twenty-three to thirty-nine years of age, they could not clearly be characterized as streetwalking boys. The sources give no hint about why, in this case, only East Germans were sentenced. Did the West Berlin court, like the SED, fear contacts between gay men from the East and the West? The six men were sentenced to between two and four weeks in prison, with three years of probation during which they were prohibited from visiting the bar where they had been arrested or, in one case, even all homosexual bars in West Berlin. The raids brought no progress in the investigations of the murders of five homosexual men. In the press, the position of the bar owner was again given precedence, whereas the police's failure was cause for gleeful comment. "No Success for Chief Cop during

Nightly Hunt," *nacht-depesche* titled about the raid on Amigo-Bar.[90] The bar owner was quoted as saying:

> Why do they give me a permit first and then ruin my business with such methods. It is known that I cater to homosexuals, but I make sure that streetwalking boys cannot take up space in my bar by letting in only members or their acquaintances.[91]

The statement highlights the tremendous risk that bar owners took, and it demonstrates the uncoordinated and at times contradictory policies of different state authorities. The district office had given the bar a permit without regard to its clientele, but the police raided it. Whereas Amigo-Bar's owner distanced his bar from streetwalking boys, the owner of Robby-Bar explained that, with the streetwalking boys gone, the other guests stopped coming too, resulting in severe damage to his business.[92]

Massive raids were the most spectacular and scary form of police surveillance. Throughout his service as chief of West Berlin's detective squad, Sangmeister asserted that their purpose was not the persecution of homosexuals but only the crackdown on streetwalking boys and progress in murder investigations of homosexual men. The outcome of the raids – bar patrons arrested on the grounds of §175 – belied his claim, however. The raids endangered bar patrons' and owners' livelihoods. They demonstrated police power and created a climate of constant risk. Despite these severe restrictions, queer Berliners continued going out, enjoying the coziness and conversation, the dancing and flirting with others from near and far that West Berlin's bars offered.

In 1959, representatives of the police and city government began a regular exchange in the "Rowdy Commission." Since the mid-1950s, psychologists, politicians, and police in both West and East Germany occupied themselves with teenagers and young adults who embraced US popular culture, distanced themselves visibly and audibly from bourgeois respectability, and became known as "Rowdies" or "*Halbstarke*."[93] After jazz and rock n' roll concerts in West Berlin in 1956 and 1957 had resulted in rioting young fans, the "Rowdy Commission" was set up to deal with the problem, made up of representatives of the Senator for the Interior, the Senator for the Economy, and the Senator for Youth and Sport, as well as high-ranking police officers.[94] In the commission's meetings and its decisions for action, streetwalking boys remained a central figure of contention, as authorities worried that "dubious bars" would expose young men to "a criminal infection."[95] Here, the discourses about criminality and homosexuality overlapped, with queer bars acting as sites of infection. Even if the commission's initial focus was on juvenile delinquency generally, the close cooperation between the police, the judiciary, the Senate, and the district offices created the foundation for a massive campaign against queer bars in the 1960s.

Police raids did not present the only disturbance of queer sociality at the bars. While the angry crowd in front of Elli's dispersed on the night of the raid, three weeks later, the bar was attacked by a group of about fifteen youth, who beat up patrons and destroyed furniture.[96] A similar attack is described in Peter Thilo's novel manuscript. In the late 1950s, protagonist Karl, now a law student, rewards himself for having studied hard by paying Elli's a visit, a place that he appreciates because of its patrons' non-normative gender:

> After being surrounded by all the conforming students at university ... Karl wanted to be among homosexuals again who affirmed their sexuality and who had gaily made themselves at home in it. That was not true for Karl; he no longer had to hide at home, but in the presence of his fellow students, he could not even inconspicuously wiggle his butt or speak in a nelly way, not even for fun. Here at Elli's, a nelly demeanour of different varieties was the custom.[97]

Karl and his friend find a table and begin drinking when noise from the entrance commands their attention. While most guests flee to the back of the bar room and hide behind sofas and under tables, Karl joins the "four waiters in their white jackets" who "tried barring the entrance to a group of new guests."[98] These new guests, Karl finds out soon, are "a kind of rocker or biker gang, clad in leather, at first sight six or eight strong figures" who were "not well intentioned towards the homosexuals."[99] The "rockers" fight the waiters and bar patrons with bar stools and ransack the bar area by throwing bottles, glasses, and ashtrays against the mirrored shelves. Karl, hit on the head with a bar stool for the third time, faints and awakes in his own blood. The bar owner, Elli, anxious to return to business as usual, rejects his plea to call the police, an ambulance, or a taxi. Stabilized by his friend, Karl walks to a nearby hospital, where his cut is stitched, and then takes the subway back to his home in the suburb of Dahlem. The next day, the doctor prescribes multiple weeks of rest. The lighthearted narrative voice contradicts the violence captured in this episode and the terror that Elli's guests must have felt. Elli herself is portrayed as a no-nonsense businesswoman whose concern lies with the reputation of her bar rather than her guests' well-being. The episode further demonstrates the risks that queer bar-goers took upon themselves for a night out. Again, these risks were distributed unevenly; those whose gender was non-normative, the feminine men and transvestites, were in danger, whereas normatively masculine men had less to fear. Episodes recounted in two oral history interviews demonstrate this range of experiences. Whereas feminine Orest Kapp felt terror at the sight of groups of youth on his way to or from a bar, conventionally masculine Fritz Schmehling had the privilege of passing as one of them and then returning to the bar that his friends had disrupted, even making it his regular joint.

Teenage Orest Kapp and his friends would go to bars in Schöneberg where he met "really sweet men, often still boys," for instance at Trocadero and later Black Molly.[100] But the way to the bar was dangerous, and before entering, Kapp took precautions:

> You could never let yourself be seen on the streets. Especially not alone. And when you saw a group of youths, you'd best make yourself scarce. And at the bars that we went out to, there were bells, and you'd never go inside without checking if anyone is watching you.[101]

By contrast, Fritz Schmehling's normative masculinity made for an entirely different bar-going experience. Schmehling came to West Berlin in 1963, a few days after his twenty-first birthday, to explore the city's gay subculture. A carpenter, he had taken the opportunity to commit to two years of employment in West Berlin in exchange for evading the mandatory military service.[102] Asked by the interviewer if he identified as "homosexual" when he moved to Berlin, Schmehling responded:

> No ... That makes you a pansy, and end of story! But I never felt like the female part. Up to today I can make very little of that. [laughs] Maybe that has to do with my trade too, I don't know. A craftsman remains a craftsman, right?[103]

Schmehling hence did not identify as a "homosexual" because, to him, the term signified femininity. His masculinity, which he links to his trade here, allowed him to pass for straight among his colleagues. His first experience of a gay bar then came as part of a group of young men – a clique – seeking to "go on a rampage" in a gay bar during a Saturday night tour of the red-light district of Potsdamer Straße.

> I had a few colleagues at the company where I worked as carpenter. They said, Ooh, Saturday we'll explore Potsdamer [Straße.] Well, I said, ok, good, I'll come, right? Well and so you got to know the different establishments.

Watched the ladies who think they'll get ahead quicker by walking slowly. And then one of them said, now let's go to Winterfeldtplatz to a gay bar and go on a rampage. Ok, why don't you go along, at least you'll know where to go. So we went into the old Trocadero and [ahem] well, you misbehaved a little bit, tipped beer into the ashtray, turned the ashtray on its head, etc. Then they kicked us out. We continued back towards Potsdamer [Straße] and I somehow split, said, I'm done for today. So I walked back to Winterfeldtplatz, knocked on the door, thinking, let's see if they let me in. An older gentleman opened the door and said, I thought that you weren't one of them. And he let me in. From then on, this Trocadero was my starting point.[104]

In Schmehling's narration, causing a stir at a gay bar is part of a fun night out in West Berlin's red-light district for a group of young tradesmen: visiting "different establishments" – the term could refer to bars or to brothels – going "on a rampage" at a gay bar, and then returning to Potsdamer Straße, whether to continue drinking or to purchase sexual services from one of the streetwalkers. Compared to the violence at Elli's described by Peter Thilo, the disturbances Schmehling mentions – creating a mess by tipping over beer-soaked ashtrays – appear benign, like a prank. But to someone like Orest Kapp, who was a regular guest at Trocadero and whose femininity would have made him a "pansy" in Schmehling's eyes, the group's disruption of the familiar space of the gay bar would have been terrifying. Schmehling's normative masculinity allowed him to pass for straight among his colleagues. While his entry to the world of gay bars came as part of a group of hostile youths, the fact that he was let back in suggests that he did not play a leading role in the disturbances and that the experienced older doorman was able to distinguish his normative masculinity from heterosexuality.

As seen in the patron lists from Elli's and Robby-Bar, East Berliners could be found in West Berlin bars, though in small numbers only: going out in the West was attractive, but expensive. Dog groomer Rita "Tommy" Thomas, whose photo collection I discussed in chapter 1, had friends in West Berlin. She and her girlfriend Helli spent their Friday and Saturday nights exploring the bars. In an oral history interview, Tommy remembers exchanging five Ostmarks for one Westmark, which made for a frugal nightlife experience:

We were pretty spartan, we maybe ordered one schnapps and one lemonade, and held on to that all night. While the others drank wine. Or we drank a bottle of wine, not a bottle, a glass. When there were a few of us, a bottle and then everyone got a glass. So as I said, you could have a conversation there. And that was a lot. That was pretty good.[105]

Tommy's lack of means affected her experience of queer nightlife, but it did not exclude her from queer sociality. She was introduced to her first queer bar, Bei Rudi in Schöneberg, by friends.

Well, somebody said, I don't know who it was, some acquaintance or so, I met a lot of people, after all. Why don't you come along! So I went along and looked around. That was the first time I was in a club like that. I just looked, yeah. There was dancing there too, but I was too strange still, and I was also very young.[106]

Tommy describes having been "too strange" to join in the dancing during her first visit at a queer bar, as well as being "very young." But later, when she had become familiar with queer nightlife, she continued to be a talker rather than a dancer. She describes the typical course of an evening at a lesbian bar as follows: "You sat down and talked some and drank some and maybe made a date."[107] Bei Rudi was named after its owner, a woman whose elegant masculinity impressed Tommy. "Rudi was wearing a tie, and always a suit, and always had red lips, and ran the show."[108] Rudi later took over Fürstenau, a club in the backyard of Adalbertstraße 21 in Kreuzberg.[109] This bar became Tommy and Helli's regular haunt, an integral part of their everyday life, as seen in chapter 1.

Tommy also remembers Eldorado, where her Charlie Chaplin costume once won the first prize at a masquerade ball, and Kathi und Eva in Schöneberg, where an all-women band played for dancing late at night. Bei Rudi and Kathi und Eva were women-only in her memory, though it is unclear in the interview whether these spaces were exclusively female all the time or just for one night. Fürstenau and Kathi und Eva were also remembered by Renate, an older lesbian woman interviewed in the 1980s.[110] Renate and her girlfriend Klara, both born in the 1920s, were a working-class couple living in Spandau, a western suburb. They worked heavy manual labour jobs, as Trümmerfrauen, women who helped clear the ruins after the Second World War, as welder, and as turner, but were also out of work for longer periods of time. Nevertheless, they made their way downtown to visit a queer bar now and then.

I learned of the bars from acquaintances, after the war. There was the bar in Adalbertstraße, in Kreuzberg, by the Wall. It had an upper floor where the heteros were. Everybody took the same entrance. On the lower floor, it belonged to two girls who were a little older already. You should have seen them! That was around '60. We went along with a co-worker once. It was like this: back then, they were all still coming from East Berlin. They sat there in suits, tailcoats, smoking fat cigars. There was a round table, a kind of regulars' table. Then there was a dance floor, not located separately, but by the entrance. An all-male band was playing on the dance floor ... Suddenly a girl was peeking through the door. They were fighting. Every so often there are pretty intense scenes of jealousy! We only went there twice because I did not like it so much. Then we'd always go to Fuggerstraße, there was a bar there, "Eva und ..." They had a music box. What I did not like so much about it was, to be honest, that there were rich women there. We could not consume anything there, after all. We did always drink our martini, though. Then the two of us talked, but you did not get in touch with others there. It was so upper class, we couldn't really keep up. And it was pretty much the same on Goethestraße.[111]

In Renate's account, class divisions across lesbian bar spaces become apparent. Fürstenau, situated in the heart of proletarian Kreuzberg and very close to the zonal boundary, was popular with East Berliners and masculine women wearing suits and dress coats and smoking cigars. The direct sequence of these two groups in her narration – East Berliners, masculine women – may express that women from East Berlin frequently adhered to a style of female masculinity that is known from photographs of 1920s lesbian bar culture.[112] Fights between women, caused by jealousy, were not uncommon according to Renate. This fact, too, evokes historical precedent: in his 1914 description of homosexual community life, Magnus Hirschfeld had described women's bars as "more rowdy" than men's.[113] By contrast, Kathi und Eva in Schöneberg catered to a wealthy audience. In Renate's narrative, her and Klara's poverty prevented the couple from socializing with other patrons: it was so "upper class" that they "couldn't keep up." Still, she says they "always" came there, and "always" drank their martini, suggesting that, despite the class difference, they were regulars at Kathi und Eva. The place on Goethestraße that Renate describes as similar to Kathi und Eva was likely the lesbian bar L'Inconnue, discussed later in this chapter.

Hans-Joachim Engel, born in 1935 and a resident of East Berlin since the late 1950s, was aware of queer bars in East Berlin, but they were not of interest to him. "Before the Wall was built, I never went out in the East. Because what was I supposed to do there?" he put it, suggesting that bars in East Berlin had little appeal, at least to him.[114] Engel's first experience of a gay bar was the Kleist-Kasino, one of West Berlin's most popular and most long-running bars. He described this visit, most likely in 1958, in ambivalent terms.

> It was strange, we met at Kleist-Casino, and, well, I was so shocked there after all, and he was the only one who came up to me, he came up to me in a really nice way, and so I, well, dancing was exaggerated, but, in any way, we made a date for the following Saturday at Kleist-Casino. So I dressed up and made myself look pretty, and he showed up too, but nothing happened. I mean, we had a good conversation, we were entertained, all of that ... And it was almost lights out, and I say, what now? [The other man said:] I know a café that's open a little longer. But I wanted something else entirely ... So I said, listen. What's going to happen now, my place or yours. And he hesitated briefly, then said, well, we can go to my place. In Rudow.[115]

Like Tommy, Engel did not feel comfortable during his first visit to a queer bar: he expresses his shock, though without vocalizing what exactly was shocking to him. Nevertheless, his visit was a success, as he met a "nice" man. A week later, after a night spent together at the other man's apartment in Rudow, a suburb in the city's southeast, Engel would find out that his lover was a West Berlin police officer. The two kept dating until the Wall separated them permanently.[116]

In my in-depth analysis of the 1950s, the practices of both queer bar-goers and the West Berlin police have come to the fore. The latter gave up its traditional stance of the surveilled tolerance of queer bars in 1954, shifting to a policy of intense repression through raids instead. Reasons for this change may include the return of former Nazis and military personnel to the police force, as well as the conservative city government's desire to satisfy its voters. Mounting tensions between East and West may also have contributed to the change in police strategy, as suggested by the temporal proximity between the scandalizing news coverage of West German intelligence service president Otto John's disappearance and reappearance in the GDR in July 1954 and reporting on the raids in queer bars in September of the same year.

The significance of embodied gender for queer bar-goers' experience of West Berlin nightlife has been another focus of this section. It was predominantly those whose masculinity or femininity attracted attention as non-normative who had to fear a police arrest or thug violence. Additionally, young bar-goers were automatically suspected of being "streetwalking boys." Over the course of the 1950s, the public began to regard them as dangerous criminals rather than as victims of the difficult times, and police intensified their persecution. In West Berlin,

streetwalking boys were increasingly perceived as East Germans prof-
iting from the open border, though authorities in both East and West
were wary of their mobility. The West Berlin press reported critically
on police repression of queer bars, at times giving ample page space to
statements of bar owners and patrons affected by raids. In the 1960s,
queer bar owners would no longer limit their response to complaints in
the press: now, they began to fight back.

The 1960s: The Wall, Continuing Raids, and a Growing Resistance among Bar Owners

In her oral history interview, Tommy, the East Berlin dog groomer,
describes returning home to Friedrichshain from a night out at the
Kreuzberg bar Bei Rudi in the early morning hours of Sunday, 13
August 1961.

> That night we were out in West Berlin, at Rudi's, Adalbertstraße. And early
> in the morning, around one, two, we got to the border at Oberbaumbrücke
> ... There were some policemen standing around there, and we chatted
> with them, a little drunk as we were [points to her head]. And then the
> policeman said: "Well, if you cross now, then you're over there. And will
> never be allowed back here. Think about that." ... Well, we did not have
> the intention [to stay in the West]. I had all my animals here in the garden,
> and Helli [her girlfriend] ... The West Berlin police said: "You can cross,
> but then you can't come back." They were informed already. Well, and
> since then, we could not come to West Berlin. That was the last day. One
> doesn't mourn after things, then, after all, we had our life here. Only that,
> a little bit, the going out, because we did not have that here, we did miss
> that a little bit, right?[117]

While Tommy, using the impersonal pronoun "one," concludes that
there was no point in mourning what had been, her last sentence suggests that the transition to life behind the Wall was not so smooth and
painless after all. "Only that, a little bit, the going out, because we did
not have that here, we missed that a little bit," she continues. Despite
her repeated use of the diminutive "a little bit," the lack that Tommy
felt, suddenly unable to spend her weekend nights in the company of
other lesbian women in queer public spaces, becomes palpable here.
Hans-Joachim Engel found himself having to make the same decision:
staying in the West or going home to the East, forever? He was dating
the West Berlin police officer, but his main employment as a decorator was in East Berlin (figure 2.8). He had recently married a pregnant

Figure 2.8. Hans-Joachim Engel photographed by Mark B. Anstendig at his job as decorator. Courtesy of the artist.

friend who needed a father for her child, and the three shared an apartment in Stalinstadt. Since the baby was born, Engel helped provide for the child, taking on odd jobs in West Berlin to have some Westmark to buy *"Penaten* baby lotion, bananas, and what else you need as a young father."[118] In August 1961, he was working night shifts as a reception clerk at a friend's guesthouse in West Berlin. On Saturday, 12 August, he was out at an artists' bar on Kurfürstendamm when he received the news from West Berlin actors returning from their performance at East Berlin's variety theatre Friedrichstadtpalast. Staying in the West was not an option for him, however.

> I would not have stayed there. First off, I had family. And then I explained to everyone, this will last four weeks, maybe, then they'll wall us in around Berlin, and then the Saxons can't flee anymore and that's that. Because in Berlin, nobody fled to the West. People could visit their grandma every day, and you could work a little bit in the West, you know. The farmers sold eggs in the West, etc. Well, that was it ... That was that famous night.[119]

"First off, I had family," Engel explains – he had married his friend and helped provide for the baby. He also did not expect the city's division to be permanent. The everyday reality of the divided, but entangled city, where visiting the other part for leisure or work remained common despite the escalating Cold War, had become so entrenched as to appear normal and unchangeable. When prompted if the separation from his West Berlin boyfriend was not painful, Engel responded:

> That is the only thing [that was painful], otherwise it did not really affect me much. I'm not sure why, I had a good job, I had a circle of friends here. I still had all my family ... I had to return, come hell or high water. And you had to console yourself, whole families were torn apart, I mean, that [his own situation] was sad, too, but ... And, I don't know ... the first year, [I thought] still, that can't work for long. A few people thought that ... And then I have to say, we were on the Island of the Blissful. We had Western radio, Western television, we were up to date. When I visited my friends in Dresden, [they were living in the] Valley of the Clueless.[120]

At least in retrospect, Hans-Joachim Engel soon accommodated himself with the new situation. Whereas for Tommy the Wall meant being shut off from public spaces of lesbian sociality until a small activist queer scene developed in East Berlin ten years later, Engel now discovered that there were gay bars in East Berlin too. For a while, he became a regular at City-Klause and Esterhazy-Keller, both in the immediate vicinity of the Friedrichstraße train station, where all of East Berlin's queer venues in the 1960s were congregated.

City-Klause, a small venue run by an Austrian, served as a workman's pub during the day. Engel remembers the men working at the hauling companies around Friedrichstraße going there for breakfast. At night, the entrance was barred off, and a doorman controlled access. Its interior as described by Engel, four tables and a bar complete with a *Hungerturm*, a glass cabinet showcasing sandwiches, was reminiscent of traditional Berlin pubs such as the Mulackritze, preserved in Charlotte von Mahlsdorf's *Gründerzeitmuseum*.[121] One of the four tables was the regulars' table, where, according to Engel, a rich fishmonger held court with her circle of young gay men, "a real pansy club" that spent their summer vacation together in Ahrenshoop, on the Baltic coast.[122] Engel does not elaborate the relationship between the fishmonger and the young feminine men, but his phrasing that "she had at least five or six" suggests that they may have worked as "streetwalking boys" for her. Stasi informant "Franz Moor" reported on female-led male prostitution at City-Klause and the nearby Esterhazy-Keller in February 1961. He described two women, allegedly "former lesbian girlfriends," running a streetwalking boy business that doubled as the spy ring "Ring of the Nibelung." In his report, "Moor" writes that the men were to report on their tricks' "political views" and that they were working for the "MfS," the Stasi ministry.[123] Their job thus appears to have been spying on fellow GDR citizens primarily, not on Westerners.

Another bar that Hans-Joachim Engel remembered was the Mokka-Bar in the Sofia House, also on Friedrichstraße. This bar was run by "two ladies" as Engel recalls. He describes it as a "transit" place, where "you'd meet one another" but then move on.[124] Lesbian Stasi informant "Maria Jahn" mentioned Mokka-Bar as "the meeting spot for lesbian women" in a report from 1967.[125] Next to Mokka-Bar, there was the G-Bier-Bar, which "Jahn" described as a "meeting place for homosexuals and lesbians."[126] All queer bars on Friedrichstraße, with the exception of Mokka-Bar, had to close by the end of the 1960s for unknown reasons.[127] Mokka-Bar itself was shut down in the mid-1970s to make way for an Intershop, a store where high-quality products that were generally not available for purchase in the GDR could be bought with Western currency.[128] Clearing Friedrichstraße of queer bars may thus have been motivated by the dual goals of presenting visitors with a respectable facade of the Cold War front city and using the prime location, just a short walk from the central transit station of Friedrichstraße, to generate much-needed Western currency for the GDR economy.

In West Berlin, police raids continued throughout the decade, but bar owners began protecting their businesses in the 1960s, countering the harassment in two ways: introducing physical barriers to control access to their bars and challenging the legality of the raids.[129] What is more, as West Berlin's isolation from West Germany solidified over the course of the 1960s and the city became a centre of student unrest and political protest, the consensus on keeping checks on the city's queer subculture, if there had ever been one, eroded. The police, different levels of city administration, and the city's tourist office now all pursued different interests in regulating nightlife.

Even in the late 1940s, bar-goers in some queer bars had to ring a bell to be allowed entry.[130] As seen earlier, this practice was no protection from violent thugs or police raids, but it served at least as a modest obstacle to disruptions. State authorities tolerated the practice until the 1960s, when bar owners began shutting police out. The first record of concerns about a bar restricting police access is from 1960, when the Senator for the Economy inquired with the police if a bar owner could lock his doors while guests were present inside.[131] The inquiry was prompted by a Schöneberg host who had lost the dancing license for his bar and now opened his doors only upon knocking. The police replied cautiously that "the facilitation of surveillance alone" would not be enough to force a host to keep doors open but "indecent acts committed in the closed bar" would provide a valid reason.[132]

In 1963, the Neukölln bar Jansa-Hütte came under police scrutiny for keeping its doors shut. Frequent police patrols – two or three times a week – often found the bar closed, or, if open, access was limited by a sign on a door reading "private party." During a "Japanese lampion celebration," a patrol report noted "male patrons in women's cloth-ing," and unknown guests were turned away by the owner himself. Summoned to the precinct, twenty-two-year-old owner Peter Raudonis explained that he kept the bar closed because it was a meeting place for homosexuals.[133] In the report to the district office, the police expressed their concern that "by consciously making his bar a meeting place for homosexuals," Raudonis was promoting indecency, and they proposed to run another background check on the owner.[134] They also noted that a youth centre had just opened in the bar's immediate vicinity and sug-gested that the bar might thus run counter to public interest. Jansa-Hütte remained open under Raudonis's direction, however. It does not reappear in the police files until 1967, indicating that the young bar owner's self-confident stance towards police surveillance had been successful.

By the mid-1960s, protecting one's patrons and one's own livelihood from police raids by installing bell and light systems had become a widely followed practice of West Berlin bar owners.[135] These systems doubled as protection from police and homophobic bullies, warning customers inside of possible danger. The police's frustration about hampered surveillance led to a heightened concern with "indecency" and crimes associated with queer bars among authorities. Ultimately, this concern resulted in the reformation of the "Rowdy Commission" and a massive, multiple-year campaign against queer bars, as well as against other bars considered hosts of deviance. Apart from bar own-ers' securing of doors, two elements contributed to this campaign: First, West Berlin's description as a homosexual haven in the West German press led to worries about the city's reputation among police and some city officials. Second, a series of violent incidents at West Berlin bars prompted police and the Senate to take action against bar owners con-sidered "irresponsible," blaming them for allowing crime to happen or, worse, for promoting it. The ensuing exchanges in the reconvened Rowdy Commission demonstrate competition over who could control nightlife. If the proponents of an unrestricted nightlife prevented some, though not all, of the suggested regulations, it had less to do with a Berlin tradition of laissez-faire. Rather, West Berlin's geographical isola-tion, and its separation from many of the city's major sights by the Wall, meant that its infamous nightlife was a precious part of its economy, an asset that the city could not afford to lose through the imposition of stricter regulations.[136] However, queer bars did not enjoy such freedom, but rather suffered more intense surveillance as a result of closer cooperation between police, Senate, and district offices.

In a 1965 issue, national weekly *Der Spiegel* described West Berlin as a "meeting place" of homosexuals, citing as evidence the 12,000 men registered as homosexuals by the West Berlin police since 1948, half of whom resided in West Germany.[137] This kind of unwanted press attention contributed to the reconvening of the Rowdy Commission in 1966, though now with a particular focus on queer bars.[138] The incidents that immediately triggered the commission's reformation, however, paradoxically were instances of sexual violence perpetrated by heterosexual men against women and trans people.[139] In one of the cases, a man abducted an eighteen-year-old woman on the street, dragged her into his car, took her to the Schöneberg bar Crazy Horse, and raped her there. Then he and a group of other men continued to another bar, Black Molly, where they violently forced a present transvestite to accompany them to one of the perpetrators' apartments.[140] In the commission's meetings, the police repeatedly complained that district offices, whose economic departments oversaw bar licensing, did not respond to their reports about irresponsible bar owners who allowed, or even promoted, criminal or indecent behaviour in their establishments. One measure to be taken against the "excesses" was the reintroduction of a curfew in the city.[141] Early on, a near consensus was formed between the police and representatives of different Senate departments – the Departments of the Interior, Justice, Youth and Sport, Health, and Finances – to follow this path, albeit with "generous exceptions."[142] The single committee member to disagree was the Economy Department's representative, who argued that "introducing a curfew ran counter to Berlin's metropolitan character and might lead to a 'purification' of Berlin's nightlife."[143] Within a few months, however, this economic argument gained force, and at an October 1966 meeting of the commission, the tide had turned against limitations on nightlife. Reintroducing a curfew or prescribing brighter bar lighting ran counter to Berlin's status as "*Weltstadt*," or cosmopolitan city, representatives of the Senate's Economy Department insisted.[144] They were backed by the city's tourism office, whose representative strongly advised against restrictions. She explained that the lack of a curfew had increased tourism: travel agencies no longer complained about the "unsatisfactory Berlin nightlife."[145] She was concerned, however, about visitors getting caught up in a raid, and asked to be informed of so-called *Schwerpunktlokale* (focus bars).[146] That was the police term for bars that they considered hotbeds of crime, "bars patronized exclusively or predominantly by asocials and criminals, and which have garnered attention for an accumulation of criminal offences."[147] At the meeting, the police distinguished these focus bars, which required tight regulation, from the city's nightlife more generally, which they claimed they had no intention to curtail. Among the focus bars were "*Homo-Lokale*" (homo bars), and the attending officers pointed out the "special problem" presented by "the homosexuals." They stated that the number of "homosexuals" had risen significantly, as well as that of "transvestites," who now made up "50% of service staff" in some bars. The city occupied a leading position in the number of homo bars. The officers also described the protocol for changes in the ownership of queer bars: the new owners were informed in writing of the behaviours that were considered "*polizeiwidrig*" (contrary to police regulations): "kissing, hugs" as well as "close dancing."[148] The police representatives further explained that they informed the districts' economy departments – the only authorities capable of imposing restrictions – of criminal incidents happening at bars and of untrustworthy bar owners, but that these briefings frequently remained without response.[149]

While the Senate ultimately declined to reintroduce a curfew, the meetings of the Rowdy Commission did have the effect of improved communication between police, Senate, and district offices. Furthermore, they resulted in a streamlined effort to tighten regulation of the focus bars, in some cases forcing bar owners to uninstall bell systems and give police complete access to bars again.[150] In November 1966, the Senator for the Economy wrote to the district departments for the economy, providing a list of focus bars and bell bars, and asking district authorities to require bar owners to uninstall their bell or light systems and guarantee access to their bars. In Charlottenburg, for instance, the Senator noted three bars patronized chiefly by "homosexuals, lesbians, and streetwalking boys," who presented a "danger for decency" for the other guests and staff.[151] The police continued sending district offices updated lists of bell bars throughout the following years, prompting the Senator to clarify to the district offices that only those bell bars that presented "moral dangers" to guests and staff could be required to reverse their entry restrictions.[152] District offices, in turn, asked the owners of these bars to take down the bell and keep their doors open. If they did not comply, they could be issued tickets of up to 500 Marks.[153] Some bar owners fulfilled the provision immediately, but many did not, instead filing a formal appeal, hiring a lawyer, or just ignoring the new demand. The owner of the Schöneberg bar Black Molly explained to the patrolling cop that "he must be a new officer who did not know yet that the vice squad had nothing against closed doors."[154] Peter Raudonis, owner of Jansa-Hütte in Neukölln, told a patrolling officer that "he was not willing to comply with the district office's demand to take down the bell and keep the bar open."[155] Raudonis hired a lawyer who protested the provision, involving the Senator for the Economy too.[156] Gerda Ritzhaupt, owner of Weinrestaurant Ritzhaupt in Charlottenburg, engaged in lengthy negotiations with the district office, which in turn consulted with the police to determine if it should grant the bar an exception. The police reply revealed the thin ground on which the police were treading, relying on assumptions, hearsay, and observation of behaviours that were not illegal to construct the "moral danger" necessary to impose the no-bell provision.

> The above-mentioned restaurant continues to be a meeting place of homosexual persons where male guests socialize predominantly. *Despite repeated controls and observations, no culpable behaviour could be found* in the bar itself. During a control on 12 October 1967, a detective heard by way of conversation that a drunk transvestite *supposedly* undressed on 17 September 1967. During another observation on 5 December 1967, the detectives *merely* noted that they were "sized up" by the older men present who were sitting at the bar, in the same way that is common in other bars where homosexuals socialize when younger, yet unknown male guests enter. During another observation on 12 December 1967, the detectives observed two male guests leaving the bar together, *making the impression* of a homosexually inclined couple ... Another male guest at the Ritzhaupt was recognized as a homosexual looking for a partner by one of the detectives. During the time of observation, men were repeatedly found dancing to recorded music too. Even if these *perceptions do not yet present culpable acts*, they do justify the *suspicion* that homosexuals also come to "Ritzhaupt" to look for a partner. For this reason, it would be unavoidable to examine carefully if the incontestable restriction should be rescinded with the possibility of creating a precedent.[157]

The use of the subjunctive, of words such as "impression" and "perception," and modifiers that indicate limitations, such as "despite," "even if," "however," or "merely," demonstrates clearly that the police had no reliable proof for the moral dubiousness of Ritzhaupts Weinstube. But the "suspicion" that the bar was frequented by homosexuals who looked for sex sufficed for the intense scrutiny shown by the police. The district office eventually followed the police's recommendation, charging Ritzhaupt a penalty of 300 Marks. The Schöneberg bars Le Punch and Pink Elephant, which had also appealed the no-bell provision, were equally unsuccessful. In the case of Le Punch, the police could point to the bar's listing in the homosexual travel guide *Eos-Guide* as incriminating evidence. In addition, the rejection letter of Le Punch's appeal gave a long list of police observations to prove that the bar's owner, by controlling access to the bar via a bell, "had made it possible for the persons socializing there to give in to their abnormal inclinations."[158] The observations included a familiar range of activities that were mostly not illegal: men dancing with men and women with women, men kissing men and women kissing women, the presence of transvestites, and in one case, a young man masturbating an older one under the table.[159] Even after West Germany reformed its homosexuality law in 1969, legalizing sex between men over twenty-one years of age, authorities did not stop their surveillance. In 1970, West Berlin's police president assured the Senator for the Economy that he would continue to inform the district offices of queer bars that restricted police access through a bell and welcomed men under twenty-one. It seems very likely that this practice applied to most venues.[160]

Lesbian women, despite not being threatened by §175, were part and parcel of the group of people considered criminal and dangerous because of their sexuality. In a police memo on the legal grounds of conducting bar patrols from the late 1960s, the customers necessitating police controls are described as follows:

> From experience, we know that some bars serve as gathering points for homosexuals, lesbians, streetwalking boys, and other asocial or criminal people. These bars thus pose dangers to public safety and order, because they are often the origin or scene of criminal acts, and in addition give cause for police measures in terms of health and vice authorities.[161]

Consequently, police surveillance extended to bars that were patronized primarily or exclusively by queer women. In 1967, the police informed the Charlottenburg district office that the bar L'Inconnue "has been known as a meeting place of lesbian women since around 1960."[162] Recently, the new female bar owner had restricted access through a bell, and the female bouncer only let policemen in after they showed their badge. Once inside, the bar owner requested that police identify themselves and explain the reasons for their visit. The women running the bar thus stood up to the intrusions by the police, holding law enforcement accountable rather than cooperating in the surveillance. The letter continued, saying that although

> women's homosexuality is not punishable per se ... we cannot rule out that criminal acts might be perpetrated by this circle of people either ... The possibility exists indeed that women or girls who may be wanted or underage can be found in a bar of this character too.[163]

Despite the frequent use of the conjunctive form here and the officer's concession that "no observations of this kind have been made so far," the district office did not seem to doubt the necessity of continued police patrols of L'Inconnue. Surveillance of the bar continued even beyond the reform of §175 in 1969.[164]

Conclusion

Bars were important sites of queer space-making throughout the post-war period. In West Berlin, despite intense repression efforts by the police, queer Berliners could pick among a diverse landscape of night-life haunts to socialize, dance, and be entertained. Bars catered to differ-ent patrons specified by age, class, and gender, with those addressing a higher class crowd and/or queer or straight tourists located in Schöne-berg and Charlottenburg. Kreuzberg was a hub of working-class queer bars whose traditional, turn-of-the-century interiors appealed to diverse crowds. In East Berlin, a small number of bars along Friedrich-straße catered to gay men and, to a lesser extent, lesbian women. State policy towards queer bars went through phases of tolerance and repres-sion. In the Scheunenviertel in the early 1950s, the district office actively shut down queer bars. During the 1950s and 1960s, the queer bars on Friedrichstraße could operate, though they were under surveillance by Stasi informants, often queers themselves whose homosexuality had been used to pressure them into the job. The Stasi also actively used these spaces to recruit additional informants. By the late 1960s, most Friedrichstraße bars had to close, and the only remaining spot, Mokka-Bar, did not survive beyond the mid-1970s. In West Berlin, after a brief period of toleration, the police conducted raids on queer bars from the mid-1950s until the end of the 1960s. The rationale for the raids shifted from a campaign against the "streetwalking boy plague" to a concern about the bars' role as places of "indecency" and "crime." As I have shown, the association of queerness and criminality extended beyond those affected by §175, legitimating the surveillance of lesbian bars too. In their treatment of queer bar patrons, West Berlin police differentiated by gender performance and age. Men who looked like they might be underage were suspected of being streetwalking boys, and they and transvestites, cross-dressing men or trans women, suffered the most direct form of police harassment. For all others, the raids functioned "as deterrent," as Clayton Whisnant has put it.[165] Everyone present at a queer bar during a raid was registered on a "pink list," their (suspected) homosexuality now in the hands of all kinds of state authorities, with unforeseeable consequences for careers and personal lives. But these sources also demonstrate that queer bar-goers and bar owners were not discouraged by the massive repression they faced. Patrons spoke up during raids and expressed their anger to journalists, whose reporting was often sympathetic to their cause. Bar owners restricted access to their venues, protecting their customers from police and thugs, and sought legal help in their dealings with the police and district offices. Finally, the documents also show that, over the course of the 1960s, an economic discourse took precedence over the moral one, as some in West Berlin's administration argued for queer bars' value as draws for tourists.

3 Passing Through, Trespassing, Passing in Public Spaces

Oh beloved Guy, you are the only one for whom I have shed tears. In Lugano and here in Berlin. The tears came into my eyes as I saw you drive off in the omnibus, and I was glad that I could keep my countenance on the S-Bahn at least. Here at home I cannot anymore. And Mutti always wants to know if I want something to eat instead of leaving me alone.

> – Eberhardt Brucks to Guy Morris, 18 December 1949[1]

When we kissed yesterday in the waiting room and in front of the omnibus, it became terrifically clear to me again. When I saw you disappear in the omnibus, I could no longer hold the tears back.

> – Eberhardt Brucks to Guy Morris, 19 December 1949[2]

My love, I dreamt of you again last night. We were sitting in a restaurant and eating. All at once you took your hand and stroked mine which was lying on the table, all the people were looking at us and when I saw everyone looking at us, I took your head towards me and kissed you on the mouth – it was so wonderful to feel your mouth again that it made me overjoyed.

> – Eberhardt Brucks to Guy Morris, 16 January 1950[3]

The heartbreak of saying goodbye to a lover at the bus station; the need to keep the tears and the sadness at bay until reaching the privacy of home, where one's concerned but clueless mother won't even leave one alone; the joy of reuniting with the lover, if only in a dream; daring to kiss farewell in the anonymous space of the station; and celebrating a kiss in the imagined public of a restaurant in his dream: Eberhardt Brucks's letters to his American lover Guy Morris speak of the realities and fantasies of queering public spaces in postwar Berlin. Brucks and Morris had met in Lugano, Switzerland, in 1948, where Brucks, a thirty-year-old visual artist and native Berliner, was spending a year to recover from a liver illness. Guy Morris, a car sales representative of the same age, was in Europe for work. The two fell in love, and reunited in Berlin in 1949, where Brucks was sharing an apartment with his mother in the suburban district of Lankwitz in the city's southwest.[4] The letters serve as a passionate and poetic introduction to some of the themes of this chapter, which will examine how queer Berliners perceived the city's public spaces, how they moved in them, how their movements and actions were shaped by laws and policing, and how they subverted public spaces' intended uses, queering them for their own purposes. Some of these spaces, like streets and train lines, are transitory, avenues of movement and connection. Others, such as squares, parks, and train stations, are stationary, islands of rest, bringing the busy traffic to a halt. In the city's queer topography, these spaces take on meaning beyond their primary functions. They are spaces not only of seeing and being seen, of flirting, cruising, and sex, but also spaces of slurs, name-calling, and assault, of surveillance and arrest.

While Berliners of all genders passed through the city's public spaces, my analysis in this chapter is limited to the experience and policing of cis men and trans women. In the oral histories I used, gay men frequently mention public spaces as important sites, but they hardly come up in the narratives of the interviewed cis women. Police records about the patrolling and raiding of public spaces focus on "homosexuals," "streetwalking boys," and male-to-female "transvestites," making no mention of lesbian women or female-to-male "transvestites." Women who sold sexual services to men were heavily policed, and they often appear side by side with other sexual deviants in police records. Many of them had relationships with other women, and historians have recently pointed out that queer history would do well to study sources on female sex workers, both as an entryway to lesbian working-class lifeworlds and as a way to overcome its "overreliance on the modern sexual identity categories that serve as our point of departure," instead taking seriously the categorizations of the historical archive.[5] While I wholeheartedly agree with both points, female sex workers are not part of this chapter because, in their presence in public space, they were not perceived as queer.

In Eberhardt Brucks's letters, the station appears as the site of a romantic farewell between lovers. In the literature on queer Berlin, this space is more commonly associated with anonymous, sometimes commercial sex between men. These aspects are explored in detail by historian Jennifer Evans, who in her analysis of sexual sites in postwar Berlin has described the changing meaning of train stations from being "part of Nazi genocide ... [to] sites of transit to places of combat and sexual transgression."[6] Stations as cruising grounds for men looking for sex with other men are recorded in police and Stasi files, as well as in gay men's oral history accounts. Klaus Born, who was born in 1944, moved to West Berlin from his native Westphalia on 28 August 1965. For him, tales of the city passed along from other gay men had turned West Berlin into a metonym for a worry-free gay sexuality. A trained electrician, he quickly found a job and was put up by his employer in a hotel in the Neukölln district. In an oral history interview conducted for the Archive of Other Memories, he recalled:

> Then came ... September. Then I met a guy. Near the Gedächtniskirche [Memorial Church]. That was on the street, though. He must have been at the Zoo and not gotten any. Or he'd been elsewhere and not gotten any. Anyways: Our glances met. Faithful as we are. Smiles. And then we were a couple all at once.[7]

What is implied in Born's narration is that "Zoo" refers to West Berlin's train station, named Berlin Zoologischer Garten, or abbreviated, Zoo, and that the station was one of the main cruising grounds for gay men.[8] "He had not gotten any" hence refers to sex: the other man had not found a sex partner yet. In Born's narration, both men immediately understand the meaning of the glances and smiles they exchange. Their communication moves quickly to determining a place to have sex.

> Where do we go? I say: We can't go to mine. I live in a hotel. In Neukölln. And the bars, well, we can't do anything there ... He says: We can't go to mine either. I have a sublease. I say: Typical Berlin. Everyone's got a sublease. Yeah, he says: But that's how it is. You can't get an apartment here. Take a look around: Everything's destroyed. [breathes in] Well, what are we going to do? Well, I know a nice parking lot. There's no lights there. Nobody can peep in. And it's nice and large and empty. And there aren't any cars there. Ok, fine. Let's do it. Kantstraße ... So we drove onto it. It was really dark. He switched the lights off on Kantstraße already, though. Says, I [know] this by heart. I know exactly where to park. And above it, the S-Bahn passed by.[9]

Born's account sketches out some of the coordinates of gay sex in West Berlin in the 1960s. Twenty years after the war had ended, parts of the city were still in ruins, even in the very centre, by the Gedächtniskirche and the Zoo, which meant a lack of housing: "You can't get an apartment here ... Everything's destroyed." Transient accommodation, such as hotel rooms or sublets, did not provide the privacy needed for intimate encounters. At the same time, the ruined cityscape opened up uninhabited spaces that could be used for short get-togethers, such as the dark parking lot in between busy Kantstraße and the S-Bahn. Born's partner demonstrated knowledge of the site ("I [know] this by heart") and the necessary precautions, as he switched off the lights before entering the parking lot.

> Then we groped each other some. And then some more. Yeah, and then we put the seats right. So that you can fuck properly. Well, and then the fucking began. Then we were really going at it, yeah. And then the next shock came. All of a sudden big flashlights went on in four spots. Four spots. [breathes in] I could not say anything. Right? So how about you stop the fucking first, I heard somehow. Ok, and now come out. Then we had to get dressed first. We were naked in there after all. We were doing it! Yeah. What were these? [They] were cops. Police. [breathes in] ... And then he had to lock the car and leave it there. And then we had to go along. These cars were standing on the street already ... These cars with the bars. And then [we] were shoved in there. I did not know why. I really did not know why. And then we were driven to Keithstraße ... That's where that criminal building is [the LKA]. Yeah, so drove in there. I was crying. I did not know what to do. I did not, did not know why I was there. I just did not know. Right? For me that was a perfectly normal thing to do it. Yeah. And then it started. You have this and that. Section 175. You are temporarily detained. You do not have a permanent residence. I say: Yes I do, I live at Hotel Süden. You can ask there. That is not a permanent residence. Your ID says Benninghausen. Well, and then the next car had already arrived ... And in there were others that they had picked up, of course ... And then we were off to Moabit.[10]

Rather than the sexual paradise he had envisioned, Klaus Born's first sexual encounter in West Berlin led him directly to prison. Moabit, the West Berlin district just north of Tiergarten, housed the city's prisons, and the district name was used synonymously with them. Born's narration presents a spin on the well-rehearsed story of young queers coming to the big city to find, variously, sex/love/community/themselves. Despite a troubled youth as an out-of-wedlock war orphan who had suffered psychological, physical, and sexual abuse growing up, Born had perceived his sexual encounters with other men in his hometown as "perfectly normal." It was in West Berlin, a purported haven of gay sex, that he was first confronted with the culpability of his erotic desires. Ironically, his Westphalian acquaintances who had raved to him about Berlin's supposed liberality had also warned him about the danger of punishment: "[In] West Germany you've got to watch out. [I]n Berlin you don't have to watch out at all."[11] When the flashlights abruptly disrupted his encounter with the stranger, he was caught by surprise, in shock and clueless as to what was happening. Only at the police station did he learn that §175 was the reason for his arrest. Born's narrative introduces two of the contrasting meanings and possibilities that the West Berlin streets could hold for a same-sex desiring man: quick, anonymous sex, on the one hand, and police persecution, on the other.

A third aspect comes up in Orest Kapp's 2014 oral history interview, also at the Archive of Other Memories. His narrative highlights how non-normative gender presentation attracted attention in public spaces and what the consequences could be. Kapp moved to West Berlin from West Germany in the late 1950s when he was in his late teens, after a devastating stay at a psychiatric hospital where electroshocks were used to "cure" him of his homosexuality. In the interview, he describes his life in Berlin: "I found friends, we had a lot of sex and that was quite okay, but it was dangerous. You could never let yourself be seen on the streets. Especially not alone."[12] Later, Kapp elaborates what "never let[ting] *yourself* be seen on the streets" meant: changing his gender performance by learning to be a "man," that is to appear to be normatively masculine.

> Well, the time ... in Berlin ... it was always a catastrophe. You had to be cautious to not, by any means, move in a wrong way, walk, or talk in a wrong way. [–] It cost me **years**, at least five, six years it cost me, that I would act **manly** [–] that I would walk a **manly** stride [–] that I would make **manly** motions [–] that I would have manly conversations [–] that I would pass as a **man** in a pub or bar. [–] Yes, that was my great, my absolute must, my great must. That's what I **must** do, that's what I must achieve, then I can survive.[13]

Kapp here enumerates the requirements for passing as a "man," a learning process that took him "five, six years": to "act manly ... walk a manly stride ... make manly motions ... have manly conversations." His narration deconstructs in acute precision the work of performing normative masculinity as encompassing the whole body (motions) and mind (conversations), as an effort that demanded a total relearning of physical and social skills. His explanation of the process offers an eloquent vernacular illustration of what Judith Butler has theorized as the performative constitution of gender. In their essay "Performative Acts and Gender Constitution," Butler writes:

> Gender is in no way a stable identity or locus of agency from which various acts proceed; rather, it is an identity tenuously constituted in time – an identity instituted through a *stylized repetition of acts*. Further, gender is instituted through the stylization of the body and, hence, must be understood as the mundane way in which bodily gestures, movements, and enactments of various kinds constitute the illusion of an abiding gendered self.[14]

In Kapp's enumeration of the steps necessary for becoming a "man," normative masculinity becomes visible exactly how Butler describes gender: a stylized repetition of acts, of bodily gestures, movements, and enactments of various kinds. His agitation at recapitulating these efforts is visible in the transcription of his narration. Words that he stresses are printed in bold, and short breaks in his speech, caused by him drawing fresh breath before describing another step of this labour of transformation, are indicated by bracketed dashes. In their essay, Butler also notes that "performing one's gender wrong initiates a set of punishments both obvious and indirect." If the painstaking work of becoming a "man" was an indirect punishment for Orest Kapp's non-normative masculinity, he was also faced with a more obvious punishment. Asked by the interviewers if he was ever insulted in the streets, Kapp again addresses his enactment of gender and sexuality.

> Yes, when you could discern it, back then during the first years, that I am gay, I did look it [look gay], that's why I learned to become a **man** then, after all, in my motions, and generally. Yes, you were confronted with that, especially when it was cliques, about four to six persons, they enjoyed doing that. Yes, I am afraid of that to this day.[15]

The terror he experienced when groups confronted him in public thus haunts Orest Kapp into the present, more than five decades later. The tales of terror and joy, romance and thrill, pleasure and powerlessness relayed by Orest Kapp, Klaus Born, and Eberhardt Brucks have served as an introduction to the main threads running through this chapter: Berlin's public spaces as sites of sex, of police surveillance and persecution, of violence at the hands of homophobic thugs, and as sites of transgressing normative gender. In the following, I first juxtapose the oral testimony with records of the West and East Berlin police as well as the Stasi, attending to moments of connection and disjuncture between a queer phenomenology of public spaces, their legal framework, and authorities' as well as Berliners' practices of policing queer gender and sexuality. Second, I return to the Berlin Wall and its significance for the city's queer public. Beyond separating relationships and cutting off East Berliners from West Berlin's bars, I argue that, through the case of Günter Litfin, the first person to be shot dead at the Wall, queer East Berliners in particular came to associate the Wall with death. By contrast, it served as a thrilling erotic fantasy for West German and Swiss readers of the homophile magazine *Der Kreis*.

Sex in Public

When you'd been in the city on the weekend and eventually had to ride back to Spandau, for me there was the last tram at Kantstraße, the [line] 75 and the [line] 76. And I would always make another stop at the Charlottenburg courthouse, where there is a wonderful wooden cottage.[16]

The stop at the "wonderful wooden cottage" by the Charlottenburg courthouse was a beloved part of Fritz Schmehling's weekend routine in the early 1960s, a last moment of pleasure before he returned to his home and his job as a carpenter in suburban Spandau. Like Klaus Born, Schmehling had moved to West Berlin from West Germany because of its reputation as a gay haven as soon as he turned twenty-one. Living in a Nissenhütte, Schmehling, like Klaus Born, had little choice but to pursue sex outside the home. *Klappen*, public toilets sought out for gay sex, were fixed points not just on his, but on many gay men's mental maps of the city, regular stops on their movements to and from work and leisure. It seems ironic that Schmehling's fondly remembered cottage was in close proximity to the courthouse, the site where gay men were prosecuted, publicly shamed, and often sentenced to time in prison. This vicinity did not seem to hamper his pleasure, however. He relates an unexpected encounter at his favourite *Klappe*:

One night I was standing in there, thinking, maybe something else will come around, maybe not. All of a sudden, the door opens, a cop comes in, in a white traffic coat. I packed mine in when he said, leave it out, we're doing it together. [laughs] Now my heart started pounding. I'm thinking, is this a real cop? It was a real cop. [laughs] The last tram was gone, of course. I had to walk over to Otto-Suhr-Allee, of course, where the tram to Hakenfelde was. And then I hitchhiked from Hakenfelde to Heerstraße at night. [laughs] So it goes when you're greedy. [laughs] That was one of my experiences that have really stuck with me.[17]

The sight of a "real cop" made Schmehling's heart pound. Whether from sexual excitement, from fear, or both, the episode had a happy end as the policeman was looking for sex, not an arrest. Of course, not everyone was so lucky.

Klappen were not only sites of fleeting sexual encounters. Sometimes these turned into lasting relationships: Klaus Born met his partner of thirty-five years at a Klappe on Sophie-Charlotte-Platz in Charlottenburg. Klappen were monitored closely by the police, who patrolled them and often conducted raids. Unless police caught the men during sex, they could not arrest them. They did, however, record their personal information and took them to the precinct where they were instructed about the laws governing public toilets.[18] The legal basis for this temporary detention was §15 of the *Polizeiverwaltungsgesetz* (Police Administration Law), which postulated that persons could be taken into police custody "to relieve a disturbance of public safety or order that has already occurred or to fend off an imminent danger, if no other measures can be taken."[19]

If they were discovered having sex in public, men could be prosecuted under §175 as well as §183. This section, titled literally "Public Causation of a Sexual Nuisance," criminalized those "who cause a public nuisance by acting indecently."[20] This is what happened to Orest Kapp, who at age seventeen was caught having sex with a friend and arrested by the West Berlin police. The place of arrest is unclear in the interview; since Kapp frequently had sex in public toilets, it may well have been a Klappe.

> That was when I got caught with the friend, [–] when we, well, I don't want to go into detail, let's just say, when we were behaving sexually. And, well, yeah, the policemen were not very friendly … I got blows on my belly, got an arm, an elbow rammed into my belly, or, hm, my head was pushed down and then pushed back with the knee, it was not very friendly with us. They showed us, hm, exactly what they thought of us, what we were, as I keep remembering it: you faggot, what are you doing? Hm, you ought to, you ought to be executed, you ought to be gassed, you, all the things they told me I ought to be.[21]

After being abused by the police, Kapp spent months in jail, then had his trial, and was finally let go because he was underage. Though he was arrested only once, he faced repeated abuse by the police, often during raids of public toilets. "The police provoked us, after all. Yeah, they wanted us to fight back or to talk back, and then they would, they would show us their power," he recalled.[22]

Klappen could be found throughout the city. Those known to be cruising grounds were also regular stops for police patrols in East and West Berlin.[23] Train stations, where thousands of people crossed paths every day, provided innumerable opportunities for sexual encounters with strangers. They were also crucial workspaces for men (and women) selling sexual services, which put them at the centre of the police's attention. The Zoo train station represented a central node for anonymous sex between men in West Berlin. But stations of regional transit, where the S- and U-Bahn stopped, were also regularly patrolled. The East Berlin police focused their attention on Mitte district, particularly the Friedrichstraße, Nordbahnhof, and Alexanderplatz stations, and the public toilets on Neuer Markt in the immediate vicinity of Alexanderplatz.[24]

Jennifer Evans has offered an in-depth analysis of train stations and their policing in postwar West and East Berlin. In particular, she has examined stations as the workspace of "streetwalking boys," who, she has argued, occupied both a central and precarious position in postwar discourses. Evans rightly stresses the vilification of streetwalking boys, who faced the scorn of both state authorities and homophile activists. However, some of the streetwalking boys were at the same time perpetrators, mugging their clients, blackmailing them, and sometimes murdering them. Part of what makes it so tricky to interpret them is their overlap with gangs of male youth and young men known as juvenile delinquents, "Halbstarke," "Rocker," or "rowdies," whose violence in the streets and, as seen in chapter two, in bars was at times directed against queers. A connected reason for their analytical elusiveness is that authorities used both homophobic and non-homophobic rhetoric to justify their persecution. Police wanted them off the streets and far from the stations because their presence damaged public space's respectable and heteronormative appearance, but they also arrested them to prevent violence against gay men.

This entanglement of different persecutory motives is demonstrated by a 1952 report from the East Berlin criminal squad. The report noted that, in the year's first quarter, two out of a total of three murder victims had been homosexual men. It continued:

> In the Mitte precinct (station hall Friedrichstraße train station) the streetwalking boy activity has again emerged as a focus area. Two massive raids were conducted, though with the goal of determining the murderers of homosexuals. Simultaneously, however, streetwalking boys could be given over to the [respective] working group for intense examination ... Resulting from these operations, measures were prepared to cleanse the train station of streetwalking boys before 1 May.[25]

Hence, the stated goal of resolving murders allowed for massive policing and the "cleansing" of public space. The measures alluded to here
are spelled out in the report for the following quarter. Every night in
April 1952, police patrolled the station from 8 p.m. to midnight. They
claimed that this intense surveillance resulted in a decline in blackmail
and muggings.[26]

Homophobic attacks at the hands of young men were often committed in groups. In 1952–53, a group of nine persons aged sixteen to
twenty-two committed "50 crimes, such as robberies and predatory
blackmail" in a nine-month period.[27] The police report noted that "in
ca. 90 cases, the accused have engaged in homosexual activities. It
was in this context, then, that the predatory blackmail occurred too."[28]
Members of the group had thus blackmailed the men with whom they
had sex. The phrasing "engaged in homosexual activities [*homosexuell
betätigt*]" shows that the definitional line between homosexuality and
commercial sex among men could sometimes blur in police parlance.
East Berlin police recorded streetwalking boys variously under prostitution and juvenile delinquency, suggesting that, apart from their
lingering in public spaces that were meant for rapid transition, it was
young people's banding up in cliques that made them conspicuous to
authorities. Indeed, the East German government moved to codify the
criminalization of both these aspects within the next decade and a half
in laws targeting "asocials" and "rowdies."

In 1957, a group of eight males, four of them minors, robbed gay men
in the city's Eastern and Western sectors by acting as streetwalking boys
at the Zoo, Lehrter, and Friedrichstraße stations. In the report on their
crimes, the East Berlin police described their actions and linked their
criminality to "asociality":

> All the accused admit to having robbed homosexuals ... by acting as
> streetwalking boys, luring the "johns" into ruins or remote spots, and
> then, depending on the situation, through blows or other force stealing
> the wallet, rings, or watches. This incidence is a typical example where
> the formation of a gang occurs through the association of asocial youths.[29]

In their reports, police forces in both East and West Berlin forged a connection between streetwalking boys, juvenile delinquents, and asocials.
As seen in chapter 2 on bars, the West Berlin police deployed the term
"asocial" to describe sexual deviants into the late 1960s. Recent studies
on "asociality" have shown how the term took on a dramatically different legal meaning in the East and West German states, though. Initially,
it functioned "as a self-evidently and unreflectively used umbrella term

for people with a lifestyle that deviated from the norm of the majority ... in East and West."[30] But in West Germany, the term "asociality"
never entered the books, and the acts and attitudes associated with it in
§361 of the criminal law – vagrancy, begging, homelessness, "idleness,"
being "work-shy," and prostitution – were decriminalized in the late
1960s and early 1970s.[31] In the GDR, however, "asociality" and "rowdyism" were theorized as "the socially other inside the GDR" and codified
in criminal law in the 1960s.[32] The 1961 "Ordinance about the Limitation
of Stay" and §249 of the new criminal code, "Endangering Public Order
through Asocial Behaviour," promulgated in 1968, allowed the state
to prohibit citizens from entering certain areas as well as force them
to work if they were found to be "work-shy." These laws were used
against different groups who deviated from the socialist norm, in particular people who did not hold a steady job, defiant youth, and women
selling sexual services. Prostitution was explicitly mentioned in §249.
While streetwalking boys are not mentioned in the laws or the scholarly
literature, "from the perspective of the state authorities and the jurists,
homosexuals and people suffering from sexually transmitted diseases
moved into the vicinity of 'asocials.'"[33] Streetwalking boys and conspicuous queers thus were likely also targets of these laws. Those who
were convicted under the 1961 ordinance or the 1968 law could be sent
to "labour education commandos," as well as prohibited from visiting
the GDR's "Windows to the West," East Berlin and the convention city
Leipzig, where they might encounter Western visitors. §249 allowed for
prison sentences too, and courts made frequent use of it throughout the
existence of the GDR.[34] An in-depth examination of how these asociality
laws were used to penalize queer subjectivities, while beyond the scope
of this book, would address larger questions of how normalcy and deviance were constructed in the GDR.

As seen in chapter 2, groups of young men attacking queer bars, harass-
ing and at times severely injuring patrons and staff, as well as causing
significant material damage, made going out in the purported queer paradise a risky pleasure. West Berlin police, while very much invested in persecuting queers and curtailing the formation of a queer public, also kept
records on homophobic crimes. The criminal squad in 1958 listed eleven
"incidents in connection with homosexuals" over a fourteen-month
period, nine of them in squares and parks in the West Berlin district of
Wilmersdorf, all committed by youths, usually in groups.[35] The number
is not small, given that many men who were assaulted did not notify the
police, because doing so made them vulnerable to prosecution. Indeed, in
the brief descriptions of the incidents, it is evident that, even when police
investigated homophobic crime, the criminalization of homosexuality

meant that its victims were always equally under scrutiny. For instance, the fact that attackers were often arrested on scene, sometimes after their victim had cried out for help, suggests that police were in the immediate vicinity, surveilling the park. The descriptions of incidents often make note, too, of a *victim*'s previous arrests on site or their status of being "so far unfamiliar" to the police. Suggesting that a victim was homosexual may also have worked as a strategy of defense for the youths' crimes. In one case, seven youths who brutally beat up a man and tried to rob him claimed that he was homosexual. The report of the incident notes "investigations are still ongoing," raising questions as to who and what was being investigated, the thugs or their victim. Finally, one of the accounts describes the victim as a "homo," a clearly derogatory term.

Trespassing the Borders of Normative Gender

Orest Kapp's traumatic memories of having to "become a man" and facing violent threats from groups of youth have illustrated the dangers that feminine men faced in public spaces in the 1950s and 1960s in West Berlin. Despite these dangers, some consciously used elements of feminine style to draw attention to themselves. A person interrogated by the East Berlin Stasi in 1955 explained:

> To meet men, I applied make-up, pencilling over my brows, rouging my lips with a lipstick, and undulating my hair, so that when I visit a bar in this made-up state, or go for a walk, I become conspicuous as a homosexual.[36]

While the interrogated appears to have limited their use of feminine style to modifying their head, others cross-dressed completely, donning women's clothing too. Indeed, while the speaker identifies as a "homosexual" here and is described as a "man" in the report, the statement might also be read as a trace of a non-binary or trans subjectivity. Whereas this source does not allow a definite conclusion as to the arrested person's gender identity, Klaus Born told interviewers about his acquaintance Manuela, a West Berlin trans woman. After his incarceration and trial for §175, Born had lost his accommodation, the hotel room in Neukölln. During the following year, he lived "underground," as he put it, "hopping from bed to bed."[37]

> Then I met someone, her name was Manuela. I stayed with her for a whole two months even. I always had to look out for her, though. Because she was frequently out of luck. She always got beaten up, very often, because she walked around in drag all the time.[38]

In the interview, Born explains that Manuela worked "as a transvestite" in bars, among them the well-known Chez Nous. The two thus helped each other out. Manuela gave the homeless Born a place to stay, and he used his normative masculinity to protect her from street violence.

People whose embodied gender did not read as conventionally masculine or feminine could also run into trouble with the law. Wearing the clothing of the other gender was not forbidden, but causing a public nuisance was punishable in Germany under §183 and §360 of criminal law. Both sections originated in the nineteenth century and continued to be effective in this form until the postwar era. §183, "Public Causation of a Sexual Nuisance," punished those "who give a public nuisance by acting indecently" with up to two years in prison or a fine of up to 500 Marks, and additionally allowed for the revocation of civil rights.[39] §360 made "engaging in disorderly conduct" punishable by a fine of 150 Marks or imprisonment.[40] These laws remained in place in both German postwar states until the reforms of the late 1960s: the new socialist criminal law codified in the GDR in 1968 and the West German Great Criminal Law Reform of 1969. Cross-dressers and trans people could hence run into problems if they became conspicuous in public: that is, if they failed to pass. As early as 1910, Magnus Hirschfeld had addressed this question, and following his proposal, the Berlin police had issued *Transvestitenscheine* (transvestite passes). These documents stated that their bearer was known to the police to wear the clothing of the other sex and included their photograph in their everyday, transvestite appearance.[41] Part of the cooperation between sexual scientists, activists, and police, this practice reinforced the notion that public order depended on the gender binary. At the same time, the practice also acknowledged that gender could be separate from the body, that the body people were born with might not correspond to the gender they felt they belonged to. As I show in the following pages, the West Berlin police stopped issuing *Transvestitenscheine* around 1960.

The transvestite passes, which other German cities had adopted during the Weimar years, continued to be issued in Berlin well into the Nazi period.[42] For postwar East Berlin, Ulrike Klöppel has shown that the authorities continued to issue transvestite passes into at least the second half of the 1950s.[43] In West Berlin, the police continued the policy throughout the 1950s, but then discontinued it in the 1960s, as a file at the Police Historical Collection Berlin suggests.[44] The correspondence archived in the file sheds light on a local, on-the-ground negotiation about the definition of gender between trans people, the police, and city administration during the decades in which medical and legal experts in West and East Germany struggled over the mutability of gender and its repercussions for the law, and ultimately fortified the system of binary gender.[45]

In the early 1950s, "wearers of women's clothing" who were "known and registered with the police" could be issued a confirmation that included their photo in female attire.[46] The case of a Kreuzberg trans woman, F. Krüger, gave occasion to the police to come up with a policy for issuing regular identity cards to people whose outer appearance differed from the gender in their documents. The police administrative department II, in charge of issuing passports and ID cards, collaborated with the criminal squad. The local precinct had confiscated Krüger's identity card. When applying for a substitute, Krüger asked to include their portrait in women's clothing because their old identity card, which had their portrait in male appearance, "caused trouble."[47] The dissimilarity between Krüger's photo and live appearance was likely the reason why the police seized the ID card in the first place. Police department II reported that Krüger had "refused to cut his hair short just so that photos for the preliminary ID card could be made; further he was no longer in possession of men's clothing."[48] The officer in charge followed Krüger's argumentation, noting to his colleagues at the detective squad that "his objections … cannot readily be denied."[49] He thus suggested to go along with Krüger's wish to include a photo in female attire and to add a note stating:

> This Identity Card is only valid in connection with the confirmation issued by the Police President, Department K, from [date], that the holder of this Identity Card is known and registered as a wearer of women's clothing.[50]

The detective squad agreed, noting that, since the "tiresome matter" had led to disagreements in the past, it welcomed a lasting solution to the issue.[51]

Two years later, in 1952, an inquiry from the Munich police prompted the West Berlin police to explicate the procedure in more detail.[52] A Munich trans person had informed the local police of Berlin's *Transvestitenschein* practice, and the Bavarian officers were curious to learn more, apparently unaware that Munich police had issued them during the Weimar Republic.[53] In their response, the West Berlin detective squad explained that transvestites could apply for an identity card with their photo in female attire with the detective squad. Their statement was recorded at the police station, and they had to have a doctor's statement, which they had to pay for themselves.[54] If the doctor found that the person was a "pure transvestite, and there is no danger of him practising a deviant sexual inclination ... in public (suspicion of homo-sexuality)," the confirmation could be issued.[55]

Sexologists during Nazism used the notions of "pure" and "impure" transvestitism to differentiate heterosexual transvestites, on the one hand, from homosexual transvestites and cross-dressing male sex work-ers, on the other.[56] While the terms were of Nazi origin, the distinction itself was not; rather, it was a key feature of sexological theories of trans-vestitism as well as discourses among transvestites since the beginning of the century.[57] In addition to the continued use of Nazi terminology, the phrasing in the letter ("practising a deviant sexual inclination ... in public") suggests that the police amalgamated concepts of homosexu-ality and male prostitution. The West Berlin police further explained to their Munich colleagues that "his [the applicant's] outward appear-ance in women's clothing must not give cause to a public nuisance."[58] Hence, to get the recognition that the *Transvestitenschein* represented, trans women had to perform a seamless version of normative feminin-ity before the authorities; they had to be able to pass to get a pass.

In 1960, the West Berlin police changed this practice. An inquiry to the detective squad from police department II B, in charge of passport matters, relayed that recently, three passports had been issued to "per-sons of male sex who appear in female clothing and hairstyles."[59] The writer continued:

> In my opinion, for reasons of public order, only such passport photos should be used that correspond to the personal information recorded in the passport and indicating the sex, for instance the first name, the profes-sion. On the other hand, one could demand for reasons of identification that the photographs show the passport holder in the garb and look that he usually appears in. I have presented these questions to the Senator for the Interior who is interested in the position that the criminal squad and the Federal Criminal Police Office, respectively, take in this matter. One would also have to entertain the question whether persons of female sex should be allowed to bring photographs showing them in male clothing. Do you have any experience in how far men have tried to evade a penalty for a violation of §175 by using female clothing?[60]

The writer distinguished between the upholding of public order and an effective identification, two interests that had previously been understood as related, if not identical. Whereas the practice of issuing *Transvestitenscheine* was based on the understanding that public order depended on the possibility of the state to identify people in public space, the writer argued that public order did not so much rely on the congruence of outward appearance and the ID photograph, but instead on the concurrence of the photograph with the markers of gender that the document contained, "first name" and "profession." Identity cards and passports at the time did not record their holders' gender. Also, the three people whose passports prompted the inquiry apparently did not apply for a name change to go by gender-neutral names, as was often the case.

How did the criminal squad respond to this inquiry? Interestingly, the file contains two versions of the reply. The first one proposes a continuation of the transvestite pass policy, noting that cases of persons cross-dressing to escape criminal persecution "are rare and do not give occasion for special measures."[61] But then, the person in charge, likely criminal squad director Wolfram Sangmeister, had a change of mind. The second version of the response expresses agreement that the photographs in passports should correspond to the "personal information noted in the passport and indicating the gender, as well as the description of the person."[62] Further, should a search for a transvestite occur, "identification would not be hampered because the circle of transvestites is generally known," and the police could "fall back on photographs displaying the transvestites in their everyday garb and look." The police hence kept a comprehensive register of transvestites. Though the second version of the letter also acknowledged that cross-dressing to escape criminal persecution was a negligible phenomenon, it concluded with reinforcing the necessity for police control. Proclaiming that "it is, however, a fact derived from experience that transvestites essentially only wear the clothing of the other sex to camouflage their homosexual practice," the letter again amalgamated transvestitism, homosexuality, and male prostitution. Such arguments were in line with the position taken by most judges dealing with trans claimants' applications for a change of gender at the time. In a 1957 case where the West Berlin Senator of the Interior contested a marriage because the husband, though identifying as male, appeared to be biologically female, the Court of Appeals annulled the marriage, ruling that "according to the general and undisputed opinion relevant here, a human's gender depends crucially on his physical constitution. It is of no import to the question of his gender whether he feels like a man or a woman irrespectively of this constitution."[63] Since the case involved the Senator of the Interior, who was in charge of both the register offices and the police, it is likely that this ruling influenced the change in police policy.

Since the file only contains the drafts of the two letters, it is unclear which one was sent in reply to the passport department's inquiry. The crime squad did, however, ask the Federal Criminal Police Office to put the matter on the agenda for the upcoming meeting of the working group of the directors of the Federal and State Criminal Offices (Bundes- und Landeskriminalämter).[64] An excerpt from the minutes of that meeting suggests that the inquiry, prompted by the three passports issued to West Berlin transvestites, had far-ranging consequences. Not only did the discussants agree that passport photographs should correspond to their holders' gender as recorded at birth: "a person of male gender must be pictured as man, a person of female gender as a woman."[65] The group also made a recommendation for changing the design of future identification documents, noting that "additionally it would be desirable if, in the future, forms for passports and identification cards would designate a category for stating the person's gender." Correspondence from various state criminal offices from the 1970s shows, however, that states continued to pursue their own policies regarding photographs in passports, suggesting that the push for a unified federal policy was not successful.[66]

In summary, the *Transvestiten* file from the West Berlin police attests to a continuation of the Berlin police practice of issuing transvestite passes into at least the early 1950s. Throughout the 1950s, police even issued passports with photographs that showed their bearers in their everyday transvestite presentation. At least for trans women, this liberal policy depended on their seamless performance of a normative gender and sexuality, however, demonstrating the long-lasting effects of early sexologists' differentiation between heterosexual and homosexual transvestites, taken up by Nazi sexology as "pure" and "impure" transvestitism. The West Berlin police's change in transvestite policy after 1960, from a tolerance dependent on passing to a disavowal of trans subjectivities, is in line with both contemporary legal discourses and practices towards trans people and the development towards a more repressive queer bar policy, particularly the intense policing of transvestites in bars seen in chapter 2.

The Wall: Dividing the City's Queer Public

When the GDR constructed the Wall on 13 August 1961 and over the following days and weeks, queer East Berliners were sealed off from West Berlin's queer public. As seen in chapter 2, the Wall separated couples such as Hans-Joachim Engel and his boyfriend. It also cut off bar-goers like Tommy and Helli from their beloved queer bars. The loss that this separation entailed remained largely unspoken in their testimony. Their silence in remembering lost love and sociability may express more than the difficulty to remember and speak about a painful period in their own lives. That the construction of the Wall was an especially traumatic event for queer East Berliners is suggested by the case of Günter Litfin, the first person to be shot dead by GDR border troops while trying to escape to the West. Litfin's queerness, used by the East to vilify him as a criminal, was not mentioned in Western coverage of his death, and in fact remains unacknowledged to the present in official commemorations.

Günter Litfin was born in 1937 and grew up in the Weissensee district in Berlin's northeast.[67] After completing an apprenticeship as a tailor, he worked for a custom tailor close to the Zoo train station in West Berlin while continuing to live in Weissensee. He was thus one of the thousands of *Grenzgänger* (border crossers), Berliners who resided in one part of the divided city but worked in the other.[68] When East Berlin authorities increasingly harassed border crossers, he rented an apartment in the Charlottenburg district in West Berlin. He put off registering with West Berlin authorities, however, so as not to be counted as *republikflüchtig*, as the GDR termed its citizens who fled to the West. Leaving the country without a permit was a crime that could carry up to three years in prison.[69] Those deemed "refugees of the Republic" were hence subject to arrest when returning to the GDR; registering in West Berlin would have meant that Litfin could no longer visit his family in Weissensee in East Berlin. When the border was closed on 13 August 1961, Litfin was in Weissensee with his family. On the afternoon of 24 August 1961, he attempted to cross the border by swimming through the Spree River between the Friedrichstraße and Lehrter Bahnhof S-Bahn stations, close to where the city's main train station is located today. He was spotted by the East Berlin police, however, who fatally shot him in the head.[70]

Dieter Berner has shown how the East Berlin press used Litfin's homosexuality to vilify him as a criminal and to detract attention from its murderous border regime.[71] At first, East Berlin newspapers printed only a brief report by the People's Police, which claimed that "a person persecuted for criminal deeds" had ignored multiple demands to give themselves up to the People's Police. The report stated – inaccurately – that the person had fallen into the water after being hit by an aimed shot and had probably drowned.[72] A week after Litfin's death, however, the East Berlin press felt compelled to report in more detail. On 29 August, East Berlin border police had shot and killed another refugee who had also tried to escape by swimming, and West Berlin newspapers had reported widely on his death, printing photographs of his failed flight.[73] The East German government hence was under tremendous pressure to justify the killing of the refugees.

In reaction, East Berlin newspapers mixed Stasi knowledge of Litfin's persecution under §175 in West Berlin, neighbourhood talk of his feminine masculinity, and discourses of predatory homosexuality and "work-shy" "streetwalking boys." Combined with the site of his attempted flight and murder in the vicinity of the Friedrichstraße train station, widely known as a location of male prostitution, the result was toxic. *Berliner Zeitung* titled its article "Front City Press Turns Criminal into Hero":

> One does not even shy away from playing up politically ... a criminal with a history of multiple offences who was caught doing criminal deeds by our detective squad in the proximity of Friedrichstraße train station on 24 August. This work-shy element, who was widely known under his moniker "Puppe" [doll] among homosexual circles in West Berlin, and who had been looking for victims in democratic Berlin since 13 August, had tried to resist his arrest through the People's Police, jumped into Humboldt Harbour, and died in the process.[74]

Immediately after Litfin's death, the Stasi collected information about him in the Weissensee neighbourhood that was home to his family. Neighbours stated that he had been known as *"Puppe"* (doll) in their neighbourhood, a term long used to designate feminine gay men. They shared their estimation that Litfin was "homosexually inclined because he has not had a closer connection to any girl so far."[75] They told the Stasi that Litfin often went out by himself and that neighbours would then gossip that he was going on a "doll stroll" (*Puppentour*). Litfin had not become "suspicious in this regard" in the neighbourhood itself, though. Another Stasi report dated 31 August 1961 and addressed to Erich Honecker, who was at the time the SED Central Council's secretary for security, repeated this information but added that Litfin had been incarcerated under §175 in West Berlin in 1957–58.[76] This report's emphasis, however, was on Litfin's membership in the youth group of the local chapter of the illegal Christian Democratic Union (CDU), his participation in a trip organized by its educational foundation, and his parents' long-term involvement in the CDU.

The Stasi was correct about Litfin's prosecution for §175 in West Berlin. His name comes up in the prisoner file of Hans-Ulrich H., who was arrested in August 1957 under the suspicion of having established a "traitorous relationship" with the Stasi and the East German labour union FDGB over a period of two years.[77] H. was arrested and incarcerated for both treason and transgression of §175 in 1957. The arrest warrant for the latter crime accused H. of sex with Litfin on multiple occasions in the summer of 1957.[78] The file also contains a note that H. was to be brought before court in November 1957 to testify in the criminal case against Günter Litfin and others.[79] While the file thus documents that Litfin was arrested and brought before court under §175, it does not confirm his incarceration.

If the West Berlin court found Litfin guilty of having had sex with a man, the denotation of Litfin as a "criminal" that the *Berliner Zeitung* used was factual, illustrating once more the power of §175 to turn a consensual sexual encounter into a crime that ruined reputations. Since Litfin's attempt to escape was a crime too, it was not wrong that he was "caught doing criminal deeds."[80] However, the phrasing "committing criminal deeds in the vicinity of the Friedrichstraße train station" combined with the adjective "work-shy," the moniker "doll," and the claim that Litfin had been popular with "homosexual circles" in West Berlin mobilized images of a "streetwalking boy" looking for clients. The article failed to mention Litfin's employment at the West Berlin custom tailor. Finally, the claim that he "had been looking for victims in democratic Berlin since 13 August" reinforced the idea of homosexuals as dangerous criminals preying on the innocent.

In light of the international attention that Litfin's death attracted – *Life Magazine* printed a photo of his lifeless body being dragged out of the water, for instance – East Berlin media further escalated its rhetoric.[81] The newspaper *Neues Deutschland* compared West Berlin efforts to memorialize Litfin with the Nazis' celebration of Horst Wessel, a young SA leader who was shot by a Communist in 1930. It thus insinuated both West Germany's fascist character and the equal depravity of Litfin's homosexuality and Wessel's alleged work as a pimp.[82] And a year later, when a memorial stone was set for Litfin at the western side of Humboldt Harbour, commentary on GDR television again drew on the Horst Wessel comparison. Television host Karl-Eduard von Schnitzler showed footage of the memorialization ceremony from a West German station in his weekly show *Der schwarze Kanal* (The Black Channel), a propaganda program that contrasted Western footage of current problems in West German society with images of GDR success.[83] Schnitzler described the site as a "memorial for a professional homosexual." In case viewers had not yet caught on to the insinuation, he continued: "That's what this Litfin was. He was living on our side and had his worksite at Zoo train station."[84] Again, his audience would have understood his mention of the Zoo station as a code word for commercial sex between men.

The case of Günter Litfin helps explain East Berliners' silence about the meaning of the Wall. "For the SED propaganda, the physical extermination of the refugee was not enough, he also had to be eliminated in reputation and in the public's consciousness," Dieter Berner wrote.[85] Put another way, just weeks after its construction, the Wall came to signify queer death in multiple ways: the death of a queer man as well as the death of queer sociability. As seen in the bar chapter, by cutting off queer bar-goers from West Berlin bars, the Wall isolated queer East Berliners, who took years to recover a queer social life. Through the vicious defamation of Günter Litfin in the East German public sphere, the Wall also became associated with a notion of homosexuality as utterly shameful: as commercial, as criminal, and as predatory. I will return to Günter Litfin and the lasting effects that the SED's defamation had for his memorialization even beyond the fall of the Wall in this chapter's conclusion.

While the Wall came to signify queer death, it also served as a queer erotic fantasy in a short story published in homophile magazine *Der Kreis* in 1963.[86] The trilingual magazine featured articles in German, French, and English, and was published in Zurich, Switzerland, and read worldwide. The story, titled "Behind the Wall," met with strong reactions from readers. Some rejected it as irresponsible kitsch; others appreciated that the author had treated the heavy subject with a light hand. The discussion of the two-page story filled ten pages over three issues of the magazine.

The story is the account of Michael, a West German of unknown age, who visits East Berlin on a Saturday in the winter of 1962. Michael knows Berlin: "He wanted to take a peek behind 'The Wall,' visit all the familiar sites that had once endeared Berlin to him."[87] He arrives in East Berlin by S-Bahn, going through border controls at Friedrichstraße train station. While waiting in line to have his passport checked and get a day permit, he makes eye contact with a young officer who is patrolling the waiting line, picking out "old people and those who he saw were about to collapse" for immediate passport controls.[88]

Once he has passed border controls, Michael walks down an empty Unter den Linden boulevard, feeling "an unusual chill that hurt."[89] At Palace Square, he visits the closeby Café Bukarest.[90] At this wine bar, Michael re-encounters the border control officer, and they begin a conversation that becomes more relaxed as they evade the issue of politics.[91] Michael then asks the officer to join him at the opera, and they see a performance of *La Traviata*. During the performance, the officer's hand reaches for Michael's, and they once again exchange glances. The story then jumps ahead to the two of them walking slowly on Unter den Linden towards Friedrichstraße train station, where Michael will catch the S-Bahn back to West Berlin and the officer will begin his night shift.

The narrator explains that Michael knew that their relationship would not last:

> Over there was a wall that prevented that, and maybe there was even more there; but they had not talked about that. They had only lived the moment in the shadows of a ruin; more had not been granted to them.[92]

Hence, besides the Wall, here trivialized by the use of the indeterminate article as just *a* wall, there might have been other obstacles to Michael and Eberhard's – the officer is now named – continued relationship, such as an existing boyfriend or a wife. But that possibility is never mentioned. All that time allows is quick sex in a ruined building. Before they get to Friedrichstraße station, they say their goodbyes. The boulevard is empty, facilitating a tender farewell:

> All alone they were standing on the walking path between the linden trees and were holding hands. Gently, Eberhard took Michael's head between his hands and tenderly kissed him on the mouth. "Let us never forget this hour," he added.[93]

The story ends with Michael hurrying towards his hotel along West Berlin's Kurfürstendamm boulevard, which, in contrast to its Eastern counterpart, is "flushed with traffic," whereas "Eberhard began his control walk along the Wall."[94] The remaining space on the page is filled with a schematic illustration of a wall.

The goodbye scene between Eberhard and Michael is reminiscent of the farewell between Eberhardt Brucks and Guy Morris, which introduced this chapter: a kiss in public, rendered in melodramatic tone. Volker, the story's author, represented the two parts of divided Berlin as different, but not too much so, and the Wall as an obstacle that could easily be overcome, at least for a West German; it is not a deadly barrier but a brief delay for a young man promenading through the city's public spaces. The humane treatment he receives from the border officer and the experience of being checked out by him gives the wait at the border a new meaning. In the story, East Berlin appears as a succession of landmarks within a half mile radius of Friedrichstraße, sights that would have been easily recognizable to *Der Kreis*'s readership. And while West Berlin's bright lights and traffic signal modernity, the backwardness of East Berlin, expressed in its emptiness, darkness, and the ruins, makes possible the intimacy between officer Eberhard and visitor Michael.

Critical readers of the story took offence at its poor style, pointing out that the formulaic melodrama had missed the very real drama that the

Wall signified for queer Berliners. "A 'Wall-tearjerker' with the undertone 'They aren't that bad after all,' decorated with a cute construction kit wall," summarized reader Horst from West Berlin. His scathing critique of the story opened and set the frame for the intense debate that followed between readers, editor, and author.[95] In his letter to the editor, which was as long as the story itself, he offered trenchant comments on the stylistic and substantial problems of "Behind the Wall."

> The whole story shows that the "Eastern Wanderer" has barely made an effort to engage with the human tragedy of the Wall. He has merely tried for the facades: Unter den Linden – Café Bukarest with the mellifluous violin music – State Opera – and, what coincidence, the young officer! He, too, pardon me, the facade of a probably attractive-looking man. Neither did our "Eastern Wanderer" look behind the scenes, not those of the representative of the Eastern gentlemen [the SED party leaders], either, because – they did not talk about politics. Not about humanity, either, because certainly, the "shadows of the ruin" where they later "lived the moment" was already casting its shadows before them, obscuring everything else.[96]

The superficial description, Horst argued, made not only for poor style. To get across what the author had failed to grasp by not going beyond appearances, Horst polemically continued the story.

> Certainly Michael did not consider that good Eberhard, after they parted at 21.45, theoretically and also very practically, by virtue of his order, might have, already at 22.05 when he began his control walk, shot down a human being, who possibly, just as coincidentally, might have been one of us, and whom a stronger bond than a Saturday afternoon romance might have given the strength and the courage to flee over the Wall. To flee to his West Berlin boyfriend, who after all cannot go to East Berlin for a café and opera visit.[97]

Horst hence insisted on the reality of divided Berlin in response to Volker's fantasy of a queer encounter between West and East outside the political. As West Berliners, neither Horst nor the "West Berlin boyfriend" he imagined could visit East Berlin in 1962–63. Visits only became possible in December 1963 with the first of the *Passierscheinabkommen*, the treaties that allowed West Berliners to come to East Berlin for a brief time. Horst also confronted "Behind the Wall" with the reality of the Wall as queer death. His description of "one of us" being killed by a border guard while trying to flee to his boyfriend in West Berlin can be read as a possible reference to the case of Günter Litfin. As a West

Berliner, Horst might have known Litfin personally; at least it is likely that queer West Berliners were aware of the SED's smear campaign against Litfin and would have discussed it with friends. In his letter, Horst does not refer to Litfin directly, however. Indeed, the following sentences suggest that he may be referring to another case.

> The gunned down man was a soldier and was guarding the Wall, he was separated from his boyfriend on 13 August 1961, he no longer had the strength to endure the separation, and he no longer wanted to live "the moment" over and over again.[98]

The change in grammatical mood, from subjunctive to indicative, may signify a change in genre from fiction to non-fiction. The definitiveness of the simple past implies factuality; the letter's tone shifts from the polemical to the authentic, maybe even autobiographic. Was this soldier Horst's boyfriend? Is he telling his own story? Horst brings back "Officer Eberhard," the fictional figure from the story, in the next sentence. But historical reality surfaces again in the final sentence, when he describes Eberhard as "the murderer of a human whose only 'crime' consisted of having dreamt, since 13 August 1961, of once again being kissed gently and tenderly by his boyfriend."[99] The word "crime," I posit, can be read as a reference to the vilification of Günter Litfin as a "criminal" engaging in "criminal deeds" by GDR media. The multiple layers of reference in Horst's letter, expressed in varying registers of grammar and voice, destabilize the fictional framework of the story and make historical reality shimmer through the fictional facade of "Behind the Wall."

Horst also addresses historical reality directly. Referring to the publisher's location in Switzerland, far away from East-West tensions, he writes:

> Certainly, it is difficult to grasp the problem of the Wall comprehensively from Zurich; just how hard it is can be gauged by the fact that not even the West Germans succeed in it, as the mindless example of the story shows ... Believe me, there must be thousands of cases where couples of friends [Freundespaare] were separated by this deed of impotence by a hated regime, just like families, marriages, fiancés, and all scales of human bond were recklessly torn apart.[100]

The reactions to Horst's letter were split, with some readers enthusiastically agreeing with him and others, including the publisher and author, reading his response as tainted with Cold War fury, failing to engage with his criticism, and displaying a remarkable naiveté. "Why should he [the young officer] shoot right away? Normally, we especially are not so trigger-happy, here as there," reader Klaus from Geneva wrote, postulating a gay exceptionalism of peacefulness.[101] He believed that the story, because it was "not drenched in hate," could show readers that there were "people 'over there' too, who sense and feel like humans."[102] Author Volker shared Klaus's incomprehension over Horst's outrage. "Why turn a story into a drama, a coincidental encounter of two young people into a political problem right away?" he asked.[103] He was concerned "not with the facade, but with the purely human," he claimed. His response ended with the call: "Let us not look at the uniform, but through it!"[104] That suggestion was gladly taken up by editor Rolf, who found it adequate to extend such a gener-ous ignorance of uniforms to those who had worn them less than two decades earlier.[105]

> It is as utterly wrong today to see in an officer of the Eastern police only a henchman of the regime as it was wrong during the Thousand-Year Reich to see a sadist devoted to Hitler in every bearer of an SS uniform. We know today that some – certainly not enough – let themselves be roped in so as to be able to prevent some of the monstrous, and did so too.[106]

To Rolf, the concern that the officer in the story had shown for the old and infirm waiting in line at the border was proof enough that he would not coolly execute the command to shoot illegal border crossers. He could find no fault with the story whose singular point he described as "the vital spark of eros stopping before no border and no wall and no 'enemy,'" and he reproached critics for wanting to "attach such heavy weights to everything."[107]

Despite his disagreement with the critics, editor Rolf gave them more room in the pages of his magazine. In the May 1963 issue, discussion took up another three pages. Reader Rolf C. rejected the editor's talk of "heavy weights," instead repeating Horst's point that the story's trivi-ality was incompatible with its subject's gravity. "What is demanded here is solely the right relation of topic and form of discussion," he wrote. "It is also called tact."[108] He saw no contradiction between his call for keeping the right measure and his own juxtaposition of the walled-in GDR with the Nazi concentration camps. "The Wall has created the most modern KZ, and we would find a schmaltzy portrayal of human episodes in a Nazi KZ unbearable today," he wrote. Horst from West Berlin, whose letter sparked the discussion, responded to his critics and addressed their resistance against imagining the border guard as a killer. He pointed out that those who became officers in the People's Police did so voluntarily and enlisted for a minimum of ten years, suggesting their ideological commitment to the GDR. He denied that being "one of us" made anyone less trigger-happy.[109] But editor Rolf continued to be unmoved by arguments about the inadequacy of the story, insisting that it "neither could nor wanted to grasp or artistically shape the ground of the Berlin Wall in its whole breadth and depth, but only show a small adventure and a quiet cheerfulness that had strayed into the ruins."[110] This statement was his final word, wrapping up the discussion once and for all: he stood by his opinion that printing "Behind the Wall" had been the right decision.

"Behind the Wall" and the heated debate it elicited show a clash of everyday experiences and fantasies of the Berlin Wall and of Berlin as a queer space. As the story's critics pointed out, the Wall served as mere decoration in this narrative, East Berlin as mere facade for telling a titillating tale of quick sex with a man in uniform. The reluctance to imagine gay men in uniform as murderers and the readiness to grant them superior, benevolent motives for joining both oppressive regimes, apparent in many of the readers' responses, is disturbing to the contemporary reader. Perhaps even more shocking is the casual use of the Nazi concentration camps as simile for the walled-in GDR, which was, however, a feature of much Western reporting on the Wall.[111] Whereas the Nazi comparisons remained unchallenged in *Der Kreis*, the story's treatment of sex was met with ample comment. In its tame, yet comparatively explicit mention of the sexual encounter – multiple readers mentioned that the sex scene took up an unusually central place in the narrative – and its more pronounced description of public tenderness between men, the story reinforced Berlin's image as a haven for queer love. More than fifteen years after the war ended, the city's ruins remained part of the "moral geography of danger and desire" articulated by Jennifer Evans.[112] As the responses to the story and its critique by West Berliner Horst demonstrate, the lethal reality of the Wall for queer East Berliners could easily be ignored by the magazine's West German and Swiss readership, which appears to have been unaware of Günter Litfin's case. At the same time, multiple readers asked whether the magazine had subscribers in East Germany, conveying genuine interest in the situation of their Eastern "comrades," a term often used to express community with other homophiles. Editor Rolf did not answer this question, and East German voices were not represented in the discussion, suggesting that there were no East German subscribers beyond medical professionals and institutes.

Conclusion

This chapter set out to examine how queer Berliners perceived the city's public spaces, how they moved in them, how their movements and actions were shaped by laws and policing, and how they subverted public spaces' intended uses, queering them for their own purposes. In gay men's oral histories, stopping at *Klappen* for anonymous sex emerged as a beloved routine, albeit one whose thrill came with the danger of violence, arrest, and incarceration. "Streetwalking boys," many of whom worked in public spaces, appear as ambivalent and contradictory figures in this chapter. Authorities' desire to cleanse public space of signs of sexual deviance and commercial sex meant that they were heavily policed. At times, a man's presence in a space known for male prostitution was enough to be arrested. The GDR's formalized persecution of individuals whose lifestyle did not conform to socialist ideals of work and family through the "asociality" law may have affected streetwalking boys too. But streetwalking boys could be perpetrators as much as victims, robbing, blackmailing, physically hurting, and even killing the men who purchased their services.

Free passage through public spaces was predicated upon a normative performance of gender: to pass as a man, queer Berliners could not be feminine, but had to pick up the gestures, movements, and language of normative masculinity. To pass as a woman, trans women had to perform a seamless version of normative femininity. In West Berlin, police recognition of transvestite subjectivities ended in 1960 at the latest, as the practice of issuing *Transvestitenscheine* and passports that showed their bearers in their chosen everyday appearance was abolished.

In 1961, the construction of the Wall materialized Berlin's border and ended the porousness that had characterized the inner-city division since the beginning of the Cold War. It broke apart the queer public that had existed up to this point in the postwar city, despite the economic inequalities and political and legal differences in East and West. When the SED regime's violent enforcement of the new order hit a gay man as its first victim, and it then leveraged homophobic prejudice to legitimize his killing, the Wall came to signify queer death to queer Berliners.

Even beyond the end of the GDR, the SED's defamation had lasting effects for the memorialization of Günter Litfin. His portrait on the Chronicles of the Wall website, a project by three major federal institutions documenting the history of the Wall and commemorating its victims, mentions neither his homosexuality nor East German media's homophobic abuse for propagandistic purposes.[113] The website stresses his family's membership in the CDU and their Catholicism, accompanied by Litfin's first communion photograph (figure 3.1). His sense of

Victims at the wall

Back to overview

Günter Litfin

born on January 19, 1937
shot dead on August 24, 1961

in the Humboldt Harbor near Charité Hospital
at the sector border between Berlin-Mitte and Berlin-Tiergarten

Günter Litfin, photo: ca. 1960 (Photo: private)

Günter Litfin: Memorial cross for Günter Litfin at the Reichstag building in Berlin, 2005 (Photo: Hans-Hermann Hertle)

It was just after 4 p.m. when Günter Litfin began his attempt to reach West Berlin by fleeing between the Friedrichstrasse and Lehrter train stations. According to reports from the East Berlin police, he crossed Charité Hospital grounds and climbed over a wall bordering the bank of the Spree River when members of the transport police discovered him.

Günter Litfin: First communion (photo; ca. 1947) (Photo: private)

Günter Litfin was born in Berlin on January 19, 1937 and lived in the city district of Weissensee. He grew up during the Second World War and later experienced the country's reconstruction and the gradual division of the city. His father Albert worked as a butcher and in 1945 helped found the local CDU district chapter, which his wife Margarete also joined. The four sons were baptized Catholic and attended the St. Joseph School in Berlin-Weissensee. The family was clearly rooted in a milieu that was not supportive of the East German government and its mission to 'establish socialism.'[1] The sons continued to maintain this attitude as adults: In 1957 Günter Litfin and his younger brother, Jürgen, joined the West Berlin CDU, which unlike the CDU block party in East Germany, existed illegally in the eastern part of the city. [2]

After completing an apprenticeship as a tailor, Günter Litfin got a job in a West Berlin tailor workshop. He was fashion conscious, dressed elegantly and dreamed of becoming a costume maker for the theater. At first the young man commuted daily from his parents' apartment in Weissensee to his job near the Bahnhof Zoo. But 'border-crossers,' as people who worked in the West and lived in the East were called, were under increasing pressure in East Germany. To avoid conflict Günter Litfin found an apartment in the West Berlin district of Charlottenburg, but he did not register his new address with the police because that would have made him a 'republic fugitive' - someone who has deserted East Germany - and would have meant that he could no longer visit his relatives in East Berlin. Günter Litfin's brother later described him 'as the calming force in the family and the one everyone could confide in.'[3] After his father died in May 1961, Günter strongly felt it was his responsibility to be there for his mother.

Consequently, he postponed his permanent move to West Berlin - until it was too late. The construction of the Berlin Wall suddenly put an end to his plans for the future. Günter Litfin spent August 12, 1961, a Saturday, with his mother and brother visiting relatives on the west side of the city. When they took the S-Bahn back to Weissensee late that evening, they had no idea that measures were being prepared to close the border. The shock was great the next morning when they heard on the radio that the sector border had been completely sealed off during the night. Günter Litfin, unable to accept the existence of the Wall, began poking into fashion is mentioned too, not without the addition that it "corresponds to his profession" as a tailor.[114] This portrayal of Günter Litfin as a Christian, conservative young man whose impeccable appearance was an expression of his professional ethics and his good upbringing continues the efforts of his brother Jürgen Litfin, three years his junior, who until his death in 2017 made it his life's work to commemorate his older brother. In 2003, he opened a memorial to his brother and the other victims of the Wall in a former guard tower close to the site of Günter's attempted escape.

In his 2006 memoir, Jürgen Litfin remembers his brother and their relationship, Günter's death, and the repercussions for him and his family. Growing up, the brothers Günter and Jürgen had been close. Jürgen Litfin's pride in his brother shines through in his account of Günter's "excellent work and courteous nature," his tailoring work for well-known actors, "his good manners," "good looks, tall (182 centimetres), slender, dark hair, and dark eyes," his "warm, outgoing manner."[115] Günter supported his brother and his parents financially, and the brothers also socialized together, going on bike tours and out to dance. In this context, Jürgen Litfin mentions "my brother's girlfriend ... Monika."[116] At the same time, he also describes that Günter had to endure "derisive criticism" on the streets of Weissensee for his elegant wardrobe.[117] Whereas Günter appears as an exceptionally well-dressed, well-mannered heterosexual man in Jürgen Litfin's characterization, the sneering comments that he suffered for his looks hint at the fragility of this image of heterosexual masculinity, and at his brother's awareness of it.

The day after Günter Litfin's shooting, without knowing what had happened, Jürgen Litfin was interrogated for hours by the Stasi.[118] His questioners confronted him with two contradictory theories about his brother, both of which he describes as "slander": that Günter was homosexual and that he had sexually harassed a female nurse at the Charité Hospital.[119] When Jürgen returned home, he found his mother in despair. Their apartment had been turned upside down and partly destroyed by Stasi agents who had not bothered to inform her about the reasons for their search. The two of them only learned of Günter's violent death the following day, when the West Berlin television news reported on it. The family was then forced to keep quiet about the circumstances of Günter's passing.

After the fall of the Wall, Jürgen Litfin worked ceaselessly to rehabilitate his brother and get justice for him. He tried to find out more about the course of events that led to his brother's death, in particular the identities of the policemen who shot him. In this context, he discusses the content of the Stasi report to Erich Honecker. He mentions how the report maligned the family for their CDU membership but omits its reference to his brother's alleged homosexuality and incarceration in West Berlin. In the reprint of the report that is included in the text, the respective lines are blackened.[120]

In light of the traumatic connection between his brother's death and the state's vicious homophobic defamation, it is understandable that Jürgen Litfin glossed over all hints of Günter Litfin's homosexuality. But the result is a misrepresentation. Günter Litfin was not only a Catholic and a political conservative, but, quite likely, he also loved men. His brave attempt to flee the GDR, I would suggest, was motivated also by a need to be among friends and lovers in West Berlin and to partake in West Berlin's queer public, not only by his political leanings and his wish to continue his professional success. In addition, Jürgen Litfin's refusal to even entertain the possibility of Günter's homo- or bisexuality perpetuates the very homophobia expressed so heinously by GDR media. By uncritically following his account, official commemorations such as the Chronicles of the Wall participate in upholding a silence that signifies the shamefulness of queer love.

4 Bubis behind Bars:
Prisons as Queer Spaces

In the late 1940s or early 1950s, East Berlin dog groomer Rita "Tommy" Thomas served ten months for unlawful possession of a gun at the East Berlin women's prison at Barnimstraße (Barnim Street), just minutes from Alexanderplatz.[1] She recalled the experience in a 2016 oral history interview with the Archive of Other Memories:

> I went to Keibelstraße [the East Berlin People's Police pretrial detention site] for pretrial detention right away. Then they transferred me to Barnimstraße, Barnimstraße 10. There was a block upstairs, on the first or second floor, first floor, that was all juveniles ... They saw me downstairs and called to me from upstairs: Hey, send the Bubi to us up here. Because back then people used to say Bubi [lad] and Mäuschen [little mouse]. And well, I had to, if I wanted to or not. But it was a good time. It was like a kindergarten. There were pretty women there too. And once when we had our free hour, with one of them I got along really well, and we said, we'll celebrate our engagement here now. And there were ten of us, not more, ten or twelve, we walked around the prison yard arm in arm, and they followed. And so we celebrated our engagement, more for a joke, really. And the guards, they were [transcript unclear, could also mean "that was"] strange too, the inmates would give them nicknames. One of them had a silver tooth in her mouth, and they'd call her Blechzahnbubi [tin tooth Bubi], and the other one was called Fräulein Fuchs [Miss Fox]. And, well then I was in a cell, she [another prisoner] always wanted to make out, and I did not like that so much. There were three of us in the cell, and I asked for a single cell. And then when I did get a single cell, I wrote. I only ever wrote. The guard said I was like Chopin, that's what she said.[2]

In Tommy's narration, the prison emerges as a space marked by the articulation of queer subjectivities, the scene of inmate relationships both playful and transgressive, and a place that allowed for introspection and creativity – a veritable room of one's own. As I will demonstrate in this chapter, in East and West Berlin sources from the 1950s and 1960s, women's prisons appear as spaces in which queer relationships were lived, where queer subjectivities became visible and were formed. A closer analysis of Tommy's prison memories will guide us towards a full articulation of this argument.

Immediately upon her arrival, Tommy is called out as *Bubi* by other prisoners. "*Bubi*" has been employed as a German term for masculine-presenting, same-sex desiring women since at least the turn of the twentieth century, and historians of queer cultures of the 1920s have described gender-differentiated lesbian couples of *Bubis* and *Mädis* [girls] or *Bubis* and *Damen* [ladies].[3] By calling Tommy out as a *Bubi*, the other prisoners were hence designating her as queer. Calling her by this name also placed her in the space of the prison: she is sent "up to us here," to the group that claimed her as one of their own. Tommy does not elaborate who this group was, if it was all *Bubis*, suggesting a gendered organization of prison space, or both *Bubis* and *Mäuschen*, pointing to sexuality as ordering principle. These queer subjectivities did not apply to inmates only but also to two guards the prisoners nicknamed "Tin Tooth Bubi" and "Miss Fox."

In Tommy's story, the prison also provided space for various kinds of inmate relationships. The performance of an engagement ceremony between Tommy and another prisoner, celebrated in the presence and with the participation of other inmates in a mix of play and formality, was a demonstration of prisoner agency: the incarcerated used their free time and the comparatively open space of the prison yard to construct their own social order. In her cell, by contrast, Tommy was exposed to unwanted sexual advances. When she was granted her wish to be put in a single cell, it became a space of reflection. The guard's comparison of Tommy's creativity to the composer Frédéric Chopin was a compliment, and a sense of pride resonates in her narration of this episode. Given that she came from a working-class family, did not receive formal education beyond high school, and made a living as a dog groomer, her prolific prison writing stands out in her biography. The single cell that she occupied and the time away from everyday life afforded her a chance for reflection that she likely would not otherwise have had, and it may explain why she described her prison stay as "a good time," a perhaps surprising assessment that I will contextualize below.

Tommy's narrative introduces carceral spaces as sites where non-normatively lived genders and same-sex relationships could be found. Whether inmates arrived in prisons with queer subjectivities, whether they adopted them in prison, and whether their experiences in prison had lasting effects on their sexual subjectivities will be the questions running through this chapter. As I will demonstrate through my discussion of oral history testimony and administrative and inmate files, looking at prisons can help us see queer histories that so far have largely remained opaque, particularly in the German context, such as working-class lesbian relationships and trans subjectivities in the 1950s and 1960s. In this way, a queer historical analysis of prisons contributes to a more comprehensive history of the repression and resilience of queers, a history that takes seriously the intersections of gender, sexuality, and class, and their repercussions in queer folks' everyday lives. While my focus in this chapter is on women's prisons, it is important to note that, in postwar Germany, especially in the West, prisons were sites of the mass criminalization, degradation, and disenfranchisement of men sentenced under §175 and §175a, the laws prohibiting sex between men and male prostitution. I will offer a brief excursus on queer men in prison in West Berlin as well.[4]

In what follows, I outline the historiographies on prisons, sex, and butch-fem subjectivities. I then analyse archival documents and oral history testimonies on women's prisons in East and West Berlin. In my examination of these sources, I offer an intertwined analysis of practices (what people were doing), subjectivities (how they understood what they were doing and who they were), and discourses (how others understood what they were doing, who they were, and what the repercussions of that were) in the hope of arriving at an understanding of the prison that spotlights queer agency while remaining mindful of the very real deprivations, hostilities, and violence inflicted on queer inmates.

Prisons, Sex, and Butch-Fem Subjectivities

As a central agent of what Michel Foucault calls "the normalizing power" in modern Western societies, the prison is a prime location for studying how sexual and gender norms were produced and how non-normative sexualities and genders were disciplined.[5] Foucault famously posited that the modern prison is one institution among others, such as schools, almshouses, or social work, in a "carceral network" that, through "its systems of insertion, distribution, surveillance, observation," disciplines individuals and produces deviants.[6] Historians of sexuality and prison historians have been slow to explore the nexus of the carceral and the sexual, however, as Regina Kunzel has pointed out in *Criminal Intimacy*, her history of sexuality and prisons in the United

States.[7] She argues that the prison's location at the margins of society makes it a particularly well-suited site for examining the instabilities and anxieties that structure the broader society and that discourses about prison sex might illuminate the construction of gender and sexuality norms. Kunzel's thesis is based on her analysis of sociological studies of US prison populations from the mid-twentieth century. These studies' authors, she shows, most prominent among them Donald Clemmer and Gresham Sykes, interpreted same-sex practices and relationships between prisoners as an "understandable and compensatory response to the deprivations of incarceration" and thus without consequences for the stability of American heterosexuality more broadly.[8] These were instances of "situational" homosexuality only, they argued, and as soon as inmates left the prison "situation," they returned to the heterosexual order.[9] At the same time, however, the sociologists' assurances betrayed their realization, Kunzel argues, that prison sex also carried "potential to reveal heterosexual identity as fragile, unstable, and, itself, situational" and thus to "expose the framing beneath the edifice of heterosexuality at a key moment in its construction."[10]

The rich sociological scholarship on prison society in the United States does not have a correlate in Germany, where prisons as social spaces have been largely ignored by sociology, history, and sexology.[11] Recent publications on everyday life and sexuality in Nazi concentration camps by Insa Eschebach and Anna Hájková have begun to examine same-sex sexuality between camp inmates, as well as between inmates and guards. However, their focus has been on expressions of homophobia in camp memorializations rather than on sexual and affective practices in the camps.[12] Also, the situation of concentration camp inmates was far worse than that of prisoners in the postwar Germanies, as the goal of camp internment was death, not punishment. As I will show, German postwar prisons allowed inmates some room for negotiation of their conditions. With the postwar years characterized by what Dagmar Herzog has termed "fragile heterosexuality" and a "desperate search for normality," negotiations around sex in prisons may be particularly insightful for the making of sexual norms in Germany in this period.[13] To repurpose Kunzel's words, the postwar years in Germany were also a "key moment" in the construction of "the edifice of heterosexuality," and ideas about non-normative sexualities were crucial building blocks for it.

Beyond prison sex as a central discursive site in the construction of heterosexuality, Kunzel is also attentive to the practices of constructing the gendered and sexual selves of prisoners and the presence of queer working-class subjectivities in mid-century prisons.[14] "Populations of women's as well as men's prisons were drawn disproportionately from the working class, and the increasing importance of butch-femme dynamics and gender signification began to be apparent in women's prisons beginning in this period as well," she writes.[15] Kunzel cites Elizabeth Kennedy and Madeline Davis's oral history study of the postwar butch-fem subculture in Buffalo, New York, *Boots of Leather, Slippers of Gold: The History of a Lesbian Community.*[16] Though I have already discussed this seminal work in the chapter on homes in conjunction with Tommy's photographs of lesbian sociability in East Berlin, Kennedy and Davis's argument for the political significance of butch-fem subjectivities warrants a closer look.

> Butches defied convention by usurping male privilege in appearance and sexuality, and with their fems, outraged society by creating a romantic and sexual unit within which women were not under male control. At a time when lesbian communities were developing solidarity and consciousness, but had not yet formed political groups, butch-fem roles were the key structure for organizing against heterosexual dominance. They were the central prepolitical form of resistance.[17]

Kennedy and Davis here offered an alternative reading of US gay and lesbian history, challenging the narrative that the respectability-centred approach of the homophile movement had been the only gay and lesbian politics before Stonewall. In my analysis of German inmate files and oral history testimony, I pay keen attention to gendered performances and their verbalizations, such as Tommy's designation as Bubi in the East Berlin prison. I contend that in Germany too, the practices of butch and fem self-fashioning were key to queer community building, not just under the conditions of imprisonment but also more generally during the intensely homophobic 1950s and 1960s.

Excursus: Queer Men in Prison in West Berlin

Because only sex between men was prohibited by law, incarceration as punishment for queer sex affected only those identified by the law as men, which included those classified as male-to-female transvestites, as seen in the previous two chapters. Excerpts from the oral history interviews of Orest Kapp and Klaus Born highlight aspects of queer men's experience in prison that warrant exploration in greater depth, especially because prison time was a feature of many queer men's lives.

No statistics exist for the incarceration of queer Berliners under §175 in the postwar years.[18] However, according to historian Jens Dobler, 758 men were convicted under §175 in Berlin (East and West) between 1945 and 1948 alone. Statistics of the sentences given to men in West Germany under §175 or §175a between 1950 and 1969 show that 75 per cent received a prison term.[19] With the prosecution for §175 intensifying dramatically in West Germany over the 1950s and into the 1960s, it seems likely that thousands of men were imprisoned in West Berlin prisons for having sex with other men until the reform of the law in 1969. In East Berlin, the numbers were likely much lower. Incomplete statistics show that between 1949 and 1959, at least 202 men and male youth were sentenced under §175 and §175a.[20] But as seen in chapter 3, the GDR's laws targeting "asocials" were possibly also used against queers. Men's prisons in East Berlin thus warrant an in-depth examination as sites that played a significant role for queer men.

Orest Kapp, whose description of the painstaking process of learning normative masculinity I discussed in chapter 3, was "surprised with a friend" by the West Berlin police in the late 1950s when he was seventeen.[21] In the interview, he does not specify what they were caught doing, but he was arrested for causing a public nuisance and for §175, suggesting that he and his friend had sex in a public space. While Kapp was ultimately not convicted, he spent three months in custody. He was "ashamed to be in prison, especially as a homosexual," and told acquaintances that he was jailed for "something criminal."[22] In custody, he had sex for safety,[23] as he explains to the interviewers:

INTERVIEWER: Did you have problems in custody?
OREST KAPP: Hm, I did not, thank God, because the boss of my cell, where I was, well, the boss, he took me under his wing, to put it this way, yeah. So I was his sex partner. But in return, the others spared me.[24]

By incarcerating him for consensual sex with a friend, the state thus subjected teenage Orest Kapp to a situation in which he had to choose between acting as sex partner to the cell's "boss" or being exposed to the advances of other inmates.

Twenty-one-year-old Klaus Born's arrest during his first sexual encounter in West Berlin, with a man he met in the vicinity of the Zoo station in 1965, also led him into custody, but his experience there was different from Orest Kapp's. Born was put in a single cell and not allowed to have any contact with other prisoners. In the oral history interview, he describes the deprivations of life in prison.

And then I had my room in the uppermost floor. A so-called solitary cell. There was nothing in there. There was the bed, a table, a small chair, and the pit toilet. And that was it. And a little bit of water. [breathes in] ... So I was inside. A week. Two weeks. Three weeks. It must have been ... seven, eight weeks. How long exactly it was? I don't know. [breathes in] ... And in the time I was inside. I had no music. I had nothing to read. I had nothing to write. Nothing. I wasn't allowed to do anything either. It was like a, how do you say? Hm, hm, it was a solitary confinement ... The only thing I was allowed to do. I was allowed to. Everyday. For ten minutes. With two men. One in front. One behind. In a certain distance. To go for a round in the yard downstairs. And then I could go back upstairs. But I could not come too close to the two. I might have infected them, after all. To become gay. Right?[25]

In the transcript, Klaus Born's repeated pausing to breathe is noted, and the frequent full stops register his chopped narration, indicating that these memories are hard for him to express. He enumerates the things he did not have (music, things to write and read) in order to illustrate how he suffered from the lack of occupation and contact that his solitary confinement entailed. The only contact he describes occurs during his court rounds, and during these instances, prison staff prescribed a mandatory physical distance between him and the men walking in front and behind him, whether these were guards or other prisoners. Born sarcastically renders prison staff's pathologizing rationale for this distance, which likely explains his solitary confinement too: they pathologized him as infectious.

Continuing his narration, Klaus Born describes how he appropriated this pathologizing language and turned his court trial from a spectacle meant to shame him into an unashamed praise of sex between men.

And then the trial came. Then I said to him ... Then why do I go to trial? I'm going to make them all sick! Won't they all get sick when I get up there. No, not there. That's a court. It will sentence you, after all. Ah, ok. Hm. Well, anyway ... Now I am in the dock. And I look in the back. That was a large room. Then two school classes come in there ... They were to listen to this so that they would not get sick. Right? So that they know how it is when you lead a gay life. When you practise §175. So when you go through with it. Yeah. Then they listened to all of that. I explained it to them close and hot [brühwarm], what we did and how it was so beautiful too. I said: It was wonderful. And then all of a sudden the lamps go on and we are dis-, disturbed. That probably did not suit them either.[26]

In this part of his narration, Klaus Born appears strong and self-confident. He is aware of the efforts to pathologize him but does not let himself be affected by them. Instead, by naively asking if his presence during the trial won't infect the other people present, he demonstrates the absurdity of the idea that his homosexuality might be contagious. During the trial, when he becomes aware of his audience of high school students, he appropriates the courtroom as a stage that was meant to cast him as a shameful criminal. He "explains" to the students "close and hot," so likely in vivid and detailed language, what he and the other man did, and how "wonderful" it felt. In his rendering of his statement in court, the state's intervention comes across as a disturbance: it is not he and his sex partner who disturb public order, but the state that disturbs a "beautiful" encounter between two people. In this narration, decades after his trial, Klaus Born thus rhetorically turned the state's weapons against itself.

The Women's Prisons in Postwar East and West Berlin: Criminological Concepts and Penal Practice

Guided by different strategies for dealing with the Nazi past and competing visions for the future, the East and West German states developed different concepts of penal law and practice. In the first years after 1945, penal law in both states was almost identical to the Reich Penal Code of 1871. The purpose of punishment was retribution for the crimes committed.[27] In the West, the postwar years were characterized by continuities from the Nazi period in criminological thought and penal practice, as well as a slow process of liberalization. In the immediate post-Nazi period, biological determinism remained the predominant theory for explaining crime.[28] But over the 1950s, under the influence of the occupying powers, liberal understandings of criminality, which stressed environmental influences, gained ground in West Germany.[29] As a result, the criminal's rehabilitation, or *Resozialisierung*, became the chief reason for incarceration.

On the ground, however, many West German federal states kept the Nazi rules for prisoners in place, with only slight changes. There were significant continuities from the Nazi era among penal personnel, ranging from high-ranking civil servants in the ministries to prison directors, chaplains, and guards.[30] Many of those working directly with convicts did not believe in rehabilitation. As Greg Eghigian has noted, prison reform in West Germany was a top-down affair, "carried out and designed by academic experts, longtime federal administrators, and national politicians, who clearly and knowingly operated contrary to the general sentiment of most prison staff and the general population."[31] While prisoners were incrementally granted more rights and a new Federal Penal and Prison Order went into effect in 1962, it still stressed retribution over rehabilitation. Only in 1976 did rehabilitation become the explicitly stated goal of incarceration in the new penal law, alongside protecting the public from future crimes.[32]

East Germany pursued a more radical break with the Nazi era by removing former party members from all state offices. All Nazi judges and prison staff were dismissed.[33] The law, and by extension incarceration, was now marshalled for the goal of building socialism. The law thus served to penalize East Germans for behaviour that was regarded antagonistic to the socialist state and society.[34] Despite the stated goal of moving away from Nazi ideology, however, penal practice differed starkly from official policy throughout the existence of the GDR. While the East German authorities initially put experts in charge who had led prison reform during the Weimar Republic, they were quickly let go again.[35] In 1951, responsibility for the penal system was wrested from the judicial system and given to the Ministry of the Interior and the police, "the most unscrupulous pillars of the new regime," according to Nikolaus Wachsmann.[36] It was partly the growing number of political prisoners that motivated this change.[37] Living conditions in East German prisons were dismal, particularly in the early 1950s, and prisons were routinely overcrowded by the mid-1950s. There was also a severe shortage of qualified staff.[38] In the late 1950s, East German scepticism about rehabilitative penal measures gave way to an optimism about the potential of the social sciences to turn convicts into "socialist personalities," citizens who would abide by the new state-issued rules for everyday behaviour, such as "decency and discipline."[39] Beginning in the 1970s, the Cold War détente led East German penology to adopt international developments in correctional theory. But as Eghigian has argued, practice was much slower to change, and the shortage and poor education of prison staff meant that they remained focused on "putting prisoners to work and keeping order," and guards interpreted breaches of prison rules as "evidence of shortcomings in the 'character' of inmates."[40]

These divergent developments can also be traced in Berlin's penal system. In 1945, it came under the control of the occupying Soviet troops, including the women's prison located at Barnimstraße 10 in the city centre, very close to Alexanderplatz.[41] During the Nazi era, both Hilde Radusch and Eva Siewert had been incarcerated here – Radusch as a communist, Siewert for making fun of the Nazis. As a result of the Berlin crisis of 1948, the city was split into East and West politically and began to turn into two separate administrative, economic, and cultural entities, a process that would not be complete until the construction of the Berlin Wall in 1961, however.[42] The city's penal system was divided in 1949. Now, prison staff who resided in West Berlin could no longer enter East Berlin. Inmates who had originally been living in what was now West Berlin were transferred to prisons in the West.[43] In East Berlin, the new judiciary introduced penal reforms in the late 1940s designed to alleviate everyday life behind bars and give prisoners more control over their incarceration, such as the introduction of prisoners' councils and the opportunity to partake in cultural and educational events.[44] This liberalizing approach ceased immediately when the police took over the East German penal system in 1951. Now, rehabilitative approaches to punishment were driven out in favour of a more authoritarian, militarized regime.[45] In West Berlin, the former military prison in Moabit, a working-class district just northwest of the city's historical centre, was turned into the women's prison in 1949.[46] After briefly housing refugees in 1945, it now took in West Berlin's female convicts. The turn-of-the-century building had suffered only minor damage in the war, but it had also not been modernized in decades. For instance, until 1964 there were only buckets in the cells, no toilets.[47] The complex continued to house the city's female prisoners until 1985, when a new facility opened in Plötzensee, a district in northern Berlin.

Queer Relationships and Subjectivities in the East Berlin Women's Prison

This chapter opened with East Berlin dog groomer Rita "Tommy" Thomas's memories of the ten months she spent in the juvenile wing of the women's prison at Barnimstraße 10. In her oral history narrative, she depicted the prison as a space of play and privacy: "a kindergarten" full of "pretty women," where engagements were celebrated "for a joke" and a young working-class person could be compared to the creative genius of a Chopin. Tommy's time at Barnimstraße prison likely fell into a comparatively comfortable period in 1949–50: the worst material deprivations of the postwar years had been overcome; the prison was no longer overcrowded with women incarcerated for petty crime, prostitution, and other postwar criminality; and the socialist authorities experimented with new, more liberal approaches to penal justice.[48] Tommy's incarceration occurred during an in-between period when the chaos, uncertainty, and openness of the postwar years had not yet hardened into the full-blown articulation of socialist morality and the sexual conservatism of the early years of the GDR.[49] With a new "normal" not yet defined, the prison was less effective as an institution of normalization. These circumstances probably contributed to the "good time" that Tommy enjoyed at Barnimstraße prison.

During the oral history interview, the interviewers asked Tommy about her usage of the terms "Bubi" and "Mäuschen":

INTERVIEWERS: You just mentioned that, back then, people would always say Bubi and Mäuschen.

TOMMY: Yes, yes, that's how it was, there were many before us, after all. I met someone once, who was, she told me this, she said: "That's a hard time, when you enter there, I was Mäuschen once too." So I say: "What's that?" And she says: "Well, Mäuschen is the woman and Bubi, well, the guy, the little guy." And that's how I know that, yes, Bubi.

INTERVIEWERS: And was it always a combination of Bubi and Mäuschen or were there couples of Mäuschen and Mäuschen or Bubi and Bubi?

TOMMY: Yes, yes, yes.

INTERVIEWERS: Those existed too?

TOMMY: Yes, those existed, too, you didn't catch on to it so much. And most often those who were a little strict, back then you could really distinguish them, you would notice – you'd simply notice, pretty much. Well, they had short hair, I always had an Elvis haircut, a little longer here [points to the left and right sides of her head, by her ears], and combed to the back. And I had a suit made for myself. I bought cloth, had a custom-tailored suit made. And on the pictures, I wear a trench coat, on most Sundays I would, during the week I had to work after all, so it wasn't possible.[50]

Several aspects in this excerpt from Tommy's narrative are striking. She learned the terminology of "Bubi" and "Mäuschen" from another woman, who warned her of the "hard time" awaiting her. Since Tommy's elaboration of what a Bubi was moves away from the prison context to her everyday life in Berlin, it is not quite clear what entry the other woman was referring to ("when you first enter there"). Is she referring to prison and a gendered organization of prison subculture into Bubis and Mäuschen? Or to styles of female femininity and masculinity in lesbian subculture more broadly? Since both terms are diminutives, they may refer to young people foremost, a possibility that is also suggested by her specification that Bubi was "the little guy." Tommy here also gives an example of butch self-fashioning at mid-century: short hair, combed back and with sideburns, as well as a custom-made suit and a trench coat. Her reference to Elvis is anachronistic, though

Figure 4.1. Rita "Tommy" Thomas in 1951. Rita "Tommy" Thomas Photo Collection, Feminist FFBIZ Archives, Berlin.

the hairstyle was popular with young Germans before him too at the time. She likely modeled her masculinity after the working-class men in her environment, as well as after Hollywood depictions that she saw in West Berlin's movie theatres. A photo taken in 1951 shows Tommy with no smile, hair slicked back, wearing a button-down shirt and a light-coloured men's flight jacket, long, wide pants, and black, clunky leather shoes (figure 4.1).[51]

Apart from Tommy's narrative, queer subjectivities and relationships at Barnimstraße can also be found in official documentation. In reports from the prison, queer sex and subjectivities were noted in the 1950s and 1960s as an indication of immorality and deviance in conflict with the norm of the "decent," productive, heterosexual socialist persona of the early GDR.[52] A 1954 quarterly report written by the penal department within the police mentioned "a larger group of comrades with lesbian disposition" that could not be fired "because of the acute lack of staff."[53] A year later, another quarterly report noted the firing of five prison guards at Barnimstraße because of their "lesbian relationships with prisoners."[54] The author of the report judged these incidents to be an "expression of the class enemy's activities in our penal departments."[55] Claudia von Gélieu has suggested that, in these cases, homosexuality may have been the real grounds for dismissal, or it may have served as a label to get rid of employees who were not considered politically reliable. Either way, relationships between guards and inmates could not be tolerated because such relationships transgressed the border between criminal and normal, and destabilized prison order.

In the mid-1960s, the Barnimstraße prison saw an influx of women incarcerated as *Arbeitserziehungspflichtige* (people obligated to education through/to work) under §249 of the new penal code. Under this section the GDR formalized its criminalization of citizens who it deemed "work-shy" and prostitutes, two groups that the regime classified as *Asoziale* (asocials).[56] While the introduction of a formal law against *Asozialität* (asociality) was a genuine novelty of the socialist state, the term itself was not new. It had circulated since the late nineteenth century as a negative term for people transgressing different social norms and had gained prominence in welfare discourses during the Weimar Republic.[57] The Nazis persecuted people who did not work, as well as individuals who "repeatedly and routinely committed minor transgressions of the law," among them prostitutes, as "asocials."[58] From 1942 they were transferred from prisons to concentration camps to be "exterminated through work." At the camps, inmates marked as "asocials" were low in the prisoner hierarchy and suffered further exclusion from other groups of prisoners.[59] Insa Eschebach has shown that survivors of the Ravensbrück women's concentration camp also linked lesbianism to "asociality," ascribing lesbian behaviour solely to "asocial" and "criminal" inmates in their memoirs.[60]

In reports on Barnimstraße prison from 1966 to 1968, the police repeatedly linked "lesbian love" and disruptions of the prison's "educational work."[61] Written by the prison's warden or the responsible official within the police (*Vollzugsgeschäftsstelle*, or Corrections Office), the reports address "the fulfilment of the main tasks of the penal department" and "the enforcement of a strict discipline and order."[62] The reports' authors claimed that "not a small part of the AE" (*Arbeitserziehungspflichtige*) had "an inclination for lesbian love." "This," they wrote, found "expression in some of them consciously trying to appear 'masculine' and to position themselves at the centre of the AEs' interest through rowdyism and rioting."[63] Here, the report does not specify how these prisoners tried to "appear 'masculine,'" whether they embodied a female masculinity through hairstyle or alterations to prisoner clothing, adopted male names, or were a part of butch-fem couples. It did stress the damaging effects that "lesbian love" had on the prison's "educational work" (*Erziehungsarbeit*), however, which affected the work morale not only of the AEs but also of regular prisoners and those in custody.[64] The year's annual report claimed that the staff at Barnimstraße had "for the most part managed to normalize the situation brought about by the change from prisoners to *Arbeitspflichtige*" but that "the order and educational work [were] still negatively affected by a number of aspects of lesbian love," and deliberations were necessary concerning "how and by what means this phenomenon can be repressed."[65] A report from February 1967 about "the enforcement of a strict discipline and order" continued to locate "the by far largest part of the motives and reasons for breaches of order and discipline" in "the widespread lesbian relationships, as well as gossiping and fighting among the AEs."[66] Instead of using their free time to read the newspaper or quality literature, "they are only interested in making illegal connections and conducting primitive conversations, most often in the dirtiest fashion about love affairs." If AEs did participate in one of the existing offers for prisoners' leisure time, "they only [did] so to make friends or to make better use of their connections. These so-called pure friendships very much and very often lead to lengthy exchanges [*Kassibereien*] of pieces of clothing or letters. What happens especially frequently is that AEs with shopping limits are provided by others with tobacco and groceries, even though they know that it is forbidden and that they too will be disciplined as a result."[67] In this quote, lesbian relationships among the prisoners appear as acts of resistance against the prison's function of disciplining inmates through "education through/to work." Sexuality (the sexual content of conversations and letters is indicated by the adjectives "primitive" and "dirty") served as an alternative way of spending free time in prison and as a subversion of the institutional mission to educate. The quote also illustrates economic solidarity among prisoners, as those who were permitted to purchase food and tobacco shared with those who were not. However, aside from such expressions of solidarity, the penal administration also recorded instances of prisoners reporting others. The 1967 "annual estimate of petitions [*Eingaben*] of incarcerated persons" includes three complaints from AEs about other AEs "who disturbed the work routine and discipline through lesbian relationships."[68] These women were assigned to other work units or were isolated temporarily.

Beatrice Kühne, a former inmate of the Barnimstraße prison interviewed by Claudia von Gélieu, remembered lesbian relationships between other prisoners. Her testimony attests to how prisoners subverted prohibitions of such relationships and to the broader political relevance of living an openly lesbian life in the GDR. Kühne herself was imprisoned in Barnimstraße in 1970 and 1971 because of her plans to flee the GDR.

> GÉLIEU: There are supposed to have been many prostitutes and "aso-cials" incarcerated at Barnimstraße. Is that true?
> KÜHNE: I don't know about that. But sex did play a role. Masturbation was not spoken about but tolerated among the prisoners. And there were lesbian relationships. I was together [in a cell] with a criminal [Gélieu and Kühne distinguish prisoners between "politicals" and "criminals"], and she had a partner [*einen festen Freund*], a woman. That was well known. They had shared a cell and fallen in love but had been separated very quickly. That was a huge drama. They met in secret, exchanged gifts. Among prisoners that was consensus. I think that kind of thing was quite frequent. First-hand I only know it about this woman, a very pretty, rebellious woman. She lived that openly. That's not to be taken for granted in the GDR. In a way, she was an oppositionist [*Oppositionelle*] too.[69]

According to Kühne, lesbian relationships were not tolerated by prison administrators, but they were accepted by the other prisoners ("that was consensus"). In the case she narrates, the involved women were not isolated in single cells, as had been the practice for lesbian women at the prison during the Nazi period, but they were separated.[70] Earlier in the interview, Kühne described separating cellmates who had grown "too close" as part of "the prison management's strategy" and the "haphazard and unpredictable" way in which separations happened as "a crucial aspect of the psychological terror."[71] The lovers continued meeting and exchanging gifts. Kühne voices respect for her cellmate living "that" openly, which she describes as extraordinary for the GDR. Indeed, Kühne even states that by openly living her same-sex love, her cellmate "was an oppositionist too." Her comment destabilizes the distinction between political and criminal prisoners, and thus acknowledges the political nature of an openly lived queer life in a homophobic society such as the GDR.

The oral history narratives of Tommy on the early 1950s and Beatrice Kühne on the early 1970s, as well as the prison reports from the 1950s and 1960s, shine a spotlight on queer subjectivities and prison management's reactions to them during different phases of the early GDR. As the Ministry of the Interior and the police took over responsibility for the penal system and prison policy moved from liberal to repressive, queer practices of affection that had been quite open – Tommy's engagement ceremony in the prison yard in the very early 1950s – became much more secret, like the meetings and gift exchanges of the couple that Beatrice Kühne remembers from the early 1970s. Prison authorities' interpretations of queer sexuality in prison shifted from interpreting homosexuality as a danger coming from outside socialist society ("an expression of the class enemy's activities") in the mid-1950s to a threat destabilizing socialism from within through women whose refusal to conform to socialist norms of work and sexuality branded them as "asocials" in the mid-1960s. Queer embodiments of gender through hairstyle or clothing, a crucial feature of Tommy's prison memories, have left few traces in the Barnimstraße administrative records. By contrast, files from the West Berlin women's prison offer rich sources on prisoner relationships and butch and fem subjectivities, allowing for a deeper analysis of prison as a queer space.

Queer Relationships and Subjectivities in West Berlin Prisons

After Berlin's penal system was divided in 1949, the former military prison in Moabit district served as West Berlin's women's prison.[72] Dr. Gertrud Siemsen, who had been the prison librarian at Barnimstraße prison, served as the director of the women's prison from 1953 until 1972.[73] Two files created during her governance speak to the institution as a queer space, documenting relationships between imprisoned women, inmates' gender presentation and sexual practices, as well as prison authorities' reaction to same-sex relationships. The first archival file, titled "Special Incidents: Secret Messages" and dated from 1958, contains messages sent among inmates and intercepted by prison staff. The second one is the prisoner file of Bettina Grundmann, who was incarcerated there in 1966–67 and whose verbal and embodied presentation of female masculinity is reflected in the database entry for their file: the person who created it added the term "*Lesbierin*," an outdated term for lesbian, to their name.[74]

The 1958 file on "secret messages" contains a message from an inmate who signs as "Strolch" (rascal, tramp, thug) and who writes to "Mammi" (Mommy), also referred to as "Lisa."[75] Though I cannot determine Strolch's gender from the file, the word "Strolch" is grammatically masculine, suggesting a flexible or fluid gender identity. I will therefore use they/them/their pronouns for Strolch. The message was found in a handkerchief. Across three pages, Strolch expresses their emotions for Mammi and other prisoners, reminisces about a former relationship with a woman in an East German prison, and makes suggestions for a rendezvous, as well as plans for their time "outside," after release. In the first sentences of the letter, Strolch describes Mammi/Lisa and themselves in gendered terms. Mammi/Lisa is "resolute" and makes Strolch feel "safe and sound." "Nevertheless," Strolch does not conceive of themselves as a "hen-pecked husband."[76] While they describe their love for Mammi/Lisa as "warm and trustful," their relationship is also sexual: "Lisa, how about we find each other physically Sunday night (tomorrow) at ½ 9 [8:30 p.m.] (each on their own)? Why do you want to hit me for that??? That you are 100% as sensual in the erotic, I do believe, a woman like you!!! But I have studied since my 15th year and I know 'the school of love.'"[77]

Here, Strolch suggests that the two masturbate simultaneously at a set time, each on their own. Later in the letter, they write out a fantasy of performing cunnilingus on Mammi/Lisa. The two also made plans for acting out these physical fantasies in person by beginning a game of chess in order to distract the guards. "We'll play once or twice, until they [prison staff] are sure [that they are really playing chess and not doing anything illicit], and then I will take advantage of the opportunity, you can believe that," they assure her.[78]

What did the West Berlin prison administration make of this apparent evidence of sex between prisoners? Prison director, Dr. Gertrud Siemsen, felt that the letter, as well as two other related letters, were fake messages sent with the aim of being discovered. Whoever sent them, she thought, wanted their alleged author to be punished and possibly wanted to disrupt a relationship between prisoners.[79] In reaction, she summoned all prisoners involved to her office, those on whom the messages were found as well as their alleged authors and addressees. In her report of the subsequent disciplinary measures, she notes that she had told prisoners

> that secret messaging may not be a pleasure for us, though some may think so, but it also does not shock us. The content was always simply telling of its authors and possibly addressees. I had no intention to take care of their dirty business for them and serve as handmaid for their revenge. Neither did I have the intention to deal with the messages in detail to figure out who had written them; if secret messages were found on someone directly, however, they would be punished. What is more, secret messaging was childish since they had enough opportunity to talk to each other in their free time and in the recreation room. Subsequently, I reminded them that any business among prisoners is forbidden.[80]

Siemsen hence knew about relationships between prisoners, and she describes them matter of factly and not derogatorily as "friendships." Yet her comment that they did "not shock" the prison administration demonstrates that she was aware of their sexual content. There is also tension between the freedom of communication that she postulated – despite all socializing happening under the watchful eyes of guards and other prisoners – and her reminder that "any business among prisoners" was prohibited. While "Geschäfte" can be translated as "business" in the sense of the exchange of goods, it can also be understood as a reference to sexual relations.

Siemsen's reaction to the discovery of this letter creates the impression that the West Berlin women's prison was a rather benign place governed by a generous, understanding director. This picture is confirmed but also complicated by the prisoner file of Bettina Grundmann, who arrived at the women's prison of West Berlin eight years after this incident, in April 1966, and to whose case I now turn to make visible both queer subjectivity and the prison as a normative institution.

The "Lesbierin" File

The prisoner file of Bettina Grundmann, categorized as "*Lesbierin*" (lesbian) in the archival catalogue, includes their mugshot, documentation of their belongings, a list of visitors, exchanges between them and the prison director, and correspondence with other prisoners and letters to their family. It offers a detailed picture of life in the women's prison of West Berlin in the 1960s. Attached to the file's inside cover is Grundmann's black-and-white mugshot in profile and frontal view, showing them dressed in a light-coloured men's shirt, hair cut short in a neat crew cut. Their gaze to the camera is self-confident, even sporting a whiff of arrogance.[81] Grundmann appears as a handsome, masculine-presenting young person who was not intimidated by the camera. In their carefully groomed masculinity, they epitomize the mid-century butch. The file promises a window onto an openly lived lesbian working-class life in 1960s West Berlin and thus access to a form of lesbian subjectivity rarely preserved in the LGBTIQ* movement archives. In the course of my analysis, it became clear, however, that rather than simply a long-desired proof of lesbian working-class experience, the Grundmann file raises complex questions about queer subject formation in mid-century West Germany. Grundmann's shifting embodiment of gender within and outside prison suggests that the category "lesbian" in the 1960s was capacious, encompassing subjectivities that today might be described as trans.[82] I thus use they pronouns to refer to Grundmann. In the following, I will summarize Grundmann's court case before reconstructing the prison as lifeworld as it appears in the file.

Bettina Grundmann went to prison because the courts found them guilty of lying about the identity of their son's father and of fraudulently receiving alimony from another man whom they claimed was the father, Walter Fern.[83] Born in Berlin to a single mother in 1936, Grundmann had grown up in a foster family from infanthood. After high school, they continued to attend vocational school and then worked in a variety of manual labour jobs.[84] Grundmann met Walter Fern on a suburban train in Berlin in April 1959, and the two went on a few dates together. In January 1960, Grundmann gave birth to a son, Hans. Since Fern disputed his fatherhood, Grundmann's home district office in the West Berlin neighbourhood of Kreuzberg, acting as the legal guardian of the child, as was common practice for children born out of wedlock, filed a suit against him. Grundmann testified in court that they and Fern had had sex once and that Fern was the only man they had slept with during the possible period of their child's conception. They added that they were "a lesbian before having sex with the accused, and I am one again now. Through my relationship with the accused, I tried finding my way back to normal sex."[85] The court, believing Grundmann's testimony, sentenced Fern to pay monthly child support of 70 Marks. He appealed the sentence, however, and the court ordered an analysis of Fern's blood groups to determine whether he could be ruled out as the father. While three subsequent analyses did not reach definite results, the court followed the third expert's estimate that Fern's fatherhood was "apparently impossible."[86] He was released of all obligations to the child, and Grundmann was charged with lying under oath.[87] Judge and jury believed Fern's statement that he and Grundmann had never had sex, and their lesbianism was taken as a sign of their guilt: "Since she always had lesbian tendencies, she cannot have forgotten about an intercourse [Geschlechtsverkehr]."[88] The court hence could only imagine "intercourse" as heterosexual sex. They found Grundmann guilty of attempted fraud by trying to make Fern pay child support. They were sentenced to the minimum sentence for perjury, one year of penitentiary, and stripped of their civil rights for a duration of two years, as well as declared legally incapable of swearing an oath. Their appeal of the decision failed, but the appeals court lowered their sentence from penitentiary to regular prison because of the "significant life difficulties" that they had faced due to "her lesbian tendencies."[89]

On 22 April 1966, Grundmann arrived at the women's prison. Just under one year later, on 14 April 1967, they were released early after serving two-thirds of their sentence.[90] At the time of incarceration, they were twenty-nine years old. Their son, born in January 1960, was living with their foster parents in the West Berlin working-class district of Kreuzberg. Grundmann shared an apartment in Wedding, another West Berlin working-class district, with their girlfriend, who is noted as their "next of kin" on Grundmann's prisoner information sheet, which staff completed upon their arrival in prison.[91] Grundmann cultivated their masculinity while in prison, both by attending to their body and by engaging in romantic relationships with multiple women inside and outside. Once incarcerated, they had to exchange their butch outfit, a black leather jacket, a men's shirt, a pair of navy-blue pants, and black shoes, for prison garb, which included dresses, work aprons, an under-skirt, but no pants.[92] They were allowed to continue smoking their pipe, and their girlfriend provided them with hairstyling product during vis-iting hours. Six weeks after entering the prison, Grundmann wrote to the prison director, asking about haircuts for inmates: "Some are really in need of one, including me. I already feel quite scruffy around my head," they explained.[93] The request was granted, though the director noted, likely just to herself: "Actually, I find G's hair just right – and shorter would be less beautiful!"[94]

In keeping with the policy of isolating gay and lesbian inmates, which was standard practice in prisons in the Nazi era and in West Germany into the 1970s, Grundmann was assigned to a single cell.[95] The prison director stressed that Grundmann was "a jack of all trades [*Hans Dampf in allen Gassen*], looking for contacts constantly ... Unfortunately, it is impossible to allow her much community."[96] Indeed, Grundmann made good use of the opportunities that free time or visits to the doctor offered for connecting with other prisoners, as intercepted messages in their file demonstrate. Two and a half months into their confinement, a prison guard caught Grundmann with a secret message to another inmate, Sabine Rasinne. The message included a photo of Grundmann at a younger age, which they had managed to smuggle into their cell by claiming that it showed their six-year-old son.[97] Though reprimanded, the two continued exchanging love notes until another inmate reported them. The snitch also told prison authorities that she had seen them kissing in the bathroom during a visit to the prison doctor. Rasinne's let-ter to Grundmann illuminates the eroticism and the butch-fem dynam-ics of their relationship, conjuring up the memory of Rasinne's arrival in prison "in high heels, the tight light-blue ladies' suit, and super blonde hair," an emblem of hyper-femininity.[98] Rasinne addresses Grund-mann as "Dieter," the name with which Grundmann signed the let-ters, another aspect of Grundmann's masculinity. In Rasinne's letter, she informs them of her progress on the collars she is making for them and adds: "You'll have to make up later for all the things I'm sewing and embroidering here for you."[99] And by mentioning the music that she is listening to on the radio, she creates a mental space of sensuality: "Now they're playing '*Nur wenn Du bei mir bist*' [Only when you're with me]. That part is so beautiful, '*Wunderschön ist das Leben seitdem Du mich geküßt*' [Life is so beautiful since you kissed me]. Remember that time in remand prison? Hopefully we can continue that soon without being disturbed. You can't imagine how much I look forward to that."[100]

Despite the short duration of their relationship, Rasinne and Grundmann clearly developed a passion that they even managed to live out physically, at least once. Their affair ended after they were discovered. The prison director instructed staff that Grundmann was to be led to all medical appointments separately from now on, no longer with the other prisoners, "so that she cannot connect with others on her way to the doctor or while waiting."[101]

Grundmann's relationship with their girlfriend outside prison ended during their affair with Rasinne. Afraid that their ex-girlfriend might take more than belonged to her when she moved out of their shared apartment, Grundmann applied for prison furlough. The application was denied, but the director allowed Grundmann to go to their apartment accompanied by a guard and dressed in prison garb. Grundmann rejected this compromise, explaining that they were known in their neighbourhood as "Mr. Grundmann." Apparently, Grundmann passed as a man in their everyday life.

Now single both inside and outside the prison, Grundmann asked "Granny" – the name by which they referred to their foster-mother – to visit their "friendships [*Freundschaften*]," a term they apparently used for their romantic interests.[102] In case "Granny" could not visit them now, she was to "write a letter to them right away and include the last passport photo you have of me. Please, Granny, it's urgent and I promised," Grundmann added.[103] It is likely that Grundmann's description of prison life as "subordination with almost military drill" explains why "Granny" never received this letter, but it is also possible that the director was actively sabotaging Grundmann's relationships with women outside.[104]

Grundmann's flirtations with other prisoners continued throughout the period of their incarceration. In spring 1967, Grundmann, writing again as "Dieter," sent a message to Nadja Werner, whose discharge from prison was imminent. Dieter had big plans for their reunion in freedom. "At any rate I'm looking forward to a life with you," they wrote.[105] After this letter was discovered in Werner's cell, Grundmann lost access to radio, television, and the recreational room up to the day of Werner's discharge, effectively separating the two. A card from Werner after her dismissal was not delivered to Grundmann because

former inmates were prohibited from contacting those still in detention. When Grundmann themselves were released from prison prema-
turely in April 1967, the reunion with Nadja Werner apparently did not
come to pass. Instead, a week after being released, Grundmann wrote
to the court asking for permission to write to yet another inmate and
explaining that, in prison, they had "befriended a young woman whose
engagement no longer exists, and who is also not interested in its main-
tenance. Because she will move in with me immediately after her discharge to live with me."[106] The court forwarded the letter to the prison
director, who rejected Grundmann's request, not without noting that
they had "several irons in the fire" and scolding them for already having attempted to contact two inmates without permission.[107]

Grundmann's queerness elicited different reactions from prison
authorities, ranging from acceptance to paternalism to pathologization.
As noted earlier, Grundmann's girlfriend was designated as next of kin
in prison documentation, suggesting that the administrator adopted a
matter of fact approach to their relationship. In correspondence to the
state attorney, the prison director described Grundmann as "having a
lesbian disposition," using a medicalized but relatively neutral term.[108]
Both director and chaplain come across as accepting of Grundmann's
relationship with their girlfriend. When they were still together and
Grundmann applied for furlough to facilitate the girlfriend's inclusion
in the rental contract for the apartment they shared, the chaplain supported their request "in the interest of her own rehabilitation."[109] However, the same chaplain pathologized Grundmann in his statement on
a prisoner assessment form when he claimed that "[she] stands outside
the community legally too, because of her sexual abnormality."[110] The
director's insistence that she could not allow Grundmann much contact with others, though stated with regret, meant that, against their
wishes, Grundmann lived in a single cell and was assigned to perform
needlework by themselves rather than work in an out-of-prison setting
or with others.[111]

The prison administrators' stance towards Grundmann's female masculinity was ambivalent. The assessment forms filled out by guard and
work supervisors described Grundmann as "boyish" and repeatedly
as "self-confident," but did not pejoratively comment on their butch-
ness.[112] The director's comment on Grundmann's hair – "shorter would
be less beautiful" – may express an aesthetic ideal of longer rather than
shorter hair for women, but it also betrays her appreciation of Grundmann's looks. Grundmann themselves altered prison garb to make it
more masculine by buttoning a collar made by their prison girlfriend
on the shirts, and their petition to have a hairdresser come in and cut

inmates' hair was successful, suggesting that prisoners were allowed some freedom to modify their appearance.

The Significance of Photos in Prison

During Grundmann's stay in prison, photos repeatedly became objects of contention. House rules prohibited the possession of photos showing the prisoners themselves.[113] This prohibition bothered Grundmann much, and they expended great energy to subvert it. As discussed earlier, when first admitted to prison, Grundmann brought in some pictures of themselves at a younger age, duping prison staff by claiming that the photos showed their son. Giving their portrait as a token of love to the women they were interested in was clearly an important romantic practice for Grundmann. Being thwarted from doing so was thus a cause of great unhappiness and anger, as a letter to Grundmann's family that was censored because of its "tone" demonstrates:

> Received your dear mail with great thanks ... today ... Now there are two drops of bitterness in the letter. First, that Papa is so sick and has to go to the hospital. Second, I did not get the images of Bettina. [Note that Grundmann is referring to herself by using her given first name rather than the first-person possessive pronoun.] That makes me so upset, and again underlines the injustice here ... But I do not see why others may have family photos on which they are depicted too, just "Grundmann" can't. And then they say that I have a big mouth. Even though all I want is to be treated like others. I am trembling from suppressed anger, I can hardly write.[114]

Grundmann understood that it was partly their non-normative gender presentation that the prison sought to discipline. In March 1967, they asked the prison director for two photos to send to their hospitalized father. Grundmann described the photos as "pictures from the fifties, in which I wear women's clothing."[115] The photos were kept with their personal belongings. Siemsen granted them this wish, and Grundmann was allowed to choose the photos themselves, but prison officials simply put the photos into the letter as it was mailed rather than giving the photos to them in the cell.

Ruby Tapia has noted in her scholarship on incarcerated women in the present-day United States that "what the public 'has' of images of women's incarceration is largely fictional and spectacular, most often transmitted by women-in-prison films."[116] If self-portraits were crucially important to prisoners' relationships to themselves and others, as Grundmann's file indicates, the prison's prohibitive picture policy appears as a central aspect of curtailing inmates' subjectivities and instituting normalcy. The fact that I could not gain permission to publish Grundmann's photo, while grounded in justified concern about individual privacy, continues this absence of images.

Conclusion

As mentioned at the beginning of this chapter, sociologists who studied women's prisons in the United States in the mid-twentieth century found same-sex relationships the central feature of prisoner society but were not alarmed by these findings. They understood the gendered organization of both male and female prisons as adaptations to the deprivations of prison life and thus not as a subversion of heterosexuality.[117] However, relationships formed in prison sometimes lasted beyond incarceration, as Bettina Grundmann's example shows. Despite the prison director's intense efforts to break off all contact between Grundmann and other inmates, their persistence eventually paid off. Six years after their dismissal, in 1973, they were in a relationship with a woman they had met in prison, Monika Kurzbein, as is apparent from another prisoner file.[118] In November 1973, Grundmann had to return to prison for ten days because they could not pay a 100 DM fine for theft.[119] In the admission sheet, Kurzbein is recorded as "next of kin." For Grundmann and Kurzbein, then, incarceration had had queer effects, resulting in a long-lasting relationship. Prison had not functioned as a normalizing institution; it had not normalized Grundmann's sexuality or rehabilitated them to a law-abiding life, much less helped them gain financial stability.

In this chapter I have argued that prisons are sites where non-normatively lived genders and same-sex relationships can be found and that taking them seriously as objects of historical analysis can serve to broaden the picture of what it meant to live a queer life, in Germany and beyond. The sources from the West and East Berlin women's prisons in the years between 1945 and 1970 paint an ambivalent picture of queer experiences of prison. They were sites of romantic, erotic, and sexual relationships. They were also locations where butch-fem subcultures were significant, either as a feature of the organization of prison life or as an important category of inmates' subjectivities. Prisons facilitated queer relationships: inmates flirted with each other nonverbally, for instance by blowing kisses, and verbally by chatting during free time and by exchanging notes. Sometimes they flirted with guards or social workers too. They formed romantic relationships, sent each other love notes and portraits, exchanged gifts, and created shared romantic moments by listening to love songs. Girlfriends on the outside sent mail, visited, and provided the everyday necessities to queer prisoners, such as hairstyling products. Inmates participated in rituals of romantic bonding such as engagement ceremonies; they sent each other scripts for oral sex; and they made dates for mutual though physically separate masturbation sessions. They used rare private moments to kiss and do other pleasurable things with their bodies, and they made plans for a life together after their time in prison, which sometimes worked out and sometimes did not.

Prisons were also spaces of non-normative gender expression. Inmates overcame the restrictions imposed by prison uniforms, altering them to make them more masculine (or feminine, presumably). They petitioned for haircuts and engaged in gendered practices such as smoking pipes. In their relationships, they adopted female or male nicknames and used the appropriate pronouns. Both Tommy's memories of Bubis and Mäuschen in East Berlin and the intercepted messages from the West Berlin prison can be read as indicative of a gendered organization of women's prisons.

Despite these possibilities for and realities of queer life and love, prisons were far from utopias. Inmates categorized as lesbians were isolated by being put in a single cell rather than group cells. Cellmates known to have developed intimate relationships with each other were separated. Exchanging notes with other prisoners was forbidden and punished with loss of free time and entertainment. Released inmates were not allowed to keep in touch with girlfriends they had made inside. Since pre-existing same-sex relationships were accepted by the West Berlin prison administration, authorities were likely concerned about the corrupting influence that the same-sex environment of the prison might have on inmates read as heterosexual. Even though an understanding of homosexuality as biologically determined is prevalent in the prison files, the notion of the homosexual seducer remained powerful in West Germany in the 1960s. "Women in Prison" films, popular since the 1950s, made the stereotype of the predatory "prison lesbian" who seduced innocent heterosexual inmates a figure with much cultural purchase.[120]

This chapter has shown that analysing prisons is a promising research strategy for historians interested in the history of same-sex relationships and gender non-conforming lives, as well as for understanding how ideas of "normal" sexuality and gender were constructed. Systematic studies of prisoner files will help broaden and deepen our knowledge of prison societies and their entanglements with and effects on society at large. Certainly, though, studying prisons can "productively complicate" contemporary history, irritating our preconceptions about identities or state attitudes towards queer folk, and in this way indeed continue the work of rendering the past queer.[121]

Conclusion: Changing Queer Constellations Before and After 1970

Through its analysis of queer spaces and subjectivities in Berlin in the years between 1945 and 1970, this book has demonstrated how productive an examination of the entanglements of sexuality, gender, and class can be for (German) queer histories. As we have seen, the embodiment of gender was a crucial aspect of female, trans, and male queer lives in Germany in the mid-century. Working-class lesbian couples embodied differently gendered subjectivities that paired female masculinity with female femininity: Hilde Radusch and Eddy Klopsch described themselves as "Vati" and "Mutti"; Tommy and Helli used the terms "Bubi" and "Mäuschen." Bettina Grundmann used a male first name with their lovers and passed as a man in their neighbourhood. These queer Berliners' gendered subjectivities were expressed through hair style, clothing, gestures, and demeanour, as well as through the distribution of gendered tasks such as housework and breadwinning. While the sources we have of them – personal papers, oral histories, photographs, and state-produced archival documents – do not speak explicitly of gendered sexual practices or roles such as pleasure-giving and pleasure-receiving, they do point to how gender and desire could be connected in lesbian lives and thus allow us glimpses into "desire as a fundamental feature of self-knowledge," as Jennifer Evans has put it.[1]

Most of this book's sources about lesbian women have come from personal papers housed in feminist archives. The photos, notes, and calendars that speak of their gendered subjectivities document their private lives at home, as long-term couples that were also, in Tommy and Helli's case, part of a lively circle of friends. Their apartments and gardens provided them the privacy to safely embody and express non-normatively gendered subjectivities. The other space in which I found a pronounced lesbian presence is the prison, a site that falls outside the public/private divide. In both the West and the East Berlin women's prisons, lesbian relationships and female masculinity were connected and attracted authorities' attention. The West Berlin women's prison administration accepted Bettina Grundmann's existing relationship with a woman but sanctioned their romances with other inmates. In East Berlin, the female masculinity of inmates imprisoned for "asociality" was linked to "rowdyism" and "rioting," and regarded as a significant breach of discipline and order. For lesbian women, then, non-normatively embodied gender appears both as an important feature of the making of erotic selves and relationships *and* as an aspect that attracted the attention of state authorities and could lead to disciplining.

Whereas female masculinity became visible in the surveilled environment of the prison, it did not go on record in public space. By contrast, the non-normative gender of trans women and feminine men in bars and public spaces left plenty of traces in police sources. Even though West and East Berlin police precincts continued to issue "transvestite passes" that identified their bearers as being known to cross-dress until circa 1960, and the West Berlin police issued passports to trans women with their photo in their everyday trans look, the police apprehended transvestite bar patrons immediately during bar raids and carted them off to the precinct. Homo- and transphobic bypassers beat up trans women, and groups of thugs attacked queer bars. The police associated male femininity and trans femininity with prostitution, drawing on a connection that sexology and law enforcement had created since the early twentieth century. In the case of Günter Litfin, the first person to be killed in the attempt to cross the Berlin Wall, this long-established link between male femininity and prostitution, combined with widespread knowledge of the Zoo station as a site of male prostitution, made it easy for the East German regime to insinuate that Litfin had worked as a "streetwalking boy." To protect themselves from police or street violence, feminine men like Orest Kapp meticulously studied and practised how to act normatively masculine, and sometimes normatively masculine queer men like Klaus Born protected trans women like his acquaintance Manuela. Despite being particularly affected by police persecution and homo- and transphobic violence, feminine men, trans women, and non-binary queers like Mamita, whom we encountered at the beginning of this book, were an integral part of Berlin's queer community. They were entrepreneurs and entertainers, and as West Berlin's queer bar scene bloomed in the late 1960s despite intense police repression, they often found employment as bartenders or servers there.

This book's analysis of queer Berlin ends in 1970. Social, cultural, and legal changes that culminated around this year significantly changed the possibilities for making queer selves and spaces, particularly, though not only, in West Berlin. In 1969, the West German parliament passed a reform of §175, legalizing sex between men above twenty-one years of age. Soon after, the first small local groups of the new gay liberation movement were founded, though it was Rosa von Praunheim's 1971 film *Not the Homosexual Is Perverse, but the Situation in Which He Lives,* broadcast on public television as well as screened in cities throughout West Germany, that really started the movement.[2] Its participants, many of them students, often positioned themselves against the previous, homophile generation's politics and modes of socializing.[3] Instead of a handful of homophile magazines, always in danger of being censored or succumbing to financial problems, there was now a wave of new gay periodicals characterized by unapologetic discussions and illustrations of gay sexuality. Following angry female activists' throwing of tomatoes on their sexist male peers in the student movement in Frankfurt in 1968, West German women joined the new women's movement in masses.[4] Lesbian women in West Berlin, who had initially organized jointly with gay men in the Homosexuelle Aktion Westberlin (Homosexual Action West Berlin, HAW), soon banded with the feminist movement, articulating their specific demands and founding their own organizations such as the Lesbisches Aktionszentrum Westberlin (Lesbian Action Centre, or LAZ), publications such as the *UKZ* (*Unsere Kleine Zeitung,* our little newspaper), and archives such as the Spinnboden Lesbian Archives.[5] With these new social movements, as well as sociocultural changes such as the emergence of student communes or the advent of discotheques, new modes of subjectivity and sociability developed, and queer Berliners made new spaces and constellations.[6] Interestingly, in both gay and lesbian politics, conflicts around gender would flare up in the 1970s and 1980s. In the famous 1973 *Tuntenstreit* in West Berlin's HAW, *Tunten,* feminine men who publicly wore "*Fummel*" (dresses), were celebrated as the most radical gay activists by one faction, the "feminists," and rejected as profoundly unpolitical by the other.[7] In West Germany's version of the feminist sex wars, readers of the lesbian magazine *UKZ* in the late 1980s hotly debated the butch/ fem characters and sexual practices in Joan Nestle's short story "My Woman Poppa," translated as "Für meine Papafrau."[8]

Trans people began forming local support groups and also started lobbying for trans legislation on a local level in the 1970s.[9] Individual trans people had sought to change their legal gender through litigation since at least the early 1960s. Ambivalent legal change came in 1980 through the *Transsexuellengesetz*, or transsexual law, though already in 1971, the Federal Supreme Court of Justice (Bundesgerichtshof) had ruled that a law was needed to regulate exceptions to the principle of unchangeability of the legal gender.[10] The 1980 transsexual law created the possibility for trans people to change their legal gender, but it came at a high cost: legal gender change was open only to trans people who, in addition to psychological counselling, had undergone gender reassignment surgery and been sterilized. Hence, as Ulrike Klöppel has argued, "the modifications that have come with a more liberal handling of gender change affirm ... the gender binary."[11] Indeed, the state remained dedicated to guard the gender binary well into the twenty-first century. The self-determination of one's gender only became a prospect after the election of a government of Liberal Democrats, Greens, and Social Democrats in 2021, who in their coalition agreement pledged to abolish the transsexual law.[12]

In the GDR, trans people were an important part of queer activism from its inception in the 1970s. After all, in East Berlin too, the 1970s saw the beginnings of a gay and lesbian movement, closely intertwined with developments in the West.[13] The Homosexuelle Interessengemeinschaft Berlin (HIB, or Homosexual Interest Community Berlin), founded on the day that Rosa von Praunheim's film was broadcast on public television, brought together gay, lesbian, and trans East Berliners.[14] At the 1973 World Festival of Youth and Students in East Berlin, Australian Peter Tatchell, activist of the British Gay Liberation Front and member of the British delegation to the festival, held up a sign reading "Civil Rights for Homosexuals" at the closing ceremony, distributed thousands of leaflets, and spoke to students about gay liberation at Humboldt University.[15] Before the East German regime shut down HIB at the end of the decade, intolerant of all efforts at building community and organizing outside socialist state structures, the organization had provided support, sociability, and political pressure for an impressive six years. For many years, self-described "transvestite" Charlotte von Mahlsdorf had given HIB members space to congregate in her museum at the outskirts of Berlin.[16] Though the GDR had decriminalized male homosexuality in 1968, and thus beat West Germany to it by a year, this legal change was less significant in East Germany, where the state had ceased persecuting sex between adult, consenting men by the mid-1960s, though it continued to sanction homosexuality among its party officials and armed forces. The socialist state also introduced a new discriminatory law in 1968, §151, which addressed male-male and female-female sex between adults and minors and stipulated a different, higher age of consent for such relationships in comparison to heterosexual ones – the stereotype of the "homosexual seducer" was well alive in the GDR. Gender transitions were regulated in the GDR in 1976 – again, earlier than in the FRG – after the "courageous to desperate efforts of people seeking a legal gender change and gender reassignment surgery," as Ulrike Klöppel has found.[17] Here, too, gender reassignment surgery was required, at least in theory, before the legal gender was changed.[18] Since the regulation was not published, it had limited reach, and many trans people did not know about it. The requirement of surgery before a legal gender change indicates that the GDR was as concerned about stabilizing the gender binary as the FRG.

As seen in the chapter on prisons, non-normative gender embodiment was a feature that the SED noted among some of the women it imprisoned under its new "asociality" law. Other scholars have found that "homosexuals and people suffering from sexually transmitted diseases moved into the vicinity of 'asocials'" and that the asociality law was used as an instrument of mass incarceration.[19] Hence, the questions of how queerness and asociality were linked in the GDR and whether the asociality law served to criminalize queers after the official decrimininalization of homosexuality deserve an in-depth study and would present an important contribution to the history of "normalcy" and "deviance" in the GDR.

Many histories of queer Berlin remain to be narrated. This book has focused on the analysis of gender, sexuality, and class, but it has not considered other categories, for instance race, ethnicity, and migration. How did people of colour, for instance Black G.I.s or trans entertainers, experience and form the queer spaces of postwar Berlin? What did interactions between white queer Berliners and "guest" and "contract" workers in West and East Berlin look like, and how did they affect their sexual subjectivities?[20] How did racism manifest in queer communities? How did queer movements show themselves in solidarity with people of colour, and what roles did activists of colour play in these movements?[21] We still have a lot to learn about how queer people shaped Berlin, and how the city shaped queer cultures.

Notes

Introduction: "Mamita Invites You In"

1 O.Z., "Mamita läßt bitten!," *Der Weg* 12, no. 10 (1962): 461–2. All translations are my own, unless another translator is given.
2 See, for instance, Hacker, *Frauen* und Freund_innen*. For the history of the word's meanings in English queer history, see Bray, *The Friend*.
3 Later on, the article mentions that Mamita was also denigrated by a malicious campaign in the tabloids.
4 O.Z., "Mamita."
5 O.Z., "Mamita."
6 O.Z., "Mamita."
7 I follow Michael Thomas Taylor and Annette Timm in using "trans" when "discussing the experiences of transgender people from a point of historical remove." Taylor and Timm, "Historicizing Transgender Terminology," 253.
8 This study might be described as intersectional in its "way of thinking about the problem of sameness and difference and its relation to power," and its "conceiving of categories not as distinct but as always permeated by other categories, fluid and changing, always in the process of creating and being created by dynamics of power." However, since it does not analyze the intersection of race with gender, sexuality, and class, I have refrained from positioning it explicitly as an intersectional study. Cho, Crenshaw, and McCall, "Toward a Field of Intersectionality Studies," 795.
9 Chauncey, *Gay New York*; Houlbrook, *Queer London*.
10 Evans, *Life among the Ruins*; Beachy, *Gay Berlin*.
11 Exceptions include path-breaking works by Ilse Kokula (*Formen lesbischer Subkultur*, 1983), Hanna Hacker (*Frauen und Freundinnen*, 1987), and Claudia Schoppmann (*Zeit der Maskierung*, 1993); and more recent writing by Kirsten Plötz (*Einsame Freundinnen*, 1999) and Benno Gammerl (*Anders*

lieben, 2021) in the case of lesbians; and Rainer Herrn (*Schnittmuster des Geschlechts*, 2005) and Adrian de Silva (*Negotiating the Borders of the Gender Regime*, 2018) in the case of trans people. The short essays in the collected volume *In Bewegung bleiben* (2007) by Gabriele Dennert, Christiane Leidinger, and Franziska Rauchut give a helpful overview of lesbian history in twentieth-century Germany, but they cannot go into depth.

12 Laurie Marhoefer has made a powerful argument for such a history of "immorality" in their book on the sexual politics of the Weimar Republic. Marhoefer, *Sex and the Weimar Republic*.

13 For recent studies about Berlin's role in the emergence of modern sexual categories, see Beachy, *Gay Berlin*; Dose, *Magnus Hirschfeld*; Herrn, *Schnittmuster des Geschlechts*; Lybeck, *Desiring Emancipation*; Taylor, Timm, and Herrn, *Not Straight from Germany*; Spector, *Violent Sensations*; Sutton, "From Sexual Inversion to Trans," 185–6.

14 Samuel Huneke's *States of Liberation* offers an in-depth history of male homosexuality in both East and West Germany across the forty years of the country's division.

15 Beemyn, "A Presence in the Past," 113.

16 Namaste, "'Tragic Misreadings'"; Keegan, "Getting Disciplined," 394.

17 Amin, "Temporality," 221.

18 Sutton, "From Sexual Inversion to Trans," 185–6.

19 "Strichjungen" is often translated as "rent boys" or "call boys," but I have found "streetwalking boys" a better translation because it carries the association with public space inherent in the German "Strichjunge." Following Julia Laite, I use "women/men selling sexual services" rather than "prostitutes" to emphasize that we are talking about an activity or occupation, rather than an identity. Laite, *Common Prostitutes*, 26. Additionally, Martin Lücke has pointed out that the term's etymological roots mean "insult," "debasement," "debauchery." Lücke, *Männlichkeit in Unordnung*, 29. On the contested meanings and politics of *Tunte*, see Griffiths, *The Ambivalence of Gay Liberation*, 168–9.

20 Foucault, *The History of Sexuality*, 1:103.

21 Steakley, *The Homosexual Emancipation Movement*.

22 Verein der Freunde eines Schwulen Museums in Berlin e.V., *Eldorado*.

23 Marhoefer, *Sex and the Weimar Republic*, 19.

24 Grau, *Hidden Holocaust?*; Gerlach, "Außerdem habe ich dort mit meinem Freund getanzt," 307.

25 Grau, *Hidden Holocaust?*, 307.

26 Schoppmann, *Days of Masquerade*, 16.

27 Steinle, *Der Literarische Salon*.

28 Dobler, *Von anderen Ufern*, 182–90; Herrn, "Ich habe wohl Freude," 63.

29 Dobler, *Von anderen Ufern*; Dobler, *Verzaubert in Nord-Ost*; Evans, *Life among the Ruins*; Evans, "Bahnhof Boys"; Pretzel, *NS-Opfer unter Vorbehalt*;

Maneo, *Spurensuche im Regenbogenkiez*; Whisnant, *Male Homosexuality in West Germany*; Zur Nieden, *Unwürdige Opfer*; Pretzel, *Berlin – "Vorposten."*

30 Ilse Kokula published excerpts from oral history interviews with lesbian women who experienced queer postwar Berlin in her 1986 *Jahre des Glücks, Jahre des Leids*. Since then, the only monograph to examine lesbian subjectivities during this period is Maria Borowski's oral history study on the early GDR, *Parallelwelten*. None of her female interviewees was living in Berlin during the 1950s and 1960s, however. The Berlin Senate's brochure series on LGBTI history includes a volume on trans history (Meyer, *Auf nach Casablanca?*) that touches on trans spaces in postwar East Berlin.

31 On cis genders and heterosexual sexuality, see Peukert, "Die 'Halbstarken'"; Poiger, *Jazz, Rock, and Rebels*; Fenemore, *Sex, Thugs, and Rock'n'Roll*.

32 Zur Nieden, "Einleitung," 6–7.

33 On the "overdetermined" question of the rapes of German women by Soviet soldiers in the months before and after German capitulation, see Grossmann, "A Question of Silence."

34 For examples, see Whisnant, *Male Homosexuality in West Germany*, 24; Timm, *The Politics of Fertility*, 329–30.

35 Borneman, *Belonging in the Two Berlins*, 132.

36 Heineman, *What Difference Does a Husband Make?*, 16.

37 Plötz, "Wo blieb die Bewegung lesbischer Trümmerfrauen?," 74.

38 Plötz, *Als fehle die bessere Hälfte*, 258.

39 Pretzel, *NS-Opfer unter Vorbehalt*, 10.

40 Pretzel, 77.

41 Vormbaum, *Das Strafrecht der Deutschen Demokratischen Republik*, 378–9.

42 Hans-Joachim Schoeps quoted by Dagmar Herzog. Herzog, *Sex after Fascism*, 94.

43 Pretzel, *NS-Opfer unter Vorbehalt*, 10; Wolfert, "Zwischen den Stühlen," 89.

44 Klaus Berndl, "Zeiten der Bedrohung," 25.

45 "§183," in Ministerium für Justiz der DDR, *Strafgesetzbuch und andere Strafgesetze*, 92; "§183," in Kohlrausch and Lange, *Strafgesetzbuch mit Erläuterungen und Nebengesetzen*, 259. In 1969, disenfranchisement was struck out as part of the Great Criminal Law Reform in West Germany.

46 "§360," in Ministerium für Justiz der DDR, *Strafgesetzbuch und andere Strafgesetze*, 163–4; "§360," in Kohlrausch and Lange, *Strafgesetzbuch mit Erläuterungen und Nebengesetzen*, 463–4.

47 Korzilius, *"Asoziale" und "Parasiten" im Recht der SBZ/DDR*, 415.

48 Korzilius, *"Asoziale,"* 291–2, 301, 617–18. At the end of the GDR, almost a quarter of prison inmates were incarcerated under §249. Thomas Lindenberger, ""Asoziale Lebensweise,'" 247.

49 On the question of whether developments in East Germany warrant the term "revolution" rather than just "evolution," see McLellan, *Love in the Time of Communism*, 9.

168 Notes to pages 11–18

50 Herzog, *Sex after Fascism*, 5–6.
51 Steinbacher, *Wie der Sex nach Deutschland kam*, 15–16.
52 Heineman, *Before Porn Was Legal*, 2, 7, 14.
53 In the 1960s, the number of §175 sentences were up to four times that of the late Weimar Republic. Moeller, "Private Acts," 530; Plötz, *Als fehle die bessere Hälfte*, 255–6.
54 Heineman, *Before Porn Was Legal*, 17.
55 Steinbacher, *Wie der Sex*, 10–11, my translation.
56 McLellan, *Love in the Time of Communism*, 2.
57 Herzog, *Sex after Fascism*, 185; Greg Eghigian, "Homo Munitus," 45–7; Evans, "Repressive Rehabilitation," 303–4.
58 McLellan, *Love in the Time of Communism*, 90.
59 Frackman, "Persistent Ambivalence"; Huneke, *States of Liberation*, 31.
60 Duberman, Vicinus, and Chauncey, *Hidden from History*.
61 Doan, *Disturbing Practices*, 60–1, viii.
62 See, for instance, Houlbrook, *Queer London*, 8; Ross, *Public City/Public Sex*, 10–11.
63 Halperin, *How to Do the History of Homosexuality*, 107.
64 Marhoefer, *Sex and the Weimar Republic*, 8.
65 Marhoefer, 9.
66 Marhoefer, 9.
67 Houlbrook, *Queer London*, 10.
68 Lefebvre, *The Production of Space*.
69 Ahmed, *Queer Phenomenology*, 106.
70 Ahmed, 67.
71 Gieseking, *A Queer New York*, xvi–xvii.
72 Gieseking, 3.
73 For a recent discussion of sexuality and space, including the changing meaning of "gayborhoods," see Hubbard, "Geography and Sexuality."
74 Herzog, *Sex after Fascism*, 64.
75 The Lili Elbe Archive for Inter Trans Queer History was founded in 2013. "Selbstbild Lili-Elbe-Archiv." The archive is now called Lili-Elbe-Bibliothek, and its new website (https://lili-elbe.de/) offers a wealth of information on trans literature and films.
76 Petra Söllner, Email to Andrea Rottmann, 16 November 2016.
77 "Lila Archiv e.V."; Ursula Sillge, Email to Andrea Rottmann, 20 November 2016.
78 On the Stasi surveillance of lesbian women, see Wallbraun, "Lesben Im Visier der Staatssicherheit." Her documentary film *Uferfrauen* came out in 2020.
79 Hacker, *Frauen und Freundinnen*, 93. See also her 2015 updated edition, Hacker, *Frauen* und Freund_innen*.
80 Vicinus, "The History of Lesbian History," 574–5.

81 Two recent German studies have innovatively researched the discrimination of lesbian women: Christiane Carri has analyzed psychiatric evaluations for the disenfranchisement of lesbian women during the Weimar Republic and Kirsten Plötz has examined how judges in different *Länder* in West Germany ruled on lesbian mothers in child custody cases. Carri, ""Als erstes Symptom"; Plötz, "Entzug der Kinder"; Plötz, " … *in ständiger Angst.*"

82 Particularly helpful was a conversation with Kirsten Plötz, another one with Landesarchiv archivist Bianca Welzing-Bräutigam, as well as Christiane Leidinger's systematic research guide for historical research on lesbian women in postwar West Germany. Leidinger, *Lesbische Existenz 1945–1969.*

83 For a critical discussion of the use of oral history in US queer history, see Boyd, "Who Is the Subject?" For recent German queer studies based on oral histories, see Gammerl, *Anders fühlen*; see also Gammerl, "Erinnerte Liebe"; Borowski, *Parallelwelten.*

84 Boyd, "Who Is the Subject?," 179–80.

85 Boyd, 189.

86 The Archive of Other Memories, a growing collection of oral history interviews with lesbian, gay, bisexual, transsexual, transgender, intersexual, and queer people (LGBTTIQ), began operating in 2013. It is part of the Federal Magnus Hirschfeld Foundation, founded in 2011 by the Department of Justice with the mission "to commemorate Magnus Hirschfeld, to promote educational and research projects, and to counteract the social discrimination of … LGBTTIQ people in Germany." Bundesstiftung Magnus Hirschfeld, "Über die Stiftung."

87 Baranowski, "Das Archiv der anderen Erinnerungen der Bundesstiftung Magnus Hirschfeld."

88 On female masculinity, see Halberstam, *Female Masculinity.*

1. Homes

1 Hilde Radusch Diary, Hilde Radusch (HR) Personal Papers, Rep 500, Acc. 300, Box 6, I-6–1, Feminist FFBIZ Archives Berlin.

2 Zur Nieden, *Unwürdige Opfer*, 22–7.

3 Radusch diary, 181.

4 Radusch diary, 182.

5 Radusch diary, 183.

6 Radusch diary, 183.

7 Both terms mean "home."

8 Betts, *Within Walls*, 15.

9 Pretzel and Roßbach, *Wegen der zu erwartenden hohen Strafe*, 180.

10 Pretzel and Roßbach, 180, 181.

11 Beck, *Und Gad ging zu David*; Färberböck, *Aimée und Jaguar*. The film is based on Erica Fischer's book of the same title.

12 Freud, "Das Unheimliche (1919)," 4:241–74.
13 Honig, "Difference, Dilemma."
14 hooks, "Homeplace."
15 Young, "House and Home."
16 Pilkey et al., *Sexuality and Gender at Home*. Lauren Gutterman's study of married women's lesbian affairs in the mid-century United States has shown the subversive possibilities that homes could have even in what is commonly understood as one of the most heteronormative times and places. Gutterman, *Her Neighbor's Wife*.
17 Gorman-Murray, "Que(E)Rying Homonormativity," 151.
18 Wolfert, "Eva Siewert." If not stated otherwise, all biographical information on Siewert is from this article.
19 Amtsgericht Charlottenburg to Andrea Rottmann, 23 December 2016.
20 Dimmig, "Lebensbilder von Eva Siewert."
21 Porubsky, "Eva Siewert, die 'Luxemburger Nachtigall.'"
22 In September 1933, Joseph Goebbels had excluded Jews from German cultural life, including journalism. The 1935 Nuremberg Laws defined those with at least three Jewish grandparents as "fully Jewish" and those with two or one Jewish grandparent as "mixed-breed." Kaplan, *Between Dignity and Despair*, 27–8, 77.
23 Siewert, "Das Orakel."
24 Siewert, "Das Orakel."
25 Siewert, "Das Orakel."
26 "'Der weitere Verbleib,'" 161.
27 "'Der weitere Verbleib,'" 161.
28 In an August 1947 letter to Kurt Hiller, Siewert stated that she no longer worked for the Berliner Rundfunk. Eva Siewert, letter to Kurt Hiller, 8 August 1947. Original at Kurt Hiller Gesellschaft Neuss. Copy at Magnus-Hirschfeld-Gesellschaft, Berlin.
29 Eva Siewert, letter to Kurt Hiller, 19 March 1947. Original at Kurt Hiller Gesellschaft Neuss. Copy at Magnus-Hirschfeld-Gesellschaft, Berlin.
30 A bibliography of Siewert's works can be found on the memorial website https://eva-siewert.de/.
31 Eva Siewert, letter to Kurt Hiller, 25 March 1949. Original at Kurt Hiller Gesellschaft Neuss. Copy at Magnus-Hirschfeld-Gesellschaft, Berlin.
32 Eva Siewert, letter to Kurt Hiller, 19 August 1949. Original at Kurt Hiller Gesellschaft Neuss. Copy at Magnus-Hirschfeld-Gesellschaft, Berlin.
33 Eva Siewert, letter to Kurt Hiller, 14 April 1949. Original at Kurt Hiller Gesellschaft Neuss. Copy at Magnus-Hirschfeld-Gesellschaft, Berlin.
34 "Im Gedenken an Alice Carlé und ihre Angehörigen," Magnus-Hirschfeld -Gesellschaft e.V., 9 February 2017, http://magnus-hirschfeld.de/forschungsstelle /veranstaltungen-und-einladungen/stolpersteine-carle-2017/.

35 "In Erinnerung an Eva Siewert," Magnus-Hirschfeld-Gesellschaft e.V., https://eva-siewert.de/.
36 On Radusch's comprehensive papers, see Scheidle, "Hilde Radusch." For publications about Radusch, see, for instance, Schoppmann, *Zeit der Maskierung*; Biermann and Haffter, *Muss es denn gleich Beides sein?*
37 Registration forms in HR Papers. FFBIZ Rep. 500, Acc. 300, 2,3, 46.
38 Lebenslauf HR, Landesarchiv Berlin (LAB) C Rep 118–01 Nr. 6693.
39 Meldeschein in personal papers.
40 HR's eulogy at EK's memorial ceremony, Box 4 (hereafter cited as HR's eulogy).
41 HR's eulogy.
42 The OdF consisted of a main board on the city level, made up of prominent Communists, Social Democrats, and Liberals, and of district branches tied to the district offices. Despite the representation of different political parties on its board, it was under Communist leadership from the beginning. Zur Nieden, *Unwürdige Opfer*, 28, 34–5, 14.
43 Schreiben der KPD Bezirksleitung Gross-Berlin, 27.11.1945, FFBIZ Rep 500, Acc 300, 39, 16.
44 Schreiben der KPD an HR vom 1.1.1946, FFBIZ Rep 500, Acc 300, 39, 16.
45 Diary entries for 7 and 12 January, HR's 1946 diary, FFBIZ Rep 500 Acc 300, 5, 2.
46 Three-page letter to comrade Sidow/comrade Mai from Heinz Schwatert (?), who also wrote the letter to HR at FFBIZ. HR OdF dossier, LAB C Rep 118–01 Nr. 6693 (hereafter cited as HR OdF dossier, Nr. 6693). All spelling and grammar mistakes are left in place. Original German: "Die Frau Radusch musste ja auch deshalb gehen weil sie alle 4 Parteien gleich behandelt hat und die Anordnung von Jure auf K.P.D. Ausweis alles zu geben zurückgewiesen hat."
47 HR OdF dossier, Nr. 6693. Original German: "Genosse. Ich halte es nicht mehr länger aus in euren Augen als Lump da zu stehn ich mach deshalb dir ein Geständnis ... Vor Weihnachten sprach Jure, Binz, Krüger, Steinfort. wie kriegen wir die Radosch raus die ist uns als Weib zu klug und gefährlich ich gebe 100 Zigarren und 5 Jacken wenn uns einer hilft. Ich war gerade dabei und fragte was man da tun mus. Darauf wurde mir gesagt aus Zimmer I. ein paar Rechnungen und ein Päckchen aus den Schreibtisch gleich vor der Tür rechts raus holen. Sie sagten mir nach Weihnachten wird alles wieder reingelegt. Ich habe aber indessen festgestellt das es nicht gemacht wurde sondern sie und Fr. Radosch aus dem Amt flogen."
48 Anonymous letter to HR, FFBIZ Rep 500, Acc 300, 4, 400, 8–12.
49 The reasons for Radusch's dismissal are difficult to untangle because it coincided with the escalation of tensions between the Berlin SPD and

KPD, and between the Soviet and American occupation leaders. Upon their arrival in August 1945, the American occupiers in Schöneberg found a district administration dominated by Communists and Social Democrats. Their suspicion of a communist supremacy culminated in the city's first postwar political trial against two Schöneberg Communists, among them the above-mentioned Gerhard Jurr. The party's district leader, Jurr, and a number of other KPD members were convicted of contempt of the US military administration in Berlin, as well as of communist conspiracy, but they were quickly pardoned because of widespread criticism of the trial. Zur Nieden, *Unwürdige Opfer*, 27; Heimann, "Politisches Leben in Schöneberg/Friedenau," 72; Krenn *Krenn's Berlin-Chronik*, 118, 125.

50 In the FFBIZ letter, S. gives more details on his theft: he took 4.000 M and a few bills.

51 Two later anonymous letters to HR speak of an indictment for embezzlement. Drohbrief an HR und EK, Box 4.

52 Hilde Radusch, Oral-History-Interview mit Annemarie Tröger, 1979/80. FFBIZ. Audiodatei, bearbeitet von Christian Fink. Original German: "Ja, solange man mit den Kommunisten mitarbeitet, ja, und ihnen hilft bei der Arbeit undsoweiter, ist alles wunderschön. Aber als ich damals ausgetreten bin, da hat man mir gesagt, nun ja, also, wir würden dich ja auch wieder aufnehmen, wenn du uns versprichst, dass du deine Freundin laufen lässt. Hab mit der Faust auf den Tisch gehauen, hab gesacht, Meine Freundin geht euch gar nichts an, hab mein Parteibuch selbst eingereicht."

53 According to Claudia Schoppmann, Radusch was expelled from the Communist Party "on account of her relationship with a woman." Schoppmann, *Zeit der Maskierung*.

54 For a contemporaneous example of the stigmatization of female same-sex relationships, see Susanne zur Nieden's analysis of the revocation of two Jewish women's Opfer des Faschismus [Victim of Fascism] recognition because of lesbian relationships. Zur Nieden, *Unwürdige Opfer*. On the German "homophobic consensus," see Zur Nieden, "Einleitung," 6–7.

55 Anonymous letter to HR, FFBIZ Rep 500, Acc 300, 4, 400, 8–12. Original German: "Man wollte sie ja längst umbringen aber ihre Freundin wich ja nicht von ihrer Seite und als sie mal jemand raus warf bemerkten sie an ihr ungeahnte Kräfte die Frau muss irgendeine Ausbildung haben denn ein schwerer Mann wie Papier in die Luft werfen könnte sie sonst nicht seitdem fürchtete man sich wenn sie dabei war."

56 In her 1986 passport, Radusch's height is given as 162 cm. HR Papers, Box 2, FFBIZ Rep 500, Acc 300.

57 Info on Ackermann from "Kurzbiographien Teilnehmer." Bundeskonferenz des Kulturbunds 1947. BArch SAPMO DY 27/3484. On the Kulturbund, see Bartsch, "Kulturbund."

58 Copy of letter from GK to Dr. Ackermann, Kulturbund, 24 June 1947. Gerd Katter Papers (GKP), Magnus-Hirschfeld-Gesellschaft (MHG), Berlin.

59 See Andreas Pretzel's work on the West Berlin Gesellschaft zur Reform des Sexualstrafrechts; Jens Dobler's work on the West Berlin Bund für Menschenrecht, later named Dr. Magnus-Hirschfeld-Gesellschaft; Erik Huneke's work on East German activist Rudolf Klimmer; and Raimund Wolfert's work on Willi Pamperin. Pretzel, *NS-Opfer unter Vorbehalt*, 287–339; Dobler, "Ein Neuanfang, der keiner war," in Dobler, *Von anderen Ufern*, 226–31; Dobler, "Die Alte Magnus-Hirschfeld-Gesellschaft"; Huneke, "Morality, Law, and the Socialist Sexual Self"; Wolfert, *Homosexuellenpolitik*.

60 According to a patient report by Magnus Hirschfeld and Felix Abraham, Katter was born in Berlin on 14 March 1910. Transcript of patient report for E. Katter, 5 March 1929. GKP, MHG, Berlin. The following biographical information is from Katter's autobiographical account, written down for Ralf Dose of the MHG in 1988. Autobiographische Erzählung von Gerd Katter für Ralf Dose, 5 October 1988. GKP, MHG.

61 Autobiographical account GK, 9.

62 Autobiographical account GK, 5.

63 There are two alternative accounts of Katter's surgery. In his memoir, sexual scientist Ludwig Lévy-Lenz describes the case of a "16-year-old transvestian girl" who came to the institute to have their breasts removed. "She had had the luck, she said, to find a job as apprentice to a carpenter, and it was only her breasts which prevented her from working like the other apprentices." Lévy-Lenz describes refusing to perform the surgery because of the patient's age but having to remove the breasts after she injured them with a razor and lost a lot of blood. Katter was a carpenter's apprentice, and in a letter to Ralf Dose, he wrote of "a book whose author was a close friend of Hirschfeld's, and which strangely reached me via Cairo … in which I even found brief mention of myself." Letter GK to Ralf Dose, 3 December 1985. GK Papers, MHG Berlin. Interestingly, Katter does not mention this self-injury in his autobiographical account.

64 Autobiographical account GK, 7.

65 Letter GK to Ralf Dose, 3 December 1985. GK Papers, MHG Berlin.

66 Autobiographical account GK, 7.

67 Autobiographical account GK, 6, 12.

68 Katter did not mention any difficulties with the Nazis because of his being trans. If his application for a name change was successful, he

would not have had to re-apply for a *Transvestitenschein* and would likely not have had to deal with any authorities. For the Nazis' contradictory stance towards transsexuals, see Herrn, "'Ich habe wohl Freude an Frauenkleidern.'"

69 According to Ralf Dose's memories of conversations with Katter in the 1980s, Katter lived in Kreuzberg and was employed at Nordsternversicherung close to Rathaus Schöneberg. Telephone conversation with Ralf Dose, 14 September 2016. Katter claimed to have studied acting in an acting studio in Schöneberg led by Anna Wüllner-Hoffmann, sister of famed tenor Ludwig Wüllner. He is mentioned as one of the actors performing at her private home in a short note in *Berliner Zeitung*, 10 August 1946, 3.

70 Copy of letter from GK to Dr. Ackermann, *Kulturbund*, 24 June 1947. Gerd Katter Papers (GKP), Magnus-Hirschfeld-Gesellschaft (MHG), Berlin. All quotes in this paragraph are from the letter.

71 In his postwar letter to the Kulturbund, Katter mentioned and attached a letter he had sent to a newspaper during the Nazi reign in response to a defamatory article about Hirschfeld. Unfortunately, that letter no longer exists.

72 Katter letter to Ackermann, 24 June 1947. GKP, MHG Berlin.

73 Katter letter to Ackermann, 24 June 1947.

74 Katter letter to Ackermann, 24 June 1947.

75 Letters to GK from Friedrich Wolf, 20 March 1949; Arnold Zweig, 2 September 1949; Paul Krische, 25 October 1949; Felix Bönheim, 1 October 1949; Harry Damrow, 3 June 1948. Further support came from the VVN. Letter from the VVN signed by Karl Raddatz, 12 September 1948. GKP, MHG.

76 In the 1946–1950 volumes of *Aufbau*, there are no articles dealing with Hirschfeld or sexual science.

77 Sternburg, *Um Deutschland geht es uns*, 251; letter to GK from AZ 2 September 1949.

78 Letter from Zweig to GK, 2 September 1949, GKP, MHG. Original German: "Sie müssen sich darüber klar sein, dass es sich bei dem Verhalten der Öffentlichkeit gegenüber dem Andenken und Lebenswerk Magnus Hirschfelds ja nicht nur um einen Akt der Sexualverdrängung handelt … sondern darüberhinaus um eine Pause in der Beschäftigung mit der psychologischen Seite gesellschaftlicher Vorgänge."

79 Herzog, *Sex after Fascism*, 4.

80 McLellan, *Love in the Time of Communism*, 5–7.

81 Heinz Willmann, "Unsere Bundeskonferenz." Manuscript for *Aussprache* 3/4, 1947, BArch DY 27/3484, 17. *Aussprache* was a newsletter for members and friends of the Kulturbund Berlin.

82 There is no mention of Hirschfeld or the Institute in the files of the federal and Berlin leadership of the Kulturbund for the years 1945–1950. BArch SAPMO DY 27 1593; 3893; 1882; 757; 3480; 3481; 3482; 3484; 1026; 1030; 907; 908; 909; 910; 911; 912.

83 Letter from Damrow to GK, 18 October 1948, GKP, MHG. The annual report for the Berlin Kulturbund for 1946 did not record any talks devoted to Hirschfeld or other sexual scientists. Jahresbericht 1946, BArch DY 27/3893.

84 Brief von Dr. Kaltofen, *Zeitschrift Liebe und Ehe*, Regensburg, an GK, 8.2.1951. GK Papers, MHG Berlin.

85 Founded in 1949, the Regensburg-based magazine was censored by the Prüfstelle für jugendgefährdende Schriften and ceased publication by the end of 1951. Herzog, *Sex after Fascism*, 80–5.

86 Sigusch, *Geschichte der Sexualwissenschaft*, 391.

87 Steinbacher, *Wie der Sex nach Deutschland kam*, 155–6, 163–5.

88 Herzog, *Sex after Fascism*, 82–5.

89 Huneke, "Morality, Law, and the Socialist Sexual Self," 69–72.

90 Hiller's tribute to Hirschfeld, written in the year of his death and critically appraising his scientific and activist lifework, was reprinted in the June 1945 issue of Swiss homophile magazine *Der Kreis*. Kurt Hiller, "Der Sinn eines Lebens. In Memoriam Magnus Hirschfeld," *Der Kreis* 13, no. 6 (1945). Three years later, Hiller followed up with a more personal appreciation of his friend in the pages of the same magazine. Kurt Hiller, "Persönliches über Magnus Hirschfeld," *Der Kreis* 16, no. 5 (1948).

91 On Hiller's postwar activism, see Wolfert, *Homosexuellenpolitik*.

92 "Gedenkfeier für Magnus Hirschfeld." *Die Freunde* 2, no. 1 (1952): 28.

93 On Kressmann, see R.B., "Der Fall Willy Kressmann: Die Berliner SPD sagte sich von ihrem Querkopf los," *Die Zeit*, 7 December 1962, https://www.zeit.de/1962/49/der-fall-willy-kressmann. Other speakers were Hans Graaz, Hildegard Wegschneider, and Adolf Koch. Georgieff, *Nacktheit und Kultur*, 84, 121.

94 Dobler, "Ein Neuanfang, der keiner war," in Dobler, *Von anderen Ufern*, 226–31.

95 On the Nazis' effects on German sexology, see Sigusch, *Geschichte der Sexualwissenschaft*, 271–5. Sigusch concludes: "Sexual science will never be able to recover from the blow it was dealt by National Socialism." Sigusch, *Geschichte der Sexualwissenschaft*, 375.

96 Johannes Werres, "Bundespost Berlin hält Magnus Hirschfeld für „wenig bekannt"." *Der Weg* 20, no. 228 (1970): 59–60.

97 James Steakley's 1975 *The Homosexual Emancipation Movement in Germany* covered Hirschfeld, but it was not translated into German. The foundation of the Magnus Hirschfeld Society was one of multiple

initiatives and developments in gay and lesbian history in West Berlin in the late 1970s and 1980s, among them the foundation of the Lesbenarchiv Spinnboden, events with women who had witnessed the city's queer subculture in the Weimar Republic (among them Charlotte Wolff), the exhibition *Eldorado* at Berlin Museum in 1984, the subsequent founding of the Schwules Museum, the making of documentaries on Kitty Kuse and Hilde Radusch, and other projects. Wolff, *Magnus Hirschfeld*.

98 Letter GK to Ralf Dose, 3 December 1985. GK Papers, MHG Berlin. Original German: "zu Ehren des Humanisten Magnus Hirschfeld, und zum Wohle der Menschen, denen seine Sorge galt, eine Institution ins Leben zu rufen, bezw. wieder auferstehen zu lassen, die endlich die Lücke schliesst, die seit seiner Vertreibung aus Hitler-Deutschland und der Zerschlagung des Instituts, das er grosszügig dem Staat zur Verfügung gestellt hatte, entstanden war."

99 Letter GK to Ralf Dose, 3 December 1985.

100 Katter himself was no longer fit to travel, but West Berliners were free to visit East Berlin and the GDR since 1972, and members of the MHG visited him at home. On the lifting of travel restrictions, see Engelmann, "'Die Mauer durchlässiger machen,'" 221.

101 Ribbe, *Berlin 1945–2000*, 91.

102 In Berlin, 25 per cent of the population were refugees, or *Umsiedler*. Borneman, *Belonging in the Two Berlins*, 129.

103 Ribbe, "Wohnen im geteilten Berlin."

104 Carstens, "Die Nissenhütte," 92. The private documentation "Nissenhütten – Wellblechbaracken in Berlin" offers a wealth of information on these makeshift huts. Frenzel, "Nissenhütten – Wellblechbaracken in Berlin."

105 Lemke, *Vor Der Mauer*, 403.

106 Plötz, "Wo blieb die Bewegung lesbischer Trümmerfrauen?," 74.

107 Borneman, *Belonging in the Two Berlins*, 131.

108 Ribbe, *Berlin 1945–2000*, 94–6.

109 Borneman, *Belonging in the Two Berlins*, 205.

110 Fritz Schmehling, interview by Michael Bochow and Karl-Heinz Steinle, 24 January 2015, Archiv der anderen Erinnerungen, Bundesstiftung Magnus Hirschfeld, Berlin.

111 Martin Knop was the publisher of *Amicus-Briefbund*. Its office was located on Nollendorfplatz, and patrons were invited to stop by during office hours. *Amicus-Briefbund* ceased publication in 1953. *Amicus-Briefbund* 2/1950. Schwules Museum, Berlin; Schlüter, Steinle, and Sternweiler, *Eberhardt Brucks*, 162.

112 *Amicus-Briefbund* 2/1950.

113 "Dauerfreundschaft; Für Betätigung und Wohnung wäre ich dankbar." *Amicus-Briefbund* 2/1950. SM*B. Whisnant, *Male Homosexuality*, 70.

114 "Die Freunde sprechen zum Freund." *Die Freunde* 1, no. 2 (1951): 16. SMB.
115 "Die Freunde sprechen zum Freund." *Die Freunde* 1, no. 4 (1951): 21.
116 Plötz, "Wo blieb die Bewegung lesbischer Trümmerfrauen?," 74. Plötz's
    suggestions that same-sex relations were tolerated as long as they
    were not named is confirmed by Benno Gammerl's oral history study.
    Gammerl, "Mit von der Partie oder auf Abstand?" In his article on
    lesbian experiences in Nazi Berlin, Samuel Huneke discusses the case of
    a landlady who did not take offence at her renters' lesbian relationship.
    Huneke, "The Duplicity of Tolerance," 45.
117 Plötz, *Als fehle die bessere Hälfte*, 255–8.
118 Kuse was a co-founder of the group L 74 (Lesbos 1974) in 1974 to
    provide a space for "older, working homosexual women," working
    or retired women who did not feel at home in the student-dominated
    Lesbenaktionszentrum (LAZ). An oral history with her was featured in
    the 1984 *Eldorado* exhibition and catalogue, and she is one of the women
    portrayed in Ilse Kokula's 1986 *Jahre des Glücks, Jahre des Leids*. Christiane
    von Lengerke and Tille Ganz made a documentary about her in 1985. In
    2016, on her birthday, a memorial stone was set for her at the St. Matthäus
    cemetery in Schöneberg, within walking distance to her childhood home.
    Kokula, *Jahre des Glücks, Jahre des Leids*, 31. Lengerke et al., *Käthe (Kitty)
    Kuse*. Her papers are kept by her friend Christiane von Lengerke, who
    kindly gave me access to them at her home.
119 Kuse had gone by a male name, Fritz Förster, for part of her teens. In her
    late twenties, she had even begun the process to get a *Transvestitenschein* –
    to pass as male when going dancing with her girlfriend, she explained in
    hindsight. Kokula, *Jahre des Glücks, Jahre des Leids*, 25–6.
120 Prüfungszeugnis Sonderreifeprüfung Humboldt-Universität, 2. April
    1947, Diplom der Humboldt-Universität, 1. Juni 1951, Teilnachlass Kitty
    Kuse (TKK).
121 Leiter des Notaufnahmeverfahrens in Berlin, Aufenthaltserlaubnis
    für Käthe Kuse, 26 January 1957, TKK. Letter from Kuse to her father,
    7 February 1946, TKK. Lebenslauf Käthe Kuse, late 1950s/1960s,
    Arbeitsvertrag im Amt für Erfindungs- und Patentwesen, 1. September
    1951, Zwischenzeugnis Amt für Erfindungs- und Patentwesen, 31.3.1953,
    TKK. In 1951, Kuse earned DM 1210 at the VEM Transformatoren.
    Zeugnis der VEM Transformatoren, 20. Oktober 1951, TKK. The median
    income in the state-owned businesses in the GDR was DM 295 in 1949,
    meaning that she made more than four times the median income. In 1955,
    the median income was DM 439. Statistisches Amt der DDR, *Statistisches
    Jahrbuch*, 144.
122 After her husband returned from war imprisonment, they had moved
    in with her parents in Berlin-Lichtenberg. Lebenslauf Ruth Wilhelmine

Dorothea Zimmel, 25 July 1957, TKK. Her mother died in 1949, followed by her father in 1951. In 1952, she divorced her husband, who died in 1954. Biographische Skizze Zimmel-Fischer für Zuzugsgenehmigung, Rückseite Antragsformular, Vorgang Zuzug West-Berlin KK, TKK.

123 I have not been able to contact Zimmel's daughters to ask them if they agree with the publication of their image and therefore cannot show it.

124 Interview with Christine Loewenstein. Archiv der Anderen Erinnerungen, Berlin. 2018.

125 Loewenstein interview. Original German: "Weil ich, ich kannte auch keine lesbischen, das heißt, das stimmt nicht ganz, aber in meiner Kindheit, in meiner Jugendzeit gabs diesen Begriff eigentlich nicht. Es gab auch das Wort nicht. Das hab ich von meinem Mann, also von meinem Freund damals gehört, so lesbisch. Ja der … Das war ganz witzig, dass wir mal bei meiner Freundin zusammen zu Besuch waren, mit ihm, also als er noch da zu Besuch kam, da sagt … Gehen wir raus, und da sagt er: „Naja, Mensch, seit wann, seit wann ist denn deine Mutter lesbisch?" Und wir [gestikuliert] wussten überhaupt nicht, wie, was. Und dann stellte sich raus, dass die Mutter von meiner Freundin mit ihrer Freundin zusammenlebte. Und das war ganz offensichtlich, aber ich habs nicht ges … Wir habens beide nicht gesehen. Sie selber hats nicht gesehen. Die haben richtig son, son, son Ehebett mit rechts und links Nachttisch gehabt und haben beide da geschlafen und waren ganz klar so traditionelles Lesbenpaar. Die Frau immer so bisschen mit Anzügen, sie mit m Rock. Und wir habens nicht … Wir kannten das nicht. Wir hatten dafür kein Wort. Und deswegen, wenn man kein Wort hat, kann man ne Sache auch nicht sich ins Bewusstsein holen, ne, so. Und deswegen war das auch kein Weg für mich."

126 In my spelling of "fem," I follow historians Elizabeth Kennedy and Madeline Davis, whose book about mid-century working-class lesbians is central to my argument, as explained below. Kennedy and Davis, *Boots of Leather, Slippers of Gold*.

127 Ahmed, *Queer Phenomenology*, 67.

128 Schreiben von EK und HR: Antrag auf Pacht eines Rasenstreifens am Bahnhof Grunewald, Schreiben des Bezirksamts Prenzlauer Berg betr. Verpachtung Großküche, Waren-Eingangsbuch Ambulanter Handel. HR Papers, FFBIZ, Rep 500, Acc 300, Box 9.

129 The envelopes bear no stamps, but instead, one says "Through messengers" and the other has a delivery note attached to it reading "Put in only before 7 otherwise after dark." Anonymous letter to HR and EK, FFBIZ Rep 500, Acc 300, 4, 400, 1–3, 4–5.

130 Anonymous letter to HR and EK, FFBIZ Rep 500, Acc 300, 4, 400, 4–5.

131 Anonymous letter to HR, FFBIZ Rep 500, Acc 300, 4, 400, 1–3.

132 Anonymous letter to HR, FFBIZ Rep 500, Acc 300, 4, 400, 1–3.
133 Anonymous letter to HR and EK, FFBIZ Rep 500, Acc 300, 4, 400, 4–5.
134 Calendar entries for 12 and 13 October 1947. Box 5.
135 Schreiben des Oberstaatsanwalts Berlin-Mitte bzgl. HRs Anzeige gegen
     Frau Agnes Reuscher, 4.8.1948; Schreiben des Oberstaatsanwaltes Berlin-
     Mitte: Einbruch Januar 1948, 3. April 1948, Box 9, 41.
136 Gedankenprotokoll von überhörter Unterhaltung von zwei Spitzeln, Box 9.
137 Schreiben an das Wirtschaftsamt Schöneberg mit Antrag auf ambulantes
     Gewerbe, Box 9; Schreiben vom Bezirksamt Mitte an Firma Klopsch
     & Radusch zum Einfinden im Wohnungsamt, 29.11.1948. persönliche
     Rücksprache.
138 Handschriftliche Notiz Einbruch 24./25.1.1948, Notiz Einbruch 15.3.48,
     Notiz Einbruch 13. Mai 48, Notiz 5. Einbruch zum 9.7.48, 6. Einbruch
     17./18.7.48, Schreiben vom Bezirksamt Mitte an Firma Klopsch &
     Radusch zum Einfinden im Wohnungsamt 29.11.1948. HR Papers
     FFBIZ Rep 500, Acc 300, Box 9; Briefentwurf an SPD, 8.1.1949, Box 8;
     Briefentwurf an Entschädigungsamt 7.11.1949, Box 4; Notiz „Gewerbe
     abgemeldet", Box 9, 34.
139 Unterlagen zu verschiedenen Beschäftigungen im Notstandsprogramm
     für Angestellte, FFBIZ Rep 500, Acc 300, Box 8.
140 Dossier OdF, HR Papers, FFBIZ Rep 500, Acc 300, Box 9. See also
     Radusch's OdF file at Landesarchiv Berlin. LAB C Rep 118–01 Nr. 6693.
141 Zur Nieden, *Unwürdige Opfer*, 83.
142 Recognition as PrV, 4 January 1952, Settlement 20 March 1952, FFBIZ Rep
     500, Acc 300, Box 9.
143 Notification about disability pension, 4 December 1952, FFBIZ Rep 500,
     Acc 300, Box 9.
144 Beschied des Senators für Arbeit und Sozialwesen über Einstellung der
     Rentenzahlung, 20.2.1954. HR Papers FFBIZ Rep 500, Acc 300, 9.
145 Vergleich zw HR und dem Entschädigungsamt wg. Schaden im
     beruflichen Fortkommen. HR Papers FFBIZ Rep 500, Acc 300, 9.
146 1946 calendar, HR Papers, FFBIZ.
147 1949 calendar, HR Papers, FFBIZ.
148 1949 calendar.
149 Einschreiben an HR vom Magistrat, endgültige Aberkennung des OdF-
     Status, 4.5.1949; Schreiben des Magistrats, Abteilung für Sozialwesen,
     warum HR nicht als PrV anerkannt werden kann, 12.7.49, Box 9.
150 1949 calendar, HR Papers FFBIZ Rep. 500, Acc. 300, 1–5–3.
151 1949 calendar.
152 Housekeeping book, HR papers, FFBIZ Rep. 500, Acc 300, 395.
153 Note from Klopsch to Radusch, HR Papers, FFBIZ Rep. 500, Acc. 300,
     Box 4.

154 Note from Klopsch to Radusch, HR Papers, FFBIZ Rep. 500, Acc. 300, Box 4.
155 Note from Klopsch to Radusch, HR Papers, FFBIZ Rep. 500, Acc. 300, Box 4.
156 1946 and 1949 calendars in HR Papers. FFBIZ Rep. 500, Acc. 300, 1–5–4. For instance, in January 1946, 13 days are marked with an "x," 7 in February 1946, 12 in January 1949, and 14 in February 1949.
157 Willenserklärung EK, 20.8.1958; Vollmacht 24.8.1959, Box 4.
158 Letter from pastor to Verwaltung des Sophienfriedhofs, 25 March 1960, Box 4.
159 Letter from the II. Sophien-Kirchhof, 2 April 1960, Box 4. From a death notice in Eddy Klopsch's papers in the HR collection, it is apparent that Otto Klopsch was Eddy's father, not her husband. Whereas Radusch had apparently claimed that Eddy had no relatives, Eddy's sister Hertha Kaufmann had suggested that she had been married. The matter was complicated by the fact that the necessary papers were no longer in Berlin due to the war.
160 Letter draft to *Tagesspiegel*, 8 April 1960, Box 4.
161 Letter to Steinmetzmeister Carl Krause, 25 April 1960.
162 Fotoprojekt Rita Thomas, Feminist FFBIZ Archives Berlin, 2018; Rita "Tommy" Thomas, interview by Karl-Heinz Steinle and Babette Reicherdt, 19 November 2016, Archiv der anderen Erinnerungen. Bundesstiftung Magnus Hirschfeld. Berlin; Transkription Janina Rieck.
163 Evans, "Seeing Subjectivity," 462.
164 Evans, 438.
165 Hirschfeld, *Berlins Drittes Geschlecht*, 89–90.
166 Plötz, "Bubis und Damen," 36; Rita "Tommy" Thomas, interview by Karl-Heinz Steinle and Babette Reicherdt, 19 November 2016, Archiv der anderen Erinnerungen. Bundesstiftung Magnus Hirschfeld. Berlin; Transkription Janina Rieck.
167 Kennedy and Davis, *Boots of Leather, Slippers of Gold*.
168 Kennedy and Davis, 195.
169 Kennedy and Davis, 192.
170 Kennedy and Davis, 191.
171 Rita "Tommy" Thomas, interview by Karl-Heinz Steinle and Babette Reicherdt, 19 November 2016.
172 Rita "Tommy" Thomas, interview by Karl-Heinz Steinle and Babette Reicherdt, 19 November 2016. Original German: "aber sie war viel bei mir, und zwar in äh Garten ham wir jewohnt meistens, hm, ja, dis war schön."
173 Tommy interview. Original German: "Ja, ihre Mutter hat immer Essen für uns jekocht, da ham wa dit Essen im Topf immer mitjenommen, mit raus in Garten, wie wie jesacht, nich. Ick war ja nur in Garten."
174 McLellan, "From Private Photography to Mass Circulation," 408.

175 Rita "Tommy" Thomas, interview by Karl-Heinz Steinle and Babette
Reicherdt, 19 November 2016. Original German: "Und da hab ick weiter
also den Hundesalon gehabt und die Tiere versorgt, da hat ich auch die
ganzen Enten und Hühner, drei, drei Enten und drei Hühner, also nich
so viel so groß. Und denn sind wir immer abends sind wir weggegangen
zum, zur 21. Das war die Adalbertstraße 21. Da war Tanz abends, naja,
abends um achte war Tanz, und da war 'n bisschen Jemütlichkeit, konnte
man sich mit andern unterhalten. Meistens, da warn nur Frauen, keine
Männer."

2. Surveilled Sociability: Queer Bars

1 "Zum 3jährigen Bestehen der Boheme Dienstag den 25.10.55 zeigen wir
Ihnen eine Modenschau! ... Es ladet herzlich ein Willy Lorenz." In this
chapter, I follow the bar's own spelling of "Boheme" without an accent.
2 See also Matt Houlbrook's observation about the "dissonance" of the
archives of persecution discussed in the introduction.
3 For East Berlin, the source material is too limited to engage in a
microanalysis that could lay bare how multiple actors negotiated East
Berlin's bars. But oral histories, memoirs, and Stasi files allow at least a
tentative account of their location and characteristics.
4 Rubin, "Studying Sexual Subcultures." Rubin refers to D'Emilio,
"Capitalism and Gay Identity," as well as to Weeks, *Coming Out:
Homosexual Politics in Britain.*
5 See Magnus Hirschfeld's chapter on "Community Life and Meeting
Places of Homosexual Men and Women." Hirschfeld, *The Homosexuality of
Men and Women*, 776–803; see also Beachy, *Gay Berlin*, 58–64.
6 Beachy, *Gay Berlin*, 58.
7 Theis and Sternweiler, "Alltag im Kaiserreich," 73.
8 Beachy, *Gay Berlin*, 244; Pretzel and Roßbach, *Wegen der zu erwartenden
hohen Strafe*, 20.
9 Fout, "Homosexuelle in der NS-Zeit," 169. On queer nightlife in Cologne
and Hamburg, see also Balser, *Himmel und Hölle*; Centrum Schwule
Geschichte, *Himmel und Hölle*; Limpricht, Müller, and Oxenius, *"Verführte"
Männer*; Rosenkranz and Lorenz, *Hamburg auf anderen Wegen*.
10 The head of Berlin's Nazi-era "Homosexuals Department" within the
criminal squad was rehired in 1946 as head of the vice squad. Pretzel and
Roßbach, *Wegen der zu erwartenden hohen Strafe*, 70.
11 The most comprehensive exploration of postwar queer nightlife in
Berlin was the 2003–04 exhibition *Mittenmang: Homosexuelle Frauen und
Männer in Berlin 1945–1969* at Schwules Museum, but no catalogue was
published. The exhibition was curated by Karl-Heinz Steinle and

Maika Leffers. Documentation of the exhibition is at the Schwules Museum archives. *Mittenmang: Homosexuelle Frauen und Männer.* See also Pretzel, *NS-Opfer unter Vorbehalt;* Dobler, *Von anderen Ufern;* Dobler, *Verzaubert in Nord-Ost.* For sketches on particular bars, see the bar portraits by Karl-Heinz Steinle in Maneo, *Spurensuche im Regenbogenkiez.*

12 See Dobler, "'Den Heten eine Kneipe wegnehmen'"; Evans, *Life among the Ruins,* 170–1.

13 See, for instance, Dobler, "Ein Neuanfang, der keiner war," in Dobler, *Von anderen Ufern,* 236; Evans, *Life among the Ruins,* 174–5, 179.

14 On the project of fashioning a new socialist morality as part of creating the "New Socialist Person" in the 1950s, see Eghigian, "Homo Munitus"; Evans, "Repressive Rehabilitation."

15 O.Z. "Mamita läßt bitten."

16 Dobler, "Die Berliner Polizei und die Nachkriegsdelinquenz," 251ff.

17 Förderkreis Polizeihistorische Sammlung Berlin e.V. (Hrsg.), Berliner Kriminalpolizei von 1945 bis zur Gegenwart, Berlin 2005, 10; Tätigkeitsberichte 1948–1951, PHS D 1.10, Band 4a.

18 *Amicus-Briefbund* 2/1950. Schwules Museum* Archives.

19 *Amicus-Briefbund* 3/1950. Schwules Museum* Archives.

20 *Amicus-Briefbund* 2–8/1950.

21 *Amicus-Briefbund* 5 and 7, 1950.

22 *Amicus-Briefbund* 2/1950.

23 *Amicus-Briefbund* 5/1950.

24 It was now located in Lutherstraße in Schöneberg, moving from Fasanenstr. in Charlottenburg. *Amicus-Briefbund* 3/1952.

25 Mamita is said to have died in a car crash. Dobler, "Kreuzberg tanzt," in Dobler, *Von anderen Ufern,* 252. Mamita is identified as the keeper of the pub at Lausitzer Platz 1 in a Stasi file, too. Arrest report, 4 November 1953, BStU 1030/58.

26 Thilo, *Ein Igel weint Tränen aus Rosenholz.*

27 Thilo wrote the manuscript in 1995 and donated it to the Gay Museum. Peter Thilo, Brief ans Schwule Museum betr. Teilnachlass, 14 May 2000, Schwules Museum, Berlin. The manuscript reads like Thilo's autobiography. Kreuzberg poet Günter Bruno Fuchs, himself a regular at the bars in this part of Kreuzberg, dedicated a poem to Peter Thilo, suggesting that they were friends and that Thilo knew the Kreuzberg bar scene from his own experience. Fuchs, *Gemütlich summt das Vaterland,* 161.

28 Thilo, *Ein Igel,* 199.

29 Thilo, 199–200. Original German: "Jetzt ging Karl erst einmal in das Lokal an der südöstlichen Ecke, wie die meisten Lokale dieser Art, nach außen nur mit einer Bierreklame versehen in Leuchtschrift, dem Kenner verriet es sich durch die zugezogenen Vorhänge vor den Fenstern, die einen

Einblick von außen unmöglich machten. Karl war verlegen, er wußte auch nicht, was auf ihn zukommen würde, aber da er sich vorgenemmen [!] hatte, sich nun für Direktkontakte zu entscheiden, trat er ein. Es war dämmrig, alles in ein rötliches Licht getaucht, das die dicken roten Vorhänge und die rote Tapete reflektierte. Es war halbvoll, an einigen Tischen saßen Männer unterschiedlichen Alters, sie unterhielten sich und machten den Eindruck, sich schon länger zu kennen. An der Bar saßen auch Männer, meist jüngere, die den Eindruck machten, nur zum biertrinken [!] hergekommen zu sein … Sie wirkten freundlich, friedlich und gelangweilt … Was Karl nicht wußte, war, daß Lokale dieser Art immer erst gegen Mitternacht voll werden. Wer um diese Zeit, kurz nach neun, kommt, kommt nicht wegen irgendwelcher Abenteuer. Sie wollen Bier trinken und mit Bekannten reden … Karl hatte den Eindruck, am falschen Ort zu sein. Hier war es zu gemütlich, die Leute gingen bekannt, nicht fremd."

30 Boheme bar photo album, PHS Berlin.

31 The host is characterized as "homosexual" by the police in the album.

32 According to the archivist, these photos show members of Sparverein West. Personal communication with Jens Dobler.

33 "Transvestitenlokale" and "Homosexuellenkneipen" re-opened in the Soviet-controlled part of the city after the war had ended. Original German: "Das alte … Stammpublikum war ja plötzlich wieder da, nicht, denn es hatten ja doch etliche auch überlebt. Und die Prostituierten natürlich, die waren ja dann auch wieder da." Transcription of interview with Charlotte von Mahlsdorf, conducted on 27 July 1995. Nachlass Charlotte von Mahlsdorf 1b, Schwules Museum, Berlin.

34 LAB C Rep 303 Nr. 128. Wegweiser durch den Revierbezirk enthält "35. Lokale, zweifelhafte, a) Lokale mit weiblicher Bedienung, b) Päderasten- und schwule Weiberlokale, c) andere zweifelhafte Lokale."

35 Mahlsdorf, *Ich bin meine eigene Frau*, 141. The bar's interior is now visible in Mahlsdorf's *Gründerzeitmuseum* in the Berlin district of Mahlsdorf.

36 In the oral history interview in her personal papers at Schwules Museum, von Mahlsdorf claims possession of files about the *Mulackritze*, possibly from the district office.

37 Mahlsdorf, *Ich bin meine eigene Frau*, 145.

38 In 1961, after the Wall had been erected, the *Mulackritze* building was expropriated and then razed to make way for apartment blocks in 1963. Mahlsdorf, *Ich bin meine eigene Frau*, 146–7.

39 McLellan, *Love in the Time of Communism*, 7; Herzog, "Chapter 5: The Romance of Socialism," in *Sex after Fascism*, 184–219.

40 „Bekanntlich existieren Lokale und Treffpunkte für diese Kategorie von Menschen nur in Westberlin. Dort treffen sich biologisch

Gleichgeartete aus dem Rias, dem NWDR oder sonstiger Kreise einschliesslich der Mitarbeiter der westlichen Okkupationsmächte." Rechenschaftsbericht für das I. Quartal 1951, 31 March 1951, DRA Babelsberg, Schriftgutbestand Hörfunk: HA Personal, Personalstatistiken und -analysen.

41 Rechenschaftsbericht für das I. Quartal 1951, 31 March 1951. In the very first years of the new socialist state, *Berliner Rundfunk*'s human resources were controlled directly by the Ministry for State Security. Herbst, *Demokratie und Maulkorb*, 69. On gay men as unreliable citizens, see, for instance, Herzer, "Schwule Widerstandskämpfer."

42 Dobler, "Schwules Leben in Berlin," 152–63, 161ff. Dobler describes the "displacement" of the Friedrichstraße bars from the mid-1950s on. However, my sources suggest that many of the bars were open at least until the early 1960s, and Dobler has suggested the same elsewhere. Teresa Tammer cites a Stasi informant in 1976 complaining about the shutdown of "Mocca Bar" at Hotel Sofia on Friedrichstraße and its replacement with an "Intershop" catering to Western tourists. The statement suggests that appealing to Western visitors was one factor in the displacement of queer bars from central East Berlin. Tammer, "Verräter oder Vermittler?," 115.

43 "Berlin: Belästigung durch die Polizei," *Der Weg* 4, no. 10 (1954): 356–7. The reprinted articles were: "Die gefährliche Molle," *Telegraf*, reprinted in *Der Weg* 4, no. 10 (1954): 357; and "Großrazzia in sechs Lokalen," *B.Z.*, reprinted in *Der Weg* 4, no. 10 (1954): 356.

44 "Seltsames Vorgehen der Kripo," *nacht-depesche*, 20 September 1954.

45 "gleichgeschlechtlich empfindende Personen."

46 "Methoden … aus dem 'Tausendjährigen Reich,'" "jenseits des Brandenburger Tores."

47 Beachy, *Gay Berlin*, 83.

48 Johannes Stumm (1897–1978) served as West Berlin's police president from 1948 to 1962. In the Weimar Republic, he had worked in the Berlin criminal squad's department for political offenses. In 1933, he was dismissed and then worked as a freelancer before returning to police service after 1945. "Stumm, Johannes" in Munzinger Online/Personen – Internationales Biographisches Archiv, https://www.munzinger.de /document/00000018955 (abgerufen von Verbund der Öffentlichen Bibliotheken Berlins am 29.4.2021). Wolfram Sangmeister (1912–78) served in the West Berlin police from 1949 and led its criminal squad from 1952 until 1968. He remained silent on his membership in the SA, though it is noted in a copy of his Deutsche Studentenschaft index card kept in his personnel records. Sangmeister had studied law and worked as a lawyer for the Deutsche Umsiedlungs-Treuhandgesellschaft from 1939 to

1941. In 1941, he became a soldier. He was a prisoner of war in the Soviet Union until 1949. PHS Berlin, H 1.22.

49 Steinborn and Krüger, *Die Berliner Polizei 1945–1992*, 98.

50 Steinborn and Krüger, 112.

51 Steinborn and Krüger, 117.

52 Fenemore, "Victim of Kidnapping or an Unfortunate Defector?"

53 "Otto John: Sie nannten ihn Bumerang," *Der Spiegel*, 28 July 1954, 5–10.

54 Rolf, "Gedanken zum Fall John," *Der Kreis*, no. 8 (1954): 9.

55 Larion Gyburg-Hall, "Die sauren Konsequenzen (Der 'Fall: Dr. Otto John')," *Der Weg* 4, no. 9 (1954): 309–12.

56 Pretzel, *NS-Opfer unter Vorbehalt*, 10.

57 For dates of Sangmeister's direction of the Kripo, see Förderkreis Polizeihistorische Sammlung Berlin e.V., ed. *Berliner Kriminalpolizei von 1945 bis zur Gegenwart* (Berlin: Selbstverlag, 2005), 10; H.W., "'Der Kurier' Berlin, meldet: Männliche Prostitution stellt die Kriminalpolizei vor Neuland," *Der Ring* 1 (August 1955): 173–4. The German term used is "Strichjungenunwesen."

58 Brief aus Hauptpflegeamt an Frau Kay, gez. i.A. Kirchhoff, Betr. Artikel in "Der Abend" vom 2.7.55: "Arbeitshaus für Strichjungen." B Rep 013 Nr. 502.

59 "wiederholt auftretende und unbelehrbare Strichjungen." H.W., "'Der Kurier,' Berlin, meldet: Männliche Prostitution," 174.

60 Lücke, *Männlichkeit in Unordnung*.

61 Lücke, *Männlichkeit in Unordnung*, 17–18.

62 Lücke cites Ulrichs, Krafft-Ebing, Bloch, and Hirschfeld as describing streetwalking boys as effeminate.

63 Lücke, *Männlichkeit in Unordnung*, 115–16.

64 Evans, "Bahnhof Boys," 608.

65 Evans, 635. According to Evans's analysis of court files, being caught as a "streetwalking boy" usually led to prison time in West Berlin, and to a juvenile workhouse in East Berlin. The West Berlin files are from the mid-1950s. Evans does not give dates for the East Berlin files.

66 Brief aus Hauptpflegeamt, 21 July 1955, B Rep 013 Nr. 502.

67 Vermerk zu Widerspruch eines als "Strichjunge" zwangsgestellten und erkennungsdienstlich behandelten Mannes. Senator for the Interior. B Rep. 004 Nr. 3805. Original German: "das nicht unbeträchtliche Ansteigen der Zahl der Strichjungen zu einem erheblichen Teil auf das sogenannte Währungsgefälle und die Flüchtlingsnot zurückzuführen ist. Neben den Strichjungen, die ihren Wohnsitz im SBS oder in der SBZ haben, betätigen sich als Strichjungen auch solche männlichen Personen, die als angebliche Flüchtlinge nach Berlin gekommen sind, denen jedoch die Aufnahme nach dem Bundesnotaufnahmegesetz verweigert wurde (vgl. Schramm,

Das Strichjungenunwesen, Sonderdruck des Bundeskriminalamtes Wiesbaden, 1959.) Strichjungen sind nach den polizeilichen Erfahrungen fast immer arbeitsscheu und nur an einem mühelosen „Broterwerb" interessiert. Wenn es darum geht, mühelos Geld zu „verdienen", schrecken viele von ihnen – durch das von ihnen gewählte Milieu animiert und von den natürlichen Hemmungen befreit – weder vor einem Mord noch vor sonstigen Gewaltverbrechen zurück. Das beweist die Anzahl der Verbrechen dieser Art, die in den letzten Jahren in Berlin von Strichjungen begangen worden sind."

68 One West Mark was worth between four and six East Marks. Despite the unfavourable exchange rate, and despite prohibitions to possess the Western currency, East Berliners frequently shopped in the West simply because many things were not available in East Berlin. Ribbe, *Berlin 1945–2000*, 118–20; Lemke, *Vor der Mauer*, 346.

69 The German term used is "Strichjungenunwesen." Streetwalking boys were characterized as the source of all evil, not just by the police but also by many gay men, as continuing discussions in homophile magazines show. This characterization had partly to do with the disproportionately high number of gay men murdered by male prostitutes and the continuing problem of blackmail, but also with ideas about seduction, both of teenagers by older men and vice versa. The harsh judgment on streetwalking boys as "incorrigible" and the police's brutal suggestion of putting them in work camps led to protest within the homophile readership too. See, for instance, issues 1 and 3, 1952 of *Die Insel*, and 4/1953 of *Der Weg*.

70 *Der Abend* reported the number of patrons as 180, *nacht-depesche* as 200, *der neue Ring* as 250. "Großrazzia in Schöneberg," *Der Abend*, 28 October 1957; "Eine geheimnisvolle Großrazzia," *nacht-depesche*, 28 October 1957; SS, "sind wir wieder einmal soweit? Ungeschminkter Tatsachenbericht von großen Berliner Kesseltreiben gegen 'homophile Lokale,'" *der neue ring* 1, no. 12 (1957): 17–19. The bar advertised itself as "internationale Herrenbar" and "Tanzpalast für den verwöhnten Geschmack" in homophile magazine *Der Weg*. "Anzeige 'Amigo-Bar,'" *Der Weg* 7, no. 7 (1957).

71 Thirty-three patrons were taken to the *Landeskriminalamt*, where fourteen were found guilty of crimes, though only seven could be brought before a judge to receive arrest warrants. "Sittendezernat hatte unruhiges Wochenende," *nacht-depesche*, 11 November 1957; "sind wir wieder einmal soweit?" *der neue ring* 1.

72 "Berlin: Razzia der Kripo," *nacht-depesche*, 22 November 1957. Five *Kripo* and forty *Schupo* officers raided the bar. Half of the patrons present were taken to the *Landeskriminalamt*, but of those thirty-five, only three

could be proven to have been involved in criminal acts, and for only
one of them was the evidence strong enough to be presented to a judge.
The officer in charge of the raid explained the lack of success with the
particular character of the bar. Many of its patrons were young male
prostitutes already known to the police, he said, who were savvy in
dealing with the cops and would only admit to crimes when caught in
the act.

73 Vermerk Zuständigkeit Bekämpfung der Strichjungen. 01.11.1957. PHS
Berlin 55.25. Organizational map of the West Berlin police, 1965, PHS Berlin.

74 Report on patrol, 27 October 1957. PHS Berlin, 1956.08. It also dutifully
recorded the behaviour of the homosexuals: "Die Homosexuellen tanzten
dort eifrig nach einer Kapelle, bzw. nach der Musikbox. Interessant ist,
dass einer der Homosexuellen, der uns nicht kannte, den Landgerichtsrat
Lutter zum Tanz aufforderte." The report remains silent on whether the
judge accepted the offer.

75 Patrol report, 8 June 1959, PHS Berlin, 1956.08.

76 "Strichjungen" and "2 der dort üblichen Transvestiten." Patrol reports on
Elli's Bier-Bar, 1 November and 5 November 1957, PHS; Patrol report on
Robby-Bar, 14 November 1957, PHS.

77 The plan of action for the raid on Elli's Bier Bar features "Sofortige
Zwangsstellung der anwesenden Strichjungen" with a handwritten
addition "+ Transvestiten." No such addition can be found on the plan
for the raid on Robby-Bar.

78 List of individuals controlled during the raid at Ellis-Bierbar, 11
November 1957. The list includes three band members. PHS Berlin.

79 "sind wir wieder einmal soweit?" *der neue ring*, 1.

80 Report on raid on Robby-Bar and Kleist-Casino, 10 March 1958, PHS.

81 KK Klose, Report on raid at Elli's, 11 November 1957. PHS. Original
German: "Vor dem Lokal hatte sich eine große Menschenmenge von
mehreren hundert Personen angesammelt, die offen ihre Sympathie für
die polizeiliche Aktion bekundeten. Lediglich eine männliche Person
versuchte Unruhe zu stiften. Diese wurde jedoch zwangsgestellt … Nach
Schluß der Aktion wurde sicherheitshalber eine Gruppe Schutzpolizei
in der Nähe des Lokals gelassen, da die Wirtin Besorgnisse äußerte,
eine „aufgebrachte Menge könne nach Abzug der Polizei ihr Lokal
stürmen und demolieren!" Zu Zwischenfällen ist es jedoch nicht mehr
gekommen."

82 "Großrazzia," *Der Abend*, 28 October 1957.

83 "Kampf dem Laster. Razzia in Kreuzberg." *7 Uhr Blatt am Sonntag Abend*,
10 November 1957, volume 11, Nr. 45a, clipping in police files, PHS.

84 "Kampf." Original German: "Die Berliner Kriminalpolizei hat dem
„Strichjungen"-Unwesen, das in unserer Stadt wie eine üble Seuche

ständig um sich greift und zu einem gefährlichen Nährboden zahlreicher anderer Verbrechen geworden ist, den Großkampf angesagt. Nachdem erst vor 14 Tagen in Schöneberg ein berüchtigter Treffpunkt der meist arbeitsscheuen und jedem geordneten Leben widersätzlichen Elemente ausgehoben worden war, schlug die Polizei in der vergangenen Nacht in Kreuzberg zu."

85   "Kampf."

86   KK Klose, Report on the raid of 21/22 November 1957, 22 Nov 1957, PHS.

87   "Eine geheimnisvolle Großrazzia," *nacht-depesche*, 28 October 1957.

88   Whisnant, *Male Homosexuality*, 30.

89   Thirty-seven were temporarily detained at Amigo-Bar, thirty-three at Elli's, and thirty-five at Robby-Bar. "Sittendezernat hatte unruhiges Wochenende," *nacht-depesche*, 11 November 1957; "Berlin: Razzia der Kripo," *nacht-depesche*, 22 November 1957; "Erfolglose Nachtjagd unseres Kripochefs," *nacht-depesche*, 29 October 1957; on the sentences: File memo M II 2, 29 November 1957, PHS.

90   "Erfolglose Nachtjagd unseres Kripochefs," *nacht-depesche*, 29 October 1957.

91   "Erfolglose Nachtjagd." The reporter for the *nacht-depesche* noted, too, that the director of the police department's vice squad had not been informed about the raid, suggesting that animosities or competition within the police department may have played into the decision to raid the bars. Original German: "Warum gibt man mir erst eine Konzession, um mit derartigen Methoden mein Geschäft zu ruinieren. Es ist bekannt, dass bei mir Homosexuelle verkehren, aber ich sorge dafür, daß sich Strichjungen in meinem Lokal nicht breitmachen können, da von mir nur Klubmitglieder oder deren Bekannte eingelassen werden."

92   Streifenbericht E I (S) über Lokale in C-burg, Schöneberg, Xberg, 25.3.1958. PHS Berlin.

93   Peukert, "Die 'Halbstarken'"; Poiger, *Jazz, Rock, and Rebels*; Maase, "Establishing Cultural Democracy"; Prowe, "The 'Miracle' of the Political-Culture Shift, 451–8; Fenemore, *Sex, Thugs, and Rock'n'Roll*.

94   Treffen der Senatoren des Inneren, Justiz, Jugend und Sport, Polizeipräsidium, 03.08.1959. LAB B Rep 010 Nr. 2300.

95   Besprechung der Rowdykommission, 24.3.1960. Bestand „Bekämpfung des ‚Rowdytums.'" PHS Berlin D 4.70.

96   Police report about attack on Elli's on 29/30 November 1957. Report Vorfälle im Zusammenhang mit Homosexualität, 9 September 1958. PHS Berlin. Az. 2 Ju Js 207.58.

97   Thilo, *Ein Igel*, 335. Original German: "Karl wollte nur, nach all den angepassten Studenten, mit denen er in der Uni … zu tun hatte, wieder einmal unter Homosexuellen sein, die ihre Sexualität bejahten und die

sich heiter darin eingerichtet hatten. Das traf nun zwar für Karl nicht
zu, er brauchte sich zwar zu Hause nicht mehr verstecken, aber in der
Gegenwart seiner Kommilitonen durfte er nicht einmal unauffällig mit
dem Hintern wackeln oder tuntig sprechen, wenn auch nur zum Spaß.
Hier bei Elli war tuntiges Gehabe in den verschiedenen Windstärken
gang und gäbe."

98 Thilo, *Ein Igel*, 335.
99 Thilo, 335.
100 Orest Kapp, Interview by Andreas Pretzel and Janina Rieck, 15 October
    2014, Archiv der anderen Erinnerungen, Bundesstiftung Magnus
    Hirschfeld, Berlin.
101 Orest Kapp, Interview by Andreas Pretzel and Janina Rieck, 15 October
    2014, Archiv der anderen Erinnerungen, Bundesstiftung Magnus
    Hirschfeld, Berlin. Original German: "Ich hab Freunde gefunden, wir
    hatten viel Sex und das war ganz okay, aber es war gefährlich. Ähm,
    man durfte sich auf der Straße niemals blicken lassen. Alleine schon gar
    nicht. Und wenn man 'ne Gruppe Jugendlicher sah, dann hat man sich
    am besten verdrückt. Und in den Kneipen, in die wir dann gingen, da
    waren dann so Klingeln, und ähm, man ging auch nie rein ohne vorher
    zu gucken, ob irgendjemand zusieht."
102 Fritz Schmehling, interview by Michael Bochow and Karl-Heinz Steinle,
    24 January 2015, Archiv der anderen Erinnerungen, Bundesstiftung
    Magnus Hirschfeld, Berlin (hereafter cited as Schmehling interview).
103 Schmehling interview. Original German: "Ne ... Dann bist de halt 'ne
    Tunte, aus! Ich hab mich aber nie als weiblichen Part, hab ich mich nie
    jefühlt. Bis heute nicht, kann nix damit anfang'n. (lacht) Vielleicht hängt
    des och mit mein'm Beruf zusammen, ich weiß nich. Handwerker bleibt
    Handwerker, ne? Kein Feingeist."
104 Schmehling interview. Original German: "Wir waren also och so 'n paar
    Kollegen bei dieser Firma, bei der ich angefangen habe als Schreiner. Die
    hab'n dann mal jesagt, ouh, Samstag mach'n wir mal 'n Zug durch die
    Potsdamer. Na, ich sage, gut, ok, ich geh mit, nich? Na und dann hat man
    so verschiedene Etablissements kennen gelernt. Hat dann die Damen
    betrachtet, die denken, durch langsames Gehen schneller vorwärts zu
    kommen und da sagt dann eener von den Kerlen, jetzt jeh'n wir mal
    an den Winterfeldtplatz in 'ne schwule Kneipe und dann mach'n wir
    Bambule. Ok, da gehst de mal mit, weest de wenigstens, wo de hingehen
    musst. Also wir sind reingekommen in das alte Trocadero damals und
    (äh) naja, man hat sich dann also bisschen daneben benommen, hat Bier
    in den Aschenbecher gekippt, den Aschenbecher umgedreht und und
    und. Dann sind wir rausgeschmissen worden. Wir sind dann wieder
    Richtung Potsdamer jezogen und ich hab dann irgendwie mich abgesetzt,

sach, ich mag nich mehr. Bin also zurückgegangen zum Winterfeldtplatz, hab da an der Tür wieder jepocht, denk, mal seh´n, ob se mich rinlassen. Macht dann ´n älterer Herr auf und sagt, det hab ich mir jedacht, dass du nich zu den´n jehörst! Und hat mich rinjelassen, mhm. Fortan war dieses Trocadero für mich der Anlaufpunkt."

105 Interview mit Rita Thomas, "Tommy," BMH. 19.11.2016 (hereafter cited as Tommy interview). Original German: "Da ham wa ziemlich spartanisch, also wir ham uns denn vielleicht een Schnaps bestellt und ne Brause, und da 'n janzen Abend dran jesessen … Die andern ham ja Wein jetrunken und allet, aber. Oder wir ham ne Flasche Wein jetrunken, nee, 'ne Flasche nich, 'n Glas. Wenn wa mehrere warn 'ne Flasche und jeder hat denn 'n Glas abbekommen. Also it war nich so dass man sich da, man konnte sich, wie jesagt, unterhalten. Und dit war schon viel. War schon janz jut."

106 Tommy interview. Original German: "Ja, äh, da hat jemand jesacht, also ick weeß nich mehr, wer dit war, irgendwie Bekannte oder so, ick hab ja viel Leute kennenjelernt, äh: Komm doch mal mit! Jo, und da bin ich mitjegangen und habe dort mal mich umjeguckt. Da war ick det erste Mal da in so 'nem Club. Hab nur jeguckt, ja. Die ham da och jetanzt und so, aber da war ick noch zu fremd, da war ick och noch sehr jung."

107 Tommy interview.

108 Tommy interview.

109 Rudi is named as an owner of Fürstenau in Dobler, *Von anderen Ufern*. Dobler, "Kreuzberg tanzt," in Dobler, *Von anderen Ufern*, 252.

110 Kokula, *"Wir leiden nicht mehr,"* 115–17.

111 Kokula, 115–16. Original German: "Durch Bekannte habe ich nach dem Krieg von den Lokalen erfahren. Da war das Lokal in der Adalbertstraße, in Kreuzberg an der Mauer. Oben war noch ein Stockwerk, da waren dann die Heteros. Alle gingen durch den gleichen Eingang. Unten gehörte es zwei Mädchen, das waren auch schon ältere Kaliber. Die hättet ihr erleben müssen! Das war so um 60. Mit einer Kollegin sind wir mal mitgegangen. Das war so, da kamen sie damals alle noch aus Ostberlin. Die saßen da, in Anzügen, mit Fracks; dicke Zigarren geraucht. Es gab einen runden Tisch, so eine Art Stammtisch. Dann war da ein Tanzsaal, der war nicht separat, sondern am Eingang. Im Tanzsaal haben Männer gespielt, eine Männerkapelle … Plötzlich guckte ein Mädchen durch die Tür. Da haben die sich in der Wolle gehabt. Es spielen sich dann und wann ganz schöne Eifersuchtsszenen ab! Da waren wir nur zweimal, weil mir das nicht gefallen hat. Dann sind wir immer in die Fuggerstraße, da war eine Bar, „Eva und …" Die hatten eine Musikbox. Es hat mir insofern nicht gefallen, weil dort – ganz ehrlich – reiche Frauen waren. Wir konnten da ja nichts verzehren. Wir haben zwar immer unseren Martini getrunken. Dann haben wir uns beide unterhalten, aber mit anderen

bist du da nicht in Kontakt gekommen. Das war so vornehm, wir haben
da praktisch nicht mithalten können. Und in der Goethestraße war es
ziemlich dasselbe."

112 For instance, the photo of a lesbian club from Hirschfeld's *Geschlechtskunde*,
1931, reprinted on the cover of Dobler's *Von anderen Ufern*.

113 Hirschfeld, *The Homosexuality of Men and Women*, 787.

114 The quote is from my own interview with Hans-Joachim Engel, Berlin, 4
October 2017. Mr. Engel was one of Maria Borowski's interviewees for her
dissertation. Maria Borowski was extraordinarily generous in not only
letting me access some of her interview transcriptions (with the consent
of her interviewees), but also in putting me in touch with Hans-Joachim
Engel. Mr. Engel, in turn, was so generous to meet with me on multiple
occasions and share his memories. My sincere thanks go to him. Maria
Borowski's dissertation is published as *Parallelwelten: Lesbisch-schwules
Leben in der frühen DDR* (Berlin: Metropol-Verlag, 2017).

115 My own interview with Hans-Joachim Engel, Berlin, 4 October 2017.
Original German: "Das war ganz komisch, wir haben uns kennengelernt
im Kleist-Casino, und, äh, ich war ja so schockiert da, und es war der
einzige, der ran kam, der kam so nett ran, und dann hab ich mich
also, tanzen war ja übertrieben, aber auf alle Fälle, und da haben wir
uns verabredet für nächsten Sonnabend im Kleist-Casino. Und dann
aufgeschmückt und schön gemacht und so, und der kam auch, und
da passierte aber nichts. Also, wir haben uns da gut unterhalten, gut
amüsiert, alles, was weiß ich ... Und es war dann fast schon Schluß, und
sag ich, ja, was ist denn nun, ja, ich kenn noch ein Café, das hat noch
länger auf, und, ich wollt ja ganz was andres ... Hab ich gesagt, pass
mal uff. Was passiert denn jetzt, zu dir oder zu mir. Und dann hat er ein
bisschen gezögert, meint naja, wir können ja zu mir. Ja, Rudow."

116 After the fall of the Wall, Engel reconnected with this former boyfriend,
who still performs as *Travestiedame* for his friends. Engel interview, 4
October 2017.

117 Tommy interview. Original German: "In dieser Nacht warn wir drüben,
bei Rudi, Adalbertstraße. Und wir kommen, früh morgens natürlich, ne,
früh morgens um ein, zwei, kommen wir an die Grenze ... Oberbaum
sind wa rüber ... und da stehen Polizisten, da ham wa uns unterhalten,
hatten 'n kleenen (zeigt zum Kopf) Dröhnung drin, und da sagt sagt
der Polizist: Also wenn se jetz rüber jehn, denn sind se drüben. Also Sie
dürfen nie mehr hierher. Überlegen sich dit ... Naja, wir hatten ja nich die
Absicht ... ick hatte meine Tiere hier alle im Garten, ja, und mit Helli und ...
Bloß die West-Polizei hat jesagt: Sie können rüber, aber kommen nich
mehr hierher. Die warn schon informiert. Na, und seitdem kamen wa nie
wieder rüber. Dit war der letzte Tach. Naja man, so trauert man och nich

nach, wir hatten ja hier unser Leben. Bloß dit ´n bisschen, dit Weggehen, weil wa dit hier nich so hatten, hat uns jefehlt ´n bisschen, ne."

118 Engel interview, 4 October 2017.

119 Engel interview, 4 October 2017. Original German: "Ich wäre auch nicht da geblieben, erstens hatt ich ja Familie, und ich hab allen erklärt, das dauert vielleicht vier Wochen, dann mauern sie uns ein rund rum Berlin, und dann können die Sachsen nicht mehr abhauen und denn ist jut. Denn in Berlin ist ja keiner abgehauen nach dem Westen. Die konnten ja jeden Tag Oma besuchen und man konnte im Westen auch bissel arbeiten gehen oder, was weeß ich. Die Bauern haben Eier verkauft im Westen oder so. Nich. Na, und das war's, dann hab ich mir meine Dollar eingerahmt, und die hingen dann bestimmt zehn Jahre an der Wand. Das war's. Ja. Das war diese berühmte Nacht."

120 Engel interview, 4 October 2017. Original German: "Das ist das Einzigste [was schmerzhaft war], ansonsten hat mich das eigentlich gar nicht tangiert. Ich weiß gar nicht warum, ich hatte vernünftige Arbeit, ich hatte hier einen Freundeskreis. Ich hatte noch die ganze Familie. Und, öh, weiß ich nicht. Ich musste zurück auf Biegen und Brechen. Und dann musste man sich damit trösten, dass ganze Familien auseinandergerissen waren, also, ich mein, das war auch traurig, aber, so, nicht … Und ich, weiß ich nicht, also, für mich war das auch, das erste Jahr immer noch, das kann ja nicht lange gut gehen … Es waren mehrere, die so gedacht haben … Und dann muss ich sagen, wir waren ja auf der Insel der Glückseligen. Wir hatten West-Funk, wir hatten West-Fernsehen, wir waren ja auf dem Laufenden. Und wenn ich meine Freunde in Dresden oder so besucht hab, Tal der Ahnungslosen, ja."

121 Engel interview, 4 October 2017.

122 Engel interview, 4 October 2017. Original German: "Eine Dame herrschte da, Fischhändlerin, die regierte diesen Stammtisch irgendwie. Und hatte ihre Jungs da alle. Und die zogen dann im Sommer alle zwei Wochen nach Ahrenshoop. Aber richtig Tuntenclub."

123 BStU Gh 90/78 A, 111, 125–6. „ehemals lesbische Freundinnen," „Nibelungenring."

124 "Und dann gab es nachher dann nachher die Mokka-Bar im Haus Sofia. Da waren zwei Damen drin. Das war auch so Durchgangsverkehr, aber nicht hundert Prozent, aber man traf sich sag ich mal so."

125 BStU BV FfO AIM 412/70, Band P, 173–4.

126 BStU BV FfO AIM 412/70.

127 Dobler, "'Den Heten eine Kneipe wegnehmen,'" 167.

128 Teresa Tammer cites a Stasi informant in 1976 complaining about the shutdown of "Mocca Bar" at Hotel Sofia on Friedrichstraße and its replacement with an "Intershop" catering to Western tourists. Tammer, "Verräter oder Vermittler?," 115.

129 *Der Weg*'s March 1965 issue again mentions raids in Berlin, allegedly conducted to arrest "Strichjungen" and thus prevent the murder of homosexuals. Jack Argo, "Flickwerk und Stümperei," *Der Weg* 15, no. 3 (1965): 52–3.

130 Akantha, "Berlin tanzt!" *Der Kreis* 17 (September 1949): 8–10, 22.

131 Schreiben des Senators für Wirtschaft und Kredit an den Polizeipräsidenten, 2 September 1960. LAB B Rep 020 Nr. 7802. The host owned a bar on Augsburger Str. 5. The file gives no indication of whether the bar catered to a queer audience or not.

132 Antwort Polizeipräsident an Senator, 13 September 1960, LAB B Rep 020 Nr. 7802.

133 Polizeipräsident in Berlin, Aktennotiz Schankwirtschaft in Berlin 44, Jansastr. 11, Erlaubnisträger: Peter Raudonis, 24.10.1963; LAB B Rep 020 Nr. 7802. Information in a Stasi file suggests that Jansa-Hütte was under the direction of a homosexual owner from 1954 to 1958 too. BStU Gh 90/878 A, 178.

134 Polizeipräsident in Berlin, Aktennotiz Schankwirtschaft in Berlin 44.

135 B.Z., "Razzia ohne Voranmeldung," 16 February 1967. Newspaper clipping in LAB B Rep 020 Nr. 7802.

136 The argument that nightlife was an important economic asset in a city that lacked other attractions was not new. For instance, it was used against stricter policing of *Die goldene Reitbahn*, a bar rumoured to be host to sexual encounters, in a 1952 meeting of the city's bar council, where a representative of the Senate Department of Traffic and Business claimed that such nightspots were necessary because the city had nothing to offer culturally. Schankbeirat, Protokoll vom 22. 7. 1952, LAB B Rep 020 Nr. 6976.

137 "Treffpunkt Berlin," *Der Spiegel*, no. 34 (17 August 1965): 49.

138 Protokoll Vorbesprechung der ersten Sitzung der Rowdy-Kommission/2. Runde, 18 January 1966, LAB B Rep 020 Nr. 7803–7804.

139 According to the police, "Crazy Horse" had been transitioning to a hangout of "homosexuals, *Strichjungen* and transvestites" in recent months. Protokoll über die 1. Sitzung der Rowdykommission 2. Runde, inkl. Beschreibung der Vorfälle, die zum Senatsbeschluss führten, 15 February 1966, LAB B Rep 020 Nr. 7803–7804.

140 Protokoll über die 1. Sitzung der Rowdykommission 2. Runde

141 Schreiben PolPräs an Senator für Wirtschaft re: Verbesserungsvorschlag Bearbeitung von Anträgen auf Schankerlaubnis, 12 May 1969. LAB B Rep 020 Nr. 7802.

142 Protokoll 3. Sitzung der Rowdy-Kommission/2, Runde, 12 April 1966. LAB B Rep 020 Nr. 7803–7804 (hereafter Protokoll 3. Sitzung der Rowdy-Kommission).

143 Protokoll 3. Sitzung der Rowdy-Kommission.

144 Protokoll Besprechung Senat, Bezirksämter, Polizei zur Bekämpfung des Rowdytums in Schanklokalen, 21 October 1966, LAB B Rep 020 Nr. 7803–7804 (hereafter Protokoll Besprechung Senat).
145 Protokoll Besprechung Senat.
146 Protokoll Besprechung Senat.
147 Protokoll Besprechung Senat.
148 Protokoll Besprechung Senat. A similar, though even more detailed list of prohibited behaviours was sent to Elli of Elli's Bier-Bar in 1965 by Police Chief Sangmeister himself. Cited by Dobler, "Ein Neuanfang, der keiner war," in Dobler, *Von anderen Ufern*, 235–7.
149 Protokoll Besprechung Senat.
150 "Nachtleben soll gesäubert werden… in Berlin." *Der Kreis* 35, no. 7 (1967): 11.
151 Schreiben des Senators für Wirtschaft an Bezirksämter, Abteilung Wirtschaft, 17.11.1966, LAB B Rep 020 Nr. 7799–7800.
152 Fernschreiben Senator für Wirtschaft an Bezirksämter von Berlin, Abt. Wirtschaft, 2 February 1967. LAB B Rep 020 Nr. 7802.
153 *B.Z.*, "Razzia ohne Voranmeldung," 16 February 1967. LAB B Rep 020 Nr. 7802.
154 "Herr K. erklärte gegenüber dem Polizeibeamten, daß er wohl ein neuer Beamter sei und deshalb nicht wisse, daß die Sittenpolizei gegen verschlossene Türen nichts einzuwenden habe." Schreiben Polizeipräsident an Bezirksamt Schöneberg, 2.11.67. LAB B Rep 020 Nr. 7802.
155 Bericht des R214 über Jansa-Hütte, 7 July 1967. LAB B Rep 020 Nr. 7802.
156 Durchschrift Polizeipräsident an das Bezirksamt Neukölln betr. Klingelbars im Bezirk Neukölln, 25 January 1967; Berichte des R214 über Jansa-Hütte, 20 March 1967 and 7 July 1967; Schreiben PolPrä an Senator für Wirtschaft zur Jansa-Hütte, 19 February 1968. LAB B Rep 020 Nr. 7802. The outcome of this dispute is unknown, unfortunately.
157 Antwort PolPräs an BA Charlottenburg, 22 January 1968. My italics. B Rep 020 Nr. 7802. Original German: "Das oben bezeichnete Lokal ist nach wie vor ein Treffpunkt homosexueller Personen, in dem im wesentlichen männliche Gäste verkehren. Trotz wiederholter Kontrollen und Observationen konnte ein strafbares Verhalten in dem Lokal selbst nicht festgestellt werden. Bei einer Kontrolle am 12.10.67 wurde gesprächsweise von den Kriminalbeamten gehört, daß sich am 17.9.67 ein betrunkener Transvestit ausgezogen haben soll. Bei einer anderen Observation am 5.12.67 wurde durch die Kriminalbeamten lediglich festgestellt, daß sie von anwesenden älteren Männern, die an der Bar saßen, „abschätzig taxiert" wurden, wie es in vergleichsweise anderen Lokalen, in denen Homosexuelle verkehren, gleichfalls üblich ist, wenn jüngere männliche Gäste kommen und noch unbekannt

sind. Bei einer weiteren Observation am 12.12.67 beobachteten die Kriminalbeamten, daß zwei männliche Gäste gemeinsam das Lokal verließen, bei denen es sich dem Eindruck nach um ein homosexuell veranlagtes Pärchen handelte … Ein anderer männlicher Gast im „Ritzhaupt" wurde von einem Kriminalbeamten als partnersuchender Homosexueller wiedererkannt. Während der Beobachtungszeit wurde auch festgestellt, daß wiederholt Männer nach Schallplattenmusik tanzten. Diese Wahrnehmungen sind zwar noch keine strafbaren Handlungen, begründen jedoch den Verdacht, daß auch in dem Lokal „Ritzhaupt" Homosexuelle zur Partnersuche weilen. Aus diesem Grunde wäre es unumgänglich, genau zu prüfen, ob die unanfechtbare Auflage aufgehoben werden soll und damit möglicherweise ein Präzedenzfall geschaffen wird."

158 Zurückweisung des Widerspruchs der Wirtin des "Le Punch" gegen die ihr erteilte Auflage, 21 September 1967, LAB B Rep 020 Nr. 7802 (hereafter cited as Zurückweisung des Widerspruchs).

159 Zurückweisung des Widerspruchs.

160 Letter from police president to Senator for the Economy, 2 April 1970. B Rep 020 Nr. 7802.

161 Rechtsgrundlagen für die Durchführung polizeilicher Kontrollen in Gast- und Schankwirtschaften, insbesondere in den sog. Klingelbars. LAB B Rep 020 Nr. 7802. Original German: "Erfahrungsgemäß sind manche Lokale Sammelpunkte von Homosexuellen, Lesbierinnen, Strichjungen und sonstigen asozialen oder kriminellen Personen. Von solchen Gastwirtschaften gehen deshalb Gefahren für die öffentliche Sicherheit und Ordnung aus, denn sie sind häufig Ausgangspunkte oder Tatort krimineller Handlungen und geben auch in gesundheits- und sittenpolizeilicher Hinsicht zu Polizeimaßnahmen Anlaß."

162 Letter from police president to Charlottenburg district office, 2 November 1967. LAB B Rep 020 Nr. 7803–7804 (herafter cited as Letter to Charlottenburg district office, 2 November 1967).

163 Letter to Charlottenburg district office, 2 November 1967. Original German: "Homosexualität von Frauen ist an sich nicht strafbar. Dennoch unterliegt auch dieses Lokal der ständigen Überwachung, denn es ist auch bei diesem Personenkreis nicht auszuschließen, daß möglicherweise Straftaten begangen werden … Es besteht durchaus die Möglichkeit, daß in einem Lokal mit diesem Charakter sich auch Frauen oder Mädchen aufhalten, die gesuchte Personen sein könnten oder die sich auf Grund ihres Alters dort nicht aufhalten dürfen."

164 Letter from police president to Charlottenburg district office, 12 December 1969, B Rep 020 Nr. 7803–7804.

165 Whisnant, *Male Homosexuality*, 30.

3. Passing Through, Trespassing, Passing in Public Spaces

1 Eberhardt Brucks, Letter to Guy Morris, 18 December 1949, SMB. Original German: "Oh geliebter Guy, Du bist der einzige Mensch um den ich Tränen vergossen habe. In Lugano und hier in Berlin. Die Tränen kamen mir in die Augen als ich Dich im Omnibus wegfahren sah und ich war froh, dass ich wenigstens in der S-Bahn meine Fassung bewahren konnte. Hier zu Haus kann ich es nicht mehr. Und Mutti will immer wissen ob ich etwas zu essen haben möchte, anstatt mich allein zu lassen."

2 Eberhardt Brucks, Letter to Guy Morris, 19 December 1949, SMB. Original German: "Als wir uns gestern im Wartesaal und vor dem Omnibus küssten wurde es mir noch einmal unheimlich klar. Als ich Dich im Omnibus verschwinden sah konnte ich die Tränen nicht mehr zurückhalten."

3 Eberhardt Brucks, Letter to Guy Morris, 16 January 1950, SMB. Original German: "Liebling ich habe heute Nacht wieder einmal von Dir geträumt. Wir sassen in einem Restaurant und assen. Auf einmal nahmst Du deine Hand und streicheltest die meine die auf dem Tische lag, alle Leute guckten uns an und als ich alle uns ansehen sah, nahm ich Deinen Kopf an mich und küsste Dich auf den Mund. – Es war so wunderbar wieder Deinen Mund zu fühlen dass ich dadurch überglücklich wurde."

4 The letters were sent when Morris, after a carefree, passionate period spent together in Berlin, had to go home to New York and his wife for the holidays. While they were apart, they exchanged letters of love and longing, which Brucks collected and bequeathed to Berlin's Gay Museum as part of his voluminous collection of artworks, correspondence, magazines, and his apartment. On Eberhardt Brucks, his life and collection, see the catalogue of the 2008 exhibition "Eberhardt Brucks" at Schwules Museum, Berlin. Schlüter, Steinle, and Sternweiler, *Eberhardt Brucks*, 149.

5 For female prostitutes as understudied subjects of lesbian history, see Dobler, "Unzucht und Kuppelei." Steffi Brüning notes that Stasi files on GDR prostitutes often mention lesbian relationships. Brüning, "Verstecken, Verheimlichen, Verleugnen." Andrew I. Ross has suggested that historians' separation of male homosexuality and female prostitution, two phenomena that authorities have archived together, is an expression of "overreliance on the modern sexual identity categories that serve as our point of departure." He suggests that "instead, we should approach the archive without identifying with it in order to formulate a vision of the past that may or may not reflect our own sexual organization." Ross, "Sex in the Archives," 267.

6 Evans, *Life among the Ruins*, 103. See also her article on "Bahnhof Boys."

7 Klaus Born, interview by Michael Bochow and Michael Jähme, 5 December 2013, Archiv der anderen Erinnerungen, Bundesstiftung Magnus Hirschfeld, Berlin; Transkription Dennis Nill. In my translation, I try to transmit Born's diction. He renders conversations in direct speech and at times uses elements of Berlin dialect. To convey the colloquial tone of the conversation, I translate his frequent use of "ja" as filler word as "yeah" or "well," not as the affirmative answer word "yes." Original German: "Dann war … September. Dann hab ich einen kennengelernt. So in der Nähe von der Gedächtniskirche. Das war auf der Straße aber. Der muss entweder er war am Zoo gewesen sein – hat nichts gekriegt. Oder er war sonst wo her – nichts gekriegt. Jedenfalls: Die Blicke gewesen, von uns beiden. Treu wie wir so sind. Gelächelt. Waren dann auf Male ganz schnell 'n Paar."

8 Zoo train station, though no longer a stop on transregional train lines, continues to serve as a site for commercial sex between men. Recently, Rosa von Praunheim has explored its role as a site of sexual transactions between men in the film *Die Jungs vom Bahnhof Zoo* (2011).

9 Klaus Born interview. Original German: "Wo gehen wir hin? Sag: Bei mir geht's nicht. Ich wohn in einem Hotel. In Neukölln. Und die Kneipen, ja, da könn' wir auch nichts machen … Sagt er: Bei mir geht's auch nich. Ich wohne zur Untermiete. Ich sag: Typisch Berlin. Alles wohnt hier zur Untermiete. Ja, sagt er: Das is' aber so. Du kriegst keine Wohnung hier. Kuck mal hier: Is' doch alles kaputt. (einatmen) Ja, was machen wir denn da? Ja, ich kenn' nen schönen Parkplatz. Da is' keine Lampe. Da kann keiner reinkucken. Und der is' schön groß und frei. Und es is' kein Auto da. Na, is gut. Machen wir doch. Kantstraße … Jedenfalls sind wir darauf gefahren. Der war wirklich dunkel. Der hat aber schon in der Kantstraße das Licht ausgeschaltet. Sagt er: Ich dat auswendig. Ich weeß genau wo ich mir hinzustellen hab'. Und oben fuhr die S-Bahn lang."

10 Klaus Born interview. Original German: "Dann ham' wir so'n bisschen rumgefummelt. Und noch 'n bisschen rumgefummelt. Ja, dann haben wir die Sitze richtig hingebracht. Damit man richtig Bumsen kann. Ja, und dann ging das Bumsen los. Dann war'n wir so richtig schön dabei, ja. Und dann kam der nächste Schock. An vier Stellen große Taschenlampen ging auf Male an. Vier Stellen. (einatmen) Ich hab nichts sagen können. Nich? Ja, dann hört mal erst auf da mit dem Bumsen, hab ich irgendwie wat gehört. So, und dann kommt mal raus. Dann mussten wir uns erstmal anziehen. Wir waren ja nackig dadrin. Wir waren bei der Nummer! Ja. Was waren das? Waren Bullen. Polizei. (einatmen) Ja. Dann stand ich wieder da. Bei der Polizei. Ja. (einatmen) Und dann musste er den Wagen abschließen und stehen lassen. Und dann mussten wir mitkommen. Dann stand / standen auf der Straße schon die Wagen da …

Diese Autos mit den / mit den Gittern. Diese Kastenwagen. Und dann da reingeschubst worden. Ich wusste nich warum. Ich wusste wirklich nich warum. Und dann wurden wir zur Keithstraße gefahren ... Da is ja dieses Kriminalgebäude. Ja, da rinngefahren. Ich hab geheult. Ich wusste nich was ich machen sollte. Ich wusste / wusste gar nich warum ich da bin. Ich wusste es einfach nich. Nich? Für mich war das was ganz Normales wenn man da 'ne Nummer schiebt. Ja. Und dann ging das auf Male los. Sie haben so und so. Ja. Paragraf 175. Sie sind vorläufig festgenommen. Sie haben ja keinen festen Wohnsitz. Ich sag: doch, ich wohn' im Hotel Süden. Könn'se doch fragen. Das ist kein fester Wohnsitz. In Ihrem Ausweis steht was von Benninghausen. Ja, dann stand schon der nächste Wagen da. Auch so n Ding. Und da waren natürlich noch mehr, die sie eingesammelt haben. Von, von andern Sachen. Oder was weiß ich. Und dann durften wir da rein. Und dann ging's nach Moabit."

11 Klaus Born interview. Original German: "Westdeutschland musste aufpassen. Hier / in Berlin / brauchste gar nich aufpassen."

12 Orest Kapp, interview by Andreas Pretzel and Janina Rieck, 15 October 2014. Archiv der anderen Erinnerungen. Bundesstiftung Magnus Hirschfeld. Berlin.

13 Orest Kapp interview. Kapp's stress on some words is indicated by bold text formatting. Original German: "Ja, also die Zeit vorher in Berlin ... es war nur Katastrophe immer. Man musste nur aufpassen, sich ja nicht falsch zu bewegen, zu gehen, zu sprechen. [–] Und es hat mich, es hat mich **Jahre**, wenn nicht, mindestens fünf, sechs Jahre hat das mich gekostet, dass ich mich **männlich** verhalte [–] dass ich **männlichen** Schrittes gehe [–] dass ich männliche Bewegungen mache, dass ich mich männlich unterhalte [–] äh, so dass ich auch in irgendsoner Pinte oder so einer Kneipe glatt durchgehe als **Mann** [–] Ja, das warn meine große, mei-, meine absolute Muss, das war mein großes Muss. Das **muss** ich tun, das muss ich schaffen, dann kann ich überleben."

14 Butler, "Performative Acts," 215. Italics in original.

15 Butler, 215.

16 Fritz Schmehling, interview by Michael Bochow and Karl-Heinz Steinle, 24 January 2015. Archiv der anderen Erinnerungen. Bundesstiftung Magnus Hirschfeld, Berlin. Original German: "Wenn man dann am Wochenende in der City war und musste dann irgendwann mal wieder nach Spandau fahren, da war also für mich immer so die vorletzte Straßenbahn (äh) in der Kantstraße die 75 und die 76. Und dann hab ich jedes Mal noch mal so ´n Halt gemacht am Amtsgericht Charlottenburg, da ist ein (schwärmt) wunderbares Holzhäuschen."

17 Fritz Schmehling interview. Original German: "Ich steh eines Abends drinne, denke, vielleicht kommt noch wat, vielleicht kommt nix mehr. Uff

eemal jeht die Türe uff, kommt ´n Bulle rin, so im weißen Verkehrsmantel. Ick mein´n einjepackt, da sacht er, lass draußen, wir mach´n des zusammen. (lacht) Jetzt hab ich erst mal Herzklopfen jekriegt. Ich denke, is des jetzt ´n echter Bulle? Es war ´n echter Bulle. (lacht) Meine letzte Straßenbahn war natürlich weg (lacht). Ich musste dann natürlich rüber laufen in die Otto-Suhr-Allee, und da fuhr die Straßenbahn nach Hakenfelde. Und dann bin ich von Hakenfelde nachts noch bis in die Heerstraße jetrampt. (lacht) So geht ´s, wenn man gierig is. (lacht) Es war eins von meinen Erlebnissen, die sehr, sehr haften geblieben sind."

18 Kriminalpolizei W.-B. Sittlichkeitsdelikte, Stellungnahme zur öffentlichen Bedürfnisanstalt am Reuterplatz, 16 January 1956, 33.05 1, PHS.

19 §15b) cited by Jens Dobler. Dobler, "Ein Neuanfang, der keiner war," in Dobler, *Von anderen Ufern*, 236.

20 "§183." In 1969, disenfranchisement was struck out as part of the Great Criminal Law Reform.

21 Orest Kapp interview. Original German: "Das war damals, als ich da mit dem Freund zusammen überrascht wurde [–], wie wir uns, naja, ich will nicht ins Detail gehen, sagen wir einfach, wie wir uns sexuell verhalten hatten. Und äh, ja, die Polizisten waren nicht sehr freundlich … Ich habe also Bauchschläge gekriegt, so den Arm, den Ellenbogen in den Bauch gerammt gekriegt, oder, äh, mein Kopf wurde runtergestoßen und dann mit 'm Knie wieder zurückgestossen, es war nicht sehr freundlich mit uns. Sie haben uns also, äh, genau gezeigt, was sie von uns dachten, was wir sind, eben, so wie ich immer wieder darauf komme ist: du schwule Sau, was machst du da. Äh, du gehörst, gehörst hingerichtet, du gehörst vergast, du-, was hat man mir nicht alles gesagt, was ich gehöre."

22 Orest Kapp interview. Original German: "Die Polizei hat uns halt eben provoziert. Ja, sie wollte, dass wir uns wehren oder dass wir widersprechen oder so, und dann haben sie eben ihre, ihre Macht ge-, gezeigt."

23 In a 1957 file note, the following sites are mentioned for regular patrol: "Toilette Reichsbahndirektionsgebäude, Volkspark Wilmersdorf, Bahnhofstoilette S Gesundbrunnen (Bahnsteig), Hinterwand U-Bahn Innsbrucker Platz, S Steglitz, Düppelmarkt Steglitz, Preußenpark Wilmersdorf." Vermerk der E I (S) über zu kontrollierende Toiletten bei Nachtstreifen, 5 November 1957, 55.25, PHS.

24 VP Berlin, Quartalsbericht für das I. Quartal 1951, 10 April 1951, C Rep 303 Nr. 131, LAB; VP Berlin, Analyse über die Cliquenbildung im demokratischen Sektor von Gross-Berlin, 28 February 1952, C Rep 303 Nr. 137, LAB.

25 VP Berlin, Quartalsbericht für das I. Quartal 1952, 1952, C Rep 303 Nr. 132, LAB. Original German: "In der VPI/K Mitte (Bahnhofshalle

Bahnhof Friedrichstrasse) hat sich die Strichjungentätigkeit wiederum als Schwerpunkt herauskristallisiert. Es fanden zwei Großrazzien statt, die allerdings das Ziel haben, die Mördern an Homosexuellen zu ermitteln. Gleichzeitig wurden aber mit diesen Aktionen Strichjungen der Arbeitsgruppe C 4 Mitte zur intensiven Prüfung übergeben. Aus diesen Einsätzen resultierend wurden Massnahmen vorbereitet, um in Verbindung mit der Trapo bis zum 1. Mai den Bahnhof von Strichjungen zu säubern."

26 VP Berlin, Quartalsbericht für das II. Quartal 1952, 1952, C Rep 303 Nr. 132, LAB.

27 VP Berlin, Bericht über die Arbeit der Untersuchungsabteilung PdVP Berlin, 7 May 1953, C Rep 303 Nr. 137, LAB.

28 VP Berlin, Bericht über die Arbeit der Untersuchungsabteilung PdVP Berlin, 7 May 1953, C Rep 303 Nr. 137, LAB.

29 VP Berlin, Besonderheiten in der Cliquenbildung in den VP-Inspektionen, 2 May 1957, C 303 Nr. 26, LAB.

30 Lindenberger, "'Asoziale Lebensweise,'" 230.

31 Korzilius, "Asoziale" und "Parasiten" im Recht der SBZ/DDR, 1.

32 Lindenberger, "'Asoziale Lebensweise,'" 238.

33 Korzilius, "Asoziale" und "Parasiten" im Recht der SBZ/DDR, 415.

34 Korzilius, 291–2, 301, 617–18. The number of sentences for §249 rose from around 4,000 in the years after 1968 to 14,000 in 1973, in preparation of the World Youth Games, and decreased to 12,000 in 1982. At the end of the GDR, almost a quarter of prison inmates were incarcerated under §249. Lindenberger, "'Asoziale Lebensweise,'" 247.

35 Kriminalpolizei West-Berlin Referat E1 Raub Einbruch, Bericht betr. Vorfälle im Zusammenhang mit Homosexuellen, 10 September 1958, 55.25, PHS. The sites mentioned are Hohenzollernplatz, Olivaer Platz, Volkspark Wilmersdorf, and Preußenpark.

36 Vernehmungsprotokoll, 19 July 1955, MfS AU 309/55 Bd. 2, BStU.

37 Klaus Born interview. Original German: "Ja, und dann hab ich unge- / nich ganz ein Jahr ungefähr im Untergrund gelebt. Dann hab ich versucht – weil ich ja kein Geld mehr hatte – im Untergrund heißt: Ich hab vom einen Bett zum andern gehüpft, so."

38 Klaus Born interview. Original German: "Dann hatt' ich mal eine kennengelernt. Manuela hieß die. Bei der hab ich / () schlappe zwei Monate sogar gewohnt. Ich musste aber immer auf die aufpassen. Weil, die hatte immer Pech gehabt. Die wurde immer zusammengeschlagen. Sehr oft. Weil sie immer im Fummel rumgeloofen is'."

39 "§183," 259. In 1969, disenfranchisement was struck out as part of the Great Criminal Law Reform.

40 "§360."

41 Herrn, *Schnittmuster*, 65–6.
42 Herrn, 165. Herrn, "'Ich habe wohl Freude an Frauenkleidern," 60.
43 Klöppel, *XXOXY Ungelöst*, 551–2. In the East Berlin police files at LAB, I have found no further mention of *Transvestitenscheine*.
44 PHS D K.KK Bd. 1. Searching for "trans*" in the East Berlin People's Police files at Landesarchiv did not produce any results. The People's Police files at the Police Historical Collection Berlin are not searchable or accessible.
45 Klöppel, *XXOXY Ungelöst*, 548–84; Silva, *Negotiating the Borders*, 55–105.
46 Schreiben der Abteilung II an den Leiter der Abteilung K, Polizeipräsident West-Berlin, 10 Juni 1950, PHS D K.KK Bd 1.
47 Schreiben der Abteilung II an den Leiter der Abteilung K, Polizeipräsident West-Berlin, 10 Juni 1950, PHS D K.KK Bd 1.
48 Schreiben der Abteilung II an den Leiter der Abteilung K, Polizeipräsident West-Berlin, 10 Juni 1950, PHS D K.KK Bd 1.
49 Schreiben der Abteilung II an den Leiter der Abteilung K, Polizeipräsident West-Berlin, 10 Juni 1950, PHS D K.KK Bd 1.
50 Schreiben der Abteilung II an den Leiter der Abteilung K, Polizeipräsident West-Berlin, 10 Juni 1950, PHS D K.KK Bd 1.
51 Stellungnahme Abt. K – K.J. M II GB, 19. Juni 1950, PHS D K.KK Bd 1.
52 Schreiben des Polizeipräsidiums München an das Polizeipräsidium Berlin, 9 Juni 1952, PHS D K.KK Bd 1.
53 Herrn, "'Ich habe wohl Freude an Frauenkleidern,'" 60.
54 Response to Polizeipräsidium München, 20 Juni 1952, PHS D K.KK Bd 1 (hereafter Response to Polizeipräsidium München). The response also mentioned that the practice continued a policy followed by the Berlin police until 1942.
55 Response to Polizeipräsidium München.
56 Herrn, "'Ich habe wohl Freude an Frauenkleidern,'" 61.
57 Herrn, *Schnittmuster*, 59; see also Sutton, "From Sexual Inversion to Trans," 192.
58 Response to Polizeipräsidium München.
59 Letter to police president, 13 April 1960, PHS D K.KK Bd 1.
60 Letter to police president, 13 April 1960, PHS D K.KK Bd 1.
61 Briefentwurf Mai 1960, PHS D K.KK Bd 1.
62 Alternativer Briefentwurf Mai 1960, PHS D K.KK Bd 1.
63 Cited in Klöppel, *XXOXY Ungelöst*, 566, as well as in Silva, *Negotiating the Borders*, 94.
64 Police President in Berlin, Department K. Letter to the Federal Criminal Office. PHS Berlin.
65 Zu Punkt 5 der Tagesordnung: Ausstellung von Reisepässen – Verwendung von Lichtbildern bei Transvestiten. Excerpt from minutes of

the meeting of the working group of the leaders of the state and federal criminal offices. Police Historical Collection Berlin.

66 These are all in file PHS D K.KK Bd 1 at the Police Historical Collection Berlin.

67 Brecht, "Günter Litfin," 37.

68 Until the construction of the Wall, 53,000 East Berliners worked in the West and 12,270 West Berliners in the East. Ribbe, *Berlin 1945–2000*, 120.

69 This was regulated in the 1954 Passport Law (*Passgesetz*) and the 1957 Changed Passport Law (*Passänderungsgesetz*). Vormbaum, *Das Strafrecht der Deutschen Demokratischen Republik*, 212–13.

70 Brecht, "Günter Litfin," 37.

71 Dieter Berner, "Wie die SED-Propaganda," 38. See also Evans, "Decriminalization, Seduction, and 'Unnatural Desire,'" 553–77.

72 "Warnung mißachtet," *Neue Zeit*, 25 August 1961. Quoted in Berner, "Wie die SED-Propaganda," 38.

73 Berner, "Wie die SED-Propaganda," 40.

74 "Frontstadtpresse macht Kriminelle zu Helden," *Berliner Zeitung*, 31 August 1961. Quoted in Berner, "Wie die SED-Propaganda," 38–9.

75 Ermittlungsauftrag Litfin, Günter, 25 August 1961. BStU MfS ZAIG Nr. 526.

76 BStU MfS ZAIG Nr. 510.

77 LAB B Rep 069 Nr. 307.

78 LAB B Rep 069 Nr. 307.

79 Schreiben des Generalstaatsanwalts beim Landesgericht an Jugendstrafanstalt Plötzensee, 9 November 1957, LAB B Rep 069 Nr. 307.

80 Brecht, "Günter Litfin," Chronik der Mauer: Todesopfer. The project is a cooperation of the Federal Foundation for Political Education, the public radio station Deutschlandfunk, and the Center for Contemporary History Potsdam.

81 *LIFE Magazine*, 1 September 1961, 37.

82 Dr. K, "Mordhetze aus der Frontstadt," *Neues Deutschland*, 2 September 1961. Quoted in Berner, "Wie die SED-Propaganda," 39. Horst Wessel, a young SA leader, was shot in his Berlin apartment by a man who was both a Communist and a pimp on 14 January 1930 and died from the injuries. His death was immediately characterized as political murder by the NSDAP, whereas the KPD portrayed it as a deadly conflict between pimps. Wessel was dating a woman who offered sex for pay. According to Daniel Siemens, it is impossible to confirm or eliminate the pimp thesis. Siemens, *Horst Wessel*, 27, 106.

83 GDR television recorded West German programs as a reservoir for counterpropaganda, and *Der schwarze Kanal* had primary access to the

recordings. Dittmar, *Feindliches Fernsehen*, 200–1. More on *Der schwarze Kanal* in Caspar, *DDR-Lexikon*, 70–2.

84 Karl-Eduard v. Schnitzler, Sendemanuskript Der Schwarze Kanal, 27.8.1962. Deutsches Rundfunkarchiv Babelsberg, E065-02-04/0001 TSig. 128.
85 Berner, "Wie die SED-Propaganda."
86 Volker, "Hinter der Mauer," *Der Kreis* 31, no. 1 (1963): 8–9.
87 Volker, "Hinter," 8.
88 Volker, 8.
89 Volker, 8.
90 Volker, 8.
91 Volker, 9.
92 Volker, 9.
93 Volker, 9.
94 Volker, 9.
95 Horst, "Ein Fehlgriff der Redaktion?" *Der Kreis* 31, no. 3 (1963): 6–7.
96 Horst, "Ein Fehlgriff," 6.
97 Horst, 7.
98 Horst, 7.
99 Horst, 7.
100 Horst, 7.
101 Klaus, "Letter to the editor," *Der Kreis* 31, no. 4 (1963): 4.
102 Klaus, "Letter," 4.
103 Volker, "Response to Horst's letter to the editor," *Der Kreis* 31, no. 4 (1963): 5.
104 Volker, "Response," 5.
105 "Rolf" was the pseudonym of Karl Meier, long-time publisher of *Der Kreis*. Kennedy, *Der Kreis/Le Cercle/The Circle.*
106 Rolf, "Response to Horst's letter," *Der Kreis* 31, no. 4 (1963): 5.
107 Rolf, "Response," 5.
108 Rolf C., "Letter to the editor," *Der Kreis* 31, no. 5 (1963): 6–7.
109 Horst, "Letter to the editor," *Der Kreis* 31, no. 5 (1963): 7–8.
110 Rolf, "Ein Nachwort zur Diskussion," *Der Kreis* 31, no. 5 (1963): 11.
111 Marion Detjen, "Die Mauer," 396.
112 Evans, *Life among the Ruins*, 19–20.
113 Brecht, "Günter Litfin."
114 Brecht, "Günter Litfin."
115 Jürgen Litfin, *Tod durch fremde Hand*, 50–1.
116 Litfin, *Tod durch fremde Hand*, 53.
117 Litfin, 48–9.
118 Litfin, 69–70.
119 Litfin, 69–70.
120 Litfin, 124–5.

4. Bubis behind Bars: Prisons as Queer Spaces

1 Tommy did not remember her exact age. She was sentenced to youth custody and was thus not of legal age at the time of sentencing. In the GDR, the legal age was lowered from 21 to 18 on 22 May 1950. Tommy was born in 1931; hence her incarceration occurred before 1952.
2 Rita "Tommy" Thomas, interview by Karl-Heinz Steinle and Babette Reicherdt, 19 November 2016. Archiv der anderen Erinnerungen. Bundesstiftung Magnus Hirschfeld. Berlin; Transkription Janina Rieck.
3 Hirschfeld, *Berlins Drittes Geschlecht*; Marhoefer, "Lesbianism, Transvestism, and the Nazi State"; Lybeck, *Desiring Emancipation*; Sutton, *The Masculine Woman*; Plötz, "Bubis und Damen."
4 An analysis of men's prisons as queer spaces would represent another crucial contribution to queer German history. A first step in this direction has recently been undertaken by Maria Bormuth's study of men imprisoned under §175 in the Wolfenbüttel prison. Bormuth, *Ein Mann, der mit einem anderen Mann Unzucht treibt*. Marcus Velke, co-author of the recent research project on the persecution and repression of homosexuals in postwar Hesse, has also pointed to the lack of research on men's imprisonment because of §175 and has included a short section on male homosexuals in the Dieburg prison. Plötz and Velke, *Aufarbeitung von Verfolgung und Repression*, 190–2. The 2021 film *Grosse Freiheit* offers a fictionalized treatment of the continuity of the criminalization in incarceration of gay men.
5 Foucault, *Discipline and Punish*, 304.
6 Foucault, 304.
7 Kunzel, *Criminal Intimacy*, 4–5.
8 Kunzel, 94–103, 98.
9 Kunzel, 2.
10 Kunzel, 8–9.
11 For history, Bormuth's study mentioned above is a rare exception. In his book on Weimar and Nazi prisons, Nikolaus Wachsmann does not systematically analyse sex in prison. His study includes multiple references that would merit further exploration, however, such as criminal-biological investigations of prison inmates during the Weimar Republic or the situation of homosexual prisoners during Nazism. Wachsmann, *Hitler's Prisons*. An important exception is Barth, "Relationships and Sexuality of Imprisoned Men." On the lack of studies of sexuality in West German prisons, see Döring, "Sexualität im Gefängnis."
12 Insa Eschebach has suggested that the homophobia expressed by former inmates represents a condensed form of the social stigma attached to

female homosexuality since the late nineteenth century. Eschebach, "Homophobie, Devianz und weibliche Homosexualität," 65. Anna Hájková has pointed to the significance of sexual barter in the camps but also of sex as a means to experience "physical pleasure." She has noted, too, that continuing homophobia and the particularly transgressive nature of sex between women, and sex between camp inmates and guards, have left stories of queer sex during the Holocaust untold. Hájková, "Den Holocaust queer erzählen," 88; Hájková, "Sexual Barter in Times of Genocide"; Hájková, *The Last Ghetto*.

13 I am referring to Dagmar Herzog's chapter titles "The Fragility of Heterosexuality" and "Desperately Seeking Normality." Herzog, *Sex after Fascism*.

14 Women's prisons in nineteenth-century France were also organized by gender and kinship, suggesting that these practices have a much longer history. O'Brien, "The Prison on the Continent," 209.

15 Kunzel, *Criminal Intimacy*, 121.

16 Kennedy and Davis, *Boots of Leather, Slippers of Gold*.

17 Kennedy and Davis, *Boots of Leather, Slippers of Gold*, 6.

18 Email to author from Rainer Hoffschildt, 30 October 2018.

19 Hoffschildt, "Statistik der Kriminalisierung."

20 Berndl, "Zeiten der Bedrohung," 21.

21 Orest Kapp, interview by Andreas Pretzel and Janina Rieck, 15 October 2014. Archiv der anderen Erinnerungen, Bundesstiftung Magnus Hirschfeld, Berlin (hereafter cited as Kapp interview, Archiv der anderen Erinerungen).

22 Kapp interview, Archiv der anderen Erinnerungen. Original German: "Und ich hab dann immer, ich hab mich natürlich geschämt im Gefängnis zu sein, vor allen Dingen als Homosexueller, also hab ich immer gesagt, ich hab, äh, irgendwas Kriminelles getan und bin denn in U-Haft gekommen."

23 Sex for safety is one of the motivations enumerated by scholar of prison sexuality Brenda V. Smith. The others are sex for pleasure, trade, procreation, freedom, transgression, and love. Smith, "Analyzing Prison Sex," 114–16.

24 Kapp interview, Archiv der anderen Erinnerungen. Original German: "Interviewerin: Hatten Sie Probleme in der Untersuchungshaft? Orest Kapp: Äh, Gott sei Dank nicht, denn der Boss von der Zelle, wo ich war, äh, war eben der Boss, und der hat mich unter seine Fittiche genommen, sagen wir mal so ausgedrückt, ja. Ich war also sein Sex-Partner. Aber dafür bin ich von den anderen verschont geblieben."

25 Klaus Born, interview by Michael Bochow and Michael Jähme, 5 December 2013. Archiv der anderen Erinnerungen, Bundesstiftung

Magnus Hirschfeld, Berlin; Transkription Dennis Nill (hereafter cited as
Born interview, Archiv der anderen Erinnerungen). Original German:
"Und dann in der obersten Etage hab ich dann mein Zimmer gehabt. Eine
so genannte Einzelzelle. Es war nichts drin. Es war nur das Bett, ein Tisch,
ein Stühlchen und das Plumpsklosett. Und das war's. Und 'n bisschen
Wasser da. ((einatmen)) … Jetzt hab ich dadrin gesessen. Eine Woche.
Zwei Wochen. Drei Wochen. Das waren bestimmt (beinahe?) sieben /
ich würde sagen: Sieben, acht Wochen. Wie lang das jetzt genau war?
Ich weiß es nich. ((einatmen)) … Und in der Zeit wo ich dadrin war. Ich
habe keine Musik gehabt. Ich hab nichts zu lesen gehabt. Ich hab nichts
zu schreiben gehabt. Nichts. Ich durfte auch nichts machen. Es war wie
ein / wie sagt man das? Ähm, äh, war 'ne Einzelhaft … Dat Einzigste was
ich machen durfte. Ich durfte jeden Tag zehn Minuten. Mit zwei Mann.
Einer vorne. Einer hinten. Einen bestimmten Abstand. Zum Ausgang.
Und zwar einen Rundgang machen. Unten. Und dann durft' ich wieder
rauf. Ich durfte aber nicht zu nah an die zwei kommen. Ich hätte die ja
anstecken können. Das sie schwul werden. Nich?"

26 Born interview, Archiv der anderen Erinnerungen. Original German:
"Und dann kam auf Mal, das mit der Verhandlung. Dann sagte ich zu
dem … Warum komm ich denn dann zur Verhandlung? Ich mach' die
doch alle krank. Die werden doch jetzt alle krank, wenn ich da oben
hinkomme. Da nicht. Da is' ein Gericht. Das verurteilt dich ja. Achso.
Hmm. Naja, jedenfalls … Jetzt sitz ich da auf der Anklagebank. Dann
kuck ich so nach hinten. Das war'n großer Raum. Dann kommen zwei
Schulklassen da rein. In den zwei Schulklassen, das waren so junge Leute.
Die durften sich das anhören auf Grund deswegen, damit sie nicht krank
werden. Ja? Damit sie wissen, wie das is', wenn man schwules Leben
führt. Wenn man den Paragrafen 175 anwendet. Also durchzieht. Ja.
Dann durften sie sich das alles anhören. Ich hab denen dat brühwarm
erklärt, was wir gemacht haben und wie dat so schön war, auch. Ich hab
gesagt: Es war wunderbar. Und dann kommen auf Male die Lampen da
und dann werden wir dabei be- / ge-, gestört. Das hat die wahrscheinlich
auch nich gepasst."

27 Gödecke, "Criminal Law after National Socialism," 271.
28 Naumann, *Gefängnis und Gesellschaft*, 213–19.
29 Eghigian, *The Corrigible and the Incorrigible*, 16.
30 Wachsmann, *Gefangen unter Hitler*, 396.
31 Eghigian, *The Corrigible and the Incorrigible*, 149.
32 Wachsmann, *Gefangen unter Hitler*, 400; Naumann, *Gefängnis und
Gesellschaft*, 256–9; Eghigian, *The Corrigible and the Incorrigible*, 147.
33 Wachsmann, 400.
34 Schroeder, *Der SED-Staat*, 524.

35 Eghigian, *The Corrigible and the Incorrigible*, 59.
36 Wachsmann, *Gefangen unter Hitler*, 403.
37 Steer, *Eingeliefert nach Rummelsburg*, 44.
38 Eghigian, *The Corrigible and the Incorrigible*, 66.
39 Eghigian, "Homo Munitus," 44–5.
40 Eghigian, *The Corrigible and the Incorrigible*, 16, 81.
41 Gélieu, *Frauen in Haft*, 24.
42 See, for instance, Michael Lemke, *Vor der Mauer*, 14.
43 Gélieu, *Barnimstraße 10*, 258.
44 Gélieu, 265–6.
45 Gélieu, 281.
46 Reissig, "Militärgefängnis/Justizvollzugsanstalt," 329, 336.
47 Reissig, 328, 336.
48 Gélieu, *Barnimstraße 10*, 265–6.
49 McLellan, *Love in the Time of Communism*, 7; Huneke, "Morality, Law, and the Socialist Sexual Self," 44.
50 Rita "Tommy" Thomas, interview by Karl-Heinz Steinle and Babette Reicherdt. Original German: "Interviewer*in: Du hast gerade gesagt, dass es damals immer hieß, Bubi und Mäuschen.

Rita Thomas: Ja, ja, dit war so, et jab ja vor uns schon viele und ick mal jemand je- kennengelernt, die war, die die hat mir dit erzählt, die sagt: Dit is ´ne schwere Zeit, wenn du da äh reinkommst, ick war och mal Mäuschen. Da sag ick: Wat ist dit. Und da sagt se: Naja, Mäuschen is die Frau und Bubi, naja, der Kerl, der kleene Kerl. Und daher weeß ich dit, ja, Bubi.

Interviewer*in: Und gab´s immer die Kombination Bubi und Mäuschen oder gab´s auch äh Kombination aus, also dass Mäuschen mit Mäuschen zusammen war oder Bubi mit Bubi?

Rita Thomas: Jaja, jaja, ja.

Interviewer*in: Gab´s auch?

Rita Thomas: Jaja, it jab auch, da hat man dit nich so mitjekriecht. Und meisst so die so ´n bisschen streng warn, früher warn die ja wirklich also auseinanderzuhalten, ziemli- dit hat man jemerkt, dit hat man einfach jemerkt, ziemlich. Naja, die hatten denn kurze Haare, ick hatte so ´ne Elvis-Frisur immer, mit so bisschen hier länger (zeigt auf ihre rechte und linke Kopfseite, Richtung Ohren), und hinten ´n Schwalbenschwanz. Und da hab ick mir ´n Anzug machen lassen. Hab ick mir Stoff jekauft, hm, ´n Anzug machen lassen, nach Maß. Und da hab ich ja auf Bildern, ´nen Trenchcoat hat ick meistens an, sonntags, in de Woche musst ick ja arbeiten, da jing et nich, oder. So."
51 "Fotoprojekt Rita Thomas," FFBIZ Feminist Archives Berlin, 1 January 2018, https://www.ffbiz.de/aktivitaeten/projekte/fotoprojekt-rita-thomas.
52 Huneke, "Morality, Law, and the Socialist Sexual Self," 36.

53 Abteilung Strafvollzug, Quartalsbericht für das II. Quartal 1954 (copy), Schwules Museum, Berlin, DDR-24.

54 Abteilung Strafvollzug, Quartalsbericht für das III. Quartal 1955 (copy), Schwules Museum, Berlin, DDR-24.

55 Abteilung Strafvollzug, Quartalsbericht für das III. Quartal 1955 (copy), Schwules Museum, Berlin, DDR-24.

56 Though the new penal code was not passed until 1968, it was put into "preliminary effect" (vorläufiges Inkrafttreten) in 1965. Gélieu, *Barnimstraße 10*, 290.

57 Brüning, *Prostitution in der DDR*, 64.

58 Brüning, 65.

59 Brüning, 66.

60 Eschebach, "Homophobie, Devianz und weibliche Homosexualität," 68.

61 Strafvollzugsanstalt Berlin II, Vollzugsgeschäftsstelle, Analyse über die in der Anstalt einsitzenden Inhaftierten unter Berücksichtigung der einzelnen Haftarten, 1 August 1966, Schwules Museum, Berlin, DDR-24.

62 Präsidium der Volkspolizei Berlin, Abteilung Strafvollzug. Bericht über die Erfüllung der Hauptaufgaben des Dienstzweiges Strafvollzug mm Jahre 1966 und die Hauptaufgabenstellung für das Jahr 1967, 15 December 1966; Strafvollzugsanstalt Berlin II. Bericht über die Durchsetzung einer straffen Disziplin und Ordnung bzw. die Ursachen für Verstöße gegen Disziplin und Ordnung, 27 February 1967, Schwules Museum, DDR 24.

63 "Ein weiterer Schwerpunkt, der sich auf die Erziehungsarbeit besonders hemmend auswirkt, ist der Hang eines nicht kleinen Teils der AE zur lesbischen Liebe. Das äußert sich darin, daß ein Teil der AE 'männlich' in Erscheinung zu treten versucht und sich durch Rowdytum und Randalieren in den Mittelpunkt des Interesses der AE zu rücken versucht." Strafvollzugsanstalt Berlin II, Vollzugsgeschäftsstelle. Analyse über die in der Anstalt einsitzenden Inhaftierten.

64 Strafvollzugsanstalt Berlin II, Vollzugsgeschäftsstelle.

65 Präsidium der Volkspolizei Berlin, Abteilung Strafvollzug, Bericht über die Erfüllung der Hauptaufgaben des Dienstzweiges Strafvollzug mm Jahre 1966.

66 "Den weitaus größten Anteil für die Motive und Gründe bei Verstößen gegen die Disziplin und Ordnung nehmen die verbreiteten lesbischen Beziehungen sowie der Klatsch und Zank unter den AE ein." Strafvollzugsanstalt Berlin II. Bericht über die Durchsetzung einer straffen Disziplin und Ordnung.

67 The original German reads: "sind sie nur daran interessiert, illegale Verbindungen zu knüpfen und niveaulose Gespräche, meistens über Liebesaffären in der schmutzigsten Weise, zu führen. Es ist auch in den bestehenden Zirkeln festzustellen, daß es nicht nur an Interesse

und Mitarbeit mangelt, sondern daß die AE deshalb daran teilnehmen, um Freundschaften zu schließen bzw. ihre Verbindungen besser ausnutzen zu können. Diese sogenannten 'reinen' Freundschaften führen in starkem Maße sehr oft zu ausgedehnten Kassibereien mit Bekleidungsstücken und Briefen. Es tritt besonders verstärkt auf, daß die AE mit Einkaufsbeschränkung von anderen mit Rauchwaren und Lebensmistteln versorgt werden, obwohl sie wissen, daß es verboten ist und sie dann ebenfalls disziplinarisch zur Rechenschaft gezogen werden." Strafvollzugsanstalt Berlin II. Bericht über die Durchsetzung einer straffen Disziplin und Ordnung.

68 "3 Beschwerden von Arbeitserziehungspflichtigen über andere Arbeitserziehungspflichtige, die durch die lesbischen Beziehungen den Arbeitsablauf und die Disziplin störten, waren berechtigt. Es wurden Verlegungen aus den Kommandos bzw. zeitweilige Isolierungen veranlaßt." Präsidium der Volkspolizei Berlin, Abteilung Strafvollzug, der Leiter, Jahreseinschätzung der Eingaben inhaftierter Personen 1967, 9 January 1968. Schwules Museum, DDR 24.

69 Gélieu, *Barnimstraße 10*, 302. Original German: "Gélieu: Nach anderen Angaben sollen sehr viele Prostituierte und „Asoziale" in der Barnimstraße inhaftiert gewesen sein. Stimmt das?

Kühne: Das weiß ich nicht. Aber Sex spielte schon eine Rolle. Selbstbefriedigung wurde stillschweigend unter den Häftlingen toleriert. Und es gab lesbische Beziehungen. Ich war mit einer Kriminellen zusammen [in der Zelle], die hatte einen festen Freund, eine Frau. Das war bekannt. In einer gemeinsamen Zelle hatten sie sich verliebt, waren aber ganz schnell getrennt worden. Das war dann das Superdrama. Sie trafen sich heimlich, tauschten Geschenke aus. Unter den Gefangenen war das Konsens. Das gab's häufig, glaube ich. Konkret weiß ich es nur von dieser Frau, einer sehr hübschen, rebellischen Frau. Sie hat das ganz offen gelebt. Zu DDR-Zeiten nicht ganz selbstverständlich. In gewisser Weise war sie auch eine Oppositionelle."

70 Gélieu, *Frauen in Haft*, 60.

71 "Eigentlich gehörte es zur Strategie der Gefängnisleitung, zu enge Zellengemeinschaften zu zerschlagen. Das Verlegen war eine einschneidende Erfahrung. Es geschah immer willkürlich und unerwartet und war ein wesentliches Moment des psychischen Terrors." Gélieu, *Barnimstraße 10*, 301.

72 Reissig, "Militärgefängnis/Justizvollzugsanstalt," 329, 336.

73 LAB finding aid B Rep 65 Nr. 70, Justizvollzugsanstalt für Frauen. Siemsen's personal papers are archived at Landesarchiv Berlin but are not accessible to research. Email from archivist Dr. Martin Luchterhandt, LAB, 21 August 2018.

74 "Bettina Grundmann" is a pseudonym, as are all names of prisoners from this file. Anonymization is required by German archival law. I have chosen pseudonyms over anonymization (a person's first name and the first letter of the last name) for two reasons: first, to proceed uniformly for different protagonists in this chapter independently of archival restrictions or permissions; second, anonymized names ring of cases – medical or criminal – and thus invoke the histories of medicalization and criminalization of queer people. Giving a full name to one's historical subjects hence is a strategy to write queer histories that break with these violent pasts. Grundmann's file is the only file that a search of the archive's catalogue for the search term "lesb*" and the period between 1945 and 1970 will yield.

75 LAB Rep. 65 Nr. 70. The authorship of the letter is unclear, and none of the prisoner files for the prisoners mentioned in the file are archived.

76 LAB Rep. 65 Nr. 70. Original German: "Meine süße, gute Mammi. Dein Strolch ist so stolz auf Dich, Du verwöhnst mich so, meine Lisa! Bei Dir werde ich auch draußen geborgen sein. Du bist resolut, das gefällt mir. Ich bin trotzdem kein Pantoffelheld!"

77 LAB Rep. 65 Nr. 70. Original German: "Ja, ich habe Dich lieb, warm u. vertrauensvoll … Lisa, wie wäre es denn, wenn wir uns Sonntag Abend (morgen) um ½ 9 körperlich (jeder für sich) finden würden? Warum willst Du mich denn hauen deshalb??? Daß Du 100% so sinnlich bist in der Erotik, daß glaube ich, eine Frau wie Du!!! … Aber ich habe seit meinem 15. Jahr studiert u. kenne „die Hohe Schule der Liebe"."

78 LAB Rep. 65 Nr. 70. German original: "Wenn Du es schaffst, mit dem Schach spielen, dann werden wir ein- zweimal spielen, bis die sicher sind, dann nehme ich die Gelegenheit wahr, das kannst Du glauben."

79 File memo Dr. Siemsen, LAB Rep. 65 Nr. 70.

80 File memo Dr. Siemsen. Original German: "Darin habe ich gesagt, daß das Kassibern zwar kein Vergnügen für uns sei, was vielleicht manche glaubten, aber uns auch nicht schockiere. Der Inhalt sei immer nur kennzeichnend für die Verfasser und evtl. auch für die Adressaten. Ich hätte aber auch nicht die Absicht, ihre schmutzigen Geschäfte für sie zu erledigen und als Handlanger für ihre Rache zu dienen. Ich hätte auch nicht die Absicht, mich eingehend mit den Kassibern zu beschäftigen, um dadurch herauszubekommen, wer sie geschrieben habe, aber wenn allerdings unmittelbar Kassiber bei jemand gefunden werden, würden diese bestraft werden. Überdies sei die Kassiberei kindisch, denn sie hätten genug Gelegenheit, bei Freizeitstunde und Freizeitraum miteinander zu sprechen. Im Anschluß daran wie ich noch einmal darauf hin, daß jegliche Geschäfte der Gefangenen untereinander verboten sind."

81 Since German archival law prohibits the reproduction of person-related documents during their lifetime and ten years beyond their death, or, if the date of death is unknown, one hundred years after their birth, I cannot show the photos here. The resulting blank space is all the more lamentable since their own picture was of utmost importance to Grundmann. Email communication with Landesarchiv Berlin, December 2017.

82 On this point, see also Laurie Marhoefer's discussion of the Ilse Totzke Gestapo case. Marhoefer, "Lesbianism, Transvestism, and the Nazi State," 1192.

83 All names are changed. Sentence of the Schöffengericht Tiergarten, 10 December 1964. Copy in Grundmann's inmate file. LAB B Rep 065 Nr. 120.

84 Inmate information sheet E, curriculum vitae, 25 April 1966, LAB B Rep 065 Nr. 120.

85 Sentence of the Schöffengericht Tiergarten, 10 December 1964, LAB B Rep 065 Nr. 120. Original German: "Ich bin vor dem Verkehr mit dem Beklagten Lesbierin gewesen und auch heute wieder. Ich habe versucht, durch die Beziehung mit dem Beklagten wieder zum normalen Verkehr zu finden."

86 Sentence of the Schöffengericht Tiergarten.

87 Sentence of the Schöffengericht Tiergarten.

88 Sentence of the Schöffengericht Tiergarten. Original German: "Da sie stets lesbisch veranlagt war, kann sie einen Geschlechtsverkehr nicht vergessen haben."

89 Sentence of Landgericht Berlin, 23 November 1965. Grundmann prisoner file. Original German: "Auf Grund ihrer lesbischen Veranlagung hatte sie erhebliche Lebensschwierigkeiten."

90 Grundmann prisoner file, LAB B Rep 065 Nr. 120.

91 Inmate information sheet, Grundmann prisoner file.

92 List of prisoner clothing, Grundmann prisoner file.

93 Letter from Grundmann to Siemsen, 1 June 1966, Grundmann prisoner file. Original German: "Einige haben es wirklich nötig und ich auch. Ich komme mir nämlich um meinen Kopf, schon reichlich ungepflegt vor."

94 Letter from Grundmann to Siemsen. Original German: "Ich finde K's Haare eigentlich genau richtig – und kürzer wäre weniger schön!"

95 According to Nikolaus Wachsmann, male homosexual prisoners were separated from other inmates before Nazism too. Wachsmann, *Gefangen unter Hitler*, 147. Separating lesbian prisoners was the practice at Barnimstraße women's prison during the Nazi era. Gélieu, *Frauen in Haft*, 60. In the 1970s, Judy Andersen, who like her lover Marion Ihns was imprisoned for hiring an assassin to murder Ihns's husband, was isolated from other prisoners in a West German prison for a period of four years. Kühn, "'Haut der geilen Männerpresse.'"

96 Siemsen note in Grundmann prisoner file, June 1966. Original German: "G. ist Hans Dampf in allen Gassen, sucht laufend Kontakte … Es ist leider nicht möglich, ihr viel Gemeinschaft usw zu gestatten."
97 Note by prison guard, 7 July 1966, Grundmann prisoner file.
98 Letter from Rasinne to Grundmann, July/August 1966, Grundmann prisoner file. Original German: "D. erzählte, wie ich mit meinen Stöckelschuhen dem engen hellblauen Kostüm u. superblonden Haaren durchs U.G. getippelt bin."
99 Letter from Rasinne to Grundmann. Original German: "Das mußt Du später alles mal wieder gut machen, was ich hir so für dich nähe u. sticke."
100 Letter from Rasinne to Grundmann. Original German: "Gerade wird gespielt „Nur wenn Du bei mir bist" Die Stelle ist so schön, Wunderschön ist das Leben seitdem Du mich geküßt. Weißt Du noch im U.G.? Hoffendlich können wir das bald ungestört weiterführen. Du glaubst garnicht, wie ich mich darauf schon freue."
101 Note from Siemsen to prison staff, 17 October 1966, Grundmann prisoner file.
102 Letter from Grundmann to foster mother, 30 October 1966, Grundmann prisoner file.
103 Letter from Grundmann to foster mother. Original German: "Oma, es ist brandeilig das Du jetzt zu meinen Freundschaften fährst … Und schick das letzte Paßbild was Du von mir hast vom vergangenen Winter mit."
104 Letter from Grundmann to foster mother.
105 Message from Grundmann to Werner, 24 February 1967, Grundmann prisoner file.
106 Letter from Grundmann to the court, 22 April 1967, Grundmann prisoner file. Original German: "Ihre Verlobung besteht nicht mehr, und an einer Aufrechterhaltung dieser, ist Sie auch nicht mehr interessiert. Da Sie nach Ihrer Entlassung sofort zu mir zieht, um mit mir zu leben."
107 Letter from Grundmann to the court, 22 April 1967. Original German: "Grundmann hat ausserdem mehrere „Eisen im Feuer"."
108 Siemsen letter to state attorney, 16 August 1966, Grundmann prisoner file. Original German: "Bettina Grundmann ist lesbisch veranlagt."
109 Chaplain statement, 31 May 1966, Grundmann prisoner file.
110 Chaplain statement on Grundmann's clemency appeal, November 1966, Grundmann prisoner file. Original German: "Durch ihre sexuelle Abartigkeit steht sie auch rechtlich ausserhalb der Gemeinschaft."
111 Grundmann's work supervisor noted that she "would accomplish much more if tasked with physical work (yard or external job)." However, she added: "She would immediately take advantage of working in a community to exchange letters." Supervisor note, 13 July 1966, Grundmann prisoner file. Original German: "G. würde weit mehr leisten wenn sie mit einer körperlichen Arbeit (Hof- oder Außenkdo) beschäftigt

werden könnte. Diese Arbeit in der Gemeinschaft würde sie sofort zum Kassibern ausnutzen."

112 Staff assessment form for prisoners, Grundmann prisoner file. The German terms are "burschikos" and "selbstbewußt."

113 House rules of the women's prison, December 1967. LAB B Rep 065, Nr. 71.

114 Letter from Grundmann to parents, 6 March 1967, Grundmann prisoner file, LAB B Rep 065, Nr. 71. Original German: "Mit herzlichen Dank ... heute Eure liebe Post erhalten ... Nun hat der Brief zwei Wermutstropfen. Erstens, das Papa so krank ist, und ins Krankenhaus soll. Zweitens, habe ich nicht die Bilder von Anita bekommen. Das empört mich derartig, und unterstreicht wieder mal, die Ungerechtigkeit hier im Hause ... Aber ich sehe nicht ein, warum andere Fam.Bilder haben dürfen, wo Sie selbst auch drauf sind, nur „Grundmann" nicht. Und dann heißt es ich habe eine große Klappe. Obwohl ich nur möchte, das man mich wie andere behandelt. Ich zittere so vor unterdrücktem Zorn, das ich kaum schreiben kann."

115 Grundmann prisoner file, LAB B Rep 065, Nr. 71. Original German: "In der Kasse zwischen meinen Bildern, befinden sich zwei Aufnahmen von mir, aus den 50.ger Jahren. Auf denen ich Damengarderobe trage."

116 Tapia, "Profane Illuminations," 686.

117 Kunzel, *Criminal Intimacy*, 127.

118 Prisoner file Bettina Grundmann, LAB B Rep 065 Nr. 121.

119 Prisoner information sheet A, LAB B Rep 065 Nr. 121.

120 Freedman, "The Prison Lesbian"; Sannwald, "Der Frauenknast Als Sündenpfuhl"; Döring, "Sexualität im Gefängnis."

121 Marhoefer, "Lesbianism, Transvestism, and the Nazi State," 1191.

Conclusion: Changing Queer Constellations Before and After 1970

1 Evans, "Seeing Subjectivity," 462.

2 Holy, "Jenseits von Stonewall," 43–8.

3 See, for instance, Griffiths, *The Ambivalence of Gay Liberation*, 171–2.

4 On the "tomato throw that started the women's movement," see "Die Rede von Helke Sander für den Aktionsrat," in Lenz, *Die Neue Frauenbewegung in Deutschland*, 38–43.

5 On the LAZ, see Ledwa, *Mit schwulen Lesbengrüßen*.

6 On male homosexual subjectivity in the 1970s and 1980s, see Beljan, *Rosa Zeiten?* Benno Gammerl argues that new spatial and technical structures create new modes of feeling. Gammerl, *Anders fühlen*, 92.

7 Griffiths, *The Ambivalence of Gay Liberation*, 166–71.

8 Weinberg, "Feminist Sex Wars in der deutschen Lesbenbewegung?"

9 Silva, *Negotiating the Borders*, 145.

10 On West German court decisions about changing the legal gender, see Klöppel, *XXOXY Ungelöst*, 562–82; Silva, *Negotiating the Borders*, 90–107. On the decision of the Federal Supreme Court of Justice, see Klöppel, *XXOXY Ungelöst*, 576.

11 Klöppel, 584.

12 Brady, "LGBTQ+ Rights."

13 Tammer, "Warme Brüder im Kalten Krieg."

14 On the HIB, see McLellan, "Glad to Be Gay."

15 McLellan, "Glad to Be Gay," 110–11.

16 On Mahlsdorf, see her memoirs: *Ich bin meine eigene Frau* and *Ab durch die Mitte: Ein Spaziergang durch Berlin*.

17 Klöppel, "Geschlechtstransitionen," 84.

18 Klöppel, 89.

19 Korzilius, "*Asoziale*," 415; Lindenberger, "'Asoziale Lebensweise,'" 247.

20 On representations of men of colour in West German homophile and gay magazines, see Ewing, "'Color Him Black.'" Member of the queer migrant organization GLADT e.V. have published a collage of graphic novel and historical documents in their brochure QUEER-MIGRANT/ische Repräsen/TANZ! Queer migrant perspectives are also represented in Voß, *Westberlin – Ein Sexuelles Porträt*.

21 Foremost, of course, is Audre Lorde's crucial role for Afro-German women. See most recently, Florvil, *Mobilizing Black Germany*. On women of colour in women's movements in East and West Germany in 1989, see Piesche, *Labor 1989*.

Bibliography

Archival and Manuscript Materials

Archiv der anderen Erinnerungen, Bundesstiftung Magnus Hirschfeld

Born, Klaus. Interview by Michael Bochow and Michael Jähme, 5 December 2013. Transcription Dennis Nill. Archiv der anderen Erinnerungen, Bundesstiftung Magnus Hirschfeld, Berlin.

Kapp, Orest. Interview by Andreas Pretzel and Janina Rieck, 15 October 2014. Archiv der anderen Erinnerungen, Bundesstiftung Magnus Hirschfeld, Berlin.

Loewenstein, Christine. Interview by Babette Reicherdt, Janina Rieck, and Kamera: Katharina Rivilis, 7 July 2017. Berlin.

Schmehling, Fritz. Interview by Michael Bochow and Karl-Heinz Steinle, 24 January 2015. Archiv der anderen Erinnerungen, Bundesstiftung Magnus Hirschfeld, Berlin.

Thomas, Rita, "Tommy." Interview by Karl-Heinz Steinle and Babette Reicherdt, 19 November 2016. Transcription Janina Rieck. Archiv der anderen Erinnerungen, Bundesstiftung Magnus Hirschfeld, Berlin.

Berliner Landesbibliothek

Berliner Morgenpost
B.Z.
Der Abend
nacht-depesche

Bundesarchiv Berlin

Kulturbund der DDR Records, SAPMO DY 27

Deutsches Rundfunkarchiv Potsdam-Babelsberg

Schriftgutbestand Hörfunk:
HA Personal, Personalstatistiken
HA Personal Schriftwechsel zu Berliner Rundfunk
HA Personal vertraulich, 1940–1953
HAP 03/07
HAP 1951
Schnitzler, Karl-Eduard von. Sendemanuskript Der Schwarze Kanal. 27.8.1962.
  E065-02-04/0001 TSig. 128.

Feministisches Archiv FFBIZ, Berlin

Hilde Radusch Personal Papers
Annemarie Tröger Personal Papers

Landesarchiv Berlin

West Berlin Records

B Rep 004, Senatsverwaltung für Inneres
B Rep 010, Senatsverwaltung für Wirtschaft
B Rep 013, Senatsverwaltung für Jugend und Sport
B Rep 020, Der Polizeipräsident in Berlin
B Rep 051, Amtsgericht Tiergarten
B Rep 065, Justizvollzugsanstalt für Frauen

East Berlin Records

C Rep 104, Magistrat von Berlin, Bereich Inneres
C Rep 118–01, Hauptausschuss „Opfer des Faschismus"
C Rep 131–08, Rat des Stadtbezirks Mitte, Abteilung Handel und Versorgung
C Rep 303, Präsidium der Volkspolizei Berlin
C Rep 341, Stadtbezirksgericht Mitte

Magnus-Hirschfeld-Gesellschaft

Correspondence Kurt Hiller – Eva Siewert
Gerd Katter Personal Papers

Polizeihistorische Sammlung Berlin

Call numbers: 1956.08; 33.05–1; 35.15; 35.15/6/67; 55.25; D 4.44, vol. 1.

Schwules Museum Berlin

1. PERIODICALS
Amicus-Briefbund
Die Freunde
Der Kreis
Der Ring
der neue ring
Der Weg

2. OTHER COLLECTIONS
DDR (GDR) Collection
Eberhardt Brucks Collection
Peter Thilo Collection
Charlotte von Mahlsdorf Collection

Stasi Records Archive

BStU 1030/58
MfS AU 309/55 Bd. 2
MfS ZAIG Nr. 510
MfS ZAIG Nr. 526

Zefys Database, Staatsbibliothek zu Berlin

East German Newspapers:
Berliner Zeitung
Neues Deutschland
Neue Zeit

Other Sites

Der Spiegel online archive

"'Der Weg.'" *Der Weg. Zeitschrift für Fragen des Judentums* 1, no. 1 (1946): 1.
Engel, Hans-Joachim. Interview by Andrea Rottmann, 4 October 2017.
   Berlin.

Die Zeit online archive

Published Sources

"§175." In *Strafgesetzbuch Für Das Deutsche Reich*. 1871.

"§183." In Kohlrausch and Lange, *Strafgesetzbuch mit Erläuterungen und Nebengesetzen*, 259.

"§360." In Kohlrausch and Lange, *Strafgesetzbuch mit Erläuterungen und Nebengesetzen*, 463–4.

Ahmed, Sara. *Queer Phenomenology: Orientations, Objects, Others*. Durham, NC: Duke University Press, 2006. https://doi.org/10.1215/9780822388074.

Amin, Kadji. "Temporality." *TSG: Transgender Studies Quarterly* 1, nos. 1–2 (May 2014): 219–22. https://doi.org/10.1215/23289252-2400073.

Balser, Kristof. *Himmel und Hölle: das Leben der Kölner Homosexuellen 1945–1969*. Cologne: Emons, 1994.

Baranowski, Daniel. "Das Archiv der anderen Erinnerungen der Bundesstiftung Magnus Hirschfeld: Voraussetzungen, Leitlinien, Schwerpunkte." *Jahrbuch Sexualitäten* 4 (2019): 233–9.

Barth, Thomas. "Relationships and Sexuality of Imprisoned Men in the German Penal System – A Survey of Inmates in a Berlin Prison." *International Journal of Law and Psychiatry* 35, no. 3 (May–June 2012): 153–8. https://doi.org/10.1016/j.ijlp.2012.02.001.

Bartsch, Udo. "Kulturbund." In *Lexikon des DDR-Sozialismus: Das Staats- und Gesellschaftssystem der Deutschen Demokratischen Republik*, edited by Rainer Eppelmann, Horst Möller, Günter Nooke, and Dorothee Wilms, 361–2. Paderborn: Schöningh, 1996.

Beachy, Robert. *Gay Berlin: Birthplace of a Modern Identity*. New York: Knopf, 2014.

Beck, Gad. *Und Gad ging zu David: Die Erinnerungen des Gad Beck*. 2nd ed. Munich: dtv, 1999.

Beemyn, Genny. "A Presence in the Past: A Transgender Historiography." *Journal of Women's History* 25, no. 4 (Winter 2013): 113–21. https://doi.org/10.1353/jowh.2013.0062.

Beljan, Magdalena. *Rosa Zeiten? Eine Geschichte der Subjektivierung männlicher Homosexualität in den 1970er und 1980er Jahren der BRD*. Bielefeld: transcript-Verl, 2014.

Berndl, Klaus. "Zeiten der Bedrohung: Männliche Homosexuelle in Ost-Berlin und der DDR in den 1950er Jahren." In Marbach and Weiß, *Konformitäten und Konfrontationen*, 20–49.

Berner, Dieter. "Wie die SED-Propaganda das Stigma Homosexualität zum Rufmord an einem Maueropfer benutzte." *Capri* 4, no. 10 (1990): 38–40.

Betts, Paul. *Within Walls: Private Life in the German Democratic Republic*. Oxford: Oxford University Press, 2010.

Biermann, Pieke, and Petra Haffter, dirs. *Muss es denn gleich beides sein?* NDR, 1986.

Bormuth, Maria. *Ein Mann, der mit einem anderen Mann Unzucht treibt …*
wird mit Gefängnis bestraft: § 175 StGB – 20 Jahre legitimiertes Unrecht in
der Bundesrepublik am Beispiel des Strafvollzugs in Wolfenbüttel. Schriften
der Gedenkstätte in der JVA Wolfenbüttel, Bd. 2. Celle: Stiftung
niedersächsische Gedenkstätten, 2019.

Borneman, John. *Belonging in the Two Berlins: Kin, State, Nation.* Cambridge:
Cambridge University Press, 1992.

Borowski, Maria. *Parallelwelten: Lesbisch-schwules Leben in der frühen DDR.*
Berlin: Metropol-Verlag, 2017.

Boyd, Nan Alamilla. "Who Is the Subject? Queer Theory Meets Oral History."
Journal of the History of Sexuality 17, no. 2 (May 2008): 177–89. https://
doi.org/10.1353/sex.0.0009.

Brady, Kate. "LGBTQ+ Rights: Germany Appoints First 'Commissioner for
Queer Affairs.'" Edited by Rina Goldenberg and Kyra Levine. *Deutsche
Welle,* 6 January 2022. https://www.dw.com/en/lgbtq-rights-germany
-appoints-first-commissioner-for-queer-affairs/a-60351173.

Bray, Alan. *The Friend.* Chicago: University of Chicago Press, 2003.

Brecht, Christine. "Günter Litfin." In *Die Todesopfer an der Berliner Mauer
1961–1989,* edited by Zentrum für Zeithistorische Forschung Potsdam and
Stiftung Berliner Mauer with the assistance of Hans-Hermann Hertle and
Maria Nooke, 37–9. Berlin: Ch. Links Verlag, 2009.

– "Günter Litfin." *Chronik der Mauer: Todesopfer.* Accessed 6 May 2019.
https://www.chronik-der-mauer.de/todesopfer/171441/litfin-guenter.

Brüning, Steffi. *Prostitution in der DDR: Eine Untersuchung am Beispiel von
Rostock, Berlin und Leipzig, 1968 bis 1989.* Berlin: be.bra Wissenschaftsverlag,
2020.

– "Verstecken, Verheimlichen, Verleugnen. Prostitution in Ost-Berlin." In
Jahrbuch Sexualitäten 2017, edited by Maria Borowski, Jan Feddersen, Benno
Gammerl, Rainer Nicolaysen, and Christian Schmelzer, 199–206. Göttingen:
Wallstein Verlag, 2017.

Bundesstiftung Magnus Hirschfeld, ed. *Forschung im Queerformat: Aktuelle Beiträge
der LSBTI*-, Queer- und Geschlechterforschung.* Bielefeld: transcript, 2014.

– "Über die Stiftung." Accessed 29 June 2019. https://mh-stiftung.de
/ueber-die-stiftung/.

Butler, Judith. "Performative Acts and Gender Constitution: An Essay in
Phenomenology and Feminist Theory." In *The Performance Studies Reader,*
edited by Henry Bial and Sara Brady, 214–25. 3rd ed. London: Routledge, 2016.

Carri, Christiane. "'Als erstes Symptom einer gewissen psychischen
Abwegigkeit ist bei ihr selbst ihre homosexuelle Einstellung zu nennen.'
Diskurse um weibliche Homosexualität aus einem Entmündigungsgutachten
der Weimarer Republik." *Invertito: Jahrbuch für die Geschichte der
Homosexualitäten* 17 (2015): 48–67.

Carstens, Uwe. "Die Nissenhütte." In *Schleswig-Holsteinische Erinnerungsorte*, edited by Carsten Fleischhauer and Guntram Turkowski, 90–5. Heide: Boyens, 2006.

Caspar, Helmut. *DDR-Lexikon: Von Trabi, Broiler, Stasi und Republikflucht*. Petersberg: Michael Imhof Verlag, 2009.

Centrum Schwule Geschichte. *Himmel und Hölle: 100 Jahre schwul in Köln*. Cologne: The Center, 2003.

Chauncey, George. *Gay New York: Gender, Urban Culture, and the Making of the Gay Male World, 1890–1940*. New York: Basic Books, 1994.

Cho, Sumi, Kimberlé Williams Crenshaw, and Leslie McCall. "Toward a Field of Intersectionality Studies: Theory, Applications, and Praxis." *Signs* 38, no. 4 (2013): 785–810. https://doi.org/10.1086/669608.

D'Emilio, John. "Capitalism and Gay Identity." In *Powers of Desire: The Politics of Sexuality*, edited by Ann Snitow, Christine Stansell, and Sharon Thompson, 100–13. New York: Monthly Review Press, 1983.

Dennert, Gabriele, Christiane Leidinger, and Franziska Rauchut, eds. *In Bewegung bleiben: 100 Jahre Politik, Kultur und Geschichte von Lesben*. Berlin: Querverlag, 2007.

"Der weitere Verbleib der Genannten ist leider nicht festzustellen." "Alice Carlé (1902–1943)." In *Erinnern in Auschwitz: auch an sexuelle Minderheiten*, edited by Joanna Ostrowska, Joanna Talewicz-Kwiatkowska, and Lutz van Dijk, 156–61. Berlin: Querverlag, 2020.

Detjen, Marion. "Die Mauer." In *Erinnerungsorte der DDR*, edited by Martin Sabrow, 389–402. Munich: C.H. Beck, 2009.

"Die Rede von Helke Sander für den Aktionsrat zur Befreiung der Frauen auf der 23. Delegiertenkonferenz des SDS (1968)." In *Die Neue Frauenbewegung in Deutschland: Abschied vom kleinen Unterschied. Ausgewählte Quellen*, edited by Ilse Lenz, 38–43. Wiesbaden: VS Verlag für Sozialwissenschaften, 2009.

Dimmig, Oranna. "Lebensbilder von Eva Siewert: Aufgefächert anhand von Nachlassfragmenten." *Mitteilungen der Magnus-Hirschfeld-Gesellschaft*, no. 68 (March 2022): 29–40.

Dittmar, Claudia. *Feindliches Fernsehen: Das DDR-Fernsehen und seine Strategien im Umgang mit dem westdeutschen Fernsehen*. Bielefeld: transcript, 2010.

Doan, Laura L. *Disturbing Practices: History, Sexuality, and Women's Experience of Modern War*. Chicago: University of Chicago Press, 2013. https://doi.org/10.7208/9780226001753.

Dobler, Jens. "'Den Heten eine Kneipe wegnehmen.'" In Dobler, *Verzaubert in Nord-Ost*, 167–73.

– "Die alte Magnus-Hirschfeld-Gesellschaft." *Mitteilungen der Magnus-Hirschfeld-Gesellschaft*, nos. 39/40 (May 2008): 78–80.

– "Die Berliner Polizei und die Nachkriegsdelinquenz." In *Großstadtkriminalität: Berliner Kriminalpolizei und Verbrechensbekämpfung 1930 bis 1950*, edited by Jens Dobler, 247–57. Berlin: Metropol-Verlag, 2013.

- "Ein Neuanfang, der keiner war." In Dobler, *Von anderen Ufern*, 226–38.
- "Kreuzberg tanzt." In Dobler, *Von anderen Ufern*, 250–62.
- "Schwules Leben in Berlin zwischen 1945 und 1969 im Ost-West-Vergleich." In *Ohnmacht und Aufbegehren: Homosexuelle Männer in der frühen Bundesrepublik*, edited by Andreas Pretzel and Volker Weiß, 152–63. Hamburg: Männerschwarm Verlag, 2010.
- "Unzucht und Kuppelei. Lesbenverfolgung im Nationalsozialismus." In Eschebach, *Homophobie und Devianz*, 53–62.
-, ed. *Verzaubert in Nord-Ost: Die Geschichte der Berliner Lesben und Schwulen in Prenzlauer Berg, Pankow und Weißensee*. Berlin: Gmünder and Sonntags-Club, 2009.
-, ed. *Von anderen Ufern: Geschichte der Berliner Lesben und Schwulen in Kreuzberg und Friedrichshain*. Berlin: Gmünder, 2003.
Döring, Nicola. "Sexualität im Gefängnis: Forschungsstand und -perspektiven." *Zeitschrift für Sexualforschung* 19, no. 4 (December 2006): 315–33. https://doi.org/10.1055/s-2006-955196.
Dose, Ralf. *Magnus Hirschfeld: The Origins of the Gay Liberation Movement*. New York: Monthly Review Press, 2014.
Duberman, Martin, Martha Vicinus, and George Chauncey, eds. *Hidden from History: Reclaiming the Gay and Lesbian Past*. New York: NAL Books, 1989.
Eghigian, Greg. *The Corrigible and the Incorrigible: Science, Medicine, and the Convict in Twentieth-Century Germany*. Ann Arbor: University of Michigan Press, 2015.
- "Homo Munitus: The East German Observed." In *Socialist Modern: East German Everyday Culture and Politics*, edited by Katherine Pence and Paul Betts, 37–70. Ann Arbor: University of Michigan Press, 2008.
Engelmann, Roger. "'Die Mauer durchlässiger machen': Die Politik der Reiseerleichterungen." In *Die Mauer: Errichtung, Überwindung, Erinnerung*, edited by Klaus-Dietmar Henke, 211–26. München: dtv, 2011.
Eschebach, Insa. "Homophobie, Devianz und weibliche Homosexualität im Konzentrationslager Ravensbrück." In Eschebach, *Homophobie und Devianz*, 65–77.
-, ed. *Homophobie und Devianz: Weibliche und männliche Homosexualität im Nationalsozialismus*. Berlin: Metropol, 2012.
Evans, Jennifer V. "Bahnhof Boys: Policing Male Prostitution in Post-Nazi Berlin." *Journal of the History of Sexuality* 12, no. 4 (October 2003): 605–36. https://doi.org/10.1353/sex.2004.0026.
- "Decriminalization, Seduction, and 'Unnatural Desire' in East Germany." *Feminist Studies* 36, no. 3 (Fall 2010): 553–77.
- *Life among the Ruins: Cityscape and Sexuality in Cold War Berlin*. Basingstoke, UK: Palgrave Macmillan, 2011.

– "Repressive Rehabilitation: Crime, Morality, and Delinquency in Berlin-Brandenburg, 1945–1958." In Wetzell, *Crime and Criminal Justice in Modern Germany*, 302–26.

– "Seeing Subjectivity: Erotic Photography and the Optics of Desire." *American Historical Review* 118, no. 2 (April 2013): 430–62. https://doi.org /10.1093/ahr/118.2.430.

Ewing, Christopher. "'Color Him Black': Erotic Representations and the Politics of Race in West German Homosexual Magazines, 1949–1974." *Sexuality & Culture* 21, no. 2 (June 2017): 382–403. https://doi.org/10.1007 /s12119-016-9345-2.

Färberböck, Max, dir. *Aimée und Jaguar*. Senator Film, 1999.

Fenemore, Mark. *Sex, Thugs, and Rock'n'Roll: Teenage Rebels in Cold War East Germany*. New York: Berghahn Books, 2007.

– "Victim of Kidnapping or an Unfortunate Defector? The Strange Case of Otto John." *Cold War History* 20, no. 2 (April 2020): 143–60. https://doi.org /10.1080/14682745.2019.1689390.

Fischer, Erica. *Aimée and Jaguar: A Love Story, Berlin 1943*. Los Angeles: Alyson Publications, 1995.

Florvil, Tiffany. *Mobilizing Black Germany: Afro-German Women and the Making of a Transnational Movement*. Urbana: University of Illinois Press, 2020. https://doi.org/10.5406/j.ctv1f884c1.

Foucault, Michel. *Discipline and Punish: The Birth of the Prison*. Translated by Alan Sheridan. New York: Vintage, 1979.

– *The History of Sexuality*. Vol. 1, *An Introduction*. Translated by Robert Hurley. New York: Vintage, 1990.

Fout, John C. "Homosexuelle in der NS-Zeit: Neue Forschungsansätze über Alltagsleben und Verfolgung." In Jellonek and Lautmann, *Nationalsozialistischer Terror gegen Homosexuelle*, 163–72.

Frackman, Kyle. "Persistent Ambivalence: Theorizing Queer East German Studies." *Journal of Homosexuality* 66, no. 5 (April 2019): 669–89. https:// doi.org/10.1080/00918369.2017.1423220.

Freedman, Estelle B. "The Prison Lesbian: Race, Class, and the Construction of the Aggressive Female Homosexual, 1915–1965." In *Feminism, Sexuality, and Politics: Essays*, 141–58. Gender and American Culture. Chapel Hill: University of North Carolina Press, 2006.

Frenzel, Uwe. "Nissenhütten – Wellblechbaracken in Berlin." Accessed 23 July 2017. https://www.nissenhütten.de/.

Freud, Sigmund. "Das Unheimliche (1919)." In Mitscherlich, Richards, and Strachey, *Studienausgabe*, 4:241–74.

– *Studienausgabe*. 10 vols. Edited by Alexander Mitscherlich, Angela Richards, and James Strachey. Gesammelte Schriften. Frankfurt am Main: Fischer, 1982.

Fuchs, Günter Bruno. *Gemütlich summt das Vaterland. Gedichte, Märchen, Sprüche und allerhand Schabernack*. Munich: Hanser, 1984.

Gammerl, Benno. *Anders fühlen: Schwules und lesbisches Leben in der Bundesrepublik. Eine Emotionsgeschichte.* Munich: Hanser, 2021.

– "Erinnerte Liebe. Was kann eine Oral History zur Geschichte der Gefühle und der Homosexualitäten beitragen?" *Geschichte und Gesellschaft* 35, no. 2 (November 2009): 314–45. https://doi.org/10.13109/gege.2009.35.2.314.

– "Mit von der Partie oder auf Abstand? Biografische Perspektiven schwuler Männer und lesbischer Frauen auf die Emanzipationsbewegungen der 1970er Jahre." In Pretzel and Weiß, *Rosa Radikale*, 160–76.

Gélieu, Claudia von. *Barnimstraße 10: Das Berliner Frauengefängnis 1868–1974.* Berlin: Metropol, 2014.

– *Frauen in Haft: Gefängnis Barnimstraße. Eine Justizgeschichte.* Berlin: Elefanten Press, 1994.

Georgieff, Andrey. *Nacktheit und Kultur: Adolf Koch und die proletarische Freikörperkultur.* Vienna: Passagen Verlag, 2005.

Gerlach, Carola. "Außerdem habe ich dort mit meinem Freund getanzt." In Pretzel and Roßbach, *Wegen der zu erwartenden hohen Strafe*, 305–32.

Gieseking, Jen Jack. *A Queer New York: Geographies of Lesbians, Dykes, and Queers.* New York: New York University Press, 2020.

GLADT e.V. und QT*I*-BlPoC-Widerstand in Berlin. "QUEER-MIGRANT/ ische Repräsen/TANZ!" Berlin, 2021.

Gödecke, Petra. "Criminal Law after National Socialism: The Renaissance of Natural Law and the Beginnings of Penal Reform in West Germany." In Wetzell, *Crime and Criminal Justice in Modern Germany*, 270–301.

Gorman-Murray, Andrew. "Que(E)Rying Homonormativity: The Everyday Politics of Lesbian and Gay Homemaking." In Pilkey et al., *Sexuality and Gender at Home*, 149–62.

Grau, Günter, ed. *Hidden Holocaust? Gay and Lesbian Persecution in Germany 1933–1945.* With a contribution by Claudia Schoppmann and translated by Patrick Camiller. Chicago: Fitzroy Dearborn, 1995.

Griffiths, Craig. *The Ambivalence of Gay Liberation: Male Homosexual Politics in 1970s West Germany.* Oxford: Oxford University Press, 2021. https://doi.org/10.1093/oso/9780198868965.001.0001.

Grossmann, Atina. "A Question of Silence: The Rape of German Women by Occupation Soldiers." *October* 72 (Spring 1995): 42–63. https://doi.org/10.2307/778926.

Grundgesetz für die Bundesrepublik Deutschland [Basic Law for the Federal Republic of Germany]. In the revised version published in the Federal Law Gazette Part III, classification number 100-1, as last amended by the Act of 28 June 2022 (Federal Law Gazette I, p. 968). Translated by Christian Tomuschat, David P. Currie, Donald P. Kommers, and Raymond Kerr in cooperation with the Language Service of the German Bundestag. https://www.gesetze-im-internet.de /englisch_gg/index.html.

Gutterman, Lauren Jae. *Her Neighbor's Wife: A History of Lesbian Desire within Marriage*. Philadelphia: University of Pennsylvania Press, 2020.

Hacker, Hanna. *Frauen und Freundinnen: Studien zur "weiblichen Homosexualität" am Beispiel Österreich 1870 – 1938*. Ergebnisse der Frauenforschung 12. Weinheim: Beltz, 1987.

– *Frauen* und Freund_innen: Lesarten "weiblicher Homosexualität,"* Österreich, *1870–1938*. Vienna: Zaglossus e. U., 2015.

Hájková, Anna. "Den Holocaust queer erzählen." In *Jahrbuch Sexualitäten 2018*, edited by Janin Afken, Jan Feddersen, Benno Gammerl, Rainer Nicolaysen, and Benedikt Wolf, 86–110. Göttingen: Wallstein Verlag, 2018.

– *The Last Ghetto: An Everyday History of Theresienstadt*. Oxford: Oxford University Press, 2020. https://doi.org/10.1093/oso/9780190051778.001.0001.

– "Sexual Barter in Times of Genocide: Negotiating the Sexual Economy of the Theresienstadt Ghetto." *Signs* 38, no. 3 (Spring 2013): 503–33. https://doi.org/10.1086/668607.

Halberstam, Jack. *Female Masculinity*. Twentieth anniversary edition with a new preface. Durham, NC: Duke University Press, 2018. https://doi.org/10.1215/9781478002703.

Halperin, David M. *How to Do the History of Homosexuality*. Chicago: University of Chicago Press, 2002.

Heimann, Siegfried. "Politisches Leben in Schöneberg/Friedenau in den ersten Jahren nach Kriegsende." In Zur Nieden, Schönknecht, and Schönknecht, *Weiterleben nach dem Krieg*, 68–79.

Heineman, Elizabeth. *Before Porn Was Legal: The Erotica Empire of Beate Uhse*. Chicago: University of Chicago Press, 2011.

– *What Difference Does a Husband Make? Women and Marital Status in Nazi and Postwar Germany*. Berkeley: University of California Press, 1999.

Herbst, Maral. *Demokratie und Maulkorb: Der deutsche Rundfunk in Berlin zwischen Staatsgründung und Mauerbau*. Berlin: VISTAS Verlag, 2002.

Herrn, Rainer. "'Ich habe wohl Freude an Frauenkleidern [...], bin aber deswegen nicht homosexuell': Der Forschungsstand zum Transvestitismus in der Zeit des Nationalsozialismus." In Bundesstiftung Magnus Hirschfeld, *Forschung im Queerformat*, 59–69.

– *Schnittmuster des Geschlechts: Transvestitismus und Transsexualität in der frühen Sexualwissenschaft*. Giessen: Psychosozial-Verlag, 2005.

Herzer, Manfred. "Schwule Widerstandskämpfer gegen den Nationalsozialismus. Neue Studien zu Wolfgang Cordan, Wilfried Israel, Theoder Haubach und Otto John." In Jellonek and Lautmann, *Nationalsozialistischer Terror gegen Homosexuelle*, 127–46.

Herzog, Dagmar. *Sex after Fascism: Memory and Morality in Twentieth-Century Germany*. Princeton, NJ: Princeton University Press, 2005. https://doi.org/10.1515/9781400843329.

Hirschfeld, Magnus. *Berlins Drittes Geschlecht: Herausgegeben und mit einem Nachwort versehen von Manfred Herzer*. Mit einem Anhang: Paul Näcke, Ein Besuch bei den Homosexuellen in Berlin. Berlin: Verlag rosa Winkel, 1991.
– *The Homosexuality of Men and Women*. Translated by Michael A. Lombardi-Nash. Homosexualität des Mannes und des Weibes. English. Amherst, NY: Prometheus Books, 2000.

Hoffschildt, Rainer. "Statistik der Kriminalisierung und Verfolgung homosexueller Handlungen unter Männern durch Justiz und Polizei in der Bundesrepublik Deutschland von der Nachkriegszeit bis 1994." Hanover, 2016. https://upload.wikimedia.org/wikipedia/commons/a/a1/BRD _Paragraph_175_StGB_Statistk_1945-94%2C_Hoffschildt_2016.pdf.

Holy, Michael. "Jenseits von Stonewall: Rückblicke auf die Schwulenbewegung in der BRD 1969–1980." In Pretzel and Weiß, *Rosa Radikale*, 39–79.

Honig, Bonnie. "Difference, Dilemma and the Politics of Home." In *Democracy and Difference: Contesting the Boundaries of the Political*, edited by Seyla Behabib, 257–77. Princeton, NJ: Princeton University Press, 1996. https:// doi.org/10.1515/9780691234168-014.

hooks, bell. "Homeplace: A Site of Resistance." In hooks, *Yearning*, 41–9.
– *Yearning: Race, Gender, and Cultural Politics*. New York: Routledge, 2015.

Houlbrook, Matt. *Queer London: Perils and Pleasures in the Sexual Metropolis, 1918–1957*. Chicago: University of Chicago Press, 2005.

Hubbard, Phil. "Geography and Sexuality: Why Space (Still) Matters." *Sexualities* 21, no. 8 (December 2018): 1295–9. https://doi.org/10.1177/1363460718779209.

Huneke, Erik G. "Morality, Law, and the Socialist Sexual Self in the German Democratic Republic, 1945–1972." PhD diss., University of Michigan, 2013.

Huneke, Samuel Clowes. "The Duplicity of Tolerance: Lesbian Experiences in Nazi Berlin." *Journal of Contemporary History* 54, no. 1 (January 2019): 30–59. https://doi.org/10.1177/0022009417690596.
– *States of Liberation: Gay Men between Dictatorship and Democracy in Cold War Germany*. Toronto: University of Toronto Press, 2022. https:// doi.org/10.3138/9781487542122.

"Im Gedenken an Alice Carlé und ihre Angehörigen." Magnus-Hirschfeld -Gesellschaft e.V., 9 February 2017. http://magnus-hirschfeld.de /forschungsstelle/veranstaltungen-und-einladungen/stolpersteine -carle-2017/.

"In Erinnerung an Eva Siewert." Magnus-Hirschfeld-Gesellschaft e.V., accessed 5 July 2019. https://eva-siewert.de/.

Jellonek, Burkhard, and Rüdiger Lautmann, eds. *Nationalsozialistischer Terror gegen Homosexuelle: Verdrängt und ungesühnt*. Paderborn: Ferdinand Schöningh, 2002.

Kaplan, Marion A. *Between Dignity and Despair: Jewish Life in Nazi Germany*. Oxford: Oxford University Press, 1998.

Keegan, Cáel. "Getting Disciplined: What's Trans* About Queer Studies Now?" *Journal of Homosexuality* 67, no. 3 (February 2020): 384–97. https:// doi.org/10.1080/00918369.2018.1530885.

Kennedy, Elizabeth Lapovsky, and Madeline D. Davis. *Boots of Leather, Slippers of Gold.* New York: Routledge, 1993.

Kennedy, Hubert. *Der Kreis/Le Cercle/The Circle: Eine Zeitschrift und ihr Programm.* Bibliothek rosa Winkel. Hamburg: Männerschwarm Verlag, 1999.

Klöppel, Ulrike. "Geschlechtstransitionen in der DDR." In Meyer, *Auf nach Casablanca?*, 84–93.

– *XX0XY Ungelöst: Hermaphroditismus, Sex und Gender in der deutschen Medizin: Eine historische Studie zur Intersexualität.* Bielefeld: transcript, 2010.

Kohlrausch, Eduard, and Richard Lange, eds. *Strafgesetzbuch mit Erläuterungen und Nebengesetzen.* 39th and 40th. Guttentagsche Sammlung Deutscher Reichsgesetze 2. Berlin: Walter de Gruyter, 1950.

Kokula, Ilse. *Formen lesbischer Subkultur.* Sozialwissenschaftliche Studien zur Homosexualität 3. Berlin: Verl. rosa Winkel, 1983.

– *Jahre des Glücks, Jahre des Leids: Gespräche mit älteren lesbischen Frauen. Dokumente.* 2nd ed. Kiel: Frühlings Erwachen, 1990.

– "Wir leiden nicht mehr, sondern sind gelitten!" Lesbisch leben in Deutschland. Cologne: Kiepenheuer & Witsch, 1987.

Korzilius, Sven. *"Asoziale" und "Parasiten" im Recht der SBZ/DDR: Randgruppen im Sozialismus zwischen Repression und Ausgrenzung.* Cologne: Böhlau, 2005.

Krenn, Karl Jürgen. *Krenn's Berlin-Chronik, 1945–1950.* Berlin: trafo, 2009.

Kühn, Monne. "'Haut der geilen Männerpresse eine in die Fresse': Itzehoer Prozess-Protest 1974." In Dennert, Leidinger, and Rauchut, *In Bewegung bleiben*, 68–71.

Kunzel, Regina. *Criminal Intimacy: Prison and the Uneven History of Modern American Sexuality.* Chicago: University of Chicago Press, 2008. https:// doi.org/10.7208/chicago/9780226824789.

Laite, Julia. *Common Prostitutes and Ordinary Citizens: Commercial Sex in London, 1885–1960.* Basingstoke, UK: Palgrave Macmillan, 2012.

Ledwa, Lara. *Mit schwulen Lesbengrüßen: Das Lesbische Aktionszentrum Westberlin (LAZ).* Giessen: Psychosozial-Verlag, 2019.

Lefebvre, Henri. *The Production of Space.* Translated by Donald Nicholson-Smith. Oxford: Blackwell, 1991.

Leidinger, Christiane. *Lesbische Existenz 1945–1969: Aspekte der Erforschung gesellschaftlicher Ausgrenzung und Diskriminierung lesbischer Frauen mit Schwerpunkt auf Lebenssituationen, Diskriminierungs- und Emanzipationserfahrungen in der frühen Bundesrepublik.* Berlin: Landesstelle für Gleichbehandlung- gegen Diskriminierung, Fachbereich LSBTI, 2015.

Lemke, Michael. *Vor der Mauer. Berlin in der Ost-West-Konkurrenz 1948 bis 1961.* Cologne: Böhlau, 2011.

Lengerke, Christiane von, Tille Ganz, Gabriele Schilling, and Margarete Schäfer. *Käthe (Kitty) Kuse. 17. März 1904 – 7. November 1999*. Self-produced video, 1985/1994.

"Lila Archiv e.V." Accessed 27 June 2019. http://www.lilaarchiv.de/.

Limpricht, Cornelia, Jürgen Müller, and Nina Oxenius. *"Verführte" Männer: das Leben der Kölner Homosexuellen im Dritten Reich*. Cologne: Volksblatt, 1991.

Lindenberger, Thomas. "'Asoziale Lebensweise': Herrschaftslegitimation, Sozialdisziplinierung und die Konstruktion eines 'negativen Milieus' in der SED-Diktatur." *Geschichte und Gesellschaft* 31, no. 2 (April–June 2005): 227–54.

Litfin, Jürgen. *Tod durch fremde Hand: das erste Maueropfer in Berlin und die Geschichte einer Familie*. With the assistance of Annette Vogel. Husum: Verlag der Nation, 2006.

Lücke, Martin. *Männlichkeit in Unordnung*. Frankfurt am Main: campus, 2008.

Lybeck, Marti M. *Desiring Emancipation: New Women and Homosexuality in Germany, 1890–1933*. SUNY series in queer politics and cultures. Albany: State University of New York Press, 2014.

Maase, Kaspar. "Establishing Cultural Democracy: Youth, 'Americanization,' and the Irresistible Rise of Popular Culture." In Schissler, *The Miracle Years*, 428–50. https://doi.org/10.1515/9780691222554-026.

Mahlsdorf, Charlotte von. *Ab durch die Mitte: Ein Spaziergang durch Berlin*. Munich: dtv, 1997.

– *Ich bin meine eigene Frau*. Munich: dtv, 1995.

Maneo, ed. *Spurensuche im Regenbogenkiez: Historische Orte und schillernde Persönlichkeiten*. Maneo-Kiezgeschichte 2. Berlin: Maneo, 2018.

Marbach, Rainer, and Volker Weiß, eds. *Konformitäten und Konfrontationen: Homosexuelle in der DDR*. Hamburg: Männerschwarm Verlag, 2017.

Marhoefer, Laurie. "Lesbianism, Transvestism, and the Nazi State: A Microhistory of a Gestapo Investigation, 1939–1943." *American Historical Review* 121, no. 4 (October 2016): 1167–95. https://doi.org/10.1093/ahr/121.4.1167.

– *Sex and the Weimar Republic: German Homosexual Emancipation and the Rise of the Nazis*. Toronto: University of Toronto Press, 2015.

McLellan, Josie. "From Private Photography to Mass Circulation: The Queering of East German Visual Culture, 1968–1989." *Central European History* 48, no. 3 (September 2015): 405–23. https://doi.org/10.1017/S0008938915000813.

– "Glad to Be Gay Behind the Wall: Gay and Lesbian Activism in 1970s East Germany." *History Workshop Journal* 74, no. 1 (Autumn 2012): 105–30. https://doi.org/10.1093/hwj/dbs017.

– *Love in the Time of Communism: Intimacy and Sexuality in the GDR*. Cambridge: Cambridge University Press, 2011.

Meyer, Sabine, ed. *Auf nach Casablanca? Lebensrealitäten transgeschlechtlicher Menschen zwischen 1945 und 1980.* Berlin: Senatsverwaltung für Justiz, Verbraucherschutz und Antidiskriminierung, Landesstelle für Gleichbehandlung – gegen Diskriminierung (LADS), 2018.

Ministerium für Justiz der DDR, ed. *Strafgesetzbuch und andere Strafgesetze.* Berlin: Deutscher Zentralverlag, 1951.

Mittenmang: Homosexuelle Frauen und Männer in Berlin 1945–1969. Schwules Museum, 3 October 2003–15 February 2004. https://www .schwulesmuseum.de/ausstellung/mittenmang-homosexuelle-frauen -und-maenner-in-berlin-1945-1969/.

Moeller, Robert G. "Private Acts, Public Anxieties, and the Fight to Decriminalize Male Homosexuality in West Germany." *Feminist Studies* 36, no. 3 (Fall 2010): 528–52.

Namaste, Viviane. "'Tragic Misreadings': Queer Theory's Erasure of Transgender Subjectivity." In *Sex Change, Social Change: Reflections on Identity, Institutions & Imperialism,* edited by Viviane Namaste, 205–38. Toronto: Women's Press, 2011.

Naumann, Kai. *Gefängnis und Gesellschaft: Freiheitsentzug in Deutschland in Wissenschaft und Praxis 1920–1960.* Berlin: LIT, 2006.

O'Brien, Patricia. "The Prison on the Continent." In *The Oxford History of the Prison: The Practice of Punishment in Western Society,* edited by Norval Morris and David J. Rothman, 199–225. New York: Oxford University Press, 1995.

Peukert, Detlev. "Die 'Halbstarken.'" *Zeitschrift für Pädagogik* 30, no. 4 (August 1984): 533–48. https://doi.org/10.25656/01:14324.

Piesche, Peggy, ed. *Labor 1989: Intersektionale Bewegungsgeschichte*n aus West und Ost.* Berlin: Verlag Yilmaz-Günay, 2019.

Pilkey, Brent, Rachael M. Scicluna, Ben Campkin, and Barbara Penner, eds. *Sexuality and Gender at Home: Experience, Politics, Transgression.* London: Bloomsbury, 2017.

Plötz, Kirsten. *Als fehle die bessere Hälfte.* Königstein: Helmer, 2005.

– "Bubis und Damen: Die zwanziger Jahre." In *Butch Femme: Eine erotische Kultur,* edited by Stephanie Kuhnen, 35–47. Berlin: Querverlag, 1997.

– *Einsame Freundinnen? Lesbisches Leben während der zwanziger Jahre in der Provinz.* Hamburg: MännerschwarmSkript Verlag, 1999.

– "Entzug der Kinder durch bundesdeutsche Gerichte: Ein Aspekt juristischer Repression von lesbischer Liebe." In *Justiz und Homosexualität,* edited by Ministerium der Justiz des Landes NRW in cooperation with Michael Schwartz, 121–7. Juristische Zeitgeschichte Nordrhein-Westfalen 24. Geldern: Ministerium der Justiz des Landes NRW, 2020.

– "...in ständiger Angst...": Eine historische Studie über rechtliche Folgen einer Scheidung für Mütter mit lesbischen Beziehungen und ihre Kinder in Westdeutschland unter besonderer Berücksichtigung von Rheinland-Pfalz (1946* *bis 2000)*. Mainz: Ministerium für Familie, Frauen, Jugend, Integration und Verbraucherschutz des Landes Rheinland-Pfalz (MFFJIV), 2021. https://mffjiv.rlp.de/fileadmin/MFFJIV/Publikationen/Vielfalt/MFFJIV_BF_Forschungsbericht_Angst_RZ_14012021_barr.pdf.

– "Wo blieb die Bewegung lesbischer Trümmerfrauen?" In Bundesstiftung Magnus Hirschfeld, *Forschung im Queerformat*, 71–86.

Plötz, Kirsten, and Marcus Velke. *Aufarbeitung von Verfolgung und Repression lesbischer und schwuler Lebensweisen in Hessen 1945–1985: Bericht im Auftrag des Hessischen Ministeriums für Soziales und Integration zum Projekt 'Aufarbeitung der Schicksale der Opfer des ehemaligen §175 StGB in Hessen im Zeitraum 1945 bis 1985'*. Berlin, 2018.

Poiger, Uta G. *Jazz, Rock, and Rebels: Cold War Politics and American Culture in a Divided Germany*. Berkeley: University of California Press, 2000. https://doi.org/10.1525/9780520920088.

Porubsky, Franz. "Eva Siewert, die 'Luxemburger Nachtigall.'" *Czernowitzer Morgenblatt*, 24 December 1933, 21. Reprinted in *Mitteilungen der Magnus-Hirschfeld-Gesellschaft*, no. 68 (March 2022): 27–8.

Praunheim, Rosa von, dir. *Die Jungs vom Bahnhof Zoo*. Rosa von Praunheim, RBB, and NDR, 2011.

Pretzel, Andreas. *Berlin – "Vorposten im Kampf für die Gleichberechtigung der Homoeroten." Die Geschichte der Gesellschaft für Reform des Sexualrechts e.V. 1948–1960*. Berlin: Schwules Museum/Verlag rosa Winkel, 2001.

– "Erst dadurch wird eine wirksame Bekämpfung ermöglicht. Polizeiliche Ermittlungen." In Pretzel and Roßbach, *Wegen der zu erwartenden hohen Strafe*, 43–73.

–, ed. *NS-Opfer unter Vorbehalt: Homosexuelle Männer in Berlin nach 1945*. Berliner Schriften zur Sexualwissenschaft und Sexualpolitik. Berlin: LIT, 2002.

Pretzel, Andreas, and Gabriele Roßbach, eds. *Wegen der zu erwartenden hohen Strafe: Homosexuellenverfolgung in Berlin 1933–1945*. With the assistance of Kulturring in Berlin e.V. Berlin: Verl. rosa Winkel, 1999.

Pretzel, Andreas, and Volker Weiß, eds. *Rosa Radikale: Die Schwulenbewegung der 1970er Jahre*. Hamburg: Männerschwarm-Verl., 2012.

Prowe, Diethelm. "The 'Miracle' of the Political-Culture Shift: Democratization between Americanization and Conservative Reintegration." In Schissler, *The Miracle Years*, 451–8. https://doi.org/10.1515/9780691222554-027.

Reissig, Harald. "Militärgefängnis/Justizvollzugsanstalt für Frauen Lehrter Str. 60/61." In *Tiergarten: Teil 2: Moabit*, edited by Helmut Engel, Berthold Grzywatz, Helmut Bräutigam, Stefi Jersch-Wenzel, Wilhelm Treue, Historische Kommission zu Berlin, 327–39. Geschichtslandschaft Berlin – Orte und Ereignisse 2. Berlin: Nicolai, 1987.

Ribbe, Wolfgang. *Berlin 1945–2000: Grundzüge der Stadtgeschichte*. Berlin: Berliner Wissenschafts-Verlag, 2002.

- "Wohnen im geteilten Berlin: Stadtplanung, Architektur und Wohnverhältnisse während des Kalten Krieges im Systemvergleich." In *Konfrontation und Wettbewerb: Wissenschaft, Technik und Kultur im geteilten Berliner Alltag (1948–1973)*, edited by Michael Lemke, 161–80. Berlin: Metropol, 2008.

Rosenkranz, Bernhard, and Gottfried Lorenz. *Hamburg auf anderen Wegen: Die Geschichte des schwulen Lebens in der Hansestadt*. Hamburg: Lambda, 2006.

Ross, Andrew Israel. *Public City/Public Sex: Homosexuality, Prostitution, and Urban Culture in Nineteenth-Century Paris*. Philadelphia, PA: Temple University Press, 2019.

- "Sex in the Archives: Homosexuality, Prostitution, and the Archives de la Préfecture de Police de Paris." *French Historical Studies* 40, no. 2 (April 2017): 267–90. https://doi.org/10.1215/00161071-3761619.

Rubin, Gayle. "Studying Sexual Subcultures: Excavating the Ethnography of Gay Communities in Urban North America." In *Out in Theory: The Emergence of Lesbian and Gay Anthropology*, edited by Ellen Lewin and William L. Leap, 17–68. Urbana: University of Illinois Press, 2002. https://doi.org/10.5406/j.ctvvng2r.6.

Sannwald, Daniela. "Der Frauenknast als Sündenpfuhl: Maria Schmidts Videokompilation 'Die Pfoten bleiben über dem Laken.'" *Frauen und Film*, nos. 58/59 (July 1996): 139–44.

Scheidle, Ilona. "Hilde Radusch: Ein Kleinod der Frauen-Lesbengeschichte." Heinrich Böll Stiftung, 14 July 2014. https://www.boell.de/de/2014/07/14/hilde-radusch-ein-kleinod-der-frauen-lesbengeschichte.

Schissler, Hannah, ed. *The Miracle Years: A Cultural History of West Germany, 1949–1968*. Princeton, NJ: Princeton University Press, 2001. https://doi.org/10.1515/9780691222554.

Schlüter, Bastian, Karl-Heinz Steinle, and Andreas Sternweiler. *Eberhardt Brucks. Ein Grafiker in Berlin*. Berlin: Schwules Museum, 2008.

Schoppmann, Claudia. *Days of Masquerade: Life Stories of Lesbians During the Third Reich*. Translated by Allison Brown. New York: Columbia University Press, 1996.

- *Zeit der Maskierung: Lebensgeschichten lesbischer Frauen im "Dritten Reich."* Berlin: Fischer, 1998.

Schroeder, Klaus. *Der SED-Staat: Geschichte und Strukturen der DDR 1949–1990*. Cologne: Böhlau, 2013.

Schwarz, Richard. "Schwarz Stadtplan von Berlin." Berlin: Schwarz, 1947. https://digital.zlb.de/viewer/image/15454953/1/.

"Selbstbild Lili-Elbe-Archiv." Accessed 7 August 2019. http://www.lili-elbe-archive.org/selbstbild.html.

Siemens, Daniel. *Horst Wessel: Tod und Verklärung eines Nationalsozialisten*. Munich: Siedler, 2009.

Siewert, Eva. "Das Orakel." *Der Weg. Zeitschrift für Fragen des Judentums* 1, no. 37 (1946): 5. https://eva-siewert.de/wp-content/uploads/2019/02/Das-Orakel-von-Eva-Siewert.pdf.

Sigusch, Volkmar. *Geschichte der Sexualwissenschaft.* Frankfurt am Main : campus, 2008.

Silva, Adrian de. *Negotiating the Borders of the Gender Regime: Developments and Debates on Trans(Sexuality) in the Federal Republic of Germany.* Gender Studies. Bielefeld: transcript-Verlag, 2018.

Smith, Brenda V. "Analyzing Prison Sex: Reconciling Self-Expression with Safety." In *Interrupted Life: Experiences of Incarcerated Women in the United States,* edited by Rickie Solinger, Paula C. Johnson, Martha L. Raimon, Tina Reynolds, and Ruby C. Tapia, 112–20. Berkeley: University of California Press, 2010. https://doi.org/10.1525/9780520944565-024.

"Sonderaktionen der Polizei." In *Lexikon zur Homosexuellenverfolgung 1933–1945: Institutionen – Kompetenzen – Betätigungsfelder,* edited by Günter Grau, 280–2. Berlin: LIT, 2011.

Spector, Scott. *Violent Sensations. Sex, Crime and Utopia in Vienna and Berlin, 1860–1914.* Chicago: University of Chicago Press, 2016. https://doi.org/10.7208/9780226196817.

Statistisches Amt der DDR. *Statistisches Jahrbuch der Deutschen Demokratischen Republik, 1990,* vol. 35. Berlin: Rudolf Haufe Verlag, 1990.

Steakley, James D. *The Homosexual Emancipation Movement in Germany.* New York: Arno Press, 1975.

Steer, Christine. *Eingeliefert nach Rummelsburg: Vom Arbeitshaus im Kaiserreich bis zur Haftanstalt in der DDR.* Berlin: BeBra Wissenschaft, 2018.

Steinbacher, Sybille. *Wie der Sex nach Deutschland kam: Der Kampf um Sittlichkeit und Anstand in der frühen Bundesrepublik.* Munich: Siedler, 2011.

Steinborn, Norbert, and Hilmar Krüger. *Die Berliner Polizei 1945–1992: Von der Militärreserve im Kalten Krieg auf dem Weg zur bürgernahen Polizei?* Berlin: Berlin Verlag, 1993.

Steinle, Karl-Heinz. *Der literarische Salon bei Richard Schulz.* Berlin: Schwules Museum, 2002.

Sternburg, Wilhelm von. *Um Deutschland geht es uns. Arnold Zweig. Eine Biographie.* Berlin: Aufbau, 2004.

Strafgesetzbuch für das Deutsche Reich, 1871. Wikisource. https://de.wikisource.org/wiki/Strafgesetzbuch_für_das_Deutsche_Reich_(1871). Originally published in *Deutsches Reichsgesetzblatt* 1871, no. 24 (15 May 1871): 127–205.

Sutton, Katie. "From Sexual Inversion to Trans*: Transgender History and Historiography." In *Was ist Homosexualität? Forschungsgeschichte, gesellschaftliche Entwicklungen und Perspektiven,* edited by Florian Mildenberger, Jennifer Evans, Rüdiger Lautmann, and Jakob Pastötter, 181–203. Hamburg: Männerschwarm Verlag, 2014.

- *The Masculine Woman in Weimar Germany.* Monographs in German history, vol. 32. New York: Berghahn Books, 2011.

Tammer, Teresa. "Verräter oder Vermittler? Inoffizielle Informanten zwischen Staatssicherheit und DDR-Schwulenbewegung." In *Welche "Wirklichkeit" und wessen "Wahrheit"? Das Geheimdienstarchiv als Quelle und Medium der Wissensproduktion,* edited by Thomas Großbölting and Sabine Kittel, 107–23. Göttingen: Vandenhoeck & Ruprecht, 2019.

- "Warme Brüder im Kalten Krieg: Schwule Bewegungen in der DDR und im geteilten Deutschland in den 1970er und 1980er Jahren." PhD diss. Westfälische Wilhelms-Universität, 2020.

Tapia, Ruby C. "Profane Illuminations: The Gendered Problematics of Critical Carceral Visualities." *PMLA* 123, no. 3 (May 2008): 684–8. https://doi.org/10.1632/pmla.2008.123.3.684.

Taylor, Michael Thomas, and Annette F. Timm. "Historicizing Transgender Terminology." In *Others of My Kind: Transatlantic Transgender Histories,* edited by Alex Bakker, Rainer Herrn, Michael Thomas Taylor, and Annette F. Timm, 251–65. Calgary: University of Calgary Press, 2020.

Taylor, Michael Thomas, Annette F. Timm, and Rainer Herrn, eds. *Not Straight from Germany: Sexual Publics and Sexual Citizenship since Magnus Hirschfeld.* Ann Arbor: University of Michigan Press, 2017. https://doi.org/10.3998/mpub.9238370.

Theis, Wolfgang, and Andreas Sternweiler. "Alltag im Kaiserreich und in der Weimarer Republik." In Verein der Freunde eines Schwulen Museums in Berlin e.V., *Eldorado,* 48–73.

Thilo, Peter. *Ein Igel weint Tränen aus Rosenholz oder Die Kulturluftschiffer Berlins aus der Sicht des Bodenpersonals betrachtet.* Unpublished novel manuscript, 1995. Schwules Museum, Berlin.

Timm, Annette F. *The Politics of Fertility in Twentieth-Century Berlin.* New York: Cambridge University Press, 2010.

"Treffpunkt Berlin." *Der Spiegel,* no. 34 (17 August 1965): 49. https://www.spiegel.de/politik/treffpunkt-berlin-a-f907bf20-0002-0001-0000-000046273739.

Verein der Freunde eines Schwulen Museums in Berlin e.V., ed. *Eldorado: Homosexuelle Frauen und Männer in Berlin 1850–1950. Geschichte, Alltag und Kultur.* Katalog der Ausstellung im Berlin Museum, 26.5.-8.7.1984. Berlin: Frölich & Kaufmann, 1984.

Vicinus, Martha. "The History of Lesbian History." *Feminist Studies* 38, no. 3 (Fall 2012): 566–96. https://doi.org/10.1353/fem.2012.0043.

Vormbaum, Moritz. *Das Strafrecht der Deutschen Demokratischen Republik.* Jus Poenale 6. Tübingen: Mohr Siebeck, 2015.

Voß, Heinz-Jürgen, ed. *Westberlin – ein sexuelles Porträt.* Giessen: Psychosozial-Verlag, 2021.

Wachsmann, Nikolaus. *Gefangen unter Hitler: Justizterror und Strafvollzug im NS-Staat.* Munich: Siedler, 2006.

– *Hitler's Prisons: Legal Terror in Nazi Germany.* New Haven: Yale University Press, 2004.

Wallbraun, Barbara. "Lesben im Visier der Staatssicherheit." In *"Das Übersehenwerden hat Geschichte": Lesben in der DDR und in der friedlichen Revolution,* edited by Heinrich-Böll-Stiftung Sachsen-Anhalt and Gunda-Werner-Institut, 26–50. Halle: Heinrich-Böll-Stiftung Sachsen-Anhalt, Gunda Werner Institut für Feminismus und Geschlechterdemokratie, 2015.

Weeks, Jeffrey. *Coming Out: Homosexual Politics in Britain from the Nineteenth Century to the Present.* London: Quartet Books, 1977.

Weinberg, Lorenz. "Feminist Sex Wars in der deutschen Lesbenbewegung? Diskussionen über lesbisch_queere Sexualität und Femme/Butch in der (West-)Berliner Lesbenzeitschrift UKZ der 1980er und 90er Jahre." In *Transposing the Year of the Women,* edited by Vera Hoffmann and Schwules Museum, 68–85. Berlin: Schwules Museum, 2022. https://yearofthewomen .net/de/magazin/202201002_magazin_transposingyotw.pdf.

Wetzell, Richard F., ed. *Crime and Criminal Justice in Modern Germany.* New York: Berghahn, 2014.

Whisnant, Clayton J. *Male Homosexuality in West Germany: Between Persecution and Freedom, 1945–69.* Genders and Sexualities in History series. Basingstoke, UK: Palgrave Macmillan, 2012.

Wolfert, Raimund. "Eva Siewert (1907–1994), Kurt Hillers 'Schwester im Geiste' – 'Wilde Freundschaft für Sie im Herzen meines Hirns.'" Online-Projekt Lesbengeschichte, Berlin, 2015/2016. Edited by Ingeborg Boxhammer and Christiane Leidinger. https://www.lesbengeschichte.org/bio_siewert_d.html.

– *Homosexuellenpolitik in der jungen Bundesrepublik: Kurt Hiller, Hans Giese und das Frankfurter Wissenschaftlich-humanitäre Komitee.* Hirschfeld Lectures. Göttingen: Wallstein Verlag, 2015.

– "Zwischen den Stühlen – die deutsche Homophilenbewegung der 1950er Jahre." In Bundesstiftung Magnus Hirschfeld, *Forschung im Queerformat,* 87–104.

Wolff, Charlotte. *Magnus Hirschfeld: A Portrait of a Pioneer in Sexology.* London: Quartet Books, 1986.

Young, Iris Marion. "House and Home: Feminist Variations on a Theme." In Young, *On Female Body Experience,* 123–54. https://doi.org/10.1093/019516 1920.003.0008.

– *On Female Body Experience: Throwing Like a Girl and Other Essays.* New York: Oxford University Press, 2005. https://doi.org/10.1093/0195161920.001.0001.

Zur Nieden, Susanne. "Einleitung." In *Homosexualität und Staatsräson: Männlichkeit, Homophobie und Politik in Deutschland 1900–1945,* edited by Susanne zur Nieden, 7–14. Frankfurt am Main: campus, 2005.

– "Neuanfang in der Schöneberger Verwaltung." In Zur Nieden, Schönknecht, and Schönknecht, *Weiterleben nach dem Krieg*, 32–9.

– *Unwürdige Opfer: Die Aberkennung von NS-Verfolgten in Berlin 1945 bis 1949.* Berlin: Metropol, 2003.

Zur Nieden, Susanne, and Helga Schönknecht, Eberhard Schönknecht, eds. *Weiterleben nach dem Krieg. Schöneberg/Friedenau 1945–6.* Berlin: Bezirksamt Schöneberg von Berlin, Kunstamt, 1992.

Index

Note: A page number in *italics* denotes a figure.

240 Index

homemaking (*continued*)
documentation of, 49, 51–2;
in East Berlin, 54–62; gardens,
32, 56, *58–60*, 62–3; lesbian
subjectivity constituted through,
63; letters, notes, and calendars,
49–53; memorialization as, 37–44,
62–3; parties and celebrations
and, 59, 61; photography as, 48,
61–2; politics of, 24–5; precarity of,
49–51; privacy and, 45–7, 64; sex
and, 45–6, 53; terms for, 24
homes: class and, 45–6; in danger,
63; feminist theorizations of,
19; of Kuse and Zimmel, 47–8;
privacy of, 104; as queer spaces,
4; of Radusch and Klopsch, 32–7,
49–54, 63; §175 and, 46; of Siewert
and Carlé, 25–31, 62; of Thomas
and Helli, 54–62; transient, 106–7.
See also apartments; bars
homophile publications, 18, 42. See also
Freunde, Die; *Kreis, Der*; *Weg, Der*
homophobia: in archival sources,
16; attacks related to, 78, 85,
112–13, 186n69; in German
history, 6; "homophobic
consensus" (Zur Nieden), 9;
persistent, 13, 133; in prison,
204n12; violence and, 112
homosexuality: anxieties around, 76;
(de)criminalization, 78, 86–7, 101,
121; female sex work vs., 196n5; as
femininity, 88; Hirschfeld's writing
on, 38; historical understandings of,
158; as identity, 88; prison and, 137,
145–6; reparative attempts, 108; the
Stasi vilifying, 122; suspected, 78;
transvestitism and, 118
Honecker, Erich, 122, 133
Houlbrook, Matt, 5, 14, 181n2
Huneke, Samuel, 166n14,
177n116

identity, 19, 83, 88, 117–19
Ihns, Marion, 211n95
Inconnue, L' (Charlottenburg lesbian
bar), 101. *See also* bars
Institute for Sexual Science, 8, 23,
37–9, 42–3
intimacy, 48, 54, 66, 125, 135, 148
Iran, 26–7
Isherwood, Christopher, 8

Jansa-Hütte (Neukölln, bar), 97, 100,
193n133. *See also* bars
Jewishness, 27–9, 40, 170n22
John, Otto, 78, 92
Jolly Nine (lesbian club), 9
Jungs vom Bahnhof Zoo, Die (von
Praunheim, Sechting; film), 197n8
Jurr, Gerhard, 35, 172n49

Kaltofen, Dr., 42
Kapp, Orest, 88–9, 108–9, 111, 115,
138–9
Kathi und Eva (Schöneberg bar), 72,
90–1. *See also* bars
Katter, Gerd: Hirschfeld's impact on,
23, 37–8, 40–3, 63; letters, 173n63,
174n71; life, 37–9, 44, 173n59,
173n63, 173n68, 174n69; socio-
economic status, 63
Kaufmann, Hertha, 54, 180n159
Kennedy, Elizabeth, 55, 138, 178n126
Kinsey, Alfred, 42
Kitty Kuse papers, 17. *See also*
archives
Klappen (public toilets), 110–12, 130
Kleist-Casino (West Berlin bar), 72,
83–4, 92. *See also* bars
Klimmer, Rudolf, 42–3
Klöppel, Ulrike, 116, 163–4, 201n43,
201n45, 201n63, 214nn10–11,
214nn17–18
Klopsch, Else "Eddy": death, 53–4;
home with Radusch, 32–7, 49–54,

GERMAN AND EUROPEAN STUDIES

General Editor: Jennifer L. Jenkins

Printed and bound by CPI Group (UK) Ltd, Croydon, CR0 4YY

09/06/2025

14685789-0001

Eliot's *Objective Correlative*
Tradition or Individual Talent

Eliot's *Objective Correlative*

Tradition or Individual Talent

Contributions to the History of a *Topos*

FLEMMING OLSEN

sussex
ACADEMIC
PRESS

Brighton • Chicago • Toronto

2 4 6 8 10 9 7 5 3 1

First published 2012 in Great Britain in the United Kingdom by
SUSSEX ACADEMIC PRESS
PO Box 139   Eastbourne BN24 9BP

Distributed in North America by
SUSSEX ACADEMIC PRESS
Independent Publishers Group
814 N. Franklin Street, Chicago, IL 60610

British Library Cataloguing in Publication Data
A CIP catalogue record for this book is available from the British Library.

Library of Congress Cataloguing-in-Publication Data
Olsen, Flemming.
Eliot's objective correlative : tradition or individual talent? :   contributions to
the history of a topos / by Flemming Olsen.
p. cm.
Includes bibliographical references and index.
ISBN 978-1-84519-554-0 (p/b : acid-free paper)
1. Eliot, T. S. (Thomas Stearns), 1888–1965—Criticism and interpretation.
I. Title.
PS3509.L43Z7966 2012
821'.912—dc23

2012015909

Typeset by Sussex Academic Press, Brighton & Eastbourne.
Printed and bound by CPI Group (UK) Ltd, Croydon, CR0 4YY

CONTENTS

Note to the Reader

French quotations running to more that a couple of words are given in their original formulation in the Notes. The English version that appears in the text is my own translation.

Il y a dans le mot, dans le *verbe,* quelque chose de *sacré,* qui nous défend d'en faire un jeu de hazard.

CHARLES BAUDELAIRE

INTRODUCTION

The only way of expressing emotion in the form of art is by finding
an "objective correlative":

> in other words, a set of objects, a situation, a chain of events which
> shall be the formula of that *particular* emotion such that when the
> external facts, which must terminate in sensory experience, are
> given, the emotion is immediately evoked.

Is Eliot's "objective correlative" just an idiosyncratic rephrasing
of the conventional formulation "the right word in the right
place"? If so, critical reverence for the dictum is inversely propor-
tional to its significance. Or is it a ground-breaking contribution
to the centuries-old discussion of the relationship between *sensus*
and *verbum*? In either case, Eliot's statement is intriguing and
deserving of closer analysis. Obviously, any human communication is dependent on the participants' — the sender's and the
receiver's — choice of words. A poet is a person who is endowed
with a well-developed ear for words, and since he or she finds
himself or herself in a specific communication situation — usually,
there is no immediate response from a receiver — the demands on
his or her control of the vocabulary are especially great.

Literary critics from Antiquity and onwards have dealt, more
or less explicitly, with the capacity of language to describe what is
conventionally called reality, to account for a person's feelings or
the workings of his or her mind, or to characterize another human
being or a situation.

However, Eliot does not give any sources or investigate any origins for his statement, which is remarkable, not only in the light of his awe-inspiring erudition and the effortless roaming in, and familiarity with, European literature that he demonstrates in his essays, but also when we consider his immense preoccupation with the use of words, their notional content, and their rhythmical sound.

Eliot, whom Hugh Kenner called "the most influential man of letters of the twentieth century"[1] never wrote, and never intended to write, an *ars poetica*. His critical output is to be found in the numerous critical essays he wrote on the oeuvres of mainly English and American, but to some extent also foreign authors' works — even though it must be admitted that some of his titles seem to promise more of an in-depth treatment than is actually offered.

Most of those essays date form the 1920s and 1930s, and in remarks scattered in his later writings, Eliot was at pains to emphasize that his taste within criticism changed with the increasing amount of literature that he read, and his growing life experience. The attitude is a faint echo of what his teacher, the philosopher Francis Herbert Bradley, once said: "The usual self of one period is not the usual self of another."[2] However, the dictum about the "objective correlative", which occurred originally in the *Hamlet* essay from 1920, was incorporated unaltered in the collection of essays *The Sacred Wood*, which appeared in 1928, and was preserved in the 1969 edition of that book. Eliot's preoccupation with the verbalization aspect also appears from the fact that even in essays dealing with philosophical or theological aspects he devotes a considerable amount of attention to the formulations chosen by the author of the analysed work.

The idea of the objective correlative is another illustration of Eliot's concern with the precise rendering of a poet's reactions. It is, on the one hand, an implicit warning against the vague effusions to be found in the feeble works of the Georgian poets who dominated the scene. On the other hand, it is a contribution to the old debate about poetic diction and about the relationship between language and reality. Eliot's emphasis on the verbal aspect, and, more generally, on form, fits in nicely with concerns prevalent in the literary climate and the intellectual Zeitgeist in the first two decades of the 20th century, when a reaction against what was felt as the dry rigidity of the Positivist world picture gathered momentum. The wording of the passage in which the objective correlative is presented is reminiscent of a Positivist axiomatic statement on a point of science: it is a fact that. . . .

The point is precision, not emotionalism: *objectivity* should be the sought-for ideal, and of course there is a *correlative*, a correspondence, which does not necessarily mean a one-to-one accord, between a writer's reaction to a stimulus from his surroundings and some item or phenomenon in those surroundings. The crux of the matter is to become aware of it and to express it adequately. The poet is not specifically referred to, but Eliot's formulation leaves us in no doubt that his words are meant as advice to, or even demands on, the poet, and such demands are not up for discussion.

As in Positivist science, the truth was not only obtainable, but also one and indivisible. However, as will appear in the following pages, Eliot's objective correlative raises at least as many hares as it shoots.

This book is not a systematic review of the ideas held by critics from Antiquity and onwards on the subject of the relationship between language and reality. Such a treatment would require volumes; hence the concentration has been on authors and critics who can be said, in some sense, to anticipate Eliot's theory.

CHAPTER ONE

SOME CLASSICAL
PREDECESSORS

Aristotle

In the opening lines to the Introduction to his *Poetics*, Aristotle announces that "my design is to treat of poetry in general, and of its several species".[1] The "species" are categorized in the next paragraph: "epic poetry, tragedy, comedy, dithyrambics, as also, for the most part, the music of the flute and the lyre".[2]

Aristotle immediately proceeds to establish their common feature: they are all imitations of the actions of men. And what the Stagirite understands by 'imitation' is explained later in the *Poetics*:

> (The poet) "must represent things such as they were or are; or such as they are said to be and believed to be; or such as they should be, . . . [3]

So, Aristotle assumes that there is such a thing as a world separate form the poet. For the concept of imitation to be at all meaningful, there must be something or somebody to imitate. Equally, he presupposes the existence of one or more recipients of the poet's achievement. Already in this very early theory, we meet the triad that has become a classic in communication theory, viz.

sender, message, and receiver. And Aristotle generalizes on behalf of mankind: "All men . . . naturally receive pleasure from imitation."[4] It is postulated that it is in man's *nature* to have a positive attitude to imitation.

Aristotle is himself an adherent of imitation: in viewing the works of art, "we contemplate with pleasure, and with the more pleasure the more they are imitated".[5] In his opinion, even rhythm, melody, and verse are "means of imitation".[6] Since words play a central part where imitation is concerned, they feature prominently in *Poetics* right from the beginning: "Words have a capacity to imitate",[7] and "the *epopeia* imitates by words alone, or by verse".[8] Eliot's theory is, *mutatis mutandis*, an echo of the former of those statements.

References to words, their composition and use occur regularly in *Poetics*. A noun is "a sound composed of other sounds", and the same goes for the verb.[9] "Diction" is one of the necessary six "parts" that constitute the peculiar character or quality of a tragedy. "The excellence of diction consists in being perspicuous without being mean."[10] The art of being "perspicuous", i.e. capable of expressing things clearly, is central to Eliot's conception of the objective correlative.

The poet can work with words: the language of tragedy should be "embellished and rendered pleasurable",[11] and "the greatest (sc. excellence) of all is to be happy in the use of metaphor; for it is this alone that cannot be acquired, and which, consisting in a quiet discernment of resemblances, is a certain mark of genius".[12]

The receiver makes a rare appearance in *Poetics*, and the work does not seem to cater for a specific group of recipients. However, the existence of a target group is obviously presupposed. "We" like successful imitations, it says on one of the first pages, and what would be the purpose of "embellishing" the presentation if it were not for the benefit of a recipient?

Poetics is a study of the creation of some literary genres, and it is an attempt to devise a system for 'poetry' as Aristotle knew it. In some respects, the treatise is also a list of prescriptions to a budding poet, and the large number of quotations of outstanding poets' achievements may serve as a guide to anyone who would like to try his hand at literary pursuits.

Discreet advice to the poet is scattered throughout the work: he must be a master of formulation so as to be able to render the presentation elegant, he must find words that are appropriate to the heroic deeds he depicts, he must never lose sight of the imitation aspect, and it is desirable that he should show some competence, if not "genius", in the handling of metaphor. Aristotle sees no rigid dividing line between epic poetry and tragedy in terms of content and form: they are both written in verse, and Aristotle is obviously attracted to metre, which is "plainly a species of rhythm".[13]

It is interesting, not least for the subject of this book, that this very early example of literary criticism should devote so much space to the language issue, more particularly to the use of words. The reason why they fascinate Aristotle is that words, according to him, have the capacity to imitate, and the purpose of epic poetry and tragedy is imitation. His copious exemplification shows that what he has in mind is not onomatopoeia, but metaphoric application of the everyday vocabulary. The aim for the 'maker' — the etymological meaning of 'poet' — should be to obtain precision and elegance.

Imitation, as Aristotle sees it, 'points outwards' — the phenomenon particularly worthy of imitation is heroic action, just as Eliot found that 'a scene' might be an appropriate objective correlative for a poet's reaction. Aristotle does not talk about an inward-looking reproduction of the workings of the poet's mind. Nor does Eliot.

Demetrius of Phalerum (c. 350–263 BC)

Demetrius was both a statesman and a philosopher, an enlightened governor of Athens, an an outstanding orator, and the author of many scholarly works, among them a treatise *On Style*, which is a mixture of stock-taking and advice to prospective poets and dramatists, i.e. in many respects similar to Aristotle's *Poetics*.

Demetrius undertakes a detailed categorization of styles: the plain style, the polished style, the dignified style, etc. He dwells on sentences, especially with reference to their length, and on the choice of words suitable to each style. The treatise is the fruit of his own extensive reading, and the aim is to show how a listener or spectator — or perhaps a reader — (none of whom are ever referred to explicitly) can be influenced, impressed, or disgusted.

For the benefit of the recipient, it is important that the diction be suited to the style, and Demetrius' work lives up to its title: it is a collection of stylistic figures and their effects. Metaphors and different metres are described at great length in terms of their contributions to the creation of a total effect. But also words are given a considerable amount of attention: the arrangement of words, the coining of new words, and the role of the individual word in the context are commented on. "A rough word produces a rough effect", says Demetrius.[14]

Horace

Horace's *Epistle to the Pisos*, better known as *Ars poetica*, was probably written around 19 BC. Addressed to a father and two sons, the letter contains advice to an aspiring poet, its emphasis being on the content of especially tragedy and epic poetry. Horace, too, follows in Aristotle's footsteps.

The idea of appropriateness, or correlation, where content is concerned, appears at the very start: neither in a painting nor in a poem should a horse's neck be united to a human head.

The work is impressionistic and allusive, anything but systematic. In *Essay on Criticism* (ll. 653–54), Pope gives a succinct characterization:

Horace still charms with graceful negligence,
And without method talks us into sense.

References to the recommended treatment of words occur sporadically and always in the form of *obiter dicta* that are not further elaborated. But that Horace was aware of the part played by words is evidenced by statements like the following:

> Let the author of the proposed poem show taste and care in linking up his words; let him embrace one word and reject another. Your diction will be excellent if a clever combination renders a familiar word original.[15]

It is possible to read an allusion to metaphoric use of language into that statement. Also, Horace is aware that "words perish with old age, and others, newly born, thrive and flourish like youths".[16] That opinion is difficult to reconcile with Eliot's conception of the stability of word meanings.

And what, in Horace's view, were poets going to write about? "I would advise the well-instructed imitator to take his model from life and customs, and from this derive language faithful to life."[17] So Horace acknowledges the mimetic principle, and the *imitandum* was the world outside the poet, not what was going on in his own mind. That attitude would be heartily endorsed by Eliot.

As to the process of verbalization, Horace echoes Cato the Elder's first rule for orators: "rem tene, verba sequentur". Horace repeats the advice, in a slightly different formulation, in the same passage as the previous quotation: "Words will quickly follow when the matter is ready".[18] That is as far as this eminent critic from Antiquity goes in the handling of the thorny problem of accounting for the leap from impression to formulation.

CHAPTER TWO

SPRAT, LOCKE,
HARTMANN

Thomas Sprat

In his *History of the Royal Society* (1667), Thomas Sprat pointed to the significance of the word for the written records of scientists. He paid tribute to

> the primitive purity and shortness when men deliver'd so many things almost in an equal number of words . . . Things lie in great number before the mind, awaiting arrangement and selection. The mind, on the other hand, is wholly separate from them: things can be clearly and distinctly separated from our continuous experience of them . . . What I experience governs all thought.[1]

The statement is in accordance with the Cartesian dichotomy, and at the same time anticipates the theory of Locke. Also, it will be seen, it is a declaration of content for Positivist scientists' outlook on "reality"

John Locke

An Essay Concerning Human Understanding, published in 1690 after 30 years of epistemological speculation, refutes the theory of innate ideas, the "establish'd Opinion amongst some Men, That there are in the Understanding certain Innate Principles . . . which the Soul receives in its very first Being, and brings into the World with it". Locke's often quoted dictum "nihil in intellectu quod non prius in sensu" posits the existence of a something outside the sentient ego which is a determining factor for the operations of the human mind.

The content of our minds stems from sensory experience. Far from discussing the nature of 'reality', Locke points to the indispensability of our surroundings: without input from the outside world, man's mind would be a blank, a *tabula rasa* — apart from some instruments suitable for the reception and processing of sensory data, we must presume. Locke talks about mankind in general so the inference is that a poet, too, is dependent on 'the other' for his material.

The relevance of Locke's assumption for Eliot's theory of the objective correlative is obvious: sense data impact on the observant poet, whose special talent enables him to find 'le mot juste' to describe, characterize, or assess his sensory experience. Like Locke, Eliot not only presupposes the existence of 'reality', he also sees it as the poet's obligation to 'take it as it is' and not to 'improve' it or moralize on it, as for example the Neo-Classicists did.

Also, Locke's speculations on the 'nominal essence' of objects have some bearing on the subject dealt with in this book. According to Locke, the name we give an object represents our idea of that object. How such names come into existence remains obscure. However, some similarity can be detected with what lies at the root of Eliot's postulate about the objective correlative: by calling his reaction a name, the poet conjures up in the receiver's mind an image or an analogue of that reaction.

Hartmann

The conditions for giving verbal expression to feelings were discussed by the German philosopher Edouard von Hartmann, who, in his book *Philosophy of the Unconscious* (1869) takes the Lockean position one step further: "only in so far as thoughts can be already translated into words, only so far are they *communicable*" (his italics).[2]

CHAPTER THREE

GAUTIER, BAUDELAIRE, GOURMONT

Gautier

It is a well-known fact that English art criticism towards the end of the 19th century and in the first two decades of the 20th century was heavily indebted to contemporary French theorists. One French critic who served as a source of inspiration to Eliot was Théophile Gautier (1811–72), whose reflections on language in general and 'le mot juste' in particular were of crucial significance to Eliot's supposition about the objective correlative.

Gautier began as art critic in 1832 with only minimal knowledge about pictorial principles. His critical oeuvre, covering a multitude of aspects of painting, sculpture, architecture, drama, and music, spans some forty years.[1] Economic necessity seems to have been the root cause of his prodigious output. He produced regular *Salon* articles, collected in three books from 1847, 1855, and 1861 respectively.

"One should not neglect the craft that is an essential part of every art form," he said in 1836.[2] The formal aspect of art was what fascinated him; the sculpture and architecture of Antiquity — categories of art where form is visible and palpable — delighted him,[3] and his manifest interest in painting largely concentrated on form. The title of his collection of poetry from 1852, *Emaux et Camées*, is meant to express, in his own words,

the plan of treating small subjects in a restricted form . . . Each
piece should be a locket . . . The author only used the eight-foot
verse, which he remelted, burnished and chased with all the care
of which he is capable.[4]

One of Gautier's axioms was that there is no idea which cannot
be expressed.[5] And in a conversation with Emile Bergerat he said:

the person who is surprised by a thought, be it ever so complex,
or by a vision, be it ever so apocalyptic, without having words to
express it, is not a writer.[6]

To Gautier, poetry is primarily a linguistic art form. Its object
was neither didactic nor mimetic, but to give a representation of
the ideal beauty that all artists contain within them. The individual artist contemplates that ideal beauty through "the eyes of
the soul" in such a way that all that they see is subordinated to that
august concept.[7] By writing what occurs to him (ce qui lui vient à
la tête), the poet manages to create something that is better than
if he had slavishly copied the world around him. "When Mr.
Delacroix creates a picture, he looks into himself instead of placing
his nose at the window."[8]

In Gautier's perception, every poet should carry within him a
'microcosm', i.e. a diminutive perfect world from which he extracts
the thought and form of his work. So, unlike the Neo-Classicists,
to whom the ideal was outside the artist, to Gautier mimesis meant
a processed introspection. The stimulus came from outside, but it
was the poet's reservoir that enabled him to lick it into shape. To
Gautier, a suitable poetic subject was not a ransacking of the poet's
own mind.

In a review article from 1847 — the book being reviewed is
Rudolph Töpffer's *Réflexions et menus Propos d'un peintre genevois* —
Gautier elaborates on his theory:

A man who has not his inner world to translate is not an artist.

Imitation is the means and not the end. . . . However, it should
not be concluded that the artist is purely subjective; he is also
objective; he gives and he receives. He takes from nature the signs
he needs in order to express it. Those signs he transforms: he adds
or removes according to the type of his thinking . . . The painter
carries his picture inside him, and the canvas serves as an inter-
mediary between nature and himself.[9]

The Lockean echo is unmistakable: everything begins with
sense impressions. However, Gautier proceeds beyond this initial
stage. Once the signal has been received, the poet's imagination
starts its operations: it 'translates' the input, gently bringing it
into accordance with the components of the microcosm in the
poet's mind. Admittedly, the ontological status of the microcosm
and its ingredients, and how it all came into existence, remains
unexplained. But Gautier is one of the few literary theorists who
have acknowledged the verbalization problem, and who has dug
one spit deeper in an attempt to explain the workings of the
creative imagination.

The imagination is postulated to play a passive as well as an
active role: a subject/object relationship is held to obtain between
the outside world and the poet's mind. Before he delivers the result
to his recipients, the poet has put his individual stamp on the original sense impression.

The conclusion drawn by Gautier is that the imagination is, at
the same time, creator and judge. Thus poetry and criticism
become complementary activities. Poetic creation is more than just
a whisper from the Muse: it is the result of a conscious process, and
it requires constant contributions from the poet's awareness and
verbal competence.

Since he is a directly responsible participant in the process, it is
incumbent on the poet not to be carried away by his passions. On
the contrary, he should endeavour to control them. By the same
token, the poet should practise incessant theoretical and methodological criticism of what he has created. Thus he will be able to

achieve what is to Gautier the ultimate purpose of poetry, viz. the cultivation and encouragement of beauty.[10]

Baudelaire

Charles Baudelaire (1821–67) started his career at a time when Gautier was held in high esteem as a journalist and a man of letters. The two men met in 1845, and by 1851 they were on 'cher ami' and first-name terms. Baudelaire considered Gautier his mentor and dedicated his epoch-making poem *Fleurs du Mal* (1857) to Gautier.

Baudelaire wrote two 'studies' (*Etudes*), i.e. long essays, about Gautier. The first came out in 1859, in the periodical *L'Artiste*, the second in 1861, in *Les Poètes français.*[11] In those two studies, Baudelaire in his tribute to Gautier indirectly gives expression to some elements of his own poetic credo.

It is evident that the formal aspect of poetry is Baudelaire's primary concern in the *Etudes*: he extols the balance and precision, the rigour bordering on mathematical exactitude, that he finds in Gautier's poems. Gautier always finds the right word, 'le mot juste', and the adequate image.

Baudelaire is impressed by Gautier's "constante recherche verbale" and his technical virtuosity as versifier: Gautier was always at pains to enrich the language, to extend its limits, so as to make it 'say more'.[12] Gautier's choice of words refers to all aspects of human activity and civilization. He includes terms from technology, science, and the arts; he coins neologisms and does not shrink from using archaisms and foreign words.

Baudelaire pays tribute to the originality of Gautier's vocabulary. Words are chosen for their suggestiveness and the inherent beauty of their sounds. Gautier's use of metaphors, unexpected associations and bold *rapprochements* contribute to creating a harmonious and rhythmical effect. In a reference to Greek statues, for example, Gautier talks about "la musique des formes humaines", and about Alboni, a celebrated singer, about whom he says, "mellifluousness bursts forth from his lips like vapour with a sound attached to it".[13]

Baudelaire is respectful towards Gautier's painstaking and meticulous labour with language: the poet, in filtering the language, cleans it. Thanks to his astounding linguistic command, Gautier was able to put even the most diminutive observation in its natural place without omitting any detail. All the time, Gautier's supreme mastery of language prompts "le mot propre, le mot unique" to spring forth, and the total effect is one of immaculate order.[14]

The encomia printed above should not be taken to mean that Baudelaire was unequivocally enthusiastic about Gautier's theories of art. Thus he was sceptical with regard to the latter's vagueness about 'ideal beauty', and he decidedly distanced himself from Gautier's strong attachment to religion. It is uncertain whether the two men met after 1859.

In his early career, Baudelaire was, by most critics, considered inferior to Gautier both as poet and as critic. However, later in the 19th century Baudelaire was rehabilitated by influential poets such as Verlaine, Rimbaud, Laforgue and the Symbolists.[15] By the early 20th century, Gautier's stature as an all-round critic was on the wane, but his linguistic theories and his poetical achievements helped to shape the manifestos, and determine the poetical output, of several schools of poets in the first two decades of the 20th century, e.g. the Imagists.

Gourmont

In the Preface to the 1928 edition of *The Sacred Wood*, Eliot acknowledges his debt to Remy de Gourmont (1858–1915) and expresses his gratitude for the inspiration he has received from the Frenchman's critical writings. Eliot calls Gourmont "the critical conscience of his generation".

Gourmont was one of the most brilliant and erudite minds of the period from 1885 to 1915.[16] Essentially an essayist and a critic, he took up the cudgels for the Symbolist movement, and for many years he was editor of the influential periodical *Mercure de France*. He was one of the leading figures in contemporary social, political, and literary debates. He held very pronounced views on democracy, capitalism, communism, socialism and Cabinet responsibility — he detested them all. When he died, Ezra Pound said, "Gourmont is dead, and the world's light is darkened".[17]

Gourmont's collected works amount to more than four volumes within the genres of science, linguistics, philosophy, and art criticism. His best works of literary criticism date from the years 1900 to 1915, the year of his death: *La Culture des Idées* (1900), *Le Problème du Style* (1902), and his collection of essays, *Promenades littéraires* and *Promenades philosophiques*, which appeared periodically from 1904 until after his death.

Gourmont was something of a polymath — artist, critic, philosopher and scientist, and his reflections on 'the great schism' caused by the Cartesian dichotomy in the early 17th century probably inspired Eliot's theory about the dissociation of sensibility. After Descartes, man had become divided against himself, and some contemporary poets (e.g. the Symbolists) attempted to make him whole again. That is what made Eliot embrace Symbolism, for the Symbolists refused to accept what they saw as Descartes' separation of Reason and Feeling. Gourmont, too, was sceptical towards the capability of reason to give a generally truthful representation of reality. If thought is, in actual fact, a physiological product that differs in quality and mode of operation from one individual to another, the world can be considered unknowable since each person will draw an individual image of what he or she sees.[18]

That postulate not only delivers a powerful blow to Positivist determinism. It also gives a free rein to an artist's originality.[19] Not surprisingly, Gourmont considers the complexity and obscurity of Symbolist art an asset. Gourmont is relevant in the context of the analysis performed in this book because he looked at style from a psychological as well as a verbal point of view. Nineteenth-century French philosophers and men of letters were pre-Freudians in that they were interested in psychology and psychiatry, thus Ribot's *Imagination créatrice* (1900) devotes many pages to a study of the unconscious.

Gourmont said,

> Who says style says visual memory and metaphoric power, combined in variable proportions with the emotional memory and all the obscure contributions of the other senses.[20]

His *Problème du Style* was written as a refutation of the theories of a certain M. Albalat, who had maintained that a budding writer could learn the profession by imitating famous authors' way of writing. After all, "les beautés littéraires sont fixes".[21] Gourmont thought that Albalat was barking up the wrong tree. His theories smacked of Neo-Classical imitation of authors from Antiquity, but Gourmont saw imitation as determined by the phenomenal world:

> All imaginative literature is based on reality. Science, too takes reality as the launching pad. The difference between the two is that literature is aware that it recasts when imitating.[22]

Gourmont agrees with the Lockean maxim "nihil in intellectu quod non prius in sensu":

> The senses are the only gateway through which everything that lives in the spirit has entered . . . an idea is nothing but a sensory experience stripped of its freshness.[23]

Like Gautier, Gourmont was fascinated by the mysterious process that transformed the initial sensation. Here he invoked the assistance of psychology and pointed to the part played by the subconscious; but he does not go into any great detail.[24]

However, he also saw a close connection between sensibility and intelligence, which meant that writing is to some extent governed by reason.

Gourmont repeatedly underlines the significance of what he calls the visual memory,

> this reservoir of images from which imagination draws its nourishment for the establishment of ever new and endless combinations.[25]

The poet is a privileged person who is endowed with a particular talent:

> It is an indisputable fact that there are men in whom every word conjures up a vision, and who have never adjusted the most imaginary description without having the exact model of it before his inner eye.[26]

We may here recall what Eliot said in *The Sacred Wood*: the poet's task is not to find new feelings, but to use the ordinary ones, and, in working them up into poetry, to express an emotion which is not in the actual feelings at all. And feelings which he has never experienced before will serve his turn as well as those familiar to him.

Gourmont was confident that the senses develop thanks to what he calls "life's natural education". So it is 'life', the storehouse which is the product of regularly occurring sensory input, which will create the image.[27] The similarity with Gautier's 'microcosm' is unmistakable, and Eliot's concept of tradition is not far away either, for the person who is able to verbalize an aesthetic emotion is determined by his heredity and education and thus becomes a 'maker' and, at the same time, the guardian of a tradition.

Pure poetry has nothing to do with the feelings, said Gourmont, and that postulate is heartily endorsed by Eliot:

The end of enjoyment of poetry is pure contemplation from which
all accidents of personal emotion are removed.[28]

Burne puts it this way:

The intensity of the poetry is another thing again than the intensity of the experience which one attributes to the poet. Art
requires *sang-froid*, which it is the nature of the emotions to make
one lose.[29]

Like Gourmont, Eliot sees a radical difference between the man
who suffers and the mind which creates. In *The Sacred Wood* he
states that the more the two are separate,

the more perfectly will the mind digest and transmute the
passions which are its material.[30]

The assumption is complementary to the concept of the objective correlative: the poet must, unsentimentally, specify his
reaction in terms of 'the right word', and, analogously, the finished
product, the work, must limit and circumscribe its own emotional
potential. A "visual memory" combined with an "emotional
memory" are, in Gourmont's opinion, two indispensable prereq-
uisites for mastering the art of writing. However, more is needed:
a competent poet must have the ability, when facing an object in
the outside world, to "move back" to the emotional state that he
sight originally aroused in him.[31]

To Gourmont, the content of literature is important, but
content should always be adapted to, and subservient to, style. And
thinking activity is a fundamental ingredient of style; without that
basis, style is in a bad way.[32] Gourmont's formulation makes it
clear that he did not take mimesis in the sense of slavish copying.
"The logic of the eye and the logic of each of the other senses are
sufficient".[33] So, the senses have a logic of their own, but their
perceptions have to be approved and adjusted by the poet's visual

and emotive memory. The inference is that mere copying would be impossible, for the need for scientific exactitude risked corrupting the evidence of the senses. That, by the way, was the reason why Gourmont found the discoveries of science dubious and problematic because they were hypothetical.

To Gourmont, words are "vitalized" by the feelings they evoke:

> Words only have meaning by the force of the feeling they involve and the representation of feeling conferred on them . . . Even the most sluggish words can be vitalized by the sensibility, they can become feelings . . . Every word, every turn of phrase, even proverbs and clichés, may for the emotive writer become nuclei of emotional crystallization.[34]

It is the interdependence of word and feeling that Gourmont finds intriguing. On the one hand, he maintains that the word should correspond exactly to the thought being expressed, but on the other he had to confess (e.g. in *La Rhétorique*) that

> words and sensations are in harmony only very rarely and very poorly.[35]

An individual way of seeing and feeling inevitably leads to an individual way of using language. Gourmont was aware that the meaning of words may vary from one man to another and from one moment to another with the same person. Therefore it may be difficult to get at an exact understanding of much writing.[36] His dilemma was that, on the other hand, he had no doubt that truth depended on words, and accordingly he studied the development and evolution of meaning indefatigably. He hoped that this approach would take him closer to the crystallizations of associations which words have acquired through the centuries; what he was aiming at was a kind of dictionary of associations.

In *The Perfect Critic*, Eliot complains of the instability and incredible vagueness of words. They are losing their concreteness because we tend to substitute emotion for thought. Gourmont exerted a huge influence on Eliot. The structure, sometimes the very formulation, of much of Eliot's literary criticism is heavily indebted to the Frenchman. Eliot used quotations from Gourmont as epigraphs for section headings in *The Sacred Wood*. He agreed with Gourmont that sensuous impressions are the basis of literary activity and that the input, after being recast in the poet's crucible, should be given a formulation that would satisfy the criterion of literary beauty. The theory of the dissociation of sensibility is borrowed from Gourmont, who talked about "dissociation of ideas", and who wanted to take ideas back to their origin in sensory experience.

Eliot actually echoes Gourmont when, in the essay on Chapman,[37] he talks about "a direct sensuous apprehension of thought". The fact the Eliot became interested in the poet Laforgue's poems and refers to him respectfully in central passages of his criticism, is largely due to Gourmont, who admired Laforgue because, in the latter's poetry intelligence was closely connected with sensibility.

Eliot pays tribute to Laforgue for the same reason as Gourmont: he was possessed of an astounding linguistic inventiveness, and in his poetry as well as in Baudelaire's and Corbière's poems he finds the same

> essential quality of transmuting ideas to sensation, of trans- forming an observation into a state of mind.[38]

And the reason why the Elizabethan dramatists captivated him was that, in their work, "sensation becomes word".[39]

Ultimately, the postulate about the dissociation of sensibility derives from the philosopher F.H. Bradley, about whom Eliot had written an unpublished doctoral dissertation.[40] Eliot found Bradley's argumentation and reasoning a useful criterion for eval- uating the achievements of not only 17th century dramatists, but also the works of some of his own contemporaries.

Like Gourmont, although to a lesser degree, Eliot was concerned with the role of the unconscious in the creative process. Gourmont, however, cast his net wider than Eliot: to all intents and purposes, our moral and aesthetic judgements are nothing but unconscious generalizations of sensations, and potentially valueless without the correcting and sobering influence of intelligence. But Eliot agreed wholeheartedly with Gourmont in the latter's banning of 'personality' as a determining factor in the process of creation. And the critic was told to beware: only such emotions as are immediately provoked by the work under consideration should be granted access to the critic's assessment.[41]

However, there were several points where Eliot gradually came to oppose Gourmont's radical stance. For one thing, Gourmont was avowedly hostile to religion and religion-based morality, about which Eliot was certainly not. Consequently, in matters of sin and justice the two men were separated by an abyss.[42] Nor did Eliot share Gourmont's black pessimism on the subject of society and politics.

CHAPTER FOUR

POSITIVISM AND SOME REACTIONS AGAINST IT

Positivism is defined by OED as follows:

> A system of philosophy elaborated by Auguste Comte, which recognizes only positive facts and observable phenomena, with the objective relations of these and the laws which determine them, abandoning all inquiry into causes or ultimate origins; also, a religious system founded upon this philosophy, in which the object of worship is Humanity considered as a single corporate being.

Since Watt patented his invention of the steam engine in 1769, technological inventions had, as the 19th century progressed, transformed not only most people's world view, but also their everyday lives. Especially in the latter half of the century, the working methods of science and the results yielded by the way they formulated their questions acquired enormous prestige.

The determining factor of the Positivist paradigm was quantification: counting, weighing, and measuring were felt to be able to give answers that were immediately graspable by common sense, and the validity of the "natural laws" that were deduced was confirmed by their seeming incontestability. The consequence was that the results obtained by science obtained truth value: truth came to mean accordance with "what you could lay your hands on". What had to do with objects became of central relevance to the Positivists. Objectivity became a key concept to them. It was not only a working method, it was also an attitude to what was outside the observer, and it was a guarantor of truth.

The ultimate aim of the Positivists was to give a reliable and incontrovertible description of reality, and science seemed to have the tools to provide it. Even if the data were collected by human beings and processed by human minds, subjectivity became a derogatory term, relegated to the level of sheer whimsicality.

The word Positivism was coined in the late 18th century by the Frenchman Saint-Simon (1760–1825). His pupil Auguste Comte (1798–1857) used the designation about the way of thinking he would like to introduce into philosophy. Comte was confident that "the march of civilization" is subject to an unchangeable law based on "the way things are".[1] And he underlined that the Positivist spirit endeavours to determine the how, not the why.[2] He based his philosophical thinking on a belief in progress: history moves through a series of phases, from a lower to the highest level, which is the Positivist approach.

Leaning on Newtonian physics, prominent scientists like Lord Kelvin (1824–1907) claimed that the "natural laws" that they had discovered gave an adequate and irrefutable image of reality. Their claim was supported by the large number of technological inventions that made everyday life easier for the common man.

Positivists were satisfied that there is such a thing as universal truth. Truth is one, they said, and our picture of it has general validity, witness the reliability of the natural laws we have discovered. These laws simply demonstrate and reflect the order of the universe.

However, the question of "why" could not so easily be brushed aside. In *First Principles* (1862–93), Herbert Spencer admitted that many of the abstract and technical terms used by scientists, e.g. motion, were actually nothing but convenient labels.[3] The point implicitly made by Spencer is that science has to resort to

26 CHAPTER FOUR

metaphorical language to account for its theories, which makes their ontological status dubious.

The insufficiency of the Positivist paradigm was becoming increasingly obvious, not least where areas outside natural science were concerned. The art historian and literary critic Hippolyte Taine had to resort to a metaphysical concept, viz. "la faculté maîtresse", to give an exhaustive explanation of the creation of a successful work of literature. Measurable phenomena like "la race, le milieu et le moment" obviously did not suffice. The Neo-Classicists had found themselves in the same quandary, so they hid behind the "je ne sais quoi".

Herbert Spencer blamed contemporary science for falling short on crucial issues like the nature of the First Cause, and Positivist philosophers, moralists, theologians and what we would today call sociologists, had a feeling that there must be "something" above or behind what observation and the consequent establishment of smooth-fitting laws could teach us.[4]

Eliot's teacher at Harvard, the philosopher Francis Herbert Bradley (1846–1924), was what could be called with an oxymoron a systematic metaphysician. He saw it as the goal of philosophy to create a rational system of first principles. He acknowledges the existence of "our real world", which, he held, is not a figment of somebody's imagination or merely a fictional concept. He proved the actual existence of "our real world" by stating that

> either in endeavour to deny it, or even in attempting to doubt it, we tacitly assume its validity.[5]

In Bradley's idiolect, "our real world" is something different from "reality", which is an abstract term, viz. the ultimate logical subject of all acts of judgement.[6] As will be seen, that is a view poles apart form that of the Positivists.

In *Appearance and Reality* (1893), Bradley's thesis is that "our real world" is not susceptible of description in terms of time, space, causation or movement — another serious blow to the Positivist conception. Bradley's generally sceptic theory has metaphysical overtones, and he was led to the conclusion that ultimate truth is unobtainable, for we humans are not provided with the necessary tools to understand "the nature of things". The best we can hope for is a small number of unconditional truths about the most general features of "our real world".

Bradley considered the relation between thought and "our real world" a major philosophical problem. Language was not his prime concern, but in his usage, 'thought' was virtually inseparable from 'language'. The idea echoes Hegel's proposition that

> the forms of thought are, in the first instance, displayed and stored in human *language*. (his italics)[7]

In his explanation of the activities of the unconscious, Bradley divides the mind into levels. The first and uppermost level is what he calls "immediate experience", by which he understands visual stimulus, or a feeling. "Immediate experience", accompanied by pleasure or pain, is an undeniable feature of human and animal life, for which reason Bradley ascribes truth value to it. The problem for Bradley was to find out how thought and language respectively were capable of dealing with such a phenomenon as immediate experience.[8] He had no doubt that reason has a fundamental part to play in the processing of "immediate experiences", and it will be seen that Eliot followed in his teacher's footsteps.

Positivism was becoming gradually more vulnerable because its paradigm failed to bridge the gap between nature and spirit; slowly its adversaries acquired a greater degree of self-assurance and cogency. And very soon after the turn of the century they got a helping hand from an unexpected corner: Einstein's theories, propounded in 1905 and later, eventually shattered the Positivist conception of reality.

During the first two decades of the 20th century, we witness, on the part of poets, philosophers and critics, increasing efforts to challenge the monopoly of the Positivist world picture. Surely, reality, and, more generally, life, could not be described exclusively in terms of weighing, counting, and measuring? The opposition originated in France, where it became particularly vocal. Critics such as Ribot, Gautier and Gourmont advocated for a breakaway from the prevalent straitjacket, and poets like Baudelaire, Laforgue and Mallarmé experimented with hitherto untried poetical forms. Since they wanted to illuminate rather than to describe or to narrate, the emphasis came to be on formal aspects, more specifically the use and function of the individual word and the effects of rhythm.

> Poets in 1910 inherited a world made out of words . . . coherence was obtained by exploiting the sounds of the words and the implications concealed in their sounds,

says Hugh Kenner.[9]

The reason why those reformist tendencies caught on in England is twofold: English poetry from the two decades straddling the year 1900, as represented by for example Alfred Noyes and Henry Newbolt, was decidedly lightweight and flabby with outworn subjects, where sentiment often degenerated into sentimentality, characterized by humdrum rhythms, straitjacket-like metres, and a dull and watered down poetic diction. And literary criticism from the same period had virtually nothing to offer in the way of theoretical discussion.

A group of devoted young poets, who in most cases were also critics (Aldington, Eliot, Fletcher, Flint, Ford, H.D., Hulme, Lewis and Pound) made their voices heard in an undergrowth of manifestos and periodicals, notably *The Egoist*. For some years after 1917, Eliot was editor of that periodical.

This group devoted a considerable amount of energy to discussions of formal criteria. The role of the individual word in the formation of the successful image was naturally prioritized. In their poems, the group members broke new ground: their poems were non-stanzaic, unrhymed, and characterized by sharpness of observation in the use of images. Their poems are neither narrative nor didactic; they are momentary snapshots of everyday scenes frozen in one or two images. The task the poets set themselves was not to write a traditionally 'beautiful' poem, but rather to create what they called a 'successful' one.

CHAPTER FIVE

THE OBJECTIVE CORRELATIVE

The Theory

The only way of expressing emotion in the form of art is by finding an "objective correlative": in other words, a set of objects, a situation, a chain of events which shall be the formula of that *particular* emotion such that when the external facts, which must terminate in sensory experience, are given, the emotion is immediately evoked. If you examine any of Shakespeare's more successful tragedies, you will find this exact equivalence; you will find that the state of Lady Macbeth walking in her sleep has been communicated to you by a skilful accumulation of imagined sensory impressions . . . .The artistic "inevitability" lies in this complete adequacy of the external to emotion, and this is precisely what is deficient in *Hamlet*. Hamlet (the man) is dominated by an emotion which is inexpressible because it is in excess of the facts as they appear.[1]

This frequently quoted but rarely analysed passage occurs in the essay *Hamlet* written in 1919. It was printed in the collection *The Sacred Wood*, the first edition of which came out in 1920. In the revised edition from 1969, the title of the re-edited essay is *Hamlet and his Problems*, but this central passage has not been changed.

Eliot said himself that it is important to put a date on his critical statements since he was liable to modify or transform his opinions from time to time. Therefore, it is relevant to point out that the formulation is admitted unchanged and without any further elaboration in the later editions of the essay. Add to this, the late twenties are a crucial period in Eliot's intellectual development; those are the years when he made his attitude to central issues clear: a classicist in literature, a royalist in politics, and an Anglo-Catholic in religion, Actually, 1928 is the year of his religious conversion.

In the essay, Eliot calls *Hamlet* an artistic failure because the protagonist's reaction is disproportionate to the situation in which he finds himself:

> Hamlet is up against the difficulty that his disgust is occasioned by his mother, but that his mother is not an adequate equivalent for it, his disgust envelops and exceeds her.[3]

Eliot's treatment of Shakespeare's play may seem idiosyncratic, but the statement just quoted is a natural preparation for the more general point he is making in the essay: Gertrude's behaviour is not an appropriate objective correlative for Hamlet's emotions.

Language

Eliot never tires of stressing the importance for a poet to study and learn to master language:

> A ceaseless care, a passionate and untiring devotion to language, is the first conscious concern of the poet.[4]

In *The Use of Poetry and the Use of Criticism* he calls for "correctness of expression" in contemporary poetry,[5] and he had full confidence in the capacity of language to present the object, to be so close to the object that the two are identified.[6]

The poet has a responsibility towards his language in terms of preservation, improvement, and extension.[7] Characteristically, in his essays dealing with renowned persons past and present, Eliot devotes at least as much space to their mastery of language as to the qualities for which they are traditionally famous. In *For Lancelot Andrewes* (1927), Eliot pays tribute to Niccolo Machiavelli because

> first of all he was concerned with truth, not with persuasion, which is one reason why his prose is great prose, not only of Italian, but a model of style for any language.[8]

In the same collection of essays, Francis Bradley, Eliot's respected and beloved philosophy mentor, is complimented for his style, which is "perfectly welded with the matter": the objective correlative, as exemplified by Bradley, we must understand, makes for a felicitous coalescence of word and object.[9] Bradley's care for words is repeatedly referred to in the essay:

> Bradley, like Aristotle, is distinguished for his scrupulous respect for words, that their meaning should be neither vague nor exaggerated.[10]

The Poet's Role

Eliot chooses an impersonal formulation for his thesis. He does not say, "A poet's only way . . . " because, to him, the poet's personality is of minor importance. In *Tradition and the Individual Talent* he says that "the progress of an artist is a . . . continual extinction of personality".[11] And later in the same essay we read that

> my meaning is, that the poet has, not a 'personality' to express.

but a particular medium, which is only a medium and not a personality, in which impressions and experiences combine in peculiar and unexpected ways.[12]

The reason why Eliot rejected realist drama was that it relies so heavily on the personality of the actor.[13]

The sense impressions that the poet receives have truth value, and the poet is a transforming catalyst rather than a spontaneous creator. The poet's I and his emotions prompted by the phenomenal world are connected to that world with a strong bond. Accordingly, it is beside the point for the poet to "feel greatly" in preparation for composing a "great" poem.[14] One of Eliot's grievances against Matthew Arnold was that the latter put the emphasis in the wrong place, viz. on the poet's feelings.

In a discussion of Milton's *Lycidas*, Eliot says:

The more perfect the artist, the more completely separate in him will be the man who suffers and the mind which creates; the more perfectly will the mind digest and transmute the passions which are its material.[15]

In the essay *Four Elizabethan Dramatists* from 1924, Eliot states that "no artist produces great art by a deliberate attempt to express his personality",[16] and the gist of his dissatisfaction with *Hamlet* is that the protagonist is dominated by an emotion "which is in excess of the facts as they appear".[17]

It is worthy of notice that Eliot does not talk about an 'adequate' or an 'original' correlative. By using the term 'objective' he exploited the respectful connotations still surrounding science and its findings. Like many of his contemporary poets and critics, he aimed at obtaining parity of esteem between an objectified emotion and a scientific achievement. The resulting equivalent is held to have a status comparable to that of the objects that were science's field of study.

The Dissociation of Sensibility

In passages like those just quoted we find part of the explanation of Eliot's theory of the dissociation of sensibility. Kenner takes this use of the word 'sensibility' to be synonymous with the Bradleyan 'immediate experience', which precedes, underlies, and prompts any degree of analysis.

Eliot pays tribute to Chapman, who amalgamated learning and feeling in his dramas, and Ben Jonson as dramatist is rehabilitated by Eliot on that score.[18] Lancelot Andrewes, Bishop of Winchester, who died in 1526, seems to personify Eliot's ideal of poetic activity: in him, intellect and sensibility were in harmony:

> Andrewes's emotion is purely contemplative, it is not personal, it
> is wholly evoked by the object of contemplation, to which it is
> adequate; his emotion is wholly contained in and explained by its
> object.[19]

The thought and the terminology are clearly recognizable from Eliot's presentation of his objective correlative theory.

However, it is Eliot's contention that, after Ben Jonson, thought and feeling were separated, and thinking was no longer felt to be the province of poetry. In the centuries down to his own age Eliot sees increasing degeneration because poets' feelings and idiosyncrasies are given a free rein, thus excluding an essential element from poetry. Eliot talks repeatedly about "unity of sentiment", which he sees as a justification of the unity of action in a drama.

What Eliot attempted to do with his postulate of the objective correlative was to reinstate the intellectual aspect in its proper place. Thus, the objective correlative assertion becomes a natural corollary of his speculations about the dissociation of sensibility. The creation of poetry requires a fusion of feeling and intellect, and for that fusion to succeed, the poet's rational faculty, which Bradley calls "the principle of synthesis",[20] must play an active part. Bradley goes a step further in his long essay *The Presuppositions of Critical History*:

> Knowledge is the reception of outward impressions, and it is but natural that the copy should resemble and reproduce the original.[21]

Feeling and Emotion

In *Tradition and the Individual Talent*, Eliot establishes a distinction between feeling and emotion, feeling being sensations and impressions prompted by the immediate sensorial input. Emotion is a superordinate term, referring to the situation where intelligence has been brought to bear on feeling. It should be added, though, that the distinction is not consistently maintained by Eliot. For instance, he says in *The Sacred Wood* (1960, repr. 1969)[22] that poetry is not a *turning loose* of emotion, but a *turning away* from emotion. Here, emotion seems to be synonymous with feeling.

Be that as it may, in the objective correlative passage Eliot uses the term emotion with a specific sense: the context shows that the reference is to feeling with an intellectual component added. Feelings need to be clarified by the intellect, and the end-result of the successful blend of the two is emotion, a state of mind rather than an instance of, for example, anger or sadness. The poet's task, then, is to find an exact verbal equivalent for the emotion. and for that purpose it is incumbent on him

> not to find new emotion, but to use the ordinary ones, and, in making them up into poetry, to express feelings which are not in actual emotions at all.[23]

The formulation is not crystal clear; for example, the ontological status of 'intelligence' is obscure, and the distinction between feeling and emotion is not strictly maintained., but a description of the process may be formulated as follows:

The creative process begins in the personal experience: sense impressions, familiar ones as well as unfamiliar ones, we may take it, are registered, and thanks to the assistance and regulating influence of the intellect, the initial stimulus is filtered and stripped of its baser matter, which could be imagined to be part of the recipient's spontaneous reaction. The thinking activity is not that of the scientist or the logician. The point for the poet is to get "some order into his own instinctive reactions", as John Middleton Murry puts it. In that way the thought becomes "systematized emotion".[24]

Eliot admired Dante's *Divina Commedia* because he found it " the most *ordered* presentation of emotion that has ever been made"[25] (his italics). And in Bradley Eliot found support for the idea of the objectivity of thought: thought is objective

> not because its content excludes the self, but because it has to control tendencies which fall outside itself.[26]

Eliot had no doubt that the entire mental process was subject to control:

> That which suffers control is the entire psychical process . . . Sensations, emotions, fancies, volitions are suppressed or modified to suit the end, viz. to promote the development of the object.[27]

The fusion is worked into what Eliot calls an emotion, for which the poet rummages his mind, his visual memory and his verbal reservoir to find a suitable equivalent. Eliot views the process as a simple, almost mechanical operation, natural to the privileged person in whom the phenomenal world triggers a response, and who can draw on his reservoir — reminiscent of Gautier's *microcosme* — to furnish a truthful illustration of his reaction in the shape of "a set of objects, a situation, a chain of events".

The Implications

In order to get closer to an understanding of what Eliot was driving at, it is necessary to look into the implications of his categorical statement. The objective correlative is something from "our real world", i.e. outside the poet. Eliot took considerable interest in the unconscious, and he considered that introspection might in a few cases be a useful tool to try to account for some mental operations. Yet, even if he was not as suspicious of introspection as were the Positivists, he found that the results of introspection were not suitable for poetical treatment. So, the equivalence invoked, the basis of comparison, would be delivered by somebody or something else than the poet — even if it was he who pointed out the equivalence.

The correlative is not a word, or a synonym for an emotion. It is a context ("a set of objects . . . "). Eliot did not question Bradley's assumption that the immediate sense impressions had truth value; and Eliot extrapolated the truth value to hold for objective correlatives, too. The adjective 'objective' is a reminiscence of the thinking of the Positivists, to whom objectivity was synonymous with truth. The accordance revealed between the poet's emotion and the scene, etc., depicted, had truth value. It is not stipulated that that scene, etc., should have what is conventionally known as 'poetic' overtones.

The significant point is that, as Eliot sees it, truth can best be approached in a figurative way, through the use of one or more images. That is an echo of the Imagist conviction. They contested the Positivist pretention that truth was one, and that their working methods secured an unambiguous account of what the world was really like.

Eliot expressly distances himself from the Wordsworthian "emotion recollected in tranquillity":

For it is neither emotion, nor recollection, nor, without distortion of meaning, tranquillity.

Rather it is

> a concentration of a very great number of experiences . . . which
> does not happen consciously or of deliberation.[28]

To Locke, the mind was originally a *tabula rasa*, and Bradley
was almost just as categorical:

> In the beginning, there is nothing beyond what is presented, what
> is and is felt, or rather is felt simply. There is no memory or imag-
> ination or hope or fear or thought or will, and no perception of
> difference or likeness, no relations and no feelings, only feeling.[29]

Eliot does not conceal the fact that the composition of a poem
is, to a very great extent, a conscious undertaking, and the veracity
of the objective correlative becomes for the poet a tool to obtain
the "systematized order" that he desired. Emotion and intellect
undergo a kind of cross-fertilization: the sensory input influences
what is already 'there' in the poet's mind, but it is, in its turn, puri-
fied by the ingredients of the poet's mind.

It will be seen that the creative process implied in Eliot's postulate bears no little resemblance to what, according to Eliot,
happens when the emergence of a new poem sets its mark on the
existing tradition, which becomes modified, be it ever so slightly.

What lies behind Eliot's theory is his awareness of the fact that
most emotional reactions are notoriously insufficiently accounted
for by synonyms or dictionary definitions. The remedy he suggests
is for the poet to move into a different kind of presentation ("a situation") to give a satisfactory idea of the result of the fusion. The
outcome is the poet's victory over language, "compelling language
to conform to his mode of experience".[30] Thus it could be plausibly
argued — and the example is not Eliot's — that a person will get
a far more vivid picture of what jealousy 'is' by reading *Othello* than
by looking up the word in a dictionary of synonyms.

The Unconscious

Eliot refers to the quality and function of the unconscious on several occasions. The unconscious is the locus of impulses and feelings, but it also contains various ingredients of the conscious.[31] It is the mysterious starting-place of the creative process. Eliot talks about

> the dark embryo within him (sc. the poet) which gradually takes on the form and speech of the poem,[32]

and in *The Three Voices of Poetry* we read that a poem begins in

> an unknown dark psychic material — we might say the octopus or angel with which the poet struggles.[33]

Seen in that light, the objective correlative is what manages to bring the result of the 'dark' activities into light. However, Eliot never goes into detail with regard to the process of amalgamation that is postulated to take place between feeling and intellect.

Once more, Eliot got his inspiration from Bradley, who had proposed an analogous theory about the operations of the mind in his essay *The Presuppositions of Critical History* from 1887:

> But the mind is such a unity that it holds a contradiction in itself until the divided elements cohere, are solved and blended into another consciousness, a fresh system, a new world — new and which contains the old in a transformed shape . . . The mind is a principle of unity.[34]

The Example

Eliot's example of the objective correlative — and he gives only one — is taken from drama, viz. Lady Macbeth's state of mind in her sleepwalking scene. Perhaps Eliot chose to take his illustration from drama because the correlation will be more easily comprehensible to a reader or spectator on the basis of the actress's speeches and general pattern of behaviour.

However, the weakness of the postulate is that Eliot does not make it clear whether he refers to the poet's expressing himself precisely, or whether the point is the potential reader's reaction. Anyway, the question of the suitability of his example inevitably arises. At first sight, it may seem paradoxical that accuracy of formulation should be a virtue where emotions are concerned. But it is a natural corollary of the Positivist and Imagist craving for mathematical exactitude when a poet committed his reactions to a scene to paper. It is a well-known fact that the New Critics saw ambiguity or irony as the ultimate goal of a poetic presentation.

It is difficult to reconcile Eliot's italicized formulation, "that *particular* emotion" with the reactions that the Lady's behaviour will provoke in a spectator or a reader. What it does show is that there is not necessarily a one-to-one correspondence between stimulus and response. She is obviously thrown off her balance owing to the turn events have taken, but as to the *particular* emotion, various options seem to be open: the Aristotelian *katharsis*, i.e. mixture of pity ('What a deplorable state she finds herself in now') and fear ('The consequences turn out to be frightful when you push another person to commit a murder'). It could also be a feeling of just retribution ('She got what she deserved'), or even relief ('At last justice is done').

Eliot does not give any specimens of objective correlatives from poetry; on the whole, he refers only very sporadically to the theory in his critical oeuvre. But the theory, for all its ambiguity, is not without relevance: we might point to the famous description of his crossing of the Alps made by John Dennis (1657–1724): the emotion objectified is *the poet's* state of mind in the presence of the sublime, viz. fascination by the beauty, and horror at the forbidding enormity, of the scene. Another instance might be Wordsworth's poem *Lucy Gray* which prompts a feeling of

Aristotelian *katharsis in the recipient* — pity with the poor little girl, and fear at the cruelty of the fate that is liable to befall even completely innocent human begins. In neither case is it a *particular* emotion.

The innumerable examples in English literature of "Ode to . . .", or "Ode on . . ." present the matter more succinctly seen from the poets' point of view: they have stated what emotion they want to focus on. Elegies strike a mood in their very titles.

Eliot asserts that his postulate is valid for all arts, which means that composers, sculptors, painters and choreographers use a non-verbal medium to project and objectify their emotions. Again, as in the case of literature, titles are helpful, but not unequivocal. Portraits may be intended to, and manage to, prompt mixed responses from beholders. What does Leonardo's *La Gioconda's* smile suggest? Even compositions within the category of programme music are open to various interpretations: is Tschaikovsky's 1812 overture *only* a battle cry of triumph? And who will be prepared to give a final verdict on the mood of Mozart's symphonies?

Reality

Eliot's reflections in the crucial passage evidently hark back to Locke, but it is Locke with a grain of salt. Locke took the world outside man, *physis* in the Greek sense of the word, lock, stock, and barrel. It was *there* as an indisputable fact, and it sent signals for man to decipher. "Reality" is a precondition for the activities of the human mind. The impact of the facts of the outside world causes them to terminate in sensory experience, and to prompt a response on the part of a recipient.

To Eliot, the case is a little more problematic: he shares Locke's interest in, and respect for, "reality". Yet he does not commit himself to any definite standpoint with regard to man's position *vis-à vis* that entity:

The genesis of the common world can only be described by admitted fictions . . . On the one hand, our experiences are similar because they are of the same objects, and on the other hand the objects are only 'intellectual constructions' out of various and quite independent experiences. So, on the one hand my experience is in principle public. My emotion may be better understood by others than by myself; as my oculist knows my eyes. And on the other hand everything, the whole world, is private to myself,

he wrote in a comment on Bradley's philosophy.[35]

The problem that Eliot brings up here but does not pursue is this: what is the true character of the phenomenal world? How is it to be understood? Is "reality" simply something that pre-exists anything else, something on the status of which there is universal agreement so that all people who watch it will get the same impression? Or is it an intellectual, man-made construction, a product of man's reflections and his language? And what is the relationship between man and the phenomenal world?

Disagreement on that essential issue has been a recurrent phenomenon in the speculations and discussions of philosophers, poets, moralists, scientists and religious people down through the centuries.

In *Genesis* (II, 20) we read that

Adam gave names to all the cattle, to the fowl of the air, and to every beast of the field,

i.e. reality was created by God, who made cosmos out of chaos. Man was a later creation and was endowed with the privilege of putting a name on the items which were already there. If "reality" is an awe-inspiring edifice created by the Almighty it can *ipso facto*, claim man's unquestioning veneration.

Kant dismisses the problem of "reality" in his *De mundi sensibilis atque intelligibilis forma et principiis* from 1770. He establishes time and space as *a priori* phenomena, 'Anschauungsformen', which precede any kind of experience, and are not deduced from it. Reality must be considered as the 'something' which is the causal origin of a subject's sensations. Objects of experience conform to man's conceptions, for which reason it is impossible to say anything about an object 'before' or 'behind' experience since the idea of the object is created by a perceiving subject and thus governed by laws of concept formation. Accordingly, what we call "reality" has *a priori* existence, but Kant does not involve God in his reflections.

Eliot sits on the fence, but he agrees that in order to be able to communicate his impressions more precisely than one word can do, the poet has to invoke the assistance of an already existing 'something' outside him.

The tenor of the objective correlative passage in is perfect accordance with Imagist theorems, indeed they might be copied from one of the numerous manifestos that saw the light of day in the first decade of the 20th century. A poet like T.E. Hulme, for whom Eliot repeatedly expressed his admiration, demonstrated how observations of everyday life are capable of triggering a receptive poet's image-creating faculty without activating his emotional *engagement*. The poems of Hulme and the other Imagists are short, often a mere handful of lines, because their point is not to tell a story but rather to see and convey a scene '*à travers un tempérament*'. The poem *is* the image, and poetry is not a gushing forth of the poet's emotional qualms. Poets and critics looked upon poetry not in terms of applied ornament, but in terms of veracity, or 'successfulness' as they tended to call it. In their perception, veracity or truthfulness was obtained if and when their images reflected a valid identification with what they saw.[36]

Le mot juste

Gautier had pointed out that the criterion for the success of a formulation in, for example, a poem was that the author had

44   CHAPTER FIVE

managed to find 'the right word'. The teaching of F.H. Bradley at
Harvard left its stamp not least on Eliot's attitude to words and
language. Eliot came to see an intimate connection between the
precise use of words in a philosophic or scientific analysis of the
world and the precise treatment of words in a poem. A successful
poetic description is a profitable and pleasurable contribution to a
description of the world. And in *Knowledge and Experience in the
Philosophy of F.H. Bradley*,[37] Eliot insists on the unity and confor-
mity of feeling and objectivity.

Bradley had called Eliot's attention to the linguistic studies of
thinkers like Russell, Whitehead, and Wittgenstein.[38] According
to Russell, language is only used with precision when dealing with
sensory experience. A logically perfect language must observe a
one-to-one correspondence between each word and the thing or
relationship it describes. Eliot was deeply impressed by Russell
and Whitehead's *Principia mathematica* (1910–13), which he
considered a greater contribution to linguistics than to mathe-
matics. In *Tractatus* (1922) Wittgenstein said that the world is a
totality of facts, and that each word unit must correspond to an
object or an event in the world if the world is to have any meaning
at all. Contemporary structuralism within linguistics was
concerned with the relationship between language and object, as
is seen in for example the works of the internationally famous
Danish "grammatologist" Louis Hjelmslev. As he saw it, the
relationship was one of pure logic, and ultimately it would be
possible to calculate it by means of a system of equations
(*Prolegomena to a Theory of Language*, 1961). Charles Peirce's philosophic realism implied that our thoughts about the world are not
phenomena that are separated from or above the world, but derived
from it: man's capacity to comprehend the mechanism of nature
springs from his origin in that same nature. Man's mind is shaped
under the influence of phenomena that are governed by mechanical laws. Consequently, some concepts that are imbedded in those
laws are implanted in the mind, a fact that makes the laws easily
comprehensible. Scientific theories express real knowledge of

reality — that which Kant called *das Ding an sich* (*Reasoning and the Logic of Things*, 1992).

A different angle of approach to the significance of the word was taken by the orientalist Ernest Fenollosa (b. 1853), who was eulogized by Pound, but whose central work few contemporaries (or later theorists) seem to have actually read. Shortly before his premature death, in 1908, of a heart attack, he wrote a long seminal essay called *The Chinese Character as a Medium for Poetry*, in which he advised Anglo-Saxon poets to adopt the technique of the Chinese pictogram in their exploitation of metaphor.[39]

Thanks to what Middleton Murry calls his "personal idiosyncrasy of expression",[40] an Imagist poet — and Eliot was closely affiliated with several of the Imagists — becomes a 'maker', which is the etymological meaning of the word 'poet': the Greek verb *poiein* means 'make' or 'create'. Aristotelian mimesis was revitalized in the sense that the poet saw his task as being that of imitating. But the Imagists' imitation was a far cry from that of the Neo-Classicists: the latter strove to obtain the standards set by Homer and Horace, whereas Eliot and many of his contemporaries sought to grasp and communicate the essence of what met their eyes. A complete poem was a genuine and idiosyncratic rendering of 'the way things are'; the poet's concern was to show rather than to tell, not to win over the reader.

The Recipient

Towards the end of the theoretical part of the objective correlative passage, Eliot appears as the recipient of the poet's message. The latter does not play a prominent part in the context, but "the emotion immediately evoked" must refer to the response of the poet's opposite number, viz. the reader.

Eliot was satisfied that a relationship, common to all mankind, exists between a physical thing and a mental event. The mental events described by psychology are "probably not independent of the physical things to which they refer", as Shaff quotes him as saying.[41] Accordingly, he found it plausible that a reader's reaction will coincide with the intended aim of the author. In *The Use of Poetry and the Use of Criticism* he declares that the poetic experience presupposes the organization of various concrete experiences[42] (a favourite idea with Eliot), and he hoped that the reader would pass from selection and consequent discarding of what is useless to him, to an organization, perhaps a reorganization, of his mind. The exceptional reader will be able to compare and clarify, and in such cases enjoyment becomes appreciation. But what is supposed to give the reader that enjoyment is not necessarily the meaning of the text — actually some poets create intensity by ignoring meaning.[43]

In *Poetry and Drama* Eliot writes:

> If your poem is right to you, you can only hope the readers will eventually come to accept it . . . The approval of a few sympathetic and judicious critics is enough to begin with; and it is for future readers to meet the poet more than halfway.[44]

That rather intransigent take-it-or leave-it attitude is modified on the same page, for Eliot admits that a dramatist is forced to ensure understanding on the part of his audience. He saw it as "a function of art" (not *the* function) to force a structure on the disorderly chaos of reality.[45] When presented with that structure as reflected in a literary work, the reader may be inspired to play the poet's game, perhaps even move into areas where the poet cannot take him. But the responsibility rests with the reader, for when the poet has found an objective correlative, his job is finished.

Rhythm

The concern for structure explains Eliot's profound interest in the concept of rhythm, not only as it occurs in music, but also in verse drama and, more generally, in literary presentations. Rhythm is dependent on words and can therefore be considered an extension of the idea of the objective correlative. Eliot praised the opening scene in *Hamlet* for its verse rhythm: the lines are transparent so that

> you are consciously attending not to the poetry, but to the meaning of the poetry. The rhythm appears not only in the individual lines, but also in the dialogic exchanges.[46]

In his own works written for the stage, Eliot strove to revive the poetic drama, which was, to him, the only form of drama that was acceptable and had a chance of survival in the modern world.

Questions

Even though Eliot refers directly to the principle of the objective correlative only once, it is far from being an idiosyncratic caprice with him. It falls neatly into line with prevalent thinking in contemporary literary and critical circles, and it is a considered presentation of a significant ramification of the Zeitgeist. Hugh Kenner goes so far as to say that the idea (sc. of the objective correlative)

> makes perhaps a more general claim than Eliot intended; he could hardly have foreseen its misapplication to the job of the lyric poet.[47]

It is true that Eliot nowhere tries to apply his theory to lyrical poetry, but, as testified by the examples given earlier, it is possible to think of correlatives also in lyrical poetry. However, Eliot's categorical pronouncements raise some questions concerning the implications and consequences of the dictum. For one thing, Eliot excludes from poetic treatment the numerous situations where the stimulus comes from within the poet himself, e.g. introspective poetry. And he does not tell us what type of scenes, etc. are suitable or not suitable for his purpose. An instinctive assessment would indicate that some situations are more appropriate in poetry than others. Moreover, the use of metaphor is ignored, and a consistent application of the theory would rule out the acknowledgement of poetic diction. Elsewhere in his essays, Eliot takes up an ambivalent attitude to poetic diction. In *On Poets and Poetry* he says that the term poetic diction usually refers to obsolete words and idioms, or perhaps to words and idioms that are inappropriate in poetry. That is a remarkable assertion, and Eliot goes on to acknowledge the right of each age to have its "justified" poetic diction, which, in Eliot's perception, is neither identical with nor too distant from "current speech".[48] Thus he twists the conventional meaning of the concept of poetic diction.

The scope of correlatives is huge: an emotion like love, for example, has innumerable potentialities of illustration. The question then arises: in the case of many options, are they all equal, and, if not, who is going to decide which is the best, and what criteria for assessment can be considered valid? If the reader's reaction is not identical with the poet's, does that mean that he has misunderstood something, or that he does not benefit adequately from the reading experience? Ultimately, what is at stake, is poetic quality.

Finally, it is Eliot's contention that showing is more efficient than telling. However, showing in his case can *also* be brought about by linguistic means. A chain of events or a situation is preferable to a single word. So, poetry does have a narrative ingredient. But is the meaning of 'objective' generally agreed upon by mankind at large? Eliot would probably answer that the responsibility rests with the reader.

CONCLUSION

Eliot's critical essays often take the form of idiosyncratic but informative causeries interspersed with thought-provoking digressions. He tends to leave the subject that the title of the essay promises "in the air", and he has many personal axes to grind. He propounds a seemingly irrelevant digression, scrutinizes it, presenting it in a polemical form; sometimes he ridicules it, sometimes he rejects it, and sometimes he just proceeds to talk about what he had originally set out to do.

Eliot's theoretical reflections on what poetry 'is' or 'should be' occur as occasional remarks in his many essays. In the Preface to *The Sacred Wood* (the 1928 edition) he says that "poetry is excellent words in excellent succession",[1] and in *The Use of Poetry and the Use of Criticism* he states categorically that criticism will never arrive at a definition of poetry, or an ultimate assessment of poetry.[2] He indulges in circular reasoning: we learn what poetry is by reading good poems;[3] by the same token he says that you can learn what criticism is by reading good criticism.[4] He never wrote an *ars poetica*, and he never claimed to be the originator of a body of systematic literary doctrines or criteria. His views were too idiosyncratic to be fitted into any straitjacket.

That is not tantamount to saying that he did not take his function as critic seriously. As matter of fact, Eliot's attitude to, and treatment of, matters literary are integral parts of a larger, suggested, but never finally elaborated, social and moral edifice. Eliot almost exclusively devoted his critical acumen to poetry with drama as a close runner-up. Novels are only sporadically referred to. Sometimes he uses the word 'poetry' in the sense of literature in general; he seems to have felt that what applies to poetry, applies, *mutatis mutandis*, to other genres as well.

It is evident that to him poetry is the basic 'kind' because it illustrates and exemplifies the genuine potentialities and values of all literature. He considers drama a permanent form of art because it is able to convey greater variation, and to depict more different social types, than any other form of art.[5] No novelist worth his salt would subscribe to that statement, but the focal point of Eliot's criticism was not the novel.

And even within his two preferred genres, Eliot imposes some restrictions. He was intrigued by the concept of rhythm, so in his dealings with poetry, the emphasis is on the impact of the individual word, the concrete image, and the total rhythmical effect produced, rather than on a plot-like development as seen in epic poetry, or the lesson to be drawn from didactic poetry. To him, form goes before content. By the same token, it is a special type of drama that is admitted to the fold, viz. verse drama. There are "legitimate" demands that can only be satisfied by a drama written in verse.[6] Eliot does not elaborate the legitimacy idea, but he insists that there is a "need" among audiences for verse drama.[7] Another instance of his sometimes diffuse postulates.

"The musical phrase" is eulogized on several occasions, and it is not difficult to see a connection between the two genres favoured by Eliot. He devotes many pages to analyses of the Elizabethan dramatists' handling of blank verse, and in 20th century drama he advocates a type of prose that approaches the characteristics of the spoken language. Several of his plays are written in something reminiscent of versified prose. He admits that he finds the heroic couplet and blank verse equally unsuitable for his own purposes, but he quotes with approval numerous examples of impressive lines from Elizabethan dramatists' use of blank verse.

To him, rhythm is a scheme of organization of the way things cohere: thought, feeling and choice of words demonstrate an impeccable coalescence. What Eliot concentrates on in his dramatic analyses is the rhythmical effect of the individual speech as well as of the totality of a scene, e.g., the opening scene of *Hamlet*. The *hamartia* and the *dénouement* of a play are of decidedly peripheral significance. Social and psychological themes he finds largely irrelevant.

In his theory about the objective correlative, Eliot became an 'honest broker' between the 'out there' and the 'in here'. The existence of reality as our common sense perceives it is not questioned. The theory says nothing about the quality of the items selected as projections ("an object . . . "). The poet is the privileged seer who can visualize a similarity and thus release the poetical potential of what to other people is just "an object". In the poet's treatment, the intension of the words undergoes a change. An intimate type of interplay is thus brought about between a member of the favoured few and reality. Poets create a world of their own, based on, but different from, 'our real world', in the sense that they see parallels that remain hidden to the common man. What is to the latter just "a scene . . . " becomes to the poet an analogue of his individual response to a stimulus. Poets become a medium of interpretation of reality and impose their own vision on it. The postulate about the objective theory boils down to more than just a commonplace observation about the advantage of using 'the right word in the right place'.

Eliot implicitly agreed with the Neo-Classicists that what is ideal is best illustrated by something outside the observer. It can be justifiably argued that the Neo-Classicists' indefatigable endeavour to imitate Horace and Homer was *their* attempt at finding an objective correlative. However, what the Neo-Classicists used as their basis of comparison was not items from the phenomenal world but rather the style and themes of a select group of authors from Antiquity, who were supposed to have set covetable standards of excellence. When Neo-Classicists treated of 'our real world', as is the case in for example landscape poems, they saw the scene as an allegory. Unlike the Neo-Classicists, Eliot does not want to improve or 'heighten' the phenomena of the outside world. He took them at face value, so to speak.

And symbols do not suffice: Eliot criticizes Ben Jonson's comedies of humour for the way they depict human characters: superficially, they are human, but in reality they are nothing but a primitive instinct emerging from below the level of consciousness. They are deprived of many of the characteristics that might have provided them with a recognizable personality. Eliot's point is that they symbolize, rather than express, the given feature.[8]

Eliot was critical of the contemporary English poets who were popular with many readers. In his opinion, William Watson, Alfred Noyes and Henry Newbolt represented the nadir of English poetry. Poets and critics writing in the first decade of the 20th century had to look to France for inspiration. Eliot was fluent in French, and the diligent translations of F.S. Flint helped to familiarize his contemporaries with the novel approaches that were beginning to become perceptible across the Channel. Eliot acknowledged his debt to T.E. Hulme, who was a comrade in spirit — a classicist, a reactionary, and a fervent Christian.

French critics like Gautier, Ribot and Gourmont were instrumental in fragmenting the Positivist world picture. A central element in the rupture was an increasing focus on form rather than content. In 1912, Gustave Kahn published a seminal book on free verse (Le vers libre), and the French poet Jules Laforgue, whom Eliot came to know thanks to Arthur Symons' book The Symbolist Movement in Literature, became one of Eliot's poetical mentors owing to his linguistic inventiveness.

Gautier talked about "un tout indissociable" between the thought and the expression, i.e. the expression should be perfectly adequate to what Gautier called "l'idée".[9] Like Eliot, Gautier tended to push the reader into the background, and to both critics, the imagination became virtually synonymous with a storehouse of linguistic detail. Gourmont advocated ideas that form the germ of the dissociation of sensibility postulate. In The Use of Poetry and the Use of Criticism, Eliot echoed one of Gourmont's favourite theo-

ries: the intellectual element should go hand in hand with the original intensity of feeling,[10] for poetry is worth reflection.[11] The link
to the objective correlative idea is obvious.

Both Valéry and Mallarmé stated that poetic intensity is most
surely achieved and sentimentality most surely avoided

> by using no word that directly describes a feeling or proceeds
> directly from an affective state.[12]

Poe, whose works Eliot did not admire, was known for choosing
with mathematical accuracy just the effect and just the word which
would create a perfect intimation of the supernatural in a story.[13]
Poe also thought that a poem should have nothing in view but
itself, and as his theory of the objective correlative shows, Eliot
agreed. His grievance against the Romanticists was that they used
poetry as a substitute for religion ('the poet is the priest'),[14] and his
life-long love/hate attitude to Matthew Arnold originated in the
latter's bland conception of poetry as 'a criticism of life', a statement that became almost an obsession and a pet aversion with
Eliot.

Eliot cherished a warm friendship with Middleton Murry, who
said in *The Problem of Style* (whose title is a verbatim translation of
Gourmont's *Le Problème du Style*),

> style is the quality of language which communicates precisely
> emotions or thoughts, or a system of emotions or thoughts pecu-
> liar to the author.[15]

So, the concern for language and the use and function of the
individual word was a significant component of the critical
thinking of Eliot's contemporaries, and it is a safe conclusion that
the statement which is the inspiration for these pages is more than
a formulation that just occurs to him. In his opinion, poetry was
more than "merely a decoration, an added embellishment", as he
says in his defence of verse drama.[16]

Also as far as the concept of tradition is concerned Eliot stood on the shoulders of his predecessors. Writing about *The Presuppositions of Critical History* (1874), Bradley explained:

> Every man's present standpoint ought to determine his belief to *all* past events . . . History stands not only for the past in fact, but also for the present in record, and it implies in itself the union of these two elements . . . (History stands) not only for the past in fact, but also for the present in record; and it implies itself the union of these two elements.[17]

By way of a parenthetical digression, it may seem paradoxical that an age that glorified movement and dynamism (cf. Bergson's dubious, but acclaimed, postulate about *l'élan vital*) should find satisfaction in a theory which, at least in Eliot's interpretation, was, to all intents and purposes, based on stability and permanence. However, since, to Eliot, language "in its healthy state" not only presents the object, but gets so close to the object that the two are identified, it is unimaginable for a word to change its sense. Only in an uncultured philosophy do words tend to undergo changes of meaning.

Eliot's theory of the objective correlative can be seen as an argument for his instinctive dislike of *Hamlet*; perhaps he felt that some kind of critical basis would be appropriate, and perhaps he made amends to Shakespeare by using an example from another of the bard's plays to illustrate what he was getting at.

He touches on the idea — without using the term — sporadically in his oeuvre: in the essay *What is a Classic* from 1914, he discusses the *Aeneid*, saying that Aeneas' meeting with Dido is one of the most moving passages in all literature — complex in meaning and economical in expression. The scene conveys an impression of Aeneas' mood as well as of Dido's. Dido's behaviour is virtually a projection of Aeneas' own consciousness.[18] In the same essay he acknowledges Tennyson and Browning as poets who think; but they do not feel their thought as intimately and spontaneously as the scent of a rose.[19] And the Metaphysical Poets' forte is their search for a verbal equivalent for their states of feeling and consciousness.[20]

Eliot is rooted in the Positivist paradigm: the great challenge is understanding reality by describing it and thus mastering it. *Physis* in the Greek sense of the word is his field of interest, he acknowledges the primacy of sight among the senses, he does not assess or beautify the object of his analyses; the ideal is objectivity, and the criterion is veracity. The aim is precise rendering, and sense impressions have an immediate truth value. He agrees with Gourmont that man is born with a need for truth, and beauty — a word rarely used by Eliot — is achieved when the criterion of truth is fulfilled.

The poet depends for his inspiration on stimuli from 'our real world', and when the processing by the poet's intellect has been accomplished, the yardstick of success is again provided by items from outside the poet. That is a far cry from Montaigne's famous statement "Je suis moi-mesme le sujet de mon livre". In Eliot's theory, an intimate cooperation is established between the poet and reality. Reality has to be processed by a human mind in order to be properly appreciated. It is of crucial importance to realize that, to Eliot, the objective correlative is not necessarily a word. Even more, the point about it is not verbalization. As he sees it, it is a matter of "la situation juste" rather than "le mot juste". In "a set of objects . . . " etc., the linguistic aspect will normally not be the first feature that comes into a receiver's mind. It is Eliot's implied contention that "a set of objects . . . " can give the receiver an experience comparable to, but more precise than, the poet's own immediate sensory input, which, incidentally, is not formulated in words. His formulation, "a chain of events . . . " allows us to conclude that a narrative and descriptive component in poetry is admissible — even though, for his purposes, the prime concern of that component is not to narrate or describe, but to contribute to determining an emotion.

Eliot's originality resides in the fact that he states categorically that a poet has to seek the support of something outside him to find a suitable formula for his emotions. Somehow, items of reality are better qualified than words to meet Eliot's demands. Poets' usual escape route when it comes to pinpointing emotions has always been metaphorical language. Eliot agrees with many of his predecessors that if emotions are to be expressed, the best way to do it is to use figurative language. But whereas conventional metaphors — usually one or a few words — only serve to illuminate a given emotion, and have, accordingly, no 'independent' existence, Eliot's correlative is something that exists in its own right. Lady Macbeth's sleepwalking scene can be enjoyed without being perceived in terms of an objective correlative. He does not question French critics' assertion that everything can be expressed, but he circumvents it by invoking phenomena that are pre-linguistic, implying that showing is more efficient than telling.

One meaning of 'objective' as defined by OED is

the object of perception or thought as distinct from the perceiving or thinking subject.

But if 'objective' is defined as something separate from, or opposite to, the 'subjective', the inference is that 'objective' is non-linguistic. So, Eliot does not talk of a one-to-one correspondence between an emotion and a word. Emotions are complex and are not, he thinks, adequately represented by dictionary definitions, or even by conventional metaphorical techniques The paradox is that his own poems do not live up to his ideal demand, witness the numerous, often conflicting, interpretations of them.

Eliot's theory of depersonalization fits in nicely with Positivist rules: the exclusion of the poet's personality causes poetry to approach the condition of science.[21] "No artist produces great art by endeavouring to express his own personality", he wrote in *Four Elizabethan Dramatists*.[22]

Aldington expatiates on the same idea:

We convey an emotion by presenting the object and circumstances of that emotion, without comment. For example we do
not say 'Oh, how I admire that beautiful, that exquisite, that –
24 more adjectives — woman', or 'O exquisite, O beautiful, O
25 more adjectives, let us spoon you for ever', but we present
that woman, we make an Image of her, we make the scene convey that emotion . . . A hardness of cut stone. No slop, no
sentimentality.[23]

That statement reads like a declaration of content of Eliot's
theory.

There may be hints of the objective correlative idea in Eliot's
interest in the relationship between poetry and the social conditions in which it is written. In *The Use of Poetry and the Use of
Criticism* he dwells on the fact that poetry is influenced by "the
circumstances of life":[24] changes in the function of poetry are
matched by parallel trends in society.[25] Radical changes within
poetry are signs of deeper transformations in society, and vice
versa. For example, it is his contention that Wordsworth's social
commitment inspired him to try his hand at a novel poetic form.
In the same way he saw criticism as a continuous interplay of
literary theory and prevalent social conditions. What absorbs him
in his own dramatic criticism is the *rapport* between the play and
the social context in which it came into existence, and in which it
was performed.[26] Hence his emphasis on the playwright's duties
and function and his responsibilities towards the audience. He
rejected the idea of art for art's sake for the very reason that its
adherents disclaimed any social obligation.

The socially tinted task facing poetry and criticism is very
briefly referred to in *The Use of Poetry and the Use of Criticism*, but
in actual fact very little information is given about the use of either
of the two terms on the title page. All that we are told is that it is
incumbent on poetry and criticism to be socially responsible and
have "as civilizing influence" in times of confusion.[27] However,
since *The Use of Poetry and the Use of Criticism* was written in the

early '30s, the 'confusion' would have been obvious to many readers.

As a matter of fact it does not become clear exactly what is the use of poetry if its changes are brought about by external factors. On top of this, Eliot distances himself from sociological criticism, and he abhors Shelley's idea of poets as 'the unacknowledged legislators of mankind'.

The reader plays an unobtrusive part in the theory, but his existence is taken for granted. What matters is the poet's craft and his loyalty to his own reaction. Once the poem has been composed — and Eliot agrees with Poe that writing a poem should be as conscious and deliberate as possible[28] — the poet's job is over and done with. Eliot did not write with a reader or a particular group of readers in mind. He just sends a poem into orbit, so to speak.

The concept of *le mot juste* is an ancient *topos*: Dante advised budding poets to depict "an emotion evident in the situation",[29] and Dryden and his contemporaries saw it as the task of 'elocution' to 'dress the thought'. Analysis of, and emphasis on, the use and function of the word has been continued by the New Critics and the Deconstructionists. Eliot gave the *topos* a personal twist and lifted it out of the commonplace abyss into which it has sometimes sunk. He wanted to make the verbalization process a conscious and rational pursuit, and to demonstrate that 'expressive' does not have to be synonymous with 'sentimental'. He was concerned to prove that a description found in poetry can have the same truth value as a theorem in science. Subjectivity and objectivity are a complementary pair.

Eliot said about Ben Jonson,

He not unnaturally laid down in abstract theory what is in reality a personal point of view.[30]

The boomerang effect of that statement is obvious, but does not impair the relevance of Eliot's idiosyncratic treatment of a seeming commonplace.

It is only fair that the final words should be Eliot's description
of his own style in *Four Quartets*:

> where every word is at home
> Taking its place to support the others,
> The word neither diffident nor ostentatious
> An easy commerce of the old and new
> The common word exact without vulgarity
> The formal word precise but not pedantic,
> The complete consort dancing together.

NOTES

Introduction

1 Hugh Kenner, *The Invisible Poet: T.S. Eliot*, Preface, p. 9.
2 Ibid., p. 51.

CHAPTER ONE
SOME CLASSICAL PREDECESSORS

1 T.A. Moxon (ed.), *Aristotle's Poetics, Demetrius on Style, and other Classical Writings on Criticism*, p. 5.
2 Ibid.
3 *Aristotle's Poetics*, p. 51.
4 Ibid., p. 8.
5 Ibid., p. 9.
6 Ibid., p. 6.
7 Ibid.
8 Ibid.
9 Ibid., p. 39.
10 Ibid., p. 43.
11 Ibid., p. 15.
12 Ibid., p. 43.
13 Ibid., p. 9.
14 Ibid., p. 213.
15 Ibid., p. 62.
16 Ibid., p. 63.
17 Ibid., p. 71.
18 Ibid.

CHAPTER TWO
SPRAT, LOCKE, HARTMANN

1 Hugh Kenner, *The Invisible Poet*, p. 44.

2 John Locke, *An Essay Concerning Human Understanding*, Part I B, p. 25.

CHAPTER THREE
GAUTIER, BAUDELAIRE, GOURMONT

1 M.C. Spencer, *The Art Criticism of Théophile Gautier*, p. 2.
2 Ibid., p. 25.
3 Ibid., p. 127.
4 Philippe Terrier (ed.), *Charles Baudelaire: Théophile Gautier. Deux Etudes*, p. 246: Le dessein de traiter sous forme restreinte de petits sujets . . . Chaque pièce devait être un médaillon . . . L'auteur n'employa que les vers de huit pieds, qu'il refondit, polit et cisela avec tout le soin dont il était capable.
5 Ibid., p. 180: Il n'y a pas d'idées inexprimables.
6 Terrier, p. 210: Celui qu'une pensée, fût-ce la plus complexe, une vision la plus apocalyptique, surprend sans mots pour les réaliser, n'est pas un écrivain.
7 Ibid., p. 11.
8 Ibid., p. 17: Quand M. Delacroix compose un tableau, il regarde en lui-même au lieu de mettre le nez à la fenêtre.
9 Spencer, *The Art Criticism of Théophile Gautier*, p. 41: Tout homme qui n'a pas un monde intérieur à traduire n'est pas un artiste. L'imitation est le moyen et non le but. De tout ceci, il ne faut pas conclure que l'artiste soit purement objectif ; il est aussi objectif ; il donne et il reçoit. Il rend à la nature des signes dont il a besoin pour l'exprimer. Ces signes, il les transforme, il y ajoute, et il en ôte, selon le genre de sa pensée . . . Le peintre porte le tableau en lui-même, et, entre la nature et lui, la toile sert d'intermédiaire.
10 Terrier (ed.), *Charles Baudelaire*, p. 145.
11 Ibid., p. 43.
12 Ibid., p. 106.
13 Ibid.: La mélodie sort de sa bouche comme une vapeur sonore.
14 Ibid., p. 180.
15 Ibid., p. 13.
16 Glenn S. Burne, *Remy de Gourmont: His Ideas and Influence in England and America*, Preface, p. v.
17 Ibid., p. 19.

18 Ibid., 35.

19 Ibid., p. 21.

20 Remy de Gourmont, *Le Problème du Style*, p. 47: Qui dit style, dit mémoire visuelle et faculté métaphorique, combinées en proportions variables avec la mémoire émotive et tout l'apport obscur des autres sens.

21 Ibid., p. 98.

22 Ibid.

23 Ibid., p. 64: Les sens sont la porte unique par où est entré tout ce qui vit dans l'esprit . . . Une idée n'est qu'une sensation défraîchie, une image effacée.

24 Burne, *Remy de Gourmont*, p. 46.

25 Remy de Gourmont, *Le Problème du Style*, 35: La mémoire visuelle, ce réservoir d'images où puise l'imagination pour de nouvelles et infinies combinaisons.

26 Ibid., p. 44: Enfin il est constant qu'il y a des hommes en qui tout mot suscite une vision et qui n'ont jamais rédigé la plus imaginaire description sans en avoir le modèle exact sous leur regard intérieur.

27 Ibid., p. 73: Les sens se développent par cette éducation naturelle que donne la vie . . . C'est la vie, c'est l'habitude des sensations qui créera l'image stylistique.

28 T.S. Eliot, *The Sacred Wood*, pp. 14–15.

29 Burne, *Remy de Gourmont*, p. 44.

30 Eliot, *The The Sacred Wood*, pp. 56–58.

31 Remy de Gourmont, *Le Problème du Style*, p. 35: Si, à la mémoire visuelle, l'écrivain joint la mémoire émotive, s'il a le pouvoir, en évoquant un spectacle matériel, de se replacer exactement dans l'état émotionel que suscita en lui ce spectacle, il possède, même ignorant, tout l'art d'écrire.

32 Ibid., p. 151: En littérature, le fond des choses a une importance absolue . . . Rien ne meurt plus vite que le style qui ne s'appuie pas sur la solidité d'une forte pensée.

33 Ibid., p. 70: La logique de l'œil et la logique de chacun des autres sens suffisent à guider l'esprit.

34 Ibid., p. 39: Les mots n'ont de sens que par le sentiment qu'ils renferment et dont on leur confère la représentation . . . Les mots les plus inertes peuvent devenir sentiments . . . Tout mot, toute locution, les

proverbes même, les clichés vont devenir pour l'écrivain émotif des noyaux de cristallisation sentimentale.

35 Burne, *Remy de Gourmont*, p. 101.
36 Ibid., p. 64.
37 T.S. Eliot, 'The Metaphysical Poets' in *Selected Essays*.
38 T.S. Eliot, *Selected Essays 1917–32*, p. 249.
39 Burne, *Remy de Gourmont*, p. 134.
40 Ibid., p. 80.
41 Eliot, *The Sacred Wood*, pp. 8–12.
42 Burne, *Remy de Gourmont*, p. 147.

CHAPTER FOUR
POSITIVISM AND SOME REACTIONS AGAINST IT

1 Flemming Olsen, *Between Positivism and T.S. Eliot: Imagism and T.E. Hulme*, p. 33.
2 Ibid., p. 41.
3 Ibid., p. 29.
4 Ibid., p. 43.
5 *Appearance and Reality*, p. 310.
6 Guy Stock, 'Bradley's Theory of Judgement' in Anthony Stock Manser and Guy Stock (eds.), *The Philosophy of Francis Herbert Bradley*, p. 132.
7 Georg Wilhem Frederick Hegel, *Wissenschaft der Logik*, vol. 5, p. 20.
8 Anthony Stock Manser and Guy Stock (eds.), *The Philosophy of Francis Herbert Bradley*, p. 27.
9 Hugh Kenner, *The Invisible Poet: T.S. Eliot*, p. 8.

CHAPTER FIVE
THE OBJECTIVE CORRELATIVE

1 T.S. Eliot, *The Sacred Wood* (1969 ed.), pp. 100–102. Eliot's italics.
2 Jon Margolis, *T.S. Eliot's Intellectual Development*, p. 99.
3 T.S. Eliot, *Selected Essays*, p. 145.
4 Hugh Kenner, *The Invisible Poet: T.S Eliot*, p. 291.
5 Ibid., p. 20.
6 Kenner, p. 48.
7 *On Poetry and Poets*, p. 20.
8 Ibid., p. 65.

9 Ibid., p. 69.

10 Ibid., p. 85.

11 Eliot, *Selected Essays*, p. 17.

12 Ibid., p. 20.

13 William Skaff, *The Philosophy of T.S. Eliot*, p. 93.

14 Kenner, *The Invisible Poet*, p. 103.

15 Ibid., p. 103.

16 Eliot, *Selected Essays*, p. 114.

17 Ibid., p. 145.

18 Ibid., pp. 147 et seq.

19 The essay was written in 1926 and published in the collection of essays *For Lancelot Andrewes* in 1928; pp. 28–30.

20 Francis Herbert Bradley, *Collected Essays*, p. 67.

21 Ibid., p. 9.

22 Ibid., p. 112.

23 Eliot, *Selected Essays*, p. 21.

24 Middleton Murry, *The Problem of Style*, p. 67.

25 Eliot, *The Sacred Wood* (1928), p. 168.

26 Eliot, *Selected Essays*, p. 236.

27 Francis Herbert Bradley, *Collected Essays*, p. 208.

28 Eliot, *Selected Essays*, p. 21.

29 T. S. Eliot, 'Association and Thought', *Collected Essays*, p. 216.

30 Murry, *The Problem of Style*, p. 21.

31 Skaff, *The Philosophy of T.S. Eliot*, p. 68.

32 C.K. Stead, *The New Poetic: Yeats to Eliot*, p. 136.

33 Eliot, *Selected Essays*, p. 68.

34 Ibid.

35 Kenner, *The Invisible Poet*, p. 54.

36 Cf. Flemming Olsen, *Between Positivism and T.S. Eliot: Imagism and T.E. Hulme*.

37 Ibid., p. 115.

38 Skaff, *The Philosophy of T.S. Eliot*, p. 154.

39 Flemming Olsen, *Ernest Fenollosa: 'The Chinese Written Character as a Medium for Poetry': Ars Poetica or the Roots of Poetic Creation?*

41 Skaff, *The Philosophy of T.S. Eliot*, p. 48.

42 T.S. Eliot, *The Use of Poetry and the Use of Criticism*, pp. 18–19.

43 Ibid., p. 151.

44 Ibid., p. 24.
45 T.S. Eliot, *Poetry and Drama*, pp. 15 et seq.
46 Ibid., p. 16.
47 Kenner, *The Invisible Poet: T.S. Eliot*, p. 88.
48 Ibid., p.185.

Conclusion

1 T.S. Eliot, *The Sacred Wood*, p. iv.
2 Ibid., p. 16.
3 Ibid.
4 T.S. Eliot, *The Use of Poetry and the Use of Criticism*, p. 20.
5 *The Sacred Wood* (1969), p. 61.
6 'The Possibilities of a Poetic Drama', *The Sacred Wood* (1969), p. 61.
7 Ibid.
8 William Skaff, *The Philosophy of T.S. Eliot*, p. 97.
9 Philippe Terrier (ed.), *Charles Baudelaire: Théophile Gautier. Deux Etudes*, p. 149.
10 Ibid., p. 19.
11 Ibid., p. 18.
12 Norman Suckling, *Paul Valéry and the Civilized Mind*, p. 81.
13 Robert Regan (ed.), *Poe: A Collection of Critical Essays*, p. 52.
14 T.S. Eliot, *The Use of Poetry and the Use of Criticism*, p. 26.
15 Middleton Murry, *The Problem of Style*, p. 65.
16 T.S. Eliot, *Poetry and Drama*, p. 10.
17 Francis Herbert Bradley, *Collected Essays*, pp. 2–8.
18 T.S. Eliot, *On Poetry and Poets*, p. 62.
19 Ibid., p. 65.
20 T.S. Eliot, 'The Metaphysical Poets' in *Selected Essays* (1932), p. 289.
21 'Tradition and the Individual Talent' in *The Sacred Wood* (1969), pp. 52–53.
22 Eliot, *Selected Essays* (1932), p. 114.
23 'Modern Poetry and the Imagists', *The Egoist*, 1st March 1915.
24 p. 20.
25 p. 23.
26 Eliot, *The Use of Poetry and the Use of Criticism*, p. 27.
27 Ibid., pp. 14–15.
28 Regan, *Poe: A Collection of Critical Essays*, p. 174.

29 C.K. Stead, *The New Poetic*, p. 127.
30 Eliot, *Selected Essays*, p. 156.

BIBLIOGRAPHY

Aldington, Richard, '*Modern Poetry and the Imagists*'. *The Egoist*, 1st March 1915.

Berger, John, *Ways of Seeing*. A Pelican Original, 1976.

Bornstein, George, *Transformation and Romanticism in Yeats, Eliot and Stevens*. University of Chicago Press, 1976.

Bradley, Francis Herbert, *Appearance and Reality*. Oxford, 1897.

——, *Essays on Truth and Reality*. Oxford, 1914.

——, *The Principles of Logic*. Corrected Impression Oxford, 1928.

——, *Collected Essays, vols 1 & 2*. Oxford, Clarendon, 1935.

Bryce, A. Hamilton (ed.), *The Poems of Horace. A Literal Translation*. Bell & Sons, London, 1902.

Burne, Glenn S., *Remy de Gourmont: His Ideas and Influence in England and America*. Southern Illinois University Press, 1963.

Clarke, Graham, *T.S. Eliot, Critical Assessments*. London, Christopher Helm, 1990.

Davidson, Harriet, *T.S. Eliot*. Longman, 1999.

Debauve, J.L., *Laforgue en son temps*. Edition de la Baconnière. Neuchâtel Langages. Documents, 1972.

Dottin, Mireille (ed.), *Jules Laforgue. Textes de critique d'art*. Presses Universitaires de Lille, 1972.

Eliot, T.S., *For Lancelot Andrewes. Essays on Style and Order*. London, Faber & Gwyer, 1928.

——, *Selected Essays*. London, Faber & Faber, 1932.

——, *After Strange Gods*. New York, Harcourt, Brace & Co, 1933.

——, *The Use of Poetry and the Use of Criticism*. London, Faber & Faber, 1933.

——, *Poetry and Drama*. Harvard University Press, 1951.

——, *The Three Voices of Poetry*. Cambridge, National Book League, 1955.

——, *On Poetry and Poets*. Fifth Impression. London, Faber & Faber, 1960.

——, *Knowledge and Experience in the Philosophy of F.H.Bradley*. Faber & Faber, 1964.

——, *To Criticize the Critic*. New York, Farrar, Straus & Giroux, 1965.

——, *The Sacred Wood*. 1960, repr. 1969. Methuen, London.

Fabricius, Johannes, *The Unconscious and Mr. Eliot*. Copenhagen, 1967.

Fauconnier, G. & Turner, M., *The Way We Think*. New York, 2002.

Gardner, Helen, *The Art of T.S. Eliot*. Cresset Press, 1949, re-issue 1968.

Gautier, Théophile, *Emaux et Camées*. Paris, 1852.

——, *L'Art*. Paris, 1857.

Gourmont, Remy de, *Le Livre des Masques*. Sixième éd., Paris, Mercure de France, 1896.

——, *Promenades littéraires*. 1e série 1904, 2me série 1906, 3me série 1909, 4me série 1912, 5me série 1913. Paris, Mercure de France.

——, *La Culture des Idées*. Paris, 1900.

——, *Le Problème du Style*. Paris, 1924.

Grant, Michael, *T.S. Eliot. The Critical Heritage*. London, 1982.

Hartmann, Eduard von, *Philosophy of the Unconscious*. Transl. from German *Philosophie des Unbewussten* by William Chatterton Coupland. London, Kegan Paul, Trench, Trubner & Co. Ltd, 1931.

Hjelmslev, Louis, *Prolegomena to a Theory of Language* (1949): transl. Francis Whitfield. Madison, University of Wisconsin Press,1961.

Kenner, Hugh, *The Invisible Poet: T.S. Eliot*. London, Methuen, University Paperback, Repr. 1979.

Kojecky, Roger, *T.S. Eliot's Social Criticism*. New York, 1972.

Locke, John, *An Essay Concerning Human Understanding*. London, 1690.

Manser, Anthony Stock & Stock, Guy (eds.), *The Philosophy of Francis Herbert Bradley*. Oxford, Clarendon, 1986.

Margolis, John D., *T.S. Eliot's Intellectual Development 1922–1939*. University of Chicago Press, 1972.

Martin, C.G. (ed.), *Eliot in Perspective: a Symposium*. Macmillan, 1970.

Matthiessen, F.O., *The Achievement of T.S. Eliot*. Oxford University Press, 1947.

Moody, A. David, *The Cambridge Companion to T.S. Eliot*. Cambridge University Press, 1998.

Moxon, T.A. (ed.), *Aristotle's Poetics. Demetrius on Style. And Other Classical*

Writings on Criticism. London, Everyman's Library 901, 1943.

Murry, John Middleton, *The Problem of Style*. Sixth Impr., Oxford University Press, 1975.

Newton-De Molina, *The Literary Criticism of T.S. Eliot: NewEssays*. London, 1972.

Olsen, Flemming, *Between Positivism and T.S. Eliot: Imagism and T.E. Hulme*. University Press of Southern Denmark, 2008.

——, *Ernest Fenollosa 'The Chinese Written Character as a Medium for Poetry': Ars Poetica or the Roots of Poetic Creation?* Brighton, Portland, Toronto, Sussex Academic Press, 2011.

Peirce, Charles Sanders, *Reasoning and the Logic of Things*. Harvard University Press, 1992.

Regan, Robert (ed.), *Poe. A Collection of Critical Essays*. Prentice-Hall, 1967.

Ribot, Théodule, *L'Imagination créatrice*. Paris, 1900.

Sharpe, Tony, *T.S. Eliot, A Literary Life*. Basingstoke, Macmillan, 1991.

Skaff, William, *The Philosophy of T.S. Eliot: From Skepticism to a Surrealist Poetic 1909–1927*. University of Pennsylvania Press, 1986.

Spencer, Michael Clifford, *The Art Criticism of Théophile Gautier*. Genève, Librairie Droz, 1969.

Sprat, Thomas, *History of the Royal Society*. London, 1667.

Spurr, David, *Conflicts in Consciousness. T.S. Eliot's Poetry and Criticism*. University of Illinois Press, 1984.

Stead, C.K., *The New Poetic: Yeats to Eliot*. London, Hutchinson University Library, 1975.

Suckling, Norman, *Paul Valéry and the Civilized Mind*. London, 1955.

Sullivan Sheila (ed.), *Critics on T.S. Eliot: Readings in Literary Criticism*. London, Allen & Unwin, 1973.

Tate, Allen (ed.), *T.S. Eliot: The Man and His Work*. New York, Delacorte, New York, 1966.

Terrier, Philippe (ed.), *Charles Baudelaire. Théophile Gautier. Deux Etudes*. Neuchâtel, 1985.

Unger, Leonard (ed.), *T.S.Eliot: A Selected Critique*. Rinehart, New York, 1948.

Valéry, Paul, *Introduction à la Poétique*. Gallimard ,1938.

Williamson, George, *A Reader's Guide to T.S. Eliot*. Thames & Hudson 1955, 2nd ed. 1966.

INDEX

Printed and bound by CPI Group (UK) Ltd, Croydon, CR0 4YY

09/06/2025

14685799-0001